Human Rights Interventions

Series Editors

Chiseche Mibenge, Stanford University, Stanford, USA
Irene Hadiprayitno, Leiden University, Leiden, The Netherlands

The traditional human rights frame creates a paradigm by which the duty bearer's (state) and rights holder's (civil society organizations) interests collide over the limits of enjoyment and enforcement. The series departs from the paradigm by centering peripheral yet powerful actors that agitate for intervention and influence in the (re)shaping of rights discourse in the midst of grave insecurities. The series privileges a call and response between theoretical inquiry and empirical investigation as contributors critically assess human rights interventions mediated by spatial, temporal, geopolitical and other dimensions. An interdisciplinary dialogue is key as the editors encourage multiple approaches such as law and society, political economy, historiography, legal ethnography, feminist security studies, and multi-media.

All manuscripts in the series undergo single blind peer review both at proposal and final manuscript stage, and have to abide by the Springer Nature ethical policy statement: https://www.springer.com/gp/editorial-policies/ethical-responsibilities-of-authors.

Ebenezer Durojaye · Satang Nabaneh ·
Johanna Bond
Editors

Harmful Practices and Human Rights: An International Perspective

palgrave
macmillan

Editors
Ebenezer Durojaye
Centre for Human Rights
University of Pretoria
Pretoria, South Africa

Satang Nabaneh
Human Rights Center
University of Dayton
Dayton, OH, USA

Johanna Bond
Law School
The State University of New Je
Newark, NJ, USA

ISSN 2946-5117 ISSN 2946-5125 (electronic)
Human Rights Interventions
ISBN 978-3-031-90332-8 ISBN 978-3-031-90333-5 (eBook)
https://doi.org/10.1007/978-3-031-90333-5

This Palgrave Macmillan imprint is published by the registered company Springer Nature Switzerland AG
The registered company address is: Gewerbestrasse 11, 6330 Cham, Switzerland

Preface

Harmful practices are generally accepted to undermine human rights. The Maputo Protocol in Article 1 defines harmful practices as 'all behaviour, attitudes and/or practices which negatively affect the fundamental rights of women and girls, such as their right to life, health, dignity, education and physical integrity' Implicit in this definition is that harmful practices contain traditional or cultural practices that may undermine the rights of women and girls. These include female genital mutilation, child marriage and widowhood practices. In addition, they include practices that undermine the autonomy and rights of women and girls while seeking health care services. These will include forced sterilisation, verbal or physical abuse, name calling, tobacco use, neglect or abonnement, failure to seek consent for treatment and forced caesarean operation, and detention for failing to pay medical fees. These practices tend to violate human rights guaranteed in international and regional human rights instruments. While most of the human rights instruments at the international level do not specifically address harmful practices, the rights guaranteed in these instruments are relevant in addressing the negative consequences of harmful practices. These include the rights to life, health, dignity, non-discrimination, liberty and freedom to be free from torture, inhuman and degrading treatment. There is a misconception that harmful practices only take place in developing countries, particularly Africa and Asia. However, experience has shown that harmful practices take place virtually everywhere in the world, including in developed countries.

This book addresses gaps in literature regarding harmful practices. It adopts a rights-based approach and feminist analysis in contextualising the negative effects of harmful practices on the enjoyment of women's rights. Drawing examples across 5 continents—Africa, Asia, Europe, North America, and Australasia, the book discusses the various human rights that harmful practice undermine, examining how states have attempted to deal with harmful practices in their countries.

While the book admits that some efforts are being made to address harmful practices. it nonetheless, emphasises that these efforts required to be renewed and backed up with political commitments from states. More importantly, the international community must continue to build alliances and adopt laws and policies grounded in a rights-based approach with a view to addressing harmful practices. Policymakers, civil society groups, students, researchers and international institutions will find the book useful.

Pretoria, South Africa — Ebenezer Durojaye
Dayton, USA — Satang Nabaneh
Newark, USA — Johanna Bond

Acknowledgements The editors are grateful to Ms Keathalia Sapto of the Dullah Omar Institute, University of the Western Cape, for providing the technical assistance. Also, the editors are grateful to thank colleagues at the Centre for Human Rights, University of Pretoria, Human Rights Center, University of Dayton and Rutgers Law School, the State University of New Jersey, USA, for their support during the preparation of this book.

Contents

Notes on Contributors

Agah Deborah Achimugu-Opaluwa is a distinguished legal scholar, seasoned academic, and accomplished barrister with extensive experience in legal practice and the academia. She holds a Bachelor of Laws (LL. B) from Kogi State University, Anyigba, Nigeria (2006), and was called to the Nigerian Bar in 2007 after successfully completing her Barrister-at-Law (B.L) program at the Nigerian Law School. Furthering her academic pursuit, she obtained a Master of Laws (LL.M) from Kogi State University, Anyigba, in 2014, and later earned a Doctor of Philosophy (Ph.D.) in Law from the University of the Western Cape, South Africa, in 2024. Since her admission to the Nigerian Bar, Dr. Achimugu-Opaluwa has practiced as a Barrister and Solicitor of the Supreme Court of Nigeria, specializing in human rights law and related legal fields. She has been a lecturer in the Department of Public Law, Faculty of Law, Kogi State University, Anyigba, since 2015. She has published extensively in reputable peer-reviewed journals and has presented her research findings at various national and international academic conferences.

Toun Adebanjo (LLD, UFS) is a law researcher, consultant and human rights advocate in Queensland, Australia. She has researched and published extensively in several areas of law, including women's rights, sexual and reproductive health and rights, public health law and policy, company and insolvency law, and international law. She is co-editor of the book '*Sexual Harassment, Law and Human Rights in Africa*' (Palgrave Macmillan, 2023).

Linimose N. Anyiwe is a lecturer in Law at the Law School, York St John University (YSJ), York, England. She is a module leader for Law in a Global Context, and teaches Criminal Law, Tort Law and other foundation in Law modules including Law in Society and the Anatomy of a Crime. Prior to joining the YSJ Law School in August 2023, she studied as a doctoral researcher in Law at the University of Central Lancashire, Preston, England where she obtained her Ph.D. in Human Rights Law, Criminal Law and Access to Justice from the School of Justice, University of Central Lancashire in 2022. She is an accomplished scholar with 16 years of combined work experience as a lawyer, researcher, and academic. She has worked as a Barrister and Solicitor of the Supreme Court of Nigeria since 2009 and represented clients in civil and criminal law cases.

Upendra Bhojani MPH, Ph.D. graduated as a dentist and taught at the Government Dental College and Hospital (Ahmedabad) before transiting to public health. He did a master's degree in public health with a major in health promotion at Deakin University (Melbourne). He returned to India and joined the Institute of Public Health (Bangalore) in 2007, where he serves as a faculty and lead the Cluster on Chronic Health Conditions and Public Policy. He served as Director (2019–2023) at the Institute of Public Health Bengaluru. He holds the DBT/Wellcome Trust India Alliance Senior fellowship (2023–2028). His research interests/work includes public health, health policy, tobacco control, non-communicable diseases, chronic health conditions, urban health, political economy of health, commercial determinants of health and health inequities. He has published papers in scientific journals and often writes in popular media. He actively engages in knowledge translation. He is also an artist and is into music and pencil sketches that he also uses for public engagement around.

Johanna Bond is the dean of Rutgers Law School. At Rutgers, she is the first law school dean to oversee the Rutgers Law School campuses in both Newark and Camden. She is an expert in international human rights law and gender and the law. Bond came to Rutgers Law School from the faculty of Washington and Lee University School of Law and previously served as the Associate Dean for Academic Affairs. Bond was twice selected as a Fulbright Scholar, and her most recent book is *Global Intersectionality and Contemporary Human* Rights, published by Oxford University Press. Her scholarship has appeared in the *Southern California*

Law Review, *Emory Law Journal*, *Columbia Journal of Gender and Law*, *Yale Human Rights and Development Law Journal*, and many others.

Ebenezer Durojaye is a professor of Law at the Centre for Human Rights, University of Pretoria, South Africa. His areas of research include human rights, socio-economic rights, sexual and reproductive health and rights, and gender and constitutionalism. He has written extensively in these areas. Between 2010–2020, he served as one of the Independent Experts to the African Commission on Human and Peoples' Rights HIV Committee. He has been involved in the drafting of important norms and standards in relation to socio-economic rights and sexual and reproductive health and rights in Africa. He is the editor/co-editor of a number of books in his areas of interest.

Cowen Dziva earned a Ph.D., MA, and BA in Development Studies. He also completed post-graduate diplomas in Higher Education Teaching and Monitoring and Evaluation. He considers himself a gender and social inclusion researcher, trainer and practitioner with an in-depth understanding of applying the human rights-based approach in development management. He is a part-time Commissioner and current Chair of the Gender Equality and Women's Rights Thematic Working Group at the Zimbabwe Human Rights Commission (ZHRC). He is an Associate Professor at the Nehanda Centre for Gender and Cultural Studies at Great Zimbabwe University (GZU). He has co-authored and published over 40 book chapters and articles on democratisation, community development and social inclusion in Zimbabwe.

Eghosa O. Ekhator is Associate Professor of International Environmental Law at the University of Derby, United Kingdom. His main research areas include International Environmental Law, African International Legal History, and Natural Resources Governance. Dr. Ekhator has published extensively on his research areas and his academic papers have been cited by a plethora of public and international agencies including the United Kingdom Parliament's International Trade Committee and the United Nations Refugee Council. Dr. Ekhator is also the Chair Committee on the Teaching of International Law and the SDGs, International Law Association (Nigerian Branch) and Senior Fellow Environmental Law and Sustainable Development—Institute for Oil, Gas, Energy, Environment and Sustainable Development (OGEES Institute)

Afe Babalola University Nigeria. Dr. Ekhator is the Deputy Editor-in-Chief, the *Journal of Sustainable Development Law and Policy*, Afe Babalola University, Nigeria.

Pragati B Hebbar MDS, Ph.D. is a dentist by education, currently a public health researcher at the Institute of Public Health, Bengaluru. In the past decade she has been involved in research and policy engagement on issues of tobacco control, road safety and non-communicable diseases. She engages in teaching at the institute by contributing to ongoing courses and workshops such as the online—implementation research course, realist evaluation workshop series and is currently the Assistant Director of Research. She represents the Southeast Asia region on the board of Directors of the Health Systems Global. Currently she is leading a REALISE Lab (Realist Evaluation Advancement Lab for Implementation Strategy Explanations) supported by the DBT/Wellcome Trust India Alliance Intermediate fellowship.

Yumba Bernadette Kakhobwe is a gender and sexual and reproductive health rights researcher. She holds a BA in Media and Communication and Classical Civilisation, a BA. Honours in Classical Civilisation, an MA in Gender Studies and an M.Phil in Sexual and Reproductive Rights. She is currently pursuing a D.Phil. in Sexual and Reproductive Rights at the Centre for Human Rights, University of Pretoria. Ms Kakhobwe has an interest in gender-based violence, adolescent sexual and reproductive health and rights, child marriage, and female genital mutilation/cutting using human rights and decolonial feminist approaches.

Helen Kruuse BA, LLB, LLM, PGDHE, Ph.D. (Rhodes) is an admitted attorney of the High Court of South Africa (non-practising) and is currently an Associate Professor at Rhodes University, South Africa. She is a review editor of the *South African Law Journal* and chairs the South African Law Reform Commission's Advisory Committee on a Review of Aspects of Matrimonial Property Law.

Lea Mwambene Dip (Nursing), LLB (Hons) (UNIM), LLM, LLD (UWC) a Professor of Law in the Department of Private Law, Faculty of Law at the University of the Western Cape, South Africa, as well as the Deputy Dean for Teaching and Learning since 2018. She is also a founding member of the Centre for Legal Integration in Africa, and currently a member of the Advisory Committee on Matrimonial Property of the South African Law Reform Commission since April 2021.

Satang Nabaneh Ph.D., is Assistant Professor of Practice at the University of Dayton Human Rights Center. Her research encompasses global human rights architecture, gender equality, sexual and reproductive health and rights, democratisation, and autocratisation. She is affiliated faculty in the Centre for Human Rights, University of Pretoria and a Global Fellow at Centre on Law and Social Transformation, University of Bergen, Norway. She is the author of *Choice and Conscience: Lessons from South Africa for a Global Debate* (PULP, 2023) and co-edited *Sexual Harassment, Law and Human Rights in Africa* (Palgrave Macmillan, 2023) and *The Gambia in Transition: Towards a New Constitutional Order* (PULP, 2022) and. Her forthcoming edited volume is *Female Genital Mutilation in Africa: Politics of Criminalization* (PULP, 2025). Satang has been featured in prominent media outlets, including The New York Times, Reuters, Time, and the Council on Foreign Relations' Think Global Health. She was named one of 10 exceptionally talented African scholars to watch in 2024 by The Africa Report.

Robert Doya Nanima is Associate Professor and Head of the Department of Criminal Justice and Procedure at the University of the Western Cape's Faculty of Law in South Africa. A renowned expert in the realm of children's rights, his research explores the intersections of childhood, armed conflict, and human rights. He has published extensively and presented at national and international conferences. His academic endeavours are complemented by his service as a member of the African Committee of Experts on the Rights and Welfare of the Child, where he holds key positions, including Special Rapporteur on Children Affected by Armed Conflict, Chairperson of the Working Group on the Implementation of Decisions, and member of the Working Group on Children's Rights and Climate Change. Before his academic career, he was a prosecutor with the Directorate of Public Prosecutions, Uganda bringing a wealth of practical expertise to his scholarly pursuits.

Zainab Monisola Olaitan is Post-Doctoral fellow at the Centre for International and Defence Policy (CIDP) at Queen's University. She is a political scientist with an interest in gender and representation, peace and conflict studies, and African politics. Her research focuses on locating women across different sectors with a central question: how are women represented in Africa? She is currently working on an Afrofeminist interrogation of the women, peace, and security (WPS) agenda in Africa. She holds a Ph.D. in Political Science from the University of Pretoria, where she interrogated the impact of gender quotas on the substantive representation of women in African politics. She is the author of ***Women's Representation in African Politics: Beyond Numbers*** published by Palgrave Macmillan in 2024. She has published widely in journals, book projects, and policy briefs on themes bordering on feminist thought, gender and representation, African indigenous knowledge systems, and peace and conflict studies.

Patricia Atim P'Odong holds a Ph.D. in Disability Studies from the University of Cape Town, South Africa. I am an enrolled practicing advocate of the Courts of Judicature in Uganda. Currently, lecturing of the School of Law, Makerere University. I am also the: Head-Legal Aid Unit of the Public Interest Law Clinic (PILAC); Project Associate for the Disability Law and Rights Center (DRC), at the School of Law, Makerere University. I am a dedicated activist in rule of law, human rights and gender relations. My research and capacity building interest are mainly human rights law; family law, children's rights; gender and the law; disability rights, Administrative law, and Clinical Legal Education. I am also an advocate for social justice and public interest lawyering.

Linet Sithole is a lawyer by training who has a Ph.D. in Law (Specialising in Sexual and Reproductive Health and Rights), Master of Arts in Human Rights and a Bachelor of Laws Honours. Dr. Linet is scholar and advocate whose work primarily revolves around reproductive health, women's rights, family law and social justice issues in Africa. Her research often addresses the intersections of health, gender, and policy, with a particular emphasis on the challenges faced by marginalised women. She is currently the Head of the Public Law Department at the Africa University School of Law, and the Gender, Inclusion and Safeguarding Officer under the Transforming African Agricultural Universities to Meaningfully Contribute to Africa's Growth and Development (TAGDev 2.0) project—which is a collaborative Programme between Mastercard Foundation, RUFORUM, Global Confederation of Higher Education Associations for Agricultural and Life Sciences (GCHERA), and 12 universities from 10 African countries. She has published on women's rights, inclusion and reproductive health and rights.

Rose Wakikona is an African feminist lawyer using the law to advance human rights. She currently works as the Deputy Executive Director for the Women's Probono Initiative (WPI) in Uganda, where she does advocacy and litigation focused on the intersection of women's rights and sexual and reproductive health and rights. She obtained an LLM in Sexual and Reproductive Rights in Africa from the University of Pretoria, Centre for Human Rights, and an LLB from Makerere University in Uganda.

Susan Weaver Ph.D. is Lecturer in the Department of Political Science at the University of Dayton (UD). She specialises in gender and international relations, post-conflict development, and the politics of human rights and human security. As an ACCAP Research Fellow with the UD Human Rights Center, she investigates subnational trends in gender-based violence and violence against women in Guinea and Togo. As a Gender Equity Research Fellow at UD, she leads research on the value perceptions of women, transgender, and gender-nonconforming faculty at UD. Previously she's evaluated gender mainstreaming in World Bank development projects in conflict-affected states, specifically the extent to which development projects are inclusive of women in post-conflict spaces and supportive of the Women, Peace and Security Agenda outlined by the U.N. Security Council. She teaches courses in Global Gender Politics, International Politics, Organisations, and Development. She is passionate about reducing social, economic and political inequalities.

List of Tables

CHAPTER 1

Harmful Practices as a Human Rights Challenge

Ebenezer Durojaye, Satang Nabaneh, and Johanna Bond

1 Introduction

Harmful practices are widely practiced worldwide and impair human rights and fundamental freedoms. Across the world, a significant number of people, especially women and girls, experience one form of harmful practice or another. Although harmful practices affect both women and men, women and girls remain particularly susceptible due to patriarchy and gender inequality. For instance, the two most common forms of

E. Durojaye (✉)
Centre for Human Rights, University of Pretoria, Pretoria, South Africa
e-mail: Ebenezerdurojaye19@gmail.com

S. Nabaneh
Human Rights Center, University of Dayton, Dayton, OH, USA
e-mail: satang.nabaneh@gmail.com

J. Bond
Rutgers Law School, The State University of New Jersey, Camden, NJ, USA
e-mail: jb2225@law.rutgers.edu

E. Durojaye et al. (eds.), *Harmful Practices and Human Rights: An International Perspective*, Human Rights Interventions,
https://doi.org/10.1007/978-3-031-90333-5_1

harmful practices—female genital mutilation (FGM) and child marriage—affect millions of women and girls worldwide. An estimated 600 million women alive today have undergone child marriage, while over 200 million women have experienced FGM.[1] In different parts of the world, diverse forms of practices harmful to women and girls are carried out. Indeed, harmful practices occur in every region of the world, including both developed and developing countries.[2] While there is no universally adopted definition of harmful practices, the book uses a holistic definition provided the Office of the High Commissioner for Human Rights (OHCHR) as follows:

> Harmful practices are a violation of human rights that put women's and adolescents' sexual and reproductive health and rights at great risk.[3] A variety of harmful practices exist, including female genital mutilation (FGM), child and forced marriage, virginity testing and related practices, extreme dietary restrictions, including during pregnancy (force-feeding, food taboos), binding, scarring, branding/infliction of tribal marks, corporal punishment, stoning, violent initiation rites, widowhood practices, accusations of witchcraft, infanticide, incest and body modifications that are performed for the purpose of beauty or marriageability of girls and women.[4]

2 Some Examples of Harmful Practices

Harmful practices thrive in many societies where gender inequality is engrained. In these societies, the scope of harmful practices is vast and may differ from national to community-based practices. Some harmful practices, such as FGM, which is common in many parts of developing

[1] See OHCHR 'Information series on sexual and reproductive health and rights: Harmful practices, especially forced marriage and female genital mutilation' (2015).

[2] UNPFA *Defying the practices that harm women and girls and undermine equality: State of the world population 2020* (2020).

[3] Para 68 of the Committee on the Elimination of Discrimination Against Women & Committee on the Rights of the Child, Joint General Recommendation 31 of the Committee on the Elimination of Discrimination against Women/General Comment 18 of the Committee on the Rights of the Child on harmful practices, 14 November 2014, UN Doc CEDAW/C/GC/31-CRC/C/GC/18 (2014).

[4] Para 9 of the Joint General Recommendation (n 3). See also, World Health Organization 'Eliminating virginity testing: An interagency statement' (2018).

countries, have been found among immigrant communities in developed countries such as the United Kingdom, New Zealand and Australia.[5] Similarly, son preference, which is another discriminatory practice, is prevalent in South Asia, North Africa and the Middle East. Yet in other parts of the world, such as China, foot-binding has been practiced, which can also be harmful to the health and well-being of individuals. Harmful practices can constitute health hazards and impact the physical, mental and psychological well-being of women and girls.[6] It may also lead to socio-economic and socio-cultural consequences for women and girls. For instance, early marriage will not only deprive the girl-child of the opportunity to go to school and, therefore, become employable, but it may also perpetuate the cycle of poverty.[7] Also, son preference can lead to shorter breastfeeding times for girls, poorer nutrition, inadequate schooling and fewer inoculations. This may in turn lead to women and girls being less equipped educationally, lacking opportunities for employment and political life.[8]

In some rural communities, traditional birth practices remain the norm, and many women and girls have lost their lives as a result. Due to age-long practices coupled with shortages of skilled healthcare providers, many communities in rural areas have resorted to the use of traditional birth attendants. These attendants usually lack medical skills or knowledge but often rely on traditional knowledge and experience. Thus, when complications arise during childbirth, these attendants are unable to provide the needed medical intervention or support. This has aggravated maternal deaths and morbidities in many of the communities.

Menstruation-related taboos tend to impose patriarchal control over women's bodies and may perpetuate the low status of women. This may, in turn, lead to girls missing out on schooling, being unable to access appropriate healthcare services and being incapable of securing decent

[5] See for instance, E Dorkenoo *Cutting the rose – Female genital mutilation: The practice and its prevention* (1996). See also S Nabaneh & A Muula 'Female genital mutilation/cutting: A complex legal and ethical landscape' (2019) 145 *International Journal of Gynecology & Obstetrics* 253.

[6] UNFPA *Interwoven lives, threads of hope: Ending inequalities in sexual and reproductive health and rights: State of the World Population 2024* (2024).

[7] See JA Walker 'Early marriage in Africa – Trends, harmful effects and interventions' (2012) 16 *African Journal of Reproductive Health* 231.

[8] UNFPA (n 6).

employment. In Nepal, for example, menstrual banishment is practiced where girls and women undergoing menstruation are made to live in out-door sheds or huts.[9] This could lead to health consequences such as diarrhoea, dehydration and urinary tract infections.[10] Unfortunately, these women and girls are not allowed to seek healthcare services until the end of menstruation.[11] Most women and girls that have undergone this practice have complained of shame, abandonment, insecurity, guilt and humiliation for being treated as 'impure or unclean'.

3 Human Rights Approach to Harmful Practices

As a by-product of gender inequality, harmful practices undermine the human rights of women and girls. Various attempts have been made to condemn harmful practices as a violation of human rights guaranteed in several human rights instruments including: the Universal Declaration of Human Rights[12]; the International Covenant on Civil and Political Rights[13]; the International Covenant on Economic, Social and Cultural

[9] R Adhikar 'Bringing to an end deadly "menstrual huts" is proving difficult in Nepal' (2020) 368 *British Medical Journal* M536; H Robinson 'Chaupadi: The affliction of menses in Nepal' (2015) 1 *International Journal of Women's Dermatology* 193.

[10] S Kadariya & A Aro 'Chhaupadi Practice in Nepal – Analysis of ethical aspects' (2015) 5 *Medicolegal and Bioethics* 53; C Ranabhat and others 'Chhaupadi culture and reproductive health of women in Nepal' (2015) 27 *Asia Pacific Journal of Public Health* 785.

[11] B Dahal and others 'Chhaupadi and health of women and girls: A study on effects of Chhaupadi practices on health status of women and girls in Karnali, Nepal' (2017).

[12] UN General Assembly, Universal Declaration of Human Rights, 217 A (III), 10 December 1948.

[13] UN General Assembly, International Covenant on Civil and Political Rights, United Nations, Treaty Series, vol 999, p 171, 16 December 1966.

Rights[14]; the Convention on the Elimination of All Forms of Discrimination Against Women[15]; and the Convention on the Rights of the Child.[16]

At the African regional level, the relevant human rights instruments include the African Charter on Human and Peoples' Rights (African Charter),[17] the Protocol to the African Charter on Human and Peoples' Rights on the Rights of Women in Africa (Maputo Protocol)[18]; and the African Charter on the Rights and Welfare of the Child (African Children's Charter).[19] Both the Maputo Protocol and the African Children's Charter contain provisions specifically concerning harmful practices.[20] Virtually all the human rights guaranteed in these instruments, such as the rights to life, dignity, privacy, non-discrimination, health, freedom from torture, inhuman and degrading treatment and liberty, are relevant in the context of harmful practices. Specifically, the CEDAW requires states to take all appropriate measures to address prejudices and practices based on gender discrimination.[21] In its Joint General Recommendation 31/General Comment 18, the CEDAW Committee and Committee on the Rights of the Child note that harmful practices impair women's fundamental rights and freedoms and constitute discrimination against

[14] UN General Assembly, International Covenant on Economic, Social and Cultural Rights, United Nations, Treaty Series, vol 993, p 3, 16 December 1966.

[15] UN General Assembly, Convention on the Elimination of All Forms of Discrimination Against Women, United Nations, Treaty Series, vol 1249, p 13, 18 December 1979.

[16] UN General Assembly, Convention on the Rights of the Child, United Nations, Treaty Series, vol 1577, p 3, 20 November 1989.

[17] Organisation of African Unity (OAU), African Charter on Human and Peoples' Rights (Banjul Charter), CAB/LEG/67/3 rev 5, 21 ILM 58 (1982), 27 June 1981.

[18] African Union, Protocol to the African Charter on Human and People's Rights on the Rights of Women in Africa, African Union, 11 July 2003.

[19] Organisation of African Unity (OAU), African Charter on the Rights and Welfare of the Child, 11 July 1990, AU Doc CAB/LEG/24.9/49 (1990).

[20] See art 5 of the African Union, Protocol to the African Charter on Human and People's Rights on the Rights of Women in Africa, African Union, 11 July 2003; and art 21 of the Organisation of African Unity (OAU), African Charter on the Rights and Welfare of the Child, 11 July 1990, AU Doc CAB/LEG/24.9/49 (1990). See S Nabaneh 'Article 5: Elimination of all harmful practices' in A Rudman, CN Musembi & TM Makunya (eds) *Protocol to the African Charter on Human and Peoples' Rights on the Rights of Women in Africa: A commentary* (2023) 117-134.

[21] See for instance, art 5 of the Convention.

women.[22] The CEDAW Committee has also affirmed that harmful practices constitute acts of violence against women.[23] The African Commission and the African Committee of Experts on the Rights and Welfare of the Child (ACERWC) have expressed a similar sentiment, noting that states are expected to take appropriate measures with a view to eradicating harmful practices against women.[24]

In addition to binding human rights, consensus statements such as the International Conference on Population and Development (ICPD) of 1994, the Sustainable Development Goals (SDGs) and the ICPD + 20 all refer to harmful practices as a major concern for the health and well-being of women and girls. For instance, during the ICPD in 1994, the international community called for universal access to sexual and reproductive health services as well as the need to put an end to all forms of harmful practices. Also, Target 5.3 of the SDGs aims at ending harmful practices by 2030. These commitments reinforce the urgent need for concerted efforts to end all forms of harmful practices across the world. They reaffirm that states are obligated to eliminate all forms of harmful practices by taking concrete measures in this regard. On this point, the three-fold obligations include respect, protect and fulfil. The obligation to respect requires states to ensure that it does not interfere with women's right to be free from harmful practices. This requires states to refrain from adopting laws and policies that endorse harmful practices. A state may be said to be in breach of this obligation if, for example, it fails to enact laws or adopt policies to address harmful practices. The obligation to protect requires states to protect women from violations of human rights by a third party. In the context of harmful practices, states are required to regulate the activities of non-state actors that may undermine the rights of women. The obligation to fulfil requires states to take legal, administrative, juridical and budgetary measures to address harmful practices. In

[22] Joint General Recommendation (n 3).

[23] UN Committee on the Elimination of Discrimination Against Women (CEDAW), CEDAW General Recommendation 19: Violence against women (1992); and UN Committee on the Elimination of Discrimination Against Women (CEDAW), General Recommendation 35 (2017) on gender-based violence against women, updating General Recommendation 19 (1992), 26 July 2017, UN Doc CEDAW/C/GC/35 (2017).

[24] See Joint General Comment of the African Commission on Human And Peoples' Rights (ACHPR) and the African Committee of Experts on the Rights and Welfare of the Child (ACERWC) on ending child marriage (2017).

this regard, states will be expected to resort to legal reforms and provide resources for the implementation of laws and policies.

In a nutshell, efforts at ending harmful practices must be holistic and may include both policy and advocacy measures, including law reform and education awareness programmes. Such efforts must also include measures to address all forms of violence against women, provision of universal access to sexual and reproductive healthcare services and legal reforms to address structural and religious practices that enable these practices to thrive.

4 Background and Justification of This Book

4.1 This Book Seeks to Ask These Critical Questions:

- What are the existing international and regional human rights norms and standards related to harmful practices?
- What are the root causes and drivers of harmful practices, and how do they vary across different regions and communities?
- How have feminist movements and theories responded to harmful practices, and what strategies have been effective in addressing them?
- What are states' obligations to address harmful practices?

4.2 Objectives:

- To examine the scope and nature of harmful practices across the world.
- To understand the factors that encourage harmful practices.
- To understand the international and regional human rights norms in relation to harmful practices.
- To examine states' obligations in relation to harmful practices.
- To explore the opportunities and strategies to address harmful practices.

4.3 Justification

Despite efforts in international, regional and national law to address harmful practices, these practices have remained threats to the enjoyment of human rights. While harmful practices affect all people, in most cases, women tend to bear the brunt and consequences compared to their male counterparts. So far, no book has holistically examined the link between harmful practices and human rights from an international perspective. Most of the existing books focus on one aspect of harmful practices or a specific region, but none has taken an international perspective on the discussion. For instance, Dorkenoo's seminal book *Cutting the rose—Female genital mutilation: The practice and its prevention* (Minority Rights Group, 1996) focuses exclusively on FGM in developed and developing countries.[25] While the book tends to adopt an international perspective in its outlook, it merely focuses on one form of harmful practices. Unlike our book, it does not examine other harmful practices that can undermine the rights and well-being of women and girls. This becomes the strong selling point of this book.

A more recent book by Campbell and others *Harmful traditional practices: Prevention, protection and policing* (Springer 2020) examines various harmful practices including FGM, child marriage, breast ironing, witchcraft and honour-based abuse. However, the book focuses on prosecuting these practices rather than exploring the human rights and gender implications. Thus, while it tends to explore various forms of harmful practices, its focus is on the prosecution of these practices, and it does not engage in the gender and human rights dimensions of these practices.

Another publication on this subject, edited by Longman and Bradley, is titled: *Interrogating harmful cultural practices gender, culture and coercion* (Routledge 2020). This book draws on recent developments on harmful practices by social scientists and contributions from non-governmental organisations. It covers diverse practices, including FGM, veiling, forced marriage, honour-related and dowry violence, lip plates and sex segregation in public places. The book focuses on situations from Africa, East Asia, Europe and the United Kingdom. While this book covers diverse forms of harmful practices across the world, relying on feminist analysis, unlike our book, it does not examine these practices in other regions such as Latin America, the United States, Australia and New Zealand. To that extent, our book is more comprehensive as it seeks to cover other parts of the world not mentioned in the book by Longman and Bradley.

[25] N 5.

4.4 Focus of Our Book

The book examines different forms of harmful practices as human rights violations as guaranteed in international and regional human rights instruments. It draws examples from Africa, Asia, Latin America, Europe and Australia. The underlying point of the book is that harmful practices not only undermine the right to health, including sexual and reproductive health, but also impugn the dignity and autonomy of women and girls. Therefore, states have the obligation to take steps towards eradicating these practices.[26]

5 Intersectionality and Feminist Analyses of Harmful Practices

The lens through which the book analyses harmful practices, places emphasis on the interconnectedness of gender, race, class, culture, and other social categories in shaping the experiences of women and girls. It highlights how feminist and intersectional approaches reveal the systemic nature of these violations and their impact on dignity, autonomy, and health. From an intersectional and transnational feminist perspective, this book, as Falcon notes, can 'clarify power dynamics by recognising the specificities of comparative national contexts'.[27]

The theoretical framework of the book is grounded in feminist analyses, which seek to understand how gender inequality and patriarchy intersect with other forms of oppression to shape social structures and power dynamics. It contends that harmful practices, such as FGM, forced marriage, and honour killings, are deeply rooted in patriarchal norms and beliefs that reinforce the subordination of women and girls. Often, these harmful social norms and cultural beliefs condone violence against women, including harmful practices, and contribute to gender inequality. Feminist scholars have argued that cultural and religious practices can be inimical to the health and well-being of women and girls.[28] While Tamale

[26] R Cook 'Women's international human rights law: The way forward' in R Cook (ed) *Human rights of women: National and international perspectives* (1995) 3.

[27] M Falcon *Power interrupted: Antiracist and feminist activism inside the United Nations* (2016) 15.

[28] See N Nzegwu *Family matters: Feminist concepts in African philosophy of culture* (2006).

argues that not all cultural and religious practices pose threats to the health and well-being of women and girls, she argues that they remain serious human rights concerns.[29] They reinforce harmful stereotypes of women and undermine their dignity. Furthermore, they are a reminder of the structural inequality and power imbalances that occur in societies and the violence that women and girls face.

Violence against women and girls is rooted in gender inequality and the unequal power dynamics between men and women. In this context, the book centres around the argument that states have a responsibility to address harmful practices and uphold the right to equality. This includes adopting legal frameworks that prohibit harmful practices, providing support and services to survivors, and working to change social norms and attitudes that perpetuate these practices. Therefore, the book also explores the challenges and opportunities for cross-border cooperation and collaboration in addressing harmful practices, and how feminist analyses can be integrated into broader efforts to promote gender equality and human rights. Mohanty's perspective on 'transnational feminism' advocates for a feminism that transcends borders while remaining grounded in specific contexts, rejecting a borderless or universalist approach.[30] This avoids the universalising of women as a homogeneous group.[31]

5.1 5.1. Intersectionality and Harmful Practices

Intersectionality is an analytical framework for understanding how different forms of discrimination, like racism, sexism, and classism, overlap and interact with each other. It recognises that people's experiences are shaped by the combination of their social identities, such as race, gender, sexual orientation, and socio-economic status.

Intersectionality, a term coined by Kimberlé Crenshaw, refers to how different forms of discrimination intersect and compound, creating unique experiences of oppression for individuals with multiple

[29] See S Tamale 'The right to culture and the culture of rights: A critical perspective of women's sexual rights in Africa' (2008) 16 *Feminist Legal Studies* 47.

[30] CT Mohanty *Feminism without borders: Decolonizing theory, practicing solidarity* (2003).

[31] See CT Mohanty 'Under western eyes: Feminist scholarship and colonial discourses' (1984) 12 *Boundary* 333.

marginalised identities.[32] Crenshaw noted that due to 'intersectional identity as both women and of colour within discourses that are shaped to respond to one or the other, women of colour are marginalised within both'.[33] Thus, the intersectional framework responds to the 'lengthy history of essentialism and exclusion', by centring the 'experiences of subjects whose voices have been ignored'.[34]

Intersectionality challenges the notion that social categories like race and gender operate independently. Instead, it recognises that these categories interact in complex ways, producing distinct forms of discrimination and disadvantage. This framework is crucial for understanding the multifaceted nature of oppression faced by women, who often navigate overlapping systems of discrimination in their daily lives.[35] For instance, their experiences with discrimination and violence are influenced by the combined effects of racial, gender and class biases, which can limit their opportunities and exacerbate vulnerabilities.[36] Mohanty argues that 'multiple, fluid structures of domination ... intersect to locate women differently at particular historical conjunctures'.[37] Understanding how intersectionality—the way different forms of discrimination overlap—increases the vulnerability of women and girls, particularly from marginalised backgrounds, is critical. As Nabaneh noted 'it is crucial to recognise the intersectionality of race, gender, and class, as well as other factors such as age, socio-economic status, sexual orientation, and disability'.[38]

As observed by the Working Group on the issue of discrimination against women in law and in practice:

[32] K Crenshaw 'Mapping the margins: Intersectionality, identity politics, and violence against women of color' (1991) 43 *Stanford Law Review* 1241. For antecedents found in Black feminist thought and parallel critiques similar to the intersectionality framework see, J Bond *Global intersectionality and contemporary human rights* (2021) 6-26.

[33] As above.

[34] J Nash 'Re-thinking intersectionality' (2008) 89 *Feminist Review* 3.

[35] See PH Collins & S Bilge *Intersectionality* (2016); Bond *Global Intersectionality and Contemporary Human Rights* (2021).

[36] See b hooks *Ain't I a woman: Black women and feminism* (1981).

[37] CT Mohanty, A Russo & L Torres (eds) *Third world women and the politics of feminism* (1991) 13.

[38] S Nabaneh *Choice and conscience: Lessons from South Africa for a global debate* (2023) 123.

> Women are not a homogenous group, and their experience varies greatly between regions, countries, socioeconomic classes within countries and their identities as members of minorities, migrants, girl children, older women, or on account of single parenthood, disabilities or sexual identity, among others.[39]

These approaches provide a useful framework for understanding the complexities of patriarchy and other axes of domination and subordination.

6 Synopsis of Chapters

Chapter 1 by Durojaye, Nabaneh and Bond serves as the overview of the book providing the background and justification for the book. It also explains the meaning of harmful practices and the nexus with human rights violations. The chapter further highlights the importance of intersectionality and feminism to the discussion of harmful practices. The authors argue that harmful practices should be defined broadly to cover a number of issues that are not necessarily connected to cultural or religious practices.

In **Chapter 2**, Durojaye and Nabaneh examine the various provisions of binding and non-binding human rights instruments in relation to harmful practices. In addition, the chapter discusses the various human rights that are affected by harmful practices. It further explores the clarifications provided through the works of treaty monitoring bodies. Where necessary, relevant case law on this subject is discussed. Furthermore, the chapter discusses the obligations of states in relation to harmful practices. The chapter provides some suggestions on the steps and measures to be taken in order to address harmful practices.

Chapter 3 by Achimugu-Opaluwa discusses the various widowhood practices prevalent in most Nigerian communities as human rights violations using a feminist lens. It examines the legal framework in Nigeria to address these widowhood practices, including its consistency with the country's obligations under international human rights law. Further, the chapter also analyses factors that impede the implementation of

[39] Human Rights Council, Report of the Working Group on the issue of discrimination against women in law and in practice, 1 April 2014, UN Doc A/HRC/26/39 (2014) para. 24.

this legal framework. It argues that despite the provisions of domestic laws, international and regional human rights instruments, and judicial pronouncements on the discrimination against widows in terms of their right to equality, dignity, and property rights, widows still undergo harmful and discriminatory cultural practices in Nigeria. It concludes by noting that harmful and discriminatory widowhood practices are detrimental to the physical, emotional, and financial health of women and provides some recommendations for the way forward.

In **Chapter 4**, Mwambene and Kruuse examine the legal framework to address *ukuthwala* in South Africa. The authors ask questions relating to the appropriateness of law to address this controversial practice. Using African feminist legal theory, which 'seeks to transform the rules and principles governing particular areas of law, so as to make them more responsive to women's needs and more reflective of women's perspectives', the authors ask: Do the existing state structures adequately come to the aid and support of those who have been victims of *ukuthwala* practice? Is this in conformity with the values and ideals of South Africa and international human rights standards? Through anecdotal evidence of the community in the *Jezile* case, the authors' answers to both questions are: 'No'.

Chapter 5 of the book, by Sithole and Dzive, explores the human rights implications of the *chinamwari/khomba* practice in Zimbabwe. The authors engage in the debate between cultural relativists and universalists regarding this practice. They argue that scholars and practitioners must move away from the cultural relativism versus universalism dichotomy to a nuanced discussion that largely acknowledges the merits of universalism and the significance of culture in dealing with harmful practices such as the chinamwari practice and advancing women's rights.

In **Chapter 6,** Atim P'Odong deals with the human rights issues raised by bride wealth in Uganda. The author observes that the right to culture is guaranteed in the Ugandan Constitution, thereby raising the tension between realising this right and its implication for the enjoyment of women's rights. Premised on this point, the chapter seeks to examine the value of the customary practice of exchange of bride wealth in celebration of customary marriages in Uganda. It argues that even as the country embarks on the decolonisation agenda to re-birth and re-value African customs and practices, state regulation must continue. Only the positive cultural practices consistent with the Constitution and international human rights standards must prevail.

Chapter 7 by Hebbar and Bhojani addresses the negative impact of tobacco use as a form of harmful practice against women in India. The chapter analyses literature and examines the gender gaps in tobacco use and its negative consequences to health. The authors argue that gender has played a crucial role in shaping the tobacco epidemic and ought to play an important role in shaping tobacco control interventions. However, the authors note that it is not fully clear how gender operates and how the industry employs it in tobacco promotion implying the need for focused research using a gender lens in India and other areas. The authors conclude by noting that tobacco control policies/programmes remain largely gender blind and ought to carefully consider gender in their design/deployment.

In **Chapter 8**, Weaver and Nabaneh explore the ever-contentious issue of child marriage and human rights implications in the US. The authors argue that while efforts have been made worldwide, including in the US, to combat child marriage, many states in the US still allow child marriage. The authors note that there are still 37 states where children under 18 years of age can marry under specific circumstances. Additionally, four states do not have a minimum age requirement for marriage, leaving it up to parental or judicial waivers to determine eligibility. According to the authors, despite the efforts by the US government to combat child marriage globally, this practice persists within the country and requires a comprehensive analysis from a human rights and feminist perspective.

Chapter 9 by Adebanjo discusses intimate partner violence (IPV) in Australia and its human rights implications. The author explores the challenges that IPV poses to the realisation of fundamental rights for women and girls in Australia, showing how this group is disproportionately affected. The chapter reviews some IPV cases in Australia and examines the country's efforts to address this issue, such as the National Plan to Reduce Violence Against Women and their Children 2022–2032: Ending gender-based violence in one generation (National Plan 2010–2022), and the effectiveness of such measures. The chapter then makes recommendations for further strengthening of the protection of women and girls, and other vulnerable groups from IPV.

In **Chapter 10**, Anyiwe and Ekhator discuss human trafficking as a harmful practice in the United Kingdom. The authors note that the Palermo Protocol is a prominent international law instrument that provides a legal structure on how to define, prevent, and prosecute human trafficking. According to the authors, the United Nations Office on Drugs and Crime (UNODC) created this instrument, which serves as a tool or mechanism to combat the scourge of human trafficking. Using the United Kingdom as a case study, the authors note that unfulfilled state obligations are one of the main reasons why victims of trafficking in human beings (THB) are prosecuted for their involvement in illegal activities.

Chapter 11 by Olaitan examines the taboos related to menstrual hygiene. The chapter embarks on a broader examination of the impact of menstrual taboos on the rights of women and girls in Africa. It adopts an African feminist lens and a rights-based approach to understand the consequences of religious stigmatisation of menstruation on women and girls in Africa. The chapter finds that menstrual taboos negatively impact the right to non-discrimination, health, information, and dignity of women and girls in Africa. It recommends that governments and relevant stakeholders make concerted efforts to address menstrual taboos to protect women and girls in Africa.

In **Chapter 12**, Wakikona addresses the practice of denying pregnant teens access to education in Uganda. The chapter discusses the practice of expelling pregnant students from schools as one that seeks to control adolescent sexuality and violates the human rights of women and girls, critiquing the current solution of re-entry as being insufficient to guarantee continuity of education. It also considers the prevalence of this practice and its impact on the lives of women and girls in Uganda. It recommends that the country begin holistically addressing social protections and guaranteeing the right to education for women and girls as an obligation under human rights standards.

Chapter 13 by Nanima evaluates the argument that the normative guidance from the African Charter on the Rights and Welfare of the Child, the institutional positioning of the African Committee of Experts on the Rights and Welfare of the Child and the developing jurisprudence all form a cycle that promotes and protects the child affected by traditional harmful practices. Three sub-arguments evaluate the efficacy of this position. Normatively, the chapter unpacks the concept of traditional harmful practices followed by an institutional evaluation of the mechanisms of the African Children's Committee to deal with the problem through its working methods. Finally, the authors examine the jurisprudence of the African Children's Committee, evaluate the Committee's position on harmful practices and offer recommendations regarding the Committee's work.

In **Chapter 14**, Kakhobwe begins with the premise that as part of the process of countering the continued escalation of child marriages on the African continent, interventions must emphasise nurturing agency and bodily autonomy in girls. The author argues that in the absence of gender equality and unwavering commitment towards the eradication of child marriage across the African region, there is a need for girls to become active participants in the claiming and realisation of their rights as a form of self-advocacy and self-protection. Contentiously, this agentive disposition challenges the manner in which girls have traditionally been socialised. However, the lack of attention given to child marriage in many jurisdictions, notwithstanding the devastating socio-economic and health implications for girls, demands a layer of protection that must be initiated by girls themselves, and depends on their ability to recognise harm, name and defend their rights, as well as challenge the belief that their security is contingent on being married.

Bibliography

Adhikar, R 'Bringing to an end deadly "menstrual huts" is proving difficult in Nepal' (2020) 368 *British Medical Journal* M536

Bond, J *Global intersectionality and contemporary human rights* (Oxford University Press 2021)

Collins, PH & Bilge, S *Intersectionality* (Wiley 2016)

Cook, R 'Women's international human rights law: The way forward' in Cook, R (ed) *Human rights of women: National and international perspectives* (University of Pennsylvania Press 1995)

Crenshaw, K 'Mapping the margins: Intersectionality, identity politics, and violence against women of color' (1991) 43 *Stanford Law Review* 124

Dahal, B and others 'Chhaupadi and health of women and girls: A study on effects of Chhaupadi practices on health status of women and girls in Karnali, Nepal' (2017)

Dorkenoo, E *Cutting the rose – Female genital mutilation: The practice and its prevention* (Minority Rights Group 1996)

Falcon, M *Power interrupted: Antiracist and feminist activism inside the United Nations* (University Washington Press 2016)

hooks, b *Ain't I a woman: Black women and feminism* (South End Press, Boston 1981)

Kadariya, S & Aro, A 'Chhaupadi Practice in Nepal – Analysis of ethical aspects' (2015) 5 *Medicolegal and Bioethics* 53

Mohanty, CT *Feminism without borders: Decolonizing theory, practicing solidarity* (Duke University Press 2003)

Mohanty, CT 'Under western eyes: Feminist scholarship and colonial discourses' (1984) 12 *Boundary* 333
Mohanty, CT; Russo, A & Torres, L (eds) *Third world women and the politics of feminism* (Indiana University Press 1991)
Nabaneh, S 'Article 5: Elimination of all harmful practices' in Rudman, A; Musembi, CN & Makunya, TM (eds) *Protocol to the African Charter on Human and Peoples' Rights on the Rights of Women in Africa: A commentary* (2023) 117
Nabaneh, S *Choice and conscience: Lessons from South Africa for a global debate* (PULP 2023)
Nabaneh, S & Muula, A 'Female genital mutilation/cutting: A complex legal and ethical landscape' (2019) 145 *International Journal of Gynecology & Obstetrics* 253
Nash, J 'Re-thinking intersectionality' (2008) 89 *Feminist Review* 1
Nzegwu, N *Family matters: Feminist concepts in African philosophy of culture* (2006)
OHCHR 'Information series on sexual and reproductive health and rights: Harmful practices, especially forced marriage and female genital mutilation' (2015)
Ranabhat, C and others 'Chhaupadi culture and reproductive health of women in Nepal' (2015) 27 *Asia Pacific Journal of Public Health* 785
Robinson, H 'Chaupadi: The affliction of menses in Nepal' (2015) 1 *International Journal of Women's Dermatology* 193
Tamale, S 'The right to culture and the culture of rights: A critical perspective of women's sexual rights in Africa' (2008) 16 *Feminist Legal Studies* 47
UNPFA *Defying the practices that harm women and girls and undermine equality: State of the world population 2020* (2020)
UNFPA *Interwoven lives, threads of hope: Ending inequalities in sexual and reproductive health and rights: State of the World Population* 2024 (2024)
Walker, JA 'Early marriage in Africa – Trends, harmful effects and interventions' (2012) 16 *African Journal of Reproductive Health* 231
WHO 'Eliminating virginity testing: An interagency statement' (2018)

Human rights instruments

African Union, Protocol to the African Charter on Human and People's Rights on the Rights of Women in Africa, African Union, 11 July 2003
Committee on the Elimination of Discrimination Against Women (CEDAW), CEDAW General Recommendation 19: Violence against women (1992)
Committee on the Elimination of Discrimination Against Women (CEDAW), General Recommendation 35 (2017) on gender-based violence against

women, updating General Recommendation 19 (1992), 26 July 2017, UN Doc CEDAW/C/GC/35 (2017)

Committee on the Elimination of Discrimination Against Women & Committee on the Rights of the Child, Joint General Recommendation 31 of the Committee on the Elimination of Discrimination against Women/General Comment 18 of the Committee on the Rights of the Child on harmful practices, 14 November 2014, UN Doc CEDAW/C/GC/31-CRC/C/GC/18 (2014)

Joint General Comment of the African Commission on Human and Peoples' Rights (ACHPR) and the African Committee of Experts on the Rights and Welfare of the Child (ACERWC) on ending child marriage (2017)

General Assembly, Convention on the Elimination of All Forms of Discrimination Against Women, United Nations, Treaty Series, vol 1249, p 13, 18 December 1979

General Assembly, Convention on the Rights of the Child, United Nations, Treaty Series, vol 1577, p 3, 20 November 1989

General Assembly, International Covenant on Civil and Political Rights, United Nations, Treaty Series, vol 999, p 171, 16 December 1966

General Assembly, International Covenant on Economic, Social and Cultural Rights, United Nations, Treaty Series, vol 993, p 3, 16 December 1966

General Assembly, Universal Declaration of Human Rights, 217 A (III), 10 December 1948

Human Rights Council, Report of the Working Group on the issue of discrimination against women in law and in practice, 1 April 2014, UN Doc A/HRC/26/39 (2014)

Organisation of African Unity (OAU), African Charter on Human and Peoples' Rights (Banjul Charter), CAB/LEG/67/3 rev 5, 21 ILM 58 (1982), 27 June 1981

Organisation of African Unity (OAU), African Charter on the Rights and Welfare of the Child, 11 July 1990, AU Doc CAB/LEG/24.9/49 (1990)

CHAPTER 2

International and Regional Norms on Harmful Practices

Ebenezer Durojaye and Satang Nabaneh

1 Introduction

Harmful practices have been described as human rights violations. In a variety of ways, they tend to undermine human rights recognised in human rights instruments. While most of the human rights instruments do not specifically address harmful practices, the human rights guaranteed in these instruments are relevant in addressing the implications and consequences of harmful practices. The Protocol to the African Charter on Human and Peoples' Rights on the Rights of Women in Africa (Maputo Protocol) specifically prohibits female genital mutilation (FGM) in article 5 and the African Charter on the Rights and Welfare of the Child (African Children's Charter) addresses harmful practices against children in its

E. Durojaye (✉)
Centre for Human Rights, University of Pretoria, Pretoria, South Africa
e-mail: ebenezer.durojaye@up.ac.za

S. Nabaneh
Human Rights Center, University of Dayton, Dayton, OH, USA

E. Durojaye et al. (eds.), *Harmful Practices and Human Rights: An International Perspective*, Human Rights Interventions,
https://doi.org/10.1007/978-3-031-90333-5_2

article 21. It should be noted that the Maputo Protocol is one of the few human rights instruments that define harmful practices.[1] In article 1, it defines harmful practices as 'all behaviour, attitudes and/or practices which negatively affect the fundamental rights of women and girls, such as their right to life, health, dignity, education and physical integrity'. This holistic approach of the Maputo Protocol resonates with the sentiment shared in this book. As noted in Chapter 1, this book takes a more holistic and broad understanding of harmful practices to cover more than the traditional practices described as harmful. For many people in Africa, some of the practices often referred to as harmful are grounded in religion and culture.

However, recent developments across the world would seem to show that there are some practices that are not rooted in culture or religion but deleterious effects on human beings, especially women. Thus, this chapter examines the various provisions of binding and non-binding human rights instruments in relation to harmful practices. In addition, it discusses the various human rights that are affected by harmful practices. It further explores the clarifications provided through the works of treaty monitoring bodies. Where necessary relevant case law on this subject is discussed. Furthermore, the chapter discusses the obligations of states in relation to harmful practices. The chapter provides some recommendations on the steps and measures to be taken in order to address harmful practices.

2 Applicable Norms and Standards

2.1 Binding Instruments Relevant to Harmful Practices

Virtually all the human rights instruments at the United Nations (UN) and regional levels contain provisions that can be used to address incidence of harmful practices. Given that harmful practices are often perpetrated against marginalised and vulnerable groups, some of the human rights instruments dedicated to addressing disadvantaged groups contain provisions to address harmful practices as a human rights issue.

[1] See S Nabaneh 'Article 5: Elimination of all harmful practices' in A Rudman, CN Musembi & TM Makunya (eds) *Protocol to the African Charter on Human and Peoples' Rights on the Rights of Women in Africa: A commentary* (2023) 117–134.

For instance, the Convention on the Elimination of All Forms of Discrimination Against Women (CEDAW)[2]; the Convention on the Rights of the Child (CRC),[3] the Convention on the Rights of Persons with Disabilities (CRPD),[4] the Protocol to the African Charter on Human and Peoples' Rights on the Rights of Women in Africa (Maputo Protocol[5]; and the African Charter on the Rights and Welfare of the Child (African Children's Charter)[6] in one way or another contain provisions to address harmful practices. Even the traditional human rights instruments such as the Universal Declaration on Human Rights,[7] the International Covenant on Civil and Political Rights (ICCPR)[8]; and the International Covenant on Economic, Social and Cultural Rights (ICESCR)[9]; as well as the African Charter on Human and Peoples' Rights (ACHPR)[10] have provisions to address harmful practices. In some communities, harmful practices are fuelled by tradition, culture, religion or superstition. They include female genital mutilation, child marriage, widowhood practices, virginity testing and bride wealth. These are caused and reinforced by gender inequality including unequal power relations between women and men, rigid gender roles, norms and hierarchies, and ascribing women

[2] UN General Assembly, Convention on the Elimination of All Forms of Discrimination Against Women, United Nations, Treaty Series, vol 1249, p 13, 18 December 1979.

[3] UN General Assembly, Convention on the Rights of the Child, United Nations, Treaty Series, vol 1577, p 3, 20 November 1989.

[4] UN General Assembly, Convention on the Rights of Persons with Disabilities: Resolution adopted by the General Assembly, 24 January 2007, UN Doc A/RES/61/106 (2007).

[5] African Union, Protocol to the African Charter on Human and People's Rights on the Rights of Women in Africa, African Union, 11 July 2003.

[6] Organisation of African Unity (OAU), African Charter on the Rights and Welfare of the Child, 11 July 1990, AU Doc CAB/LEG/24.9/49 (1990).

[7] 7UN General Assembly, Universal Declaration of Human Rights, 217 A (III), 10 December 1948.

[8] UN General Assembly, International Covenant on Civil and Political Rights, United Nations, Treaty Series, vol 999, p 171, 16 December 1966,

[9] UN General Assembly, International Covenant on Economic, Social and Cultural Rights, United Nations, Treaty Series, vol 993, p 3, 16 December 1966.

[10] Organisation of African Unity (OAU), African Charter on Human and Peoples' Rights (Banjul Charter), CAB/LEG/67/3 rev 5, 21 ILM 58 (1982), 27 June 1981. See International Conference on Population and Development, Cairo, Egypt, September 1994.

lower status in society. While harmful practices can be carried out against all individuals, women and girls tend to be more affected by these practices. As will be seen below, both the CEDAW Committee and the CRC Committee as well as the African Commission and the African Committee of Experts have played pivotal role in developing norms and standards to address harmful practices. These have not only shaped our understanding of harmful practices but have also reiterated the nature of obligations imposed on states to address these practices.

Some of these practices can be described as violence against women and others undermine human rights guaranteed in human rights instruments. For instance, harmful practices tend to undermine the rights to life, dignity, autonomy, health, non-discrimination and equality, freedom from cruel, inhuman and degrading treatment and the right to liberty. The implications of harmful practices for the enjoyment of these rights are now discussed.

2.2 *Non-Binding Instruments Relevant to Harmful Practices*

In addition to the binding human rights instruments mentioned above, there exist some non-binding instruments that contain important provisions to address harmful practices. During the International Conference on Population and Development (ICPD),[11] one of the recommendations was that harmful practices against women and girls should be given more attention by states. It was agreed that these practices undermine the rights of women and further perpetuate discrimination against women. For instance, it was noted that forced marriage or child marriage undermine the right to autonomy of women and girls and reproductive choices.[12] States were further enjoined to ensure that appropriate measures are adopted with a view to addressing harmful practices that may impair women and girls from enjoying their rights and freedoms. At the Beijing Conference, it was affirmed that all forms of violence against women, including those related to harmful practices, are a violation of women's

[11] As above.

[12] As above.

and girls' rights. States were called upon to adopt appropriate measures with a view to addressing these practices.[13]

Most of the human rights bodies have issued general comments and recommendations that are relevant to harmful practices. For instance, the CEDAW Committee and the CRC Committee have issued a Joint General Recommendation/Comment on harmful practices.[14] Some of the general comments by the CESCR Committee such as General Comments 14[15] and 22[16] have a bearing on the implications of harmful practices on the enjoyment of the right to health, including, sexual and reproductive health and rights of women and girls. The Committee has urged states to ensure that barriers to sexual and reproductive health rights (SRHR) services for women and girls are removed to realise access to unhindered SRHR services for women and girls.[17]

At the regional level, the African Commission adopted some important non-binding norms that have implications on harmful practices. These include General Comments 1[18] and 2[19] on the Maputo Protocol. In 2017 the Commission adopted the Guidelines to Combat Sexual Violence and its Consequences in 2017 (Niamey Guidelines).[20] The Niamey Guidelines contain important provisions requiring states to address all

[13] United Nations Specialised Conferences, Beijing Declaration and Platform of Action, adopted at the Fourth World Conference on Women, United Nations, 27 October 1995.

[14] Committee on the Elimination of Discrimination Against Women & Committee on the Rights of the Child, Joint General Recommendation 31 of the Committee on the Elimination of Discrimination against Women/General Comment 18 of the Committee on the Rights of the Child on harmful practices, 14 November 2014, UN Doc CEDAW/C/GC/31-CRC/C/GC/18 (2014).

[15] UN Committee on Economic, Social and Cultural Rights (ESCR Committee) General Comment 14: The right to the highest attainable standard of health (Art 12 of the Covenant), 11 August 2000, UN Doc E/C12/2000/4 (2000).

[16] ESCR Committee, General Comment 22 (2016) on the right to sexual and reproductive health (article 12 of the International Covenant on Economic, Social and Cultural Rights), 2 May 2016, UN Doc E/C.12/GC/22 (2016).

[17] As above.

[18] See ACHPR, General Comment 1 on art 14(1)(d) and (e) of the Protocol to the African Charter on Human and Peoples' Rights of Women in Africa, 2012.

[19] See ACHPR, General Comment 2 on art 14(1)(a), (b), (c) and (f) and art 14(2)(a) and (c) of the Protocol to the African Charter on the Rights of Women, 2014.

[20] ACHPR, Guidelines to Combat Sexual Violence and its Consequences, adopted by the African Commission in Niamey, 2017.

forms of ***violence*** against women and girls, including those occasioned by harmful practices. Indeed, the Commission defines sexual violence to include forced pregnancy, forced sterilisation, forced marriage, forced abortion, forced pregnancy and prostitution, female genital mutilation and pornography.[21] States were enjoined to adopt measures including legislative, education and awareness as well as rehabilitation of victims of sexual violence.[22]

3 Specific Rights Implicated by Harmful Practices

3.1 The Right to Life

The right to life is guaranteed in virtually all human rights instruments. It is often regarded as the supreme right that is not subject to derogation even in the time of public emergency.[23] Traditionally, the right to life is said to impose negative obligations on states to refrain from taking lives. However, recent developments seem to indicate that this right also imposes positive obligations on states to preserve the loss of life. Thus, the Human Rights Committee has noted that states are obligated to take appropriate measures to avoid the loss of life such as preventing maternal death. This position has been echoed by the African Commission on Human and Peoples' Rights. Harmful practices can cause direct or indirect loss of life. Practices such as FGM can lead to excessive loss of blood during the mutilation process which can result in death.[24] Others such as child marriage and wife inheritance may lead to indirect death. Marrying a girl at an early age may result in early pregnancy, which is potentially dangerous and may cause death for a young girl under 18. When a woman who has lost her husband is inherited by a family member, she may be exposed to sexually transmitted infections, including HIV/

[21] As above.

[22] As above.

[23] See UN Human Rights Committee (HRC), CCPR General Comment 6: Article 6 (Right to Life), 30 April 1982; and Human Rights Committee, General Comment 35: Article 9 (Liberty and security of person), 16 December 2014, UN Doc CCPR/C/GC/35 (2014).

[24] See S Nabaneh & A Muula 'Female genital mutilation/cutting: A complex legal and ethical landscape' (2019) 145 *International Journal of Gynecology & Obstetrics* 253.

AIDS. This not only poses a hazard for her health but may ultimately result in death if not properly treated. Above all, some of these practices constitute acts of violence against women. The CEDAW Committee has noted that violence not only undermines the rights to freedoms and liberty of women but also affects them throughout their life cycle.[25] More importantly, violence against women may lead to death.[26]

3.2 *Right to Non-Discrimination and Equality*

Perhaps the most visible right implicated by harmful practices is the right to non-discrimination and equality. As noted above, patriarchal tradition and structural inequality tend to reinforce harmful practices thereby undermining the enjoyment of the right to non-discrimination and equality. The right to non-discrimination is guaranteed in virtually all the human rights instruments. Article 1 of CEDAW defines discrimination against women purposively to mean:

> [A]ny distinction, exclusion or restriction made on the basis of sex which has the effect or purpose of impairing or nullifying the recognition, enjoyment or exercise by women, irrespective of their marital status, on a basis of equality of men and women, of human rights and fundamental freedoms in the political, economic, social, cultural, civil or any other field.

This definition of discrimination is grounded in substantive equality rather than formal equality. The Maputo Protocol has echoed this sentiment by defining discrimination against women to mean:

> [A]ny differential treatment based on sex and whose objectives or effects compromise or destroy the recognition, enjoyment or the exercise by women, regardless of their marital status, of human rights and fundamental freedoms in all spheres of life.[27]

[25] Para 14 of the CEDAW Committee, General Recommendation 35 (2017) on gender-based violence against women, updating General Recommendation 19 (1992), 26 July 2017, UN Doc CEDAW/C/GC/35 (2017).

[26] As above.

[27] Art 1(f) of the Maputo Protocol.

It is clear from this definition that the Maputo Protocol aligns itself with the substantive equality approach of the CEDAW. It is also of interest that both definitions relate to all spheres of life. This would imply that harmful practices would be covered here. Article 2 of the Maputo Protocol further notes that: 'Discrimination against women is any action preventing a woman from enjoying all the rights recognized to all human beings and in all fields because of her sex'. This is further aimed at addressing the discriminatory effects of harmful practices against women and girls. Article 2 calls on African governments to take appropriate measures with a view to ending all forms of discrimination against women and girls. It specifically requires African governments to implement laws and policies that prohibit and punish harmful practices.

In addition, articles 5 of both CEDAW and the Maputo Protocol address the negative implications of harmful practices. Article 5 of CEDAW calls on states to modify social and cultural patterns that may engender prejudices, stereotypes and discriminatory practices against women. This provision speaks directly to harmful cultural practices that undermine the rights of women. Similarly, article 5 of the Maputo Protocol provides that: 'States Parties shall prohibit and condemn all forms of harmful practices which negatively affect women's human rights and which are contrary to recognized international standards'. This is an implicit recognition of the discriminatory nature of harmful practices.

In Joint General Recommendation 31/General Comment 18 it was affirmed that harmful practices are deeply rooted in social attitudes according to which women and girls are regarded as inferior to men and boys based on stereotyped roles.[28] It is further noted that:

> Harmful practices are therefore grounded in discrimination based on sex, gender and age, among other things, and have often been justified by invoking sociocultural and religious customs and values, in addition to misconceptions relating to some disadvantaged groups of women and children.[29]

The Joint General Recommendation/General Comment further emphasises that:

[28] Para 6 of the Joint General Recommendation/General Comment (n 14).

[29] Para 7 of the Joint General Recommendation/General Comment (n 14).

> Many other practices having been identified as harmful practices are all strongly connected to and reinforce socially constructed gender roles and systems of patriarchal power relations and sometimes reflect negative perceptions of or discriminatory beliefs regarding certain disadvantaged groups of women and children, including individuals with disabilities or albinism.

In one of its decisions involving Tanzania, the CEDAW Committee noted that the evictions of two widows and minor children from their home after the death of their husbands/fathers amounts to discrimination prohibited under CEDAW.[30] The Committee recognised the multiple levels of discrimination that might have occurred in this case given that the women, are poor, uneducated and from rural areas. This decision is important in the sense that it recognises the intersectional dimension of harmful practices.

It should also be noted that article 26 of the ICCPR guarantees the right to equality before the law and freedom from discrimination. In clarifying the relevance of this provision, the Human Rights Committee, responsible for the monitoring of the implementation of the ICCPR, in its General Comment 18 has explained that: 'Non-discrimination together with equality before the law and equal protection of the law without discrimination constitutes a basic and general principle relating to the protection of human rights'.[31] The Committee further explains that states should ensure that traditional, historical, religious or cultural attitudes are not used to justify violations of women's right to equality before the law and to equal enjoyment of all Covenant rights.[32]

In *Franz Nahlik v Austria*,[33] the Human Rights Committee explained that articles 2 and 26 of the ICCPR obligate a state to ensure that all individuals within its territory and subject to its jurisdiction are free from discriminatory practices, whether perpetrated in private or the public

[30] *ES & SC v Tanzania*, Communication 48/2013, UN Doc CEDAW/C/60/D/48/2013, 13 April 2015.

[31] Art 1 of the Human Rights Committee, General Comment 18: Non-discrimination (Thirty-seventh session, 1989), UN Doc HRI/GEN/1/Rev.1, 10 November 1989

[32] Art 5 of the Human Rights Committee, General Comment 28: Equality of rights between men and women (article 3), 29 March 2000, UN Doc CCPR/C/21/Rev.1/Add.10 (2000).

[33] *Franz Nahlik v Austria* Communication 608/1995, UN Doc CCPR/C/57/D/608/1995 (1996).

sphere.[34] This implies that states must take appropriate measures to address harmful practices that entrench discrimination against women and girls.

The African Commission and the Committee of Experts have both issued two Joint General Comments on harmful practices—child marriage and female genital mutilation.[35] These General Comments address the discriminatory effects of these harmful practices on girls and women. African governments are called upon to take appropriate measures to address these practices. The Commission and the Committee affirm that harmful cultural practices undermine the rights to equality and non-discrimination of women and girls.[36] Therefore, they urge African governments to embark of law reforms and public awareness programmes in order to address the incidence of harmful practices in the region.[37]

In clarifying the importance of articles 2 and 3 of the African Charter that deal with non-discrimination and equality before the law, the African Commission in *Purohit and Moore v The Gambia*[38] observed that:

> Article 2 lays down a principle that is essential to the spirit of the African Charter and is therefore necessary in eradicating discrimination in all its guises, while Article 3 is important because it guarantees fair and just treatment of individuals within a legal system of a given country. These provisions are non-derogable and therefore must be respected in all circumstances in order for anyone to enjoy all the rights provided under the African Charter.

This statement succinctly captures the broad understanding of the African Commission of the principles of equality and non-discrimination. It summarises the importance of realising the notion of substantive equality in any society. Albertyn and Goldblatt have argued that a substantive equality approach should aim at correcting structural and entrenched

[34] As above.

[35] See ACHPR & ACERWC, Joint General Comment of the African Commission on Human and Peoples' Rights (ACHPR) and the African Committee of Experts on the Rights And Welfare of the Child (ACERWC) on ending child marriage, 2017; see also, ACERWC & ACHPR, Joint General Comment on female genital mutilation, 2023.

[36] As above.

[37] As above. The chapter by Nanima in this volume deals extensively on these issues.

[38] Communication 241/2001 (2003) AHRLR 96 (ACHPR 2003).

disadvantages in society and, at the same time, aspire to maximise human development.[39] This is echoed by Nabaneh in her book, *Choice and conscience: Lessons from South Africa for a global debate* (2023), stating that the right to equality should be interpreted in a way that recognises and addresses the systemic inequalities faced by certain groups, including women.[40]

In their seminal work *Gender stereotyping transnational legal perspective* (2010), Cook and Cusack argued that a law, policy or practice will potentially discriminate against women on the basis of gender stereotype.[41] This will occur if the law, policy or practice leads to a difference in treatment; impairs or nullifies a woman from enjoying her human rights or fundamental freedoms; and if the application, enforcement or perpetuation of a gender stereotype in the law, policy or practice is unjustifiable.[42]

In its communication procedure, the African Commission has held in *Egypt Initiative for Personal Rights & INTERIGHTS v Egypt*,[43] that acts of gender-based violence against women journalists will result in harmful practices that constitute discrimination against the victims.[44] The Commission notes that acts of violence whether in public or private constitute human rights violations of women and impose obligations on states to prevent such acts. The Commission further notes that under the due diligence principle, the state remains liable for acts of violence perpetrated by individuals or non-state actors if the state fails to prevent such violence. Given that harmful practices are rooted in cultural and social practices; it has been argued that a substantive equality approach is essential to addressing the situation.

[39] C Albertyn & B Goldblatt 'Facing the challenge of transformation: difficulties in the development of an indigenous jurisprudence of equality' (1998) 14 *South African Journal on Human Rights* 248.

[40] S Nabaneh *Choice and conscience: Lessons from South Africa for a global debate* (2023) 42.

[41] RJ Cook & S Cusack *Gender stereotyping: Transnational legal perspective* (2010).

[42] As above.

[43] Communication 323/06 of 2011.

[44] As above.

3.3 *The Right to Dignity and to be Free from Cruel, Inhuman and Degrading Treatment*

The right to dignity is one of the most important rights individuals are entitled to. It means that all human beings must be treated with utmost respect and humanness. The right to dignity is guaranteed in virtually all the human rights instruments. The Preamble to the UDHR states that 'inherent dignity and … equal and inalienable rights of all members of the human family is the foundation of freedom, justice and peace in the world'.[45] Article 1 further provides that all human beings are born free and equal in dignity and rights.[46] It should be noted that the right to dignity is guaranteed in article 10 of the ICCPR.

At the regional level, article 5 of the African Charter and article 3 of the African Women's Protocol guarantee the right to dignity.[47] Article 3 of the Protocol provides that every woman shall have the right to dignity inherent in a human being and to the recognition and protection of her human and legal rights.[48]

The concept of dignity presupposes that every human being must be treated in such a way that his/her humanity is not degraded or debased. Dupre argues that dignity is closely connected to humanity, freedom and equality.[49] According to Glensy, the basis of dignity lies in the autonomy of self and a self-worth that is reflected in every human being's rights to individual self-determination.[50] It should be noted that the right to dignity intersects with other rights and a violation of the right to dignity not only affects the victim but society as a whole, in that it questions how we choose to relate with others.[51]

[45] Preamble of the UN General Assembly, Universal Declaration of Human Rights, 10 December 1948, 217 A (III).

[46] As above.

[47] Organisation of African Unity (OAU), African Charter on the Rights and Welfare of the Child, CAB/LEG/24.9/49 (1990), 11 July 1990; and the Maputo Protocol.

[48] Art 3 of the Maputo Protocol.

[49] C Dupre 'What does dignity mean in a legal context?' *The Guardian* 24 March 2011 http://www.guardian.co.uk/commentisfree/libertycentral/2011/mar/24/dignity-uk-europe-human-rights (Accessed 15 January 2025).

[50] RD Glensy 'The right to dignity' (2011) 43 *Columbia Human Rights Law Review* 66.

[51] Dupre (n 49).

Often, harmful practices undermine the rights to dignity of women and girls. They expose women and girls to inhumane and traumatic experiences, shame and ridicule.[52] These practices undermine the dignity of women and girls and treat them as second-class citizens of no value.[53] The CEDAW Committee and the CRC Committee have noted that a practice will be regarded as harmful if it 'constitutes a denial of the dignity and/or integrity of the individual and a violation of the human rights and fundamental freedoms enshrined in the two Conventions'.[54] The Committees have also noted that harmful cultural practices such as polygamy are 'contrary to the dignity of women and girls and infringes on their human rights and freedoms, including equality and protection within the family'.[55] Similarly, the Human Rights Committee has noted that forced sterilisation contravenes article 7 of the ICCPR which prohibits torture, cruel, inhuman or degrading treatment, and article 17 on right to privacy.[56]

Some special mechanisms of the UN human rights system have framed harmful practices such as obstetrics violence, including forced sterilisation, as cruel, inhuman and degrading treatment. For instance, the UN Special Rapporteur on violence against women in a 2019 report expressed deep concerns regarding the mistreatment of women seeking reproductive health care services in health facilities.[57] The Special Rapporteur notes that this phenomenon is a growing concern globally and some of these practices not only amount to violence against women but would also result in cruel, inhuman and degrading treatment.[58] The report draws examples of mistreatment of women across the globe emphasising the

[52] See for instance, E Durojaye '"Woman but not human": Widowhood practices and human rights violations in Nigeria' (2013) 27 *International Journal of Law, Policy and family* 176.

[53] See in this regard E Durojaye 'The human rights implications of virginity testing in South Africa' (2016) 16 *International Journal of Discrimination and the Law* 228.

[54] See para 16 of the Joint General Recommendation/Comment (n 14).

[55] Para 25 of the Joint General Recommendation/Comment (n 14).

[56] See paras 11 and 20 of the CCPR General Comment 28 (n 32).

[57] UN Special Rapporteur on violence against women 'A human rights-based approach to mistreatment and violence against women in reproductive health services with a focus on childbirth and obstetric violence' UN Doc A/74/137 (2019).

[58] As above.

ubiquity of the practice noting that it undermines the right to non-discrimination, dignity and freedom from cruel, inhuman and degrading treatment.[59] The UN Special Rapporteur on the right to health has echoed this concern by noting that abusive treatment of women seeking reproductive health services such as detention in health facilities due to inability to pay medical fees amounts to violations of their rights and may constitute cruel, inhuman and degrading treatment.[60]

At the regional level, the African Commission has elaborated on the meaning of the right to dignity as guaranteed in article 5 of the Charter. In its General Comment 4 the African Commission has noted that acts such as involuntary sterilisation and other mistreatment of women in health facilities constitutes torture, cruel, inhuman and degrading treatment.[61] This position has been reiterated in the Resolution 260 on Involuntary Sterilisation of Women Living with HIV as a human rights violation. The African Commission affirmed that forced sterilisation impairs the rights of HIV positive women, including the rights to dignity, non-discrimination, health, life and liberty. It should be noted that the African Commission in its Niamey Guidelines also recognised FGM as a form of sexual violence that can constitute torture or cruel, inhuman and degrading treatment. The Guidelines thus urge states parties to implement specific policies for gender equality and to combat sexual violence, including FGM.[62]

In one of its landmark cases on child and early marriage[63] and the implications for the right to dignity in article 5 of the Charter, the African Commission has noted:

[59] As above.

[60] See HRC 'Report of the Special Rapporteur on the right of everyone to the enjoyment of the highest attainable standard of physical and mental health, Tlaleng Mofokeng' UN Doc A/HRC/50/28 (2022).

[61] African Commission on Human and Peoples' Rights, General Comment 4 on the right to redress for victims of torture and other cruel, inhuman or degrading punishment or treatment (article 5), 2017.

[62] See the ACHPR 'Guidelines to combat sexual violence and its consequences in Africa' 2017.

[63] *Equality Now and Ethiopian Women Lawyers Association v Federal Republic of Ethiopia* (Communication 341/2007) [2021] ACHPR 523 (14 October 2021) para 118.

> At the core of human dignity is the idea and recognition that a human being has unique worth, value and significance that is innate, and not acquired. It also entails that a human being is a moral agent possessed with the conscience and personal volition to decide what happens to his or her body. The right to respect of dignity is a guarantee that a human being should not be subjected to acts or omissions that degrade or humiliate him or her. The worth, value and significance of a human being may not and need not be conceptualised with scientific precision

At the national level, the High Court of Kenya in *Millicent Awuor Omuya alias Maimuna Awuor v The Attorney General* held that the detention and mistreatment of the petitioners, including being made to sleep on the floors due to inability to pay medical fees after delivery, constitutes ill-treatment and undermines the right to dignity and to be free from torture, inhuman and degrading treatment.[64]

It thus clears that harmful practices undermine the enjoyment of the right to dignity. Furthermore, they may result in cruel, inhuman and degrading treatment.

3.4 The Right to Health

This right is recognised in most of the human rights instruments. However, the most authoritative provision is found in article 12(1) of the ICESCR which obligated states to ensure the realisation of the right to the highest attainable standard of physical and mental health.[65] The Committee on ESCR in its General Comment 14 has clarified the meaning of this right as guaranteed in the Covenant.[66] According to the Committee, the right to health does not imply that states must guarantee a healthy life for all people.[67] Rather it implies that states must ensure availability, accessibility, acceptability and quality access to healthcare services for all without distinctions on the basis of sex, age,

[64] *Millicent Awuor Omuya alias Maimuna Awuorv The Attorney General* (2015) Petition 562 of 2012, Kenya High Court, Constitutional and Human Rights Division.

[65] See too the UN Committee on Economic, Social and Cultural Rights (CESCR), General Comment 14: The right to the highest attainable standard of health (Art 12 of the Covenant), 11 August 2000, UN Doc E/C.12/2000/4 (2000).

[66] As above.

[67] As above.

ethnic, religious or political affiliations.[68] The Committee explains that the elements of the right to health include freedoms and entitlements. The former refers to prohibition of treatment or medical experimentation without the informed consent of the individual. This is particularly relevant in the context of harmful practices against women and girls given that some of the practices undermine the right to autonomy and liberty of women. Forced sterilisation, forced pregnancy and marriage all undermine the right to autonomy and reproductive choices of women and girls. More importantly, the aftermath of these practices can have serious implications on the health and well-being of women and girls. The Committee in General Comment 22 has affirmed that coercive medical services and mistreatment of women seeking reproductive health services is inconsistent with the right to health and reproductive rights of women and girls. Most of the harmful practices have direct implications for the physical and mental health of women. The right to health of women is guaranteed in article 12 of the CEDAW. The CEDAW in its General Recommendation 24[69] has noted that:

> Acceptable services are those that are delivered in a way that ensures that a woman gives her fully informed consent, respects her dignity, guarantees her confidentiality and is sensitive to her needs and perspectives.

The General Recommendation also states that:

> Women have the right to be fully informed, by properly trained personnel, of their options in agreeing to treatment or research, including likely benefits and potential adverse effects of proposed procedures and available alternatives.[70]

More importantly, in making the link between harmful practices and women's right to health, the Committee affirms that:

[68] As above.

[69] Para 22 of the UN Committee on the Elimination of Discrimination Against Women (CEDAW), CEDAW General Recommendation 24: Article 12 of the Convention (women and health), UN Doc A/54/38/Rev.1, chap. I, (1999).

[70] Para 20 of General Recommendation 24 (n 69).

> Harmful traditional practices, such as female genital mutilation, polygamy, as well as marital rape, may also expose girls and women to the risk of contracting HIV/AIDS and other sexually transmitted diseases.[71]

At the regional level, article 16 of the African Charter and article 14 of the Maputo Protocol guarantee the right to health of every individual. As noted above, harmful practices can have negative implications for the health of women either directly or indirectly. Some of the practices can affect women physically and mentally while others may lead to negative health consequences such as sexually transmitted infections including HIV/AIDS. In its Joint General Comment on child marriage, the Commission and Committee observe that child marriage places health burdens on women and girls as it compromises their enjoyment of the right to health and reproductive rights.[72] According to the Commission and the Committee, child marriage can lead to early pregnancy for teens, which is potentially dangerous for their health and well-being. Child marriage may result in maternal mortality or morbidity.[73] In the Joint General Comment on FGM, the Commission and Committee emphasise that this practice is rooted in cultural and religious practices and that they constitute health hazards to women and girls.

In its General Comment 2, the African Commission explains that states must ensure quality healthcare services that respect the rights of women and girls. Implicit in this statement is that practices such as forced sterilisation and other mistreatment of women will amount to the violation of women's rights.[74] The Commission further urges states to ensure the removal of administrative, cultural and social barriers to the enjoyment of the right to health and reproductive health of women.[75] Notably, the Commission notes as follows[76]:

> State parties should take all appropriate measures, through policies, sensitization and civic education programs, to remove all obstacles to the

[71] Para 18 of General Recommendation 24 (n 69).

[72] Joint General Comment on ending child marriage (n 35).

[73] Joint General Comment on FGM (n 35).

[74] Para 47 of General Comment 2 (n 19).

[75] Para 20 of General Comment 2 (n 19).

[76] Para 60 of General Comment 2 (n 19).

> enjoyment by women of their rights to sexual and reproductive health. Specific efforts should especially be made to address gender disparities, patriarchal attitudes, harmful traditional practices, prejudices of health care providers, discriminatory laws and policies, in accordance with Articles 2 and 5 of the Protocol.

This statement exemplifies the negative impact of harmful practices for the enjoyment of the sexual and reproductive health and rights of women.

4 States' Obligation to Address Harmful Practices

States are required to take appropriate measures to address harmful practices against women and girls. Like other issues, states are expected to exhibit the three-fold obligation regarding harmful practices: respect, protect and fulfil. Each of the obligations is discussed below.

4.1 Obligation to Respect

In the content of harmful practices, the obligation to respect requires the state to ensure that its act or omission does not undermine the enjoyment of a right. For instance, failure by the state to remove socio-cultural barriers that perpetuate harmful practices will amount to a breach of the obligation to respect. Similarly, the adoption of laws and policies that entrench harmful practices will result in breach of the obligation to respect. Article 5 of the CEDAW enjoins states to take appropriate measures to address all forms of discrimination against women. This obviously includes addressing harmful practices that undermine the rights of women. The CEDAW Committee has noted that:

> Each State party is under the obligation[77] to send a clear message of condemnation of harmful practices, provide legal protection for victims, enable State and non-State actors to protect women and children at risk,

[77] See arts 2(a)-(c), 2(f) and 5 of CEDAW; and UN Committee on the Rights of the Child (CRC), General Comment 13 (2011): The right of the child to freedom from all forms of violence, 18 April 2011, UN Doc CRC/C/GC/13 (2011).

> provide appropriate responses and care and ensure the availability of redress and an end to impunity.[78]

The Committee further notes that while enactment of legislation may not suffice, rather states must supplement this with other measures such as education and awareness programmes and sensitisation seminars to address these deep-rooted practices. In addition, states must strengthen their monitoring and implementation systems in order to ensure effective outcomes.

In a case involving Tanzania, where two widows and their children were forcefully evicted from their home, the CEDAW Committee[79] urged.

> Tanzania to ensure that the rights guaranteed in the CEDAW prevail over inconsistent national laws and that it repeal or amend local customary laws, 'with a view to providing women and girls with equal administration and inheritance rights upon the dissolution of marriage by death, irrespective of their ethnicity or religion'.

At the regional level, articles 2 of the Maputo Protocol and 21 of the African Children's Charter have enjoined states to address negative and harmful practices that impair women and girls from enjoying their fundamental rights and freedoms. This can be done by eliminating these practices or at the minimum discouraging their continued practices. The Commission and Committee has noted that: 'The reference to "all appropriate measures" means that a multifaceted response is envisaged in response to FGM, and that legislative measures alone would be insufficient to meet the obligations' under the Maputo Protocol and the African Children Charter.[80] The Commission and Committee further note that national legislation must specifically condemn and prohibit harmful practices such as FGM and prescribe punishments for perpetrators of such practices. The African Court in a case involving Mali held that stipulating age differences in age of marriage for boys and girls constitutes discriminatory harmful practices, which must be eliminated. The Court further

[78] Art 39 of the Joint General Recommendation/General Comment (n 14).

[79] *ES & SC v Tanzania* (n 28)

[80] See para 3 of the Joint General Comment on FGM (n 35).

enjoined Mali to embark on law reforms with a view to amending this discriminatory provision of the law.[81]

4.2 Obligation to Protect

This often requires that the state should prevent the violation of rights by a third party. Harmful practices are often perpetuated by state agents and non-state actors. Therefore, it is necessary that the state take appropriate measures to regulate the activities of these agents and individuals. The CEDAW Committee and the CRC Committee have noted that states are to develop holistic strategies that ensure the elimination of harmful practices. They further note that: 'Such a holistic strategy must be mainstreamed and coordinated both vertically and horizontally and integrated into national efforts to prevent and address all forms of harmful practices'.[82] In some situations, the CEDAW Committee has adopted the principle of due diligence to find that acts or omissions of a non-state actor that violate women's rights can be imputed to the state if the state has failed to prevent a human rights violation in this regard.[83] In some of its concluding observations to states, the CEDAW Committee has condemned the practice of healthcare providers that often recommend caesarean sections without the informed consent of women as well as the separation of new-borns from their mothers without any medical justification and the patronising attitudes of doctors.[84] Experiencing concerns with the role of healthcare providers in human rights violations of pregnant women in health facilities, the CEDAW Committee in *NAE v Spain* found the Spanish government in violation of the obligation to prevent

[81] See *APDF & IHRDA v Republic of Mali* Application (Application 046/2016) [2018] AfCHPR 9 (11 May 2018).

[82] Para 34 of the Joint General Recommendation (n 14).

[83] See for instance UN Committee on the Elimination of Discrimination Against Women (CEDAW), CEDAW General Recommendation 19: Violence against women, 1992.

[84] See paras 36 and 37 of the Committee on the Elimination of Discrimination Against Women, Consideration of reports submitted by states parties under article 18 of the Convention: Concluding Observations of the Committee on the Elimination of Discrimination Against Women: Czech Republic, 10 November 2010, UN Doc CEDAW/C/CZE/CO/5 (2010); and paras 30 and 31 of the Committee on the Elimination of Discrimination Against Women, Concluding Observations on the sixth periodic report of the Czech Republic, 14 March 2016, UN Doc CEDAW/C/CZE/CO/6 (2016).

violence against women and ensure the right to non-discrimination and quality healthcare services to for women.[85]

The UN Special Rapporteur on violence against women has noted that:

> Under international law, acts or omissions by non-State actors attributable to the State include the 'acts or omissions of private actors empowered by the law [of that State] to exercise elements of governmental authority, including private bodies providing public services, such as healthcare or education, or operating places of detention, are considered as acts attributable to the State itself'.[6]

This would seem to be the reiteration of the due diligence principle.[86]

Under the Inter-American Human Rights System, the Inter-American Court of Human Rights has found violations of the rights to personal integrity, personal freedom, private and family life, access to information and to be free from cruel, inhuman and degrading treatment, in a case concerning the involuntary sterilisation of a woman in a public hospital in the Plurinational State of Bolivia during a caesarean section.[87] In addition, the Inter-American Commission has released a statement urging 'States to document, investigate, and punish emerging forms of violence against women, girls and adolescents', including obstetric violence.[88]

At the Africa regional level, the African Commission has observed that this obligation.

> entails the formulation of standards and guidelines containing the precision that the consent and involvement of third parties, including but limited to, parents, guardians, spouses and partners, is not required when adult

[85] *NAE v Spain* CEDAW/C/82/D/149/2019 (27 June 2022).

[86] See S Nabaneh (ed) *Female genital mutilation in Africa: Politics of criminalisation* (forthcoming, 2025). Seel also A Johnson & S Nabaneh 'Limits to achieving criminal accountability for violence against women with disabilities in Africa' in A Budoo-Scholtz & EC Lubaale (eds) *Violence against women and criminal justice in Africa: Volume II. Sustainable Development Goals Series* (2022) 259–301.

[87] *IV v Bolivia*, Preliminary Objections, Merits, Reparations and Costs, Judgment, Inter-American Court of Human Rights (ser C) No 329 (2016).

[88] Inter-American Commission on Human Rights, press release 'On International Women's Day, the IACHR urges states to refrain from adopting measures that would set back respect for and protection of women's rights' (2018) http://www.oas.org/en/iachr/media_center/ PReleases/2018/044.asp (accessed 12 January 2025).

> women and adolescent girls want to access family planning/contraception and safe abortion services in the cases provided for in the Protocol.[89]

Furthermore, the Commission has held in the *Zimbabwe Human Rights NGO Forum v Zimbabwe* that failure by the state to prevent or address acts of violence perpetrated by individuals or third parties will amount to the breach of duty to protect.[90] In explaining the basis for this, the Commission notes:

> Thus, an act by a private individual and therefore not directly imputable to a state can generate responsibility of the state, not because of the act itself, but because of lack of due diligence to prevent the violation or for not taking the necessary steps to provide the victims with reparations.[91]

This is a reinstatement of the due diligence principle. Given that some harmful practices take place in private spheres, this decision becomes important in ensuring that states are held accountable for failure to address them.

4.3 Obligation to Fulfil

This requires states to take legislative, administrative, judicial and budgetary measures to address harmful practices. Such measures will include enacting laws to address harmful practices, ensuring access to justice for victims of harmful practices, and allocating adequate resources to eliminate harmful practices. The CEDAW Committee/CRC Committee has explained that states must enact, develop, implement and monitor relevant legislation in context of harmful practices. Moreover, states are to send a clear message of condemnation of harmful practices, provide legal protection for victims, enable state and non-state actors to protect women and children at risk, provide appropriate responses and care and ensure the availability of redress and an end to impunity.[92]

[89] See para 43 of General Comment 2 of the African Commission (n 2).

[90] *Zimbabwe Human Rights NGO Forum v Zimbabwe* (2005) AHRLR 128 (ACHPR 2005); see also *Egyptian Initiatives for Personal Rights v Egypt* (2011) AHRLR 90 (ACPHR 2011).

[91] *Zimbabwe Human Rights NGO Forum v Zimbabwe* (n 90) para 143.

[92] Joint General Recommendation 31 (n 14).

States are expected to adopt an inclusive approach by involving women and children in the legislative process to address harmful practices. This will ensure that the voices of marginalised and disadvantaged groups who are often victims of harmful practices are taken into consideration in the legislative drafting process.

As part of the obligation to fulfil, states are to ensure that victims of harmful practices have access to justice or remedy for the violations suffered. One of the challenges in many parts of the world is that disadvantaged groups who have experienced violations of their rights in the context of harmful practices are often denied access to remedy. More importantly, states must commit resources towards eliminating harmful practices. This requires that states consciously allocate adequate resources to efforts to combat harmful practices.

The UN Special Rapporteur on violence against women has noted that any measures adopted by states to address harmful practices must be rooted in a human rights-based approach.[93] States are further enjoined to launch investigations into various forms of harmful practices and mistreatment of women in health facilities with a view to identifying the root causes of these violations. More importantly, as part of their obligation to fulfil:

> States should establish constructive cooperation between health institutions and professional associations with women's non-governmental organizations, women's movements and independent human rights institutions dealing with reproductive and obstetric care.[94]

The African Commission and the African Committee of Experts have also noted that states should ensure legislative measures, administrative policies and procedures to prevent women and girls due to their HIV status, disabilities or ethnicity from being forced to adopt a certain treatment against their wishes.[95] The Commission and the Committee have urged

[93] UN Special Rapporteur on violence against women (n 57).

[94] Report of the Special Rapporteur on violence against women, its causes and consequences, Dubravka Šimonović 'Intersection between the coronavirus disease (COVID-19) pandemic and the pandemic of gender-based violence against women, with a focus on domestic violence and the "peace in the home" initiative' A/75/144 (24 July 2020) para 90 (l).

[95] See para 47 of General Comment 2 of the African Commission (n 19).

states to ensure the enforcement of protections of victims of harmful practices and equip courts and the judicial process to facilitate access to justice for the victims as well as appropriate punishment for perpetrators of harmful practices.[96] The Commission and Committee have further enjoined states to engage with men and traditional leaders through sensitisation programmes with a view to addressing harmful practices among communities.[97] It is further noted that states are to develop and implement National Action Plans on harmful practices. This will enable states to monitor and detect early enough possible human rights violations that may occur from a particular practice. States are enjoined to provide reparation for victims of child marriage and other harmful practices.[98]

5 Conclusion

This chapter has discussed the norms and standards to address harmful practices at intentional and regional levels. In doing this, specific human rights that may be violated by harmful practices have been discussed. These include the rights to life, non-discrimination, dignity and freedom from torture, cruel, inhuman and degrading treatment. Various human rights bodies at the international and regional levels have developed important norms and jurisprudence further explaining how harmful practices may undermine these human rights. The chapter further discusses the obligations of states to address harmful practices. These include the obligations to respect, protect and fulfil. Human rights bodies at the international and regional levels have explained the measures and steps states should adopt in order to address harmful practices. While legislative measures prohibiting and punishing harmful practices are important, this must be supplemented with other measures such as education and awareness programmes as well as engaging with men and traditional rulers with a view to soliciting their support in eradicating harmful practices. In addition, women and girls who are often victims of harmful practices should play crucial roles in decision-making to address harmful practices.

[96] Para 36 of the Joint General Comment on FGM (n 35).

[97] See para 53 of the Joint General Comment on ending child marriage (n 35).

[98] As above.

Bibliography

Albertyn, C & Goldblatt, B 'Facing the challenge of transformation: Difficulties in the development of an indigenous jurisprudence of equality' (1998) 14 *South African Journal on Human Rights* 248

Cook, RJ & Cusack, S *Gender stereotyping: Transnational legal perspective* (University of Pennsylvania Press 2010)

Dupre, C 'What does dignity mean in a legal context?' *The Guardian* 24 March 2011(2011) http://www.guardian.co.uk/commentisfree/libertycentral/2011/mar/24/dignity-uk-europe-human-rights (accessed 15 January 2025)

Durojaye, E 'The human rights implications of virginity testing in South Africa' (2016) 16 *International Journal of Discrimination and the Law* 228

Durojaye, E '"Woman but not human": Widowhood practices and human rights violations in Nigeria' (2013) 27 *International Journal of Law, Policy and Family* 176

Glensy, R 'The right to dignity' (2011) 43 *Columbia Human Rights Law Review* 66

Inter-American Commission on Human Rights press release 'On International Women's Day, the IACHR urges states to refrain from adopting measures that would set back respect for and protection of women's rights' (2018) http://www.oas.org/en/iachr/media_center/ PReleases/2018/044.asp (accessed 12 January 2025)

Johnson, A & Nabaneh, S 'Limits to achieving criminal accountability for violence against women with disabilities in Africa' in Budoo-Scholtz, A & Lubaale, EC (eds) *Violence against women and criminal justice in Africa: Volume II: Sustainable development goals series* (2022) 259

Nabaneh, S 'Article 5: Elimination of all harmful practices' in Rudman, A; Musembi, CN & Makunya, TM (eds) *Protocol to the African Charter on Human and Peoples' Rights on the Rights of Women in Africa: A commentary* (2023) 117

Nabaneh, S *Choice and conscience: Lessons from South Africa for a global debate* (Pretoria University Law Press 2023)

Nabaneh, S (ed) *Female genital mutilation in Africa: Politics of criminalisation* forthcoming (Pretoria University Law Press 2025)

Nabaneh, S & Muula, A 'Female genital mutilation/cutting: A complex legal and ethical landscape' (2019) 145 *International Journal of Gynecology & Obstetrics* 253

Case law and legal communications

APDF & IHRDA v Republic of Mali Application (Application 046/2016) [2018] AfCHPR 9 (11 May 2018)

Egypt Initiative for Personal Rights & INTERIGHTS v Egypt Communication 323/06 of 2011

ES and SC v Tanzania Communication 48/2013, UN Doc CEDAW/C/60/D/48/2013, 13 April 2015

Equality Now and Ethiopian Women Lawyers Association v Federal Republic of Ethiopia (Communication 341/2007) [2021] ACHPR 523 (14 October 2021)

Franz Nahlik v Austria Communication 608/1995, UN Doc CCPR/C/57/D/608/1995 (1996)

IV v Bolivia Preliminary Objections, Merits, Reparations and Costs, Judgment, Inter-American Court of Human Rights (ser C) No 329 (2016)

Millicent Awuor Omuya alias Maimuna Awuor v The Attorney General Petition 562 of 2012, Kenya High Court, Constitutional and Human Rights Division

NAE v Spain CEDAW/C/82/D/149/2019 (27 June 2022)

Purohit and Moore v The Gambia Communication 241/2001 (2003) AHRLR 96 (ACHPR 2003)

Zimbabwe Human Rights NGO Forum v Zimbabwe (2005) AHRLR 128 (ACHPR 2005)

International Treaties, Conventions, and Protocols

African Union, Protocol to the African Charter on Human and People's Rights on the Rights of Women in Africa, African Union, 11 July 2003

Organisation of African Unity (OAU), African Charter on the Rights and Welfare of the Child, 11 July 1990, AU Doc CAB/LEG/24.9/49 (1990)

UN General Assembly, Convention on the Elimination of All Forms of Discrimination Against Women, United Nations, Treaty Series, vol 1249, p 13, 18 December 1979

UN General Assembly, Convention on the Rights of the Child, United Nations, Treaty Series, vol 1577, p 3, 20 November 1989

UN General Assembly, Convention on the Rights of Persons with Disabilities: Resolution adopted by the General Assembly, 24 January 2007, UN Doc A/RES/61/106 (2007)

UN General Assembly, International Covenant on Civil and Political Rights, United Nations, Treaty Series, vol 999, p 171, 16 December 1966

UN General Assembly, International Covenant on Economic, Social and Cultural Rights, United Nations, Treaty Series, vol 993, p 3, 16 December 1966.

UN General Assembly, Universal Declaration of Human Rights, 10 December 1948, 217 A (III)

International Conferences and Action Plans

Beijing Plan of Action adopted during the Fourth World Conference on Women, 1995

International Conference on Population and Development, Cairo, Egypt, September 1994

General Recommendations, Comments, and Guidelines

ACERWC & ACHPR, Joint General Comment on female genital mutilation, 2023

ACHPR, General Comment 4 on the right to redress for victims of torture and other cruel, inhuman or degrading punishment or treatment (article 5), 2017

ACHPR, Guidelines to Combat Sexual Violence and its Consequences, adopted by the African Commission in Niamey, 2017

ACHPR, General Comment 1 on arts 14(1)(d) and (e) of the African Women's Protocol, adopted in 2012

ACHPR, General Comment 2 on art 14.1 (a), (b), (c), and (f) and Article 14.2 (a) and (c) of the Protocol to the African Charter on the Rights of Women, adopted in 2014

ACHPR & ACERWC, Joint General Comment of the African Commission on Human and Peoples' Rights (ACHPR) and the African Committee of Experts on the Rights and Welfare of the Child (ACERWC) on ending child marriage, 2017

CEDAW Committee, General Recommendation 35 (2017) on gender-based violence against women, updating General Recommendation 19 (1992), 26 July 2017, UN Doc CEDAW/C/GC/35 (2017)

Committee on Economic, Social and Cultural Rights (ESCR Committee), General Comment 14: The Right to the Highest Attainable Standard of Health (Art 12 of the Covenant), 11 August 2000, UN Doc E/C12/2000/4 (2000)

Committee on Economic, Social and Cultural Rights (ESCR Committee), General Comment 22 (2016) on the right to sexual and reproductive health (article 12 of the International Covenant on Economic, Social and Cultural Rights), 2 May 2016, UN Doc E/C.12/GC/22 (2016)

Committee on the Elimination of Discrimination Against Women, Concluding Observations on the sixth periodic report of the Czech Republic, 14 March 2016, UN Doc CEDAW/C/CZE/CO/6 (2016)

Committee on the Elimination of Discrimination Against Women, Consideration of reports submitted by states parties under article 18 of the Convention: Concluding Observations of the Committee on the Elimination of Discrimination Against Women: Czech Republic, 10 November 2010, UN Doc CEDAW/C/CZE/CO/5 (2010)

Committee on the Elimination of Discrimination Against Women & Committee on the Rights of the Child, Joint General Recommendation 31 of the Committee on the Elimination of Discrimination against Women/General Comment 18 of the Committee on the Rights of the Child on harmful practices, 14 November 2014, UN Doc CEDAW/C/GC/31-CRC/C/GC/18 (2014)

UN Committee on the Rights of the Child (CRC), General Comment 13 (2011): The right of the child to freedom from all forms of violence, 18 April 2011, UN Doc CRC/C/GC/13, (2011)

Human Rights Committee (HRC), General Comment 6: Article 6 (Right to Life), 30 April 1982

Human Rights Committee, General Comment 18: Non-discrimination (Thirty-seventh session, 1989), UN Doc HRI/GEN/1/Rev.1, 10 November 1989

Human Rights Committee (HRC), CCPR General Comment 28: Article 3 (The Equality of Rights Between Men and Women), 29 March 2000, UN Doc CCPR/C/21/Rev.1/Add.10 (2000)

Human Rights Committee, General Comment 35: Article 9 (Liberty and security of person), 16 December 2014, UN Doc CCPR/C/GC/35 (2014)

HRC 'Report of the Special Rapporteur on the right of everyone to the enjoyment of the highest attainable standard of physical and mental health, Tlaleng Mofokeng' UN Doc A/HRC/50/28 (2022)

CHAPTER 3

Widowhood Practices and Human Rights in Nigeria

Agah Deborah Achimugu-Opaluwa

1 Introduction

Human rights are the fundamental principles that govern our existence as human beings.[1] Every individual has these inherent rights, without discrimination or bias. The concept of human rights encompasses a wide range of legal and moral principles, including gender equality and non-discrimination rights.[2] These rights are enshrined in international human rights instruments, such as the Universal Declaration of Human Rights

[1] H Hannum and others International human rights: Problems of law, policy and practice (2023) 2–3.

[2] UK Ogu & AC Areji 'Gender equality and women's economic and sociocultural rights in Nigeria: Deconstructing the biases' (2023) 2 Journal of African Political Philosophy and Leadership: Philosophia Politica 58.

A. D. Achimugu-Opaluwa (✉)
Department of Public Law, Prince Abubakar Audu University, Anyigba, Nigeria
e-mail: agahachimugu@gmail.com

E. Durojaye et al. (eds.), *Harmful Practices and Human Rights: An International Perspective*, Human Rights Interventions,
https://doi.org/10.1007/978-3-031-90333-5_3

(Universal Declaration),[3] the International Covenant on Economic, Social and Cultural Rights (CESR),[4] the International Covenant on Civil and Political Rights (ICCPR),[5] the Convention on the Elimination of All Forms of Discrimination Against Women (CEDAW).[6] Similarly, human rights principles are enshrined in regional human rights instruments such as the African Charter on Human and Peoples' Rights (African Charter),[7] and the Protocol to the African Charter on Human and Peoples' Rights on the Rights of Women in Africa (Maputo Protocol).[8] In addition, the Constitution of the Federal Republic of Nigeria, 1999 (S.42 Nigerian Constitution 1999) also guarantees these human rights principles. Similarly, the Violence Against Persons (Prohibition) Act[9] protects widows who are deprived of their personal liberty.

However, despite the existence of these legal frameworks, instances of human rights violations persist in the realm of harmful and discriminatory practices towards widows across many communities in Nigeria.[10] Widowhood occurs when a person loses his wife or her husband to death, thereby becoming a single person all over again.[11]

Nigeria is located in West Africa with a population of approximately 200 million people, an estimated 99.13 million of these are women.[12] Widowhood practices vary across the approximately 250 different ethnic

[3] UN General Assembly, Universal Declaration of Human Rights, 217 A (III), 10 December 1948.

[4] UN General Assembly, International Covenant on Economic, Social and C ultural Rights, 16 December 1966, United Nations, Treaty Series, vol 993, 3.

[5] UN General Assembly, International Covenant on Civil and Political Rights, 16 December 1966, United Nations, Treaty Series, vol 999, 171.

[6] UN General Assembly, Convention on the Elimination of All Forms of Discrimination Against Women, 18 December 1979, United Nations, Treaty Series, vol 1249, 13.

[7] Organisation of African Unity (OAU), African Charter on Human and Peoples' Rights (Banjul Charter), 27 June 1981, CAB/LEG/67/3 rev 5, 21 ILM 58 (1982).

[8] African Union, Protocol to the African Charter on Human and People's Rights on the Rights of Women in Africa, 11 July 2003.

[9] Violence Against Persons (Prohibition) Act (VAPPA) 2015.

[10] U Kalu and O Umunna "Harmful Cultural Practice and Women's Rights in Nigeria" (2022) 3 *LASJURE 2022* 107.

[11] NJ Ezeilo Women, law and human rights: Global and national perspectives (2011) 249.

[12] AJ Kaba 'Explaining Africa's rapid population growth, 1950 to 2020: Trends, factors, implications, and recommendations' (2020) 10 Sociology Mind 226.

groups in the country.[13] In most communities in Nigeria, widows are subjected to various harmful and discriminatory practices.[14] These widowhood practices range from forced re-marriages, living in isolation, shaving of hair, compelling the widow to drink water used to wash her deceased husband's corpse, eviction from her home, and denial of her inheritance rights, to experiencing physical, emotional, and psychological abuses, which are inherent traditions given the patriarchal nature of the Nigerian society.[15] These widowhood practices are examples of gender inequality, which is embedded in patriarchal structures.[16]

Gender inequality persists all over the world, and women continue to face discrimination as a result of religious and cultural practices.[17] Women are assigned different roles in society due to culture and religion and are restricted to the roles of childbearing and homemaking in a patriarchal setting.[18] Women are still treated as children in some parts of the world, particularly in Africa, and as second-class citizens who are only seen and not heard.[19] Gender inequality is a distinction made by society that is deeply ingrained in patriarchy.[20] Over the years, patriarchy has been analysed to be the origin of men's oppression of women.[21]

Flowing from above, this chapter seeks to analyse numerous widowhood practices present in Nigerian communities and justify them as

[13] J Olukayode 'Widowhood practices in some Nigerian societies: A retrospective examination' (2015) 5 International Journal of Humanities and Social Science 67.

[14] GE Afolayan 'Widowhood practices and the rights of women: The case of South-Western Nigeria' (2011) http://thesis.eur.nl/pub/1081 (accessed 3 July 2023).

[15] A Adedara 'Persistency of the reprehensible cultural practices against widows of the widowhood classes in Nigeria: Legal analysis' (2023) 14 African Journals Online 24.

[16] E Alemika 'Family practices and violations of the rights of women' (2010) 8 University of Maiduguri Law Journal 25.

[17] S Tamale 'The right to culture and the culture of rights: A critical perspective on women's sexual rights in Africa' (2008) 16 Feminist Legal Studies 47.

[18] A Mama 'Heroes and villains: Conceptualising colonial and contemporary violence against women in Africa' in M Alexander et al (eds) Feminist genealogies, colonial legacies, democratic futures (1997) 46–62.

[19] M Ssenyonjo 'Culture and human rights of women in Africa: Between light and shadow' (2007) 51 Journal of African Law 39.

[20] C Mackinnon Sexual harassment of working women: a case of sex discrimination (1979) 3–7.

[21] C Kramarae 'The condition of patriarchy' in C Kramarae & S Dale (eds) The knowledge explosion: Generation of feminist scholarship (1993) 397.

instances of human rights violations, using a feminist lens. Additionally, to examine the legal framework in place to address these widowhood practices and to assess if these legal frameworks are consistent with international human rights law obligations. Furthermore, to investigate the challenges to safeguards against harmful widowhood practices in Nigeria and recommend ways forward for widows.

2 Widowhood Practices in Nigeria

Widowhood practices in most Nigerian communities are heavily influenced by cultural and traditional beliefs.[22] In order to preserve traditions, various detrimental and discriminatory cultural practices that are antagonistic to the welfare of widows are tenaciously retained.[23] In many parts of Nigeria, a widow is expected to undergo certain rites and practices in order to prove her innocence and loyalty to her husband's family.[24] These practices often involve the widow being forced to sleep in the same bed as her husband's corpse for several days, shaving her head completely, and being subjected to other degrading and humiliating practices.[25] The cultural and traditional beliefs that underpin these practices are largely based on the patriarchal nature of most Nigerian communities.[26] As a result, widowhood is seen as a loss of status in society and a potential threat to the entire family's honour and reputation.[27] These practices not only violate the human rights of widows but also perpetuate their exclusion from mainstream society and limit their ability to participate fully

[22] Afolayan, Gbenga—Widowhood Practices and the Rights of Women: The Case of South-Western Nigeria 2015/07/31 DO—10.13140/RG.2.1.4749.5521 (accessed 15 January 2025).

[23] E Durojaye '"Woman, but not human": Widowhood practices and human rights violations in Nigeria' (2013) 27 International Journal of Law, Policy and the Family 176.

[24] MI Nwogu 'The legal anatomy of cultural widowhood practices in South Eastern Nigeria: The need for a panacea' (2015) 3 Global Journal of Politics and Law Research 80.

[25] F Anyogu Access to justice in Nigeria: A gender perspective (2013) 98.

[26] RA Onuoha 'Discriminatory property inheritance under customary law in Nigeria: NGOS to the rescue' (2008) 10 International Journal of Not-for-Profit Law 79.

[27] AB Okoli & L Okuosa 'The role of Christianity in gender and development in Nigeria' (2020) 76 HTS Theologies Studies/Theological Studies 1.

in economic, social, and political life.[28] Thus, addressing the beliefs and attitudes that influence the treatment of widows is crucial to promoting their human rights and empowerment.

Feminists regard these practices as dehumanising, demeaning, barbarous, rude, archaic, and deeply unacceptable. The death of a woman's husband signals grave suffering, abuse, and violations of her human rights by community cultural agents, especially her spouse's family.[29] These harmful and discriminatory cultural practices are perpetuated because most Nigerian communities are patriarchal, and they include, among others:

2.1 Denial of Property Rights

In most Nigerian communities, the denial of property rights to widows is a major issue that persists despite legal reforms to protect the rights of women.[30] Widows often face eviction from their homes and family property and are left without any means of supporting themselves and their children.[31] This reflects a deeply entrenched cultural belief that widows are usually the cause of the death of their husbands.[32] When a widow is forced to leave her house because of discriminatory customary laws that deny women the right to inherit, it not only perpetuates gender inequality but may also limit women's access to economic resources and leads to poverty.[33]

Traditionally, women are excluded from ownership of land, which is culturally the exclusive preserve of men.[34] Succession in most Nigerian communities is in accordance with the prevalent traditions, customs, and practices of the local people who are subject to it. The prevailing rule in Igbo customary law is that a widow has no claim to inherit her husband's

[28] M Dube 'Isolation and its impacts on widows: Insights from low-resourced communities in Binga district Zimbabwe (2022) 11 Social Sciences 1.

[29] Y Olomojobi Human rights on gender, sex and the law in Nigeria (2021) 354–392.

[30] Ezeilo (n 10) 249–258.

[31] T Adekunle 'Succession and inheritance law in Nigeria: Resolving the discriminatory proprietary rights of widows and children' https://www.academia.edu/35665674 (accessed 3 July 2023).

[32] Adedara (n 14) 24–33.

[33] Durojaye (n 22) 176–196.

[34] Olomojobi (n 28) 249–258.

personal or property estate. This is the practice in Ugwaji-Awkunanaw Community, Enugu State, South-East Nigeria,[35] and among the Aten tribe in Riyom Local Government Area of Plateau State, widows are denied the right to inherit land belonging to their husbands.[36] Some of these practices appear to have been validated by the courts in Nigeria as can be seen in some decided cases. The Supreme Court of Nigeria ruled in *Nezianya v Okagbue*[37] that a widow under Onitsha customary law may deal with her deceased husband's property, but only with the approval of the family. Similarly, in *Nzekwu v Nzekwu*,[38] a case on a widow's right to inherit her late husband's property under Igbo (Onitsha) custom where the widow had only two female children,-the court held that her right is only possessory and not proprietary. She is allowed to occupy the building or part of it subject to good behaviour.

The Yorubas have a well-established norm that a wife is not entitled to inherit her husband's property. She is treated as a component of her late husband's inheritance under intestacy, and the family of the deceased will administer and inherit her.[39] It is believed that property inheritance follows the blood as it was decided in *Sogunro Davies v Sogunro*.[40] In *Suberu v Sunmonu*,[41] it was decided that the rule of Yoruba native law and customs prohibiting wives from inheriting their husbands' property because they are like chattels to be inherited by a relative of their husband, should be consigned to history and deemed incompatible with natural justice, equity, and good conscience. The Supreme Court in *Akinnubi v Akinnubi*[42] upheld the same judgement. However, the custom that

[35] A Ajayi 'Disinheritance: Widows in Igboland battle against culture that men love to preserve (Part 2)' ICIR (27 October 2020) https://www.icirnigeria.org/disinheritance-widows-in-igboland-battle-against-culture-that-men-love-to-preserve-part-2/ (accessed 16 July 2023).

[36] L Sadiq 'Inside Nigeria's harmful traditional practices that impede women's rights to land ownership' (2022) https://dailytrust.com/inside-nigerias-harmful-traditional-practices-that-impede-womens-rights-to-land-ownership/ (accessed 16 July 2023).

[37] 1963 (I) ALL NLR 352.

[38] 1989 (2) NWLR (pt. 104) 317.

[39] Adedara (n 14) 24–33.

[40] 1929 (2) NLR 79.

[41] 1957 (2) FSC 23.

[42] 1972 (2) UILR 313.

denies the wife the right to inheritance has been condemned by the courts as unreasonable and discriminatory.[43]

Widows generally lack the resources and support necessary to pursue legal remedies, leaving them vulnerable to economic exploitation and social exclusion.[44] The Nigerian government has taken steps to address this problem by enacting laws and establishing a National Commission for the Protection of Human Rights, but the implementation of these measures remains a challenge.[45] Ultimately, the denial of property rights to widows reflects a broader problem of gender inequality and cultural barriers to the advancement of women's rights in Nigeria. More worrisome is the fact that Nigerian courts, including the apex court, have given recognition to some of these practices, simply on the basis that the marriages were subject to native law and customs, hence, the body of law that should apply should be the principles in such native law and customs, notwithstanding that they are obnoxious and offensive to human rights as enshrined in local statutory laws and international legal instruments. Generally, Nigerian courts are expected to subject native law and customs to the repugnancy test, which requires that they must be repugnant to natural justice, equity, and good conscience.[46] It is therefore curious whether the courts, in these cases cited above, subjected these customs to the repugnancy test.

2.2 *Forced Isolation and Quasi-Imprisonment*

In Nigeria, widows in many ethnic groups are isolated from the community for a period of time.[47] Upon the death of her husband, a widow is not allowed to go out for business, work or attend a public function. She is required to mourn her husband for a period of time depending on the culture of the place. In the Igbo ethnic group, a widow is not allowed to go anywhere for 28 days after which she performs certain rituals in order

[43] Anekwe v Nweke (2014) NWLR Pt 1412.

[44] AK Adebayo 'An appraisal of customary succession in the Western and Eastern part of Nigeria' (2022) 8 Commonwealth Law Review 387.

[45] MO Imasogie 'Comparative study of aspects of gender equality under the Nigerian and the South African laws' Doctoral thesis, University of Pretoria, 2000, 169.

[46] FO Igbineweka & EO Enakireru 'Customary law in Nigeria: Interrogating the Issue of judicial notice' (2022) 3 ACARELAR 55.

[47] Durojaye (n 22) 176–196.

to regain her freedom. During the period of mourning, she is not allowed to bath, cook, work, or trade. She is confined to a dark and lonely room, where she is fed by other widows from old plates that will be thrown away after mourning. Her isolation stems from the fact that she has to prove that she had no hand in her husband's death.[48]

This practice affects the emotional and psychological well-being of the widow. This harmful and discriminatory widowhood practice does not apply to a widower. When a man loses his wife, the customary practice is that he is required to sleep with another woman to prevent the spirit of his late wife from disturbing him.[49] This practice of isolation of widows against their freewill is obviously a clear violation of their freedom of movement and association as enshrined in the Nigerian Constitution[50] and African Charter.[51] These domestic and regional legal instruments are clear on the right of persons to move freely throughout Nigeria, without restrictions, and the right to associate peacefully with anyone or group. The psychological impact of these violations is beyond quantification because it automatically and abruptly demotes the widow to the status of a prisoner. When this is visualised from the context of a person that has only recently lost a spouse, who is still grieving and perhaps worrying over her ability to take care of and fend for her children and dependents, the graveness and inhumanness of such practices is indisputable. It must be stated that Nigeria does not have a robust and reliable social safety net to cater to the welfare and well-being of the poor and vulnerable. A widow, often times is not the breadwinner of the family, and, lacks the economic ability to bear the burden of caring and providing for the family. Hence, the worry about the basic needs of survival becomes a major priority for most widows in Nigeria. This, therefore, makes the burden of forced isolation and imprisonment additional torture and results in loss of time to pursue sources of livelihood.

[48] NA Nwanegbo Challenge of widowhood (1996) 11–13.

[49] NJ Ezeilo 'Rethinking women and customary inheritance in Nigeria' (2021) 47 Commonwealth Law Bulletin 706.

[50] Secs 40 & 41.

[51] Art 6 & 10.

2.3 *Dehumanising Treatments*

Over the years, widows are subjected to primitive practices whereby a widow who is accused of killing her husband is subjected to different forms of unpleasant and dehumanising treatments to prove her innocence.[52] This is based on the false presumption that a man could not have passed away naturally. The reason for his death must therefore be determined. Unfortunately, the deceased's wife is frequently the main suspect and will have to go through these torturous practices to demonstrate her innocence.[53] In some instances, a widow is compelled to drink water used to wash the corpse of her husband in circumstances where she is suspected to have killed him.[54] These practices obviously violate the widow's right to presumption of innocence and her right to be heard fairly by a judicial body and not by a non-state body of persons that appropriate the right of adjudication to themselves and function as accuser, prosecutor, and judge at the same time.

Other dehumanising widowhood practices include a widow being made to swear to prove her innocence by crossing her husband's coffin three times or more, taking an oath before the deity of her husband's family, or being compelled to sleep alone in the same room with the corpse of her husband. In addition, a widow is made to wear rags and walk barefoot until her mourning period is over. In some parts of Nigeria, it is considered appropriate that a widow must form a routine of crying constantly to demonstrate that her husband's passing was a tremendous grief that can only be represented through constant crying. When a woman's husband dies, it is traditional for her to weep openly and exhibit a strong sense of loss. In some societies, women are compelled to weep loudly day and night.[55] Indeed, these practices offend the right to dignity of the human person as enshrined in the Constitution of Nigeria. Such practices are capable of forcing a grieving woman into panic attacks, a nervous breakdown or irreparable psychological damage. It is common to

[52] Nwogu (n 23) 80.

[53] A Oyeniyi & I Ayodeji 'Widowhood practices among the Yorubas of South West Nigeria: Are there differences in what women experience due to their status?' (2010) 8 Gender and Behaviour 3152.

[54] CB Ike & OS Akujobi 'Widowhood in lonely days: Unsung casualties' (2021) 8 Akwa Journal of English and Literary Studies 1.

[55] Adedara (n 14) 24–33.

see widows become broken and defeated after such an ordeal; in fact, this increases their chances of developing permanent health problems, which compounds their vulnerabilities and that of their children. These practices effectively cement widowhood as a plague in these communities.

Some patriarchal practices in Nigeria involve shaving a widow's head of hair when her spouse passes away. According to cultural norms, cutting the widow's hair is one way to demonstrate that she is sincerely grieving the loss of her husband, and refusing to do so could raise suspicions that she was somehow involved in his death.[56] These practices are harmful, discriminatory and constitute a violation of widows' human rights.[57] These widowhood practices reflect a lack of gender equality because widowers are not subjected to these dangerous and dehumanising ordeals. It is believed that all forms of discrimination associated with gender inequality are products of patriarchy.[58]

2.4 *Forced or Levirate Marriage*

Another common widowhood practice in Nigeria is the practice of forced or levirate marriages. This refers to the custom where a man from the deceased husband's family is expected to marry the widow as a means of continuing his lineage.[59] A widow is viewed as the husband's property.[60] When her husband dies, she is compelled to be inherited by a relative of the husband in order to preserve her position in the family.[61] This practice is often enforced through cultural and religious beliefs, as failure to carry out this practice could result in the belief that the deceased's lineage

[56] Ogu & Areji (n 2) 58–70.

[57] B Onyima 'Widows in Nigeria are sometimes treated badly: culture is no excuse to violate rights' The Conversation (22 June 2022) https://theconversation.com/widows-in-nigeria-are-sometimes-treated-badly-culture-is-no-excuse-to-violate-rights-184934 (accessed 4 July 2023).

[58] P Miller Patriarchy (2017) 84–118.

[59] GC Samuel 'Emergent issues on widowhood practices in Igbo culture: Between the video screen and reality' (2011) 8 Unizik Journal of Arts and Humanities 184.

[60] AO Otaluka The rights of widows (1992) 1.

[61] Y Kudo 'Does criminalizing discriminatory cultural practices improve women's welfare? A simple model of levirate marriage in Africa' (2021) 199 Economic Letters 109728.

has been cut off.[62] While this practice may have been well-intentioned in ancient times, it is now considered a violation of women's rights and can lead to instances of abuse and exploitation.[63] Women who do not want to participate in levirate marriages risk being ostracised from their communities. In some cases, they may even face violence or death.[64] Many women in various Nigerian communities are afraid of widowhood. This is due not just to the agony of losing their husbands, but also to the myriad of dehumanising rituals and practices associated with widowhood.

This practice is also a way of potentially forcing a widow to inadvertently become a non-consensual participant in the offence of bigamy, where her new spouse, albeit, a forced husband in a forced marriage, may be married to another wife at that time. This equally elicits the additional consequence of forcing a woman who was previously in a monogamous marriage into a polygamous setting against her will and freedom of choice, with the attendant danger of drawing animosity from the wife of the new, albeit, forced husband.

The Nigerian government must do more to protect the rights of widows and ensure that cultural practices do not impede on these rights. If there are legal measures in place to prevent forced or levirate marriages among widows, a widow who chooses to remarry will have the chance to select a partner without cultural interference.

3 Widowhood Practices and Fundamental Rights Implications in Nigeria

The significance of human rights and widowhood practices in Nigeria lies in their implications for the protection of vulnerable members of society. Human rights are fundamental rights that are inherent to all human

62 OO Fasoranti & YO Aruna (2007) 'A Cross-cultural comparison of practices relating to widowhood and widow-inheritance among the Igbo and Yoruba in Nigeria' (2007) 111 Journal of World Anthropology: Occasional Papers 373.

63 O Dominic & VO Okeyi 'Christian impact on obnoxious traditional widowhood practices in Nigeria' (2023) 4 Aku: An African Journal of Contemporary Research 117.

64 C Odimegwu & CN Okemgbo 'Gender role ideologies and prevalence of violence against women in Imo State Nigeria' (2003) 5 Anthropologist 225.

beings, irrespective of race, gender, religion, or any other distinction.[65] They include the non-discrimination rights, right to dignity and property rights among others.[66]

3.1 Non-Discrimination Rights

The Nigerian Constitution prohibits gender-based discrimination.[67] Section 42 of the Constitution becomes crucial here as it reveals how cultural and patriarchal traditions infringe upon widows' rights to both inheritance and dignity, directly contradicting the provisions of the Constitution. Within the framework of the Nigerian Constitution, which explicitly prohibits gender-based discrimination, a significant incongruity arises in the treatment of widows and widowers upon the death of a spouse.

Specifically, while the Constitution mandates equal treatment, societal norms dictate that widows endure specific challenges not shared by their male counterparts. This disparity is justified by the notion that a widow's actions are a tribute to her late husband, perpetuating the misconception that the responsibility for honouring the deceased is primarily a duty assigned to women, thus reinforcing gendered notions of respect and authority.

3.2 Right to Dignity

In the context of widowhood practices in Nigeria, human rights are particularly relevant as they provide a framework for addressing the various forms of abuse, and violence that widows may face.[68] Section 34 of the Nigerian Constitution provides that 'no person shall be subject to torture or to inhuman or degrading treatment'. Notwithstanding, widows in Nigeria are often subjected to harmful traditional practices,

65 MA Iguh & MO Ugwu 'Protecting and promoting the rights of persons with disability in Nigeria' (2023) 5 International Review of Law and Jurisprudence (IRLJ) 153.

66 E Osita Human rights in Africa: Some selected problems (1984) 4.

67 Sec 42 of the Nigerian Constitution, 1999.

68 Durojaye (n 22) 176–196; sec 34 of the Nigerian Constitution.

such as forced marriage, eviction from their homes, and denial of inheritance rights, which violate their human rights and impede their ability to participate fully in society.[69]

They are often blamed for the death of their husbands and subjected to various forms of abuse, including physical violence and forced evictions from their homes. Therefore, it is vital to promote and protect human rights and combat harmful widowhood practices to ensure the well-being and empowerment of widows in Nigeria.

3.3 Property Rights

The negative impact of widowhood practices in Nigeria is not only limited to the widows themselves. Children of widows also suffer greatly from discriminatory practices. In many Nigerian communities, children are seen as extensions of the man and his family, and not as independent human beings. Thus, when a man dies, his children are often deemed as property of his family. In such cases, the man's family takes control of the children, leaving the widows helpless and unable to protect her offspring. The children of widows are frequently subjected to emotional and physical abuse and could be denied basic rights such as education and healthcare. The lack of protection and legal measures to safeguard the rights of widows and their children perpetuates and strengthens such harmful practices. Overall, the violations of human rights through widowhood practices in Nigeria have far-reaching consequences for individuals and communities and require urgent attention and action from both the government and society as a whole.

The impact of human rights violations on widows in Nigeria cannot be overemphasised. These women often face numerous challenges, including economic marginalisation, social stigmatisation, and psychological trauma. The denial of property inheritance, forced remarriage and the pressure to perform certain rituals add to the plight of widows. These practices violate the fundamental human rights of widows and prevent them from leading a dignified life. Furthermore, the lack of legal protections for widows exacerbates their vulnerability and reinforces the cycle

[69] TS Ali and others 'Widowhood' In P Ali & MM Rogers (eds) Gender-based violence: A comprehensive guide (2023) https://doi.org/10.1007/978-3-031-05640-6_13 (accessed 4 July 2023).

of abuse.[70] Addressing human rights violations against widows in Nigeria require sustained efforts from government and civil society organisations to raise awareness, enact stronger laws, and provide support to victims. Without these measures, widows in Nigeria will continue to experience significant hardship and injustice.

4 Legal Framework That Protects Widows Against Discriminatory Practices

In Nigeria, the Constitution of the Federal Republic of Nigeria, 1999 (as amended) is a primary law and the grundnorm in the sense that it applies to everyone and supersedes all other laws. The Nigerian Constitution is the foundation of all human rights protection and has supremacy over all other laws. Section 1 (1) & (3)[71] provides that the Constitution is supreme, and its provisions have binding force on all authorities, persons, and render void any other law that is inconsistent with the provisions of the Constitution.

In addition, section 42 opposes any form of discrimination based on gender. It provides that:

> A citizen of Nigeria of a particular community, ethnic group, place of origin, sex, religion or political opinion shall not, by reason only that he is such a person:-
>
> (a) be subjected either expressly by, or in the practical application of, any law in force in Nigeria or any executive or administrative action of the government, to disabilities or restrictions to which citizens of Nigeria of other communities, ethnic groups, places of origin, sex, religious or political opinions are not made subject.

According to this provision, the Nigerian Constitution prohibits discriminatory practices against individuals based on sex. However, when a woman dies, the widower is not expected to go through the same ordeals as the widow. These rigours are explained away by the fact that she is

[70] MO Imasogie 'Violence against women: An international perspective' in JA Sokefun (eds) The family and the law (2001) 43–48.

[71] Sec 1 (1) & (3) Nigerian Constitution.

paying tribute to her late husband. This illustrates the mistaken assumption that concordance of respect is solely the domain of men, but respect for the dead is the domain of women.[72] The significance of section 42 is that the cultural or patriarchal practices highlighted above violate the Constitution's protections for widows' rights to inheritance and dignity. The Nigerian Court of Appeal in *Asika v Atuanya*[73] upheld section 42 of the Constitution while addressing a discriminating customary practice against women's inheritance. The Court held that it seems that these provisions, especially the provision as contained in section 42(2) of the Constitution, are specific and categorical that 'no citizen of Nigeria shall be subjected to any disability or deprivation merely by reason of the circumstances of his birth'.

In addition, *Ukeje v Ukeje*[74] the lower court and the superior courts both held that the Igbo customary law which denies female children from inheriting from their father's estate is in contravention of section 42 of the Nigerian Constitution. Although this decision is not about a widow's right to inherit, it suffices to say that the Nigerian Constitution prohibits gender discrimination. In *Anekwe v Nweke*[75] Maria Nweke and her six female children were deprived of her deceased husband's property because she had no male child. She argued that the court should declare her entitled to the statutory right of occupancy of a parcel of land in Amikwo village. The Supreme Court gave judgement in favour of the defendant by stating that customs that oppressed females and protect males are discriminatory.

Similarly, the dignity of human persons is guaranteed under section 34 of the Constitution. These harmful cultural practices infringe the express provisions of this constitutionally guaranteed right. The protection and advancement of human dignity of persons is one of the objectives of the Nigerian Constitution. In other words, it affirms the 'sanctity of the human person' and the human and equal rights of every citizen.[76]

[72] C Arinze-Umobi & F Anyogu 'The widow in South-East of Nigeria in legal and customary turbulence: Need for mandatory paradigm shift' (2014) 8 International Journal of Research and Development 1.

[73] (2013) LPELR—20895 (SC).

[74] (2014) 11 NWLR (PT.1418) 384.

[75] (2014) NWLR Pt 1412.

[76] Secs 33–35, 37 & 41–42 of the Nigerian Constitution.

The Constitution prohibits the dehumanising treatment of widows. For instance, cruel treatment such as forced hair-shaving, eviction from home, denial of inheritance rights, isolation, being compelled to drink the water used to wash the corpse of her deceased husband and other such harmful and discriminatory practices violate the rights of widows to human dignity, personal liberty, and peaceful association. The Nigerian Constitution protects widows from being forced to marry their deceased husband's family due to cultural practices.

Section 35 of the Nigerian Constitution protects the personal liberty of every Nigerian citizen. This includes the personal liberty of widows from isolation and restriction after the demise of their husbands.[77] In addition, section 10 of the Violence Against Persons (Prohibition) Act, 2015 (VAPP)[78] protects widows who are deprived of their liberty, criminalises and punishes those who deprive them of their liberty by being liable to a term of imprisonment not exceeding two years, 500,000 Naira or both. The perpetrators of isolation of widows after the death of their husbands under the guise of widowhood rites deprive widows of their personal liberty. This act is unconstitutional and a human rights violation.

Although the Federal Government of Nigeria is yet to enact other laws that will specifically protect widows from cruel and discriminatory practices as a measure to protect the rights of widows in accordance with the obligation of international and regional human rights instruments to which Nigeria is a signatory. However, some Nigerian states have enacted specific laws to address the harmful and discriminatory practices meted on widows. The Anambra State Malpractices against Widow and Widowers (Prohibition) Law, 2005 (ASMWW)[79] gave recognition of widows and widowers' rights by stating that the fundamental human rights as enshrined in the Constitution are inalienable and accrue to every widow and widower. Section 4 (1)(b) of the Law provides that no person shall compel a widow or widower to do any of the things stipulated in paragraphs (a)-(o) which include, drinking the water used in washing the corpse of the spouse or performing any type of ritual in order to establish innocence causing the death of the late spouse, to sleep either alone

[77] Ogu & Areji (n 2) 64.

[78] VAPP Act, 2015.

[79] The Anambra State Malpractices against Widow and Widowers (Prohibition) Law, 2005 (ASMWW).

on the same bed or to be locked in the same room with the corpse of a late spouse or to remain in compulsory confinement after death of the spouse for any given period, and so on. Section 5 provides for a fine of 20,000 Naira or imprisonment not exceeding six months, or both such fine and imprisonment. This law criminalises and punishes anyone who subjects a widow to harmful and discriminatory practices. However, it is believed that punishment is grossly inadequate considering the weight of abuse and violations that widows pass through that may even cost their lives. A fine of 20,000 Naira is definitely not commensurate to the plight of widows neither is a prison term of six months sufficient deterrence for such grossly criminal and abusive actions.

Additionally, section 4 (1) of the Enugu State Prohibition of Infringement of a Widow's and Widower's Fundamental Rights Law[80] provides that a widow shall not be subjected to any of the following:

a. permit the hairs on the head or any part of the body to be shaved;
b. to sleep either alone or on the same bed, or be locked in a room with corpse of the husband;
c. not to receive condolence visits from sympathisers during the period of the husband's burial rights;
d. to drink the water used in washing the corpse of the husband;
e. to weep and wail loudly at intervals at anytime after the death of the husband except at one's own volition or involuntary action;
f. to remain in confinement after the death of the husband for any given period;
g. to vacate the matrimonial home, and
h. to do any act that contravenes the fundamental rights entrenched in the Constitution i.e. degrading the person.

Similarly, section 4(3) of the above Law provides that a widow or widower shall not be dispossessed (of property acquired during the deceased husband/wife's lifetime) upon the death of the husband/wife without his or her consent. Furthermore, section 5sanctions violation of this Law with N5000 fine or two years in prison. This law did not only condemn this discriminatory practice of dispossessing widows of their inheritance

[80] Enugu State of Nigeria, No 3 on Prohibition of Infringement of a Widow's and Widower's Fundamental Rights Law 2001 (PIWWFRL).

rights; it also penalises such discriminatory acts. However, it is argued that the fine is inadequate and two years' prison term will not discourage the deceased husband's relatives from depriving his widow of her inheritance nor abusing her constitutionally guaranteed rights. The inadequacies of these laws to deter such conducts have inadvertently created an incentive for these practices to continue to be perpetrated because relatives of the husband of a widow are likely going to weigh their potential gain where they apply these prohibited conducts and the possible sanction and may rather opt to err on the side of violation of the law but retain other illegal gains. For example, the family of the deceased will rather attempt to seize the personal properties of the deceased which, may be worth millions of Naira, and will be emboldened and willing to face the danger of a maximum six months' imprisonment or a paltry fine.

It is for the above reasons that despite these laws, these obnoxious practices continue to exist, and many women continue to be affected. For instance, Deborah Odo sometime in April 2018, was ejected from her husband's country home in Enugu State by some family members of her deceased husband for allegedly having a hand in his death.[81] Even before the ejection, the woman had cried out against the continued harassment, intimidation, and threat of ejection from her late husband's country home by relatives of her husband. According to her, they have made life unbearable for her and the children since the death of her husband in 2017 and accused the family members of attempting to use every available tactic, false allegations, including unlawful means, to evict her and her children from the said home.[82]

The Administration of Estate Law of Lagos State and the Administration of Estate Act regulates the property of a deceased who married under the Act and died intestate. This Law protects the rights of women married under Marriage Act and not women who are married under customary law.[83] This is a major gap under the Nigerian legal system because currently, marriages can be conducted under three possible legal regimes that are marriage under the Marriage Act/Matrimonial Causes Act, marriage under customary law, or native law and customs, and

[81] 'Rising cases of harmful widowhood practices in Igbo communities' Vanguard (24 May 2023).

[82] As above.

[83] Section 49 of the Administration of Estate Law of Lagos State 2015 (AELL).

marriage under Islamic law. The protections contained in the Administration of Estate Act and similar laws in various states, apply only to marriages conducted under the Act. This, therefore, leaves the other two categories of marriages to inheritance and intestacy rules that are derived either from peculiar customs of each community or from Sharia law, where it is an Islamic marriage. Although the Supreme Court Ordinance 1914 and section 16 of the Evidence Act have prescribed the repugnancy test, several state legislations for example section 16 of the Imo State customary law limit the application of the test. The section is hereby reproduced below:

> *Subject to S. 247 and 249 of the Constitution and provisions of this law*, a Customary Court or a Customary Court of Appeal shall administer. (a) the customary law prevailing in the area of jurisdiction ... In so far as it is not repugnant to natural justice, equity, and good conscience.

It is surprising to note that the repugnancy test and requirement for compatibility of customs with equity, natural justice, and good conscience is not an absolute test because it is made subject to other provisions of the law. It is this lacuna that some courts have exploited to preserve customs that are obnoxious and have technically established precedents that have reinforced the problem.

The Nigerian government has ratified several regional human rights instruments that prohibit discrimination and foster gender equality. The major regional human rights instruments that shall be considered here, are the African Charter and the Maputo Protocol. This is because the African Charter has been domesticated in Nigeria and the Maputo Protocol although it has not yet been domesticated, considers and addresses the age-long discrimination suffered by women in Africa. The African Charter guarantees the rights of widows against discrimination. Article 2 provides that:

> Every individual shall be entitled to the enjoyment of the rights and freedoms recognized and guaranteed in the present Charter without distinction of any kind such as race, ethnic group, colour, sex, language, religion, political or any other opinion, national and social origin, fortune, birth or other status.

This article protects widows from patriarchal or cultural practices that discriminate against them by evicting them from their homes, forced remarriage to their deceased husbands' relatives, and compelling them to do what widowers will not be subjected to. A more vivid and suitable definition of discrimination against women was given by the Maputo Protocol.[84] Article 1(f) defines discrimination as any distinction, exclusion or restriction, or differential treatment based on sex with the aim of destroying the human rights of women in all spheres of life. The Maputo Protocol gave recognition to the fact that discrimination against women is based on sex. This means that the differential treatment of widows is simply because they are women and nothing more. In addition, the Nigerian government is obligated to combat all forms of discrimination against women by enacting appropriate laws and institutional measures to promote the principle of gender equality.[85] Article 3[86] promotes the right to dignity of women. Widowhood practices in Nigeria are a human rights violation and contravene the provision of this article. Similarly, most widowhood practices to which widows are subjected to are harmful. For instance, compelling a widow to drink the water used to wash the corpse of her deceased husband will not only affect her dignity but also affects her health and may lead to death.[87] Article 3 of the Maputo Protocol mandates states parties to eliminate harmful practices against widows by enacting laws, creating public awareness, and providing necessary support to victims of harmful practices. However, the Nigerian government has no programme to raise awareness of discriminatory widowhood practices. There are programmes on other issues like malaria, polio, and HIV/AIDS, but there is no awareness at the federal level of these discriminatory widowhood practices.

Further, article 5[88] provides that 'every individual shall have the right to the respect of the dignity inherent in a human to the recognition of his legal status'. This provision guarantees an individual's right to dignity. It also prohibits all forms of cruel, inhuman, and degrading treatment

[84] Maputo Protocol (n 8).

[85] Art 2 of the Maputo Protocol (n 8).

[86] Maputo Protocol (n 8).

[87] R Ehumadu 'Depriving widows inheritance rights by husbands' relatives in Nigeria' (2022) 16 Biche Journal of Education 60.

[88] African Charter (n 7).

against any human being including widows. The African Commission on Human and Peoples' Rights[89] in *Curtis Francis Doebbler v Sudan*,[90] interpreted article 5 of the African Charter to mean that it prohibits cruel, inhuman, and degrading treatment. This covers actions that cause serious physical or psychological suffering, humiliation, or force the individual to act against his will. This interpretation given by the African Commission by implication renders widowhood practices as cruel, inhuman, and degrading treatment against women. Despite this provision, widows in Nigeria are still subjected to cruel and degrading widowhood practices.

The African Charter recognises that women are being discriminated against, and it advocates for the elimination of every form of discrimination against women. Article 18(3) provides that:

> [T]he state shall ensure the elimination of every discrimination against women and also ensure the protection of the rights of the woman and the child as stipulated in international declarations and conventions.

Similarly, article 19[91] guarantees the equality of both men and women. It provides that 'all peoples shall be equal. They shall enjoy the same respect and shall have the same rights. Nothing shall justify the domination of a people by another'. The import of this is that patriarchal practices that make men dominate women by subjecting widows to cruel or inhuman and degrading treatment impede gender equality.

Article 20(1)(a)[92] specifically calls on states parties to respond appropriately to prevent women from being subjected to inhuman and degrading treatment. In addition, to combat the negative impact of widowhood practices on women, article 21[93] stipulates that widows are entitled to their fair share of the inheritance of their husband's property. The Maputo Protocol guarantees the right of widows to continue living

[89] The African Commission.

[90] Communication 236/2000, Curtis Francis Doebbler v Sudan, Sixteenth Annual Activity Report of the African Commission on Human and Peoples' Rights (Annex VII); see also, M Baderin 'Recent developments in the African regional human rights system' (2005) 5 Human Rights Law Review 133.

[91] African Charter (7).

[92] N 8.

[93] As above.

in their marital homes. If a widow remarries, she is entitled to keep her house without interference from her late husband's relatives if she owned or inherited it from her late husband. This provision seeks to correct past injustices and sufferings suffered by African women in relation to inheritance from deceased parents and husbands.[94] Despite the provisions of the Maputo Protocol, which addresses the discrimination suffered by African women, this Protocol is yet to be domesticated in Nigeria. Hence, it does not form part of Nigerian law.

Equally, the Nigerian government has signed and ratified a number of international human rights instruments.[95] The adoption of the Universal Declaration has done a great deal to better the lot of women.[96] Article 1 of the Universal Declaration provides that 'all human beings are born free and equal in dignity and rights. They are endowed with reason and conscience and should act towards one another in spirit of brotherhood'. This provision enjoins all to respect one's rights, treating everybody equally and fairly including widows. Article 5[97] provides that 'no one shall be subjected to torture or to cruel, inhuman or degrading treatment or punishment'. This shows that the subjection of widows to cruel or inhuman treatments such as shaving their hair, being made to drink water used to wash their deceased husbands' corpses, subjecting the widow to sleeping in the same room with their deceased husband's corpse alone or swearing before their deceased husband's family deity contravenes the provision of the Universal Declaration. The protection of widows' human dignity is often expressed in provisions relating to the right to be free from inhuman and degrading treatment. In addition, article 27[98] maintains that every person has the right to freely participate in a community's cultural life. The import of this provision is that the isolation of widows from interacting with other people or participating in activities during the period of mourning is a human rights violation.

[94] DM Chirwa 'Reclaiming (wo)manity: The merits and demerits of the African Protocol on Women's Rights' (2006) 53 Netherlands International Law Review 63.

[95] V Balogun & E Durojaye 'The African Commission on Human and People' Rights and the Promotion and Protection of Sexual and Reproductive Rights' (2011) 2 African Human Rights Law Journal 368.

[96] Arinze-Umobi & Anyogu (n 71) 2–9.

[97] Universal Declaration (n 3).

[98] As above.

Similarly, the CESCR and ICCPR prohibit gender discrimination and protect basic civil and political rights and the general well-being of the individual.[99] It may be apt to say that the international human rights framework that addresses specifically the plights of widows is CEDAW.[100] The Convention recognises the influence of culture and tradition in restricting the enjoyment by women of their fundamental human rights. Culture and tradition have this effect by assigning stereotypical roles to men and women. CEDAW advocates that to achieve the equality of men and women, there is a need to change the traditional role of men as well as the role of women in society and in the family.[101] Article 1 of CEDAW defines discrimination as:

> Any distinction exclusion or restriction made on the basis of which has the effect or purpose of impairing or nullifying the recognition, enjoyment or exercise by women, irrespective of their marital status, on a basis of equality of men and women, of human rights and fundamental freedoms in the political, economic, social, cultural, civil or any other field.

The implication of this definition is that any distinction, restriction, or exclusion faced by widows because of the obnoxious practices they are subjected to, amounts to discrimination. Where the law does make a distinction that has the effect of impairing women's rights in any way, it amounts to discrimination as defined by article 1 of CEDAW.[102] Article 2 emphasises the importance of the 'principle of equality' and how states parties are obligated to use 'appropriate legislation and means' to implement this guiding principle. These are guidelines that states are required to respect, safeguard, and fulfil. Although CEDAW is yet to be domesticated in Nigeria, the non-discrimination rights and the obligation of the Nigerian government under this instrument have influenced the decision of the court. In the case of *Mojekwu v Mojekwu*,[103] the court of appeal

[99] Art 2 CESR & ICCPR (n 4&5).

[100] CEDAW (n 6).

[101] Arinze-Umobi & Anyogu (n 71) 2–9.

[102] RJ Cook Human rights of women: national and international perspectives (1994) 45–68.

[103] 1997 7 NWLR (Pt 512) 283.

in determining, whether the '*oli-ekpe*'[104] customary law of succession is consistent with the constitutional rights to freedom from discrimination on the grounds of sex as guaranteed by section 42(1) of the Nigerian Constitution stated that 'we need not travel all the way to Beijing to know that some of our customs, including Nwewi "oli-ekpe" custom relied upon is inconsistent with the civilised world in which we all live today'. However, in *Mojekwu v Iwuchukwu*,[105] the Supreme Court ruled that a custom cannot be considered to be repugnant to natural justice, equity, and good conscience simply because it contradicts English law or a tenet of individual rights as interpreted in any other legal system. As a result, before ruling a custom unacceptable, the court must hear the parties and deliberate solemnly on all of the circumstances. There may be little problem in reaching a verdict in an extreme and needlessly discriminatory custom. In certain other circumstances, it may not be that simple. This is where the repugnancy principle should be evaluated and used objectively. Based on this, the Supreme Court ruled challenging the Court of Appeal on the subject of whether the oli-epke native custom is legal was appropriate.

Articles 3 and 18 of the CEDAW explicitly provide that legislation is a vital component in ensuring the realisation of women's human rights and freedoms based on 'equality with men'. In General Recommendation 19 on violence against women,[106] CEDAW stated that a state may be held liable for private acts of violence against women if the state fails to take sufficient preventive measures. Widowhood practices are most times accompanied by violent acts, such as the eviction of a widow from her home. These are violations of a woman's dignity.

Equally, article 5 of CEDAW requires states parties to modify the social and cultural norms that apply to how men and women behave in order to eliminate the inferior roles of men and women. The import of this is that if men and women are accorded the same status, widows will not

[104] According to the 'oli-ekpe' tradition, female children are not allowed to inherit their father's property, therefore if a man dies leaving only a female child, his brother will inherit him; likewise, if he leaves a male child who inherited him but subsequently passes away, his brother will inherit him as well.

[105] 2004 11 NWLR (Pt 883).

[106] CEDAW, General Recommendation 19 on Violence against Women, UN GAOR, UN Doc A/47/38 (1992).

be subjected to inhumane and degrading treatment. General Recommendation 28 states that the primary duty of states parties is to 'condemn all forms of discrimination against women'.[107] States parties are to fulfil their obligations as required by CEDAW.[108] In response to this, the 41st CEDAW Committee Shadow Report[109] recommended that there is a need for the Nigerian government to enact laws in order to protect women and girls from harmful cultural and religious practices that impede gender equality. To some extent, this report has influenced a number of laws, such as the VAPP law and the Child Rights Act (CRA).[110] However, Nigeria is yet to enact laws that expressly prohibit harmful and discriminatory widowhood practices.

5 Challenges to Safeguards Against Harmful Widowhood Practices in Nigeria

Several factors impede the effective implementation of human rights instruments that safeguard the rights of widows against harmful and discriminatory practices in Nigeria. These factors include patriarchal and cultural practices, the non-domestication of human rights instruments and Nigeria's tripartite legal system.

5.1 Patriarchal and Cultural Practices

A patriarchal society is one in which men are the dominant authority figures, with duties such as political leadership, moral authority, and property management, and fathers have ultimate authority over women and children.[111] This philosophy advocates for women's subjugation and

[107] UN Committee on the Elimination of Discrimination Against Women (CEDAW), General Recommendation 28 on the core obligations of states parties under article 2 of the Convention on the Elimination of All Forms of Discrimination against Women, 16 December 2010, UN Doc CEDAW/C/GC/28 (2010) https://www.refworld.org/docid/4d467ea72.html (accessed 10 January 2024).

[108] Art 18(1) & (2) CEDAW.

[109] International Federation for Human Rights, The Nigeria NGO Coalition Shadow Report to the CEDAW Committee, 31 July 2008.

[110] CRA, 2003.

[111] T Ann 'Patriarchy' Routledge Encyclopedia of International Political Economy (2001) 1197–1198.

dominance in cultural, political, social, and economic rights.[112] Feminist discussions have focused on women's oppression and the structure of society.[113] Patriarchy promotes gender discrimination in all societies, notably the prevention of women from inheriting.[114]

In terms of widows' rights of succession and equal opportunity under customary law, widows are treated unfairly. Widows in most Nigerian communities are subjected to all kinds of cruel and dehumanising treatment due to patriarchal and repugnant cultural practices.[115] These patriarchal and cultural practices continue to impede the implementation of gender laws in Nigeria. Gender equality cannot be achieved unless patriarchy, which gives men an advantage over women, is eliminated.[116]

5.2 *Non-Domestication of Human Rights Instruments*

The Nigerian Constitution requires that international treaties ratified by the Nigerian government would not be legally binding until confirmed by the National Assembly. Section 12(2) of the Nigerian Constitution provides that:

> no treaty between the Federation and any other country shall have the force of law except to the extent to which any of such treaty has been enacted into law by the National Assembly.

This provision makes it difficult to implement treaties that are not domesticated in Nigeria by the national assembly. At the international level, CEDAW, CESR, and ICCPR are yet to be domesticated in Nigeria. Equally, at the regional level, the Maputo Protocol is not yet domesticated in Nigeria.

112 M Strobel 'African women' (1982) 8 Signs: Journal of Women in Culture and Society 109.

113 A Mama & E Salo 'Talking about feminism in Africa: Empowering women for gender equality' (2001) 50 Agenda 58.

114 Iguh & Ugwu (n 64) 153–162.

115 T Oyewo A handbook on African laws of marriage, inheritance and succession (1999) 12–34.

116 Arinze-Umobi & Anyogu (n 62) 2–9.

The Supreme Court in the case of *General Sani Abacha v Gani Fawehinmi*[117] held that an international treaty signed by the government of Nigeria does not automatically become binding until it is adopted into law by the National Assembly, and until that time, its provisions are not enforceable in Nigerian courts.

5.3 Nigeria's Tripartite Legal System

The Nigerian government operates a federal system of government, which enables each state of the federation to apply its indigenous laws.[118] The Nigerian legal system comprises of legislation, customary and Sharia laws.[119] Customary law governs the majority of cultural discrimination and harmful widowhood practices.[120] Many of these widowhood practices are barbaric, life threatening, and inimical to progress. However, these harmful widowhood practices have become a norm in most Nigerian communities.

The combination of legislation, customary law, and Sharia law in Nigeria impedes the enforcement of these international and regional human rights instruments. There is a need for the Nigerian government to unify these legal systems to protect the rights of widows to non-discrimination as guaranteed under section 42 of the Constitution and other international and regional human rights instruments.

6 Conclusion

In exploring widowhood practices and human rights in Nigeria, it becomes evident that there exists a complex interplay between cultural traditions and the fundamental rights of widows. While traditions often govern mourning and inheritance practices, they can sometimes encroach upon the basic human rights of widows. These harmful and discriminatory practices perpetuate gender inequality, discrimination, and violence

[117] 2000 6 NWLR 228.

[118] E Malemi The Nigerian legal system: Text and cases (2021) 41–56.

[119] General Sani Abacha (n 116) 41–45.

[120] Olakayode (n 16) 67–74.

against women. Ultimately, the elimination of harmful widowhood practices in Nigeria will promote gender equality, social justice, and human rights for all.

The acknowledgement and respect for cultural heritage need to align with the principles of human rights to create a more just and equitable society for widows in Nigeria. By fostering dialogue, raising awareness, and implementing policies that safeguard the rights of widows, a balance can be struck that honours tradition while upholding human rights principles, ensuring that widows are treated with the dignity, respect, and equality they deserve.

To ensure proper and effective implementation of the rights of widows to non-discrimination, property rights, and the right to dignity, the Nigerian government has an obligation under international law to eliminate all forms of discrimination against widows and safeguard the rights of widows. To achieve this, the Nigerian government needs to amend the Constitution to protect the rights of widows by addressing the issues surrounding harmful and discriminatory practices of widows in Nigeria.

The Nigerian government must enact legislation prohibiting any harmful widowhood practices. This is specifically intended to liberate widows from the harm and suffering imposed on them by widowhood. In addressing human rights violations against widows in Nigeria, the government and civil society must prioritise the enactment and implementation of laws and policies that protect women's rights. Research has shown that widows often experience discrimination, abuse, and loss of property after the death of their husbands. Therefore, the government should make and enforce laws that protect women's rights to inheritance, property, and access to justice. Similarly, there is a need for the Nigerian government to domesticate international and regional treaties that Nigeria signed and ratified. The domestication of these treaties would enhance the effective promotion and protection of widows from harmful and discriminatory practices.

Additionally, local traditional leaders have a role to play in eliminating harmful practices and promoting cultural and social practices that advance widows' rights and dignity. Traditional and cultural practices must be carefully examined and modified to align with human rights principles. Communities must be educated on the harmful impact of these practices and the importance of protecting widows' rights. Further, widows must be empowered to participate in decision-making processes in their communities and have access to resources and support.

The Nigerian government and civil society organisations must work towards ending these practices and ensuring that widows' rights are protected and respected. This requires significant efforts in education, advocacy, community outreach programmes, and policy reforms.

Bibliography

Adebayo, AK 'An appraisal of customary succession in the Western and Eastern part of Nigeria' (2022) 8 *Commonwealth Law Review* 387

Adedara, A 'Persistency of the reprehensible cultural practices against widows of the widowhood classes in Nigeria: Legal analysis' (2023) 14 *African Journals Online* 24

Adekunle, T 'Succession and inheritance law in Nigeria: Resolving the discriminatory proprietary rights of widows and children' https://www.academia.edu/35665674 (accessed 3 July 2023)

Afolayan, GE 'Widowhood practices and the rights of women: The case of South-Western Nigeria' (2011) http://thesis.eur.nl/pub/1081 (accessed 3 July 2023)

Ajayi, A 'Disinheritance: Widows in Igboland battle against culture that men love to preserve (Part 2)' *ICIR* (27 October 2020) https://www.icirnigeria.org/disinheritance-widows-in-igboland-battle-against-culture-that-men-love-to-preserve-part-2/ (accessed 16 July 2023)

Alemika, E 'Family practices and violations of the rights of women' (2010) 8 *University of Maiduguri Law Journal* 25

Ann, T 'Patriarchy' (2001) *Routledge Encyclopedia of International Political Economy* 1197

Anyogu, F *Access to justice in Nigeria: A gender perspective* (Ebenezer Productions 2013)

Arinze-Umobi, C & Anyogu, F 'The widows in South-East of Nigeria in legal and customary turbulence: Need for mandatory paradigm shift' (2014) 8 *International Journal of Research and Development* 1Baderin, M 'Recent developments in the African regional human rights system' (2005) 5 *Human Rights Law Review* 133

Balogun, V & Durojaye, E 'The African Commission on Human and People' Rights and the promotion and protection of sexual and reproductive rights' (2011) 2 *African Human Rights Law Journal* 368

Chirwa, DM 'Reclaiming (wo)manity: The merits and demerits of the African Protocol on Women's Rights' (2006) 53 *Netherlands International Law Review* 63

Cook, RJ *Human rights of women: National and international perspectives* (University of Pennsylvania Press 1994) 45

Dominic, O & Okeyi, VO 'Christian impact on obnoxious traditional widowhood practices in Nigeria' (2023) 4 *Aku: An African Journal of Contemporary Research* 117

Dube, M 'Isolation and its impacts on widows: Insights from low-resourced communities in Binga district Zimbabwe (2022) 11 *Social Sciences* 1

Durojaye, E '"Woman, but not human": Widowhood practices and human rights violations in Nigeria' (2013) 27 *International Journal of Law, Policy and the Family* 176

Ehumadu, R 'Depriving widow's inheritance rights by husbands' relatives in Nigeria' (2022) 16 *Bichi Journal of Education* 60

Ezeilo, NJ *Women, Law and human rights: Global and national perspectives* (Acena 2011)

Ezeilo, NJ 'Rethinking women and customary inheritance in Nigeria' (2021) 47 *Commonwealth Law Bulletin* 706

Fasoranti, OO & Aruna, YO 'A Cross-cultural comparison of practices relating to widowhood and widow-inheritance among the Igbo and Yoruba in Nigeria' (2007) 111 *Journal of World Anthropology: Occasional Papers* 373

Igbineweka, FO & Enakireru, EO 'Customary law in Nigeria: Interrogating the issue of judicial notice' (2022) 3 *ACARELAR* 55

Iguh, MA & Ugwu, MO 'Protecting and promoting the rights of persons with disability in Nigeria' (2023) 5 *International Review of Law and Jurisprudence* (IRLJ) 153

Ike, CB & Akujobi, OS 'Widowhood in lonely days: Unsung casualties' (2021) 8 *Akwa Journal of English and Literary Studies* 1

International Federation for Human Rights, The Nigeria NGO Coalition Shadow Report to the CEDAW Committee, 31 July 2008

Kaba, AJ 'Explaining Africa's rapid population growth, 1950 to 2020: Trends, factors, implications, and recommendations' (2020) 10 *Sociology Mind* 226

Kramarae, C 'The condition of patriarchy' in Kramarae, C & Dale, S (eds) *The knowledge explosion: Generations of feminist scholarship* (London: Teachers College Press 1993)

Kudo, Y 'Does criminalizing discriminatory cultural practices improve women's welfare? A simple model of levirate marriage in Africa' (2021) 199 *Economic Letters* 109728

Mackinnon, C 'Sexual harassment of working women: a case of sex discrimination' (1980) 80 *Columbia Law Review* 1686

Malemi, E *The Nigerian legal system: Text and cases* (Princeton Pub Co 2021)

Mama, A 'Sheroes and villains: Conceptualising colonial and contemporary violence against women in Africa' in Alexander, M et al (eds) *Feminist genealogies, colonial legacies, democratic futures* (Routledge 1997)

Mama, A & Salo, E 'Talking about feminism in Africa: Empowering women for gender equality' (2001) 50 *Agenda* 58

Nwanegbo, NA *Challenge of widowhood* (Sonnie Organization Ltd 1996)

Nwogu, MI 'The legal anatomy of cultural widowhood practices in South Eastern Nigeria: The need for a panacea' (2015) 3 *Global Journal of Politics and Law Research* 80

Odimegwu, C & Okemgbo, CN 'Gender role ideologies and prevalence of violence against women in Imo State Nigeria' (2003) 5 *Anthropologist* 225

Ogu, UK & Areji, AC 'Gender equality and women's economic and sociocultural rights in Nigeria: Deconstructing the biases' (2023) 2 *Journal of African Political Philosophy and Leadership: Philosophia Politica* 58

Okoli, AB & Okuosa, L 'The role of Christianity in gender and development in Nigeria' (2020) 76 *HTS Theologies Studies/Theological Studies* 1

Olomojobi, Y *Human rights on gender, sex and the law in Nigeria* (Princeton & Associates Publishing Co Ltd 2021)

Olukayode, J 'Widowhood practices in some Nigerian societies: A retrospective examination' (2015) 5 *International Journal of Humanities and Social Science* 67

Onuoha, RA 'Discriminatory property inheritance under customary law in Nigeria: NGOS to the rescue' (2008) 10 *International Journal of Not-for-Profit Law* 79

Onyima, B 'Widows in Nigeria are sometimes treated badly: Culture is no excuse to violate rights' *The Conversation* 22 June 2022 https://theconversation.com/widows-in-nigeria-are-sometimes-treated-badly-culture-is-no-excuse-to-violate-rights-184934 (accessed 4 July 2023)

Osita, E *Human rights in Africa: Some selected problems* (Nigeria Institute of International Affairs 1984)

Otaluka, AO *The rights of widows* (FIDA: Anambra Family Law Centre Publication 1992)

Oyeniyi A & Ayodeji I 'Widowhood practices among the Yorubas of South West Nigeria: Are there differences in what women experience due to their status?' (2010) 8 *Gender and Behaviour* 3152

Oyewo, T *A Handbook on African Laws of Marriage, Inheritance and Succession* (Jator Pub Co 1999) 12

Sadiq, L 'Inside Nigeria's harmful traditional practices that impede women's rights to land ownership' (2022) https://dailytrust.com/inside-nigerias-harmful-traditional-practices-that-impede-womens-rights-to-land-ownership/ (accessed 16 July 2023)

Samuel, GC 'Emergent issues on widowhood practices in Igbo culture: Between the video screen and reality' (2011) 8 *Unizik Journal of Arts and Humanities* 184

Ssenyonjo, M 'Culture and human rights of women in Africa: Between light and shadow' (2007) 51 *Journal of African Law* 39

Strobel, M 'African women' (1982) 8 *Signs: Journal of Women in Culture and Society* 109

Tamale, S 'The right to culture and the culture of rights: A critical perspective on women's sexual rights in Africa' (2008) 16 *Feminist Legal Studies* 47

Vanguard 'Rising cases of harmful widowhood practices in Igbo communities' (24 May 2023).

Case law

Anekwe v Nweke (2014) NWLR Pt 1412.

Asika v Atuanya (2013) LPELR—20895 (SC).

Curtis Francis Doebbler v Sudan Sixteenth Annual Activity Report of the African Commission on Human and Peoples' Rights (Annex VII).

Mojekwu v Iwuchukwu 2004 11 NWLR (Pt 883).

Mojekwu v Mojekwu 1997 7 NWLR (Pt 512) 283.

Ukeje v Ukeje (2014) 11 NWLR (PT.1418).

Legislation

African Charter on Human and Peoples' Rights ("Banjul Charter"), 27 June 1981, CAB/LEG/67/3 rev. 5, 21 ILM.L.M. 58 (1982).

Convention on the Elimination of All Forms of Discrimination Against Women, 18 December 1979, United Nations, Treaty Series, vol. 1249, p. 13.

International Covenant on Civil and Political Rights, 16 December 1966, United Nations, Treaty Series, vol. 999, 17.

International Covenant on Economic, Social and Cultural Rights, 16 December 1966, United Nations, Treaty Series, vol. 993, 3.

Protocol to the African Charter on Human and People's Rights on the Rights of Women in Africa, 11 July 2003.

Universal Declaration of Human Rights, 217 A (III), 10 December 1948, 217 A (III).

CHAPTER 4

Beyond the Legal Debates: An African Legal Feminist Response to Support Victims of *Ukuthwala* in South Africa

Lea Mwambene and Helen Kruuse

1 Introduction

Ukuthwala is an indigenous African custom that involves the mock abduction of a girl as a precursor to a customary marriage.[1] *Ukuthwala* in the Nguni languages of isiXhosa and isiZulu literally means 'to carry

[1] See also definitions by K Rice 'Understanding *ukuthwala*: Bride abduction in the rural Eastern Cape South Africa' (2018) 77 *African Studies* 394; D Koyana & JC Bekker 'The indomitable *ukuthwala* custom' (2007) 40 *De Jure* 139; N Karimakwenda 'Deconstructing characterisations of rape, marriage, and custom in South Africa' (2020) 63 *African Studies Review* 763; L Mwambene & J Sloth-Nielsen 'Benign accommodation? *Ukuthwala*, "forced marriage" and South African Children's Act' (2011) 11 *African Human Rights Law Journal* 1; E Moore & C Himonga 'Living customary law and families in Africa' (2018) *South African Child Gauge* 61 at 63.

L. Mwambene (✉)
University of the Western Cape, Bellville, South Africa
e-mail: lmwambene@uwc.ac.za

H. Kruuse
Rhodes University, Makhanda, South Africa

E. Durojaye et al. (eds.), *Harmful Practices and Human Rights: An International Perspective*, Human Rights Interventions,
https://doi.org/10.1007/978-3-031-90333-5_4

away'.[2] The practice of the custom has resulted in contested and strong debates about its place in a constitutional democracy.[3] Part of the challenge is that it is hard to decipher or even distinguish the original practice from the current form, which may be accompanied by violence and abuse of children or young women.[4] In more recent times, the practice has also been linked to the perception that poverty plays a role in the persistent abuse of the practice.[5]

While the work of some scholars on *ukuthwala* has highlighted the human rights violations that are linked to the practice,[6] our thesis goes further and analyses ways in which the state's current laws and policies supporting victims of *ukuthwala* are problematic.[7] Viewed through the lens of African feminist legal theory, we suggest that the state's approach

e-mail: h.kruuse@ru.ac.za

[2] J Mubangizi 'A South African perspective on the clash between culture and Human Rights, with particular reference to gender-related cultural practices and traditions' (2012) 13 *Journal of International Women's Studies* 39.

[3] M van der Watt & M Ovens 'Contextualising the practice of *Ukuthwala* in South Africa' (2012) 13 *Child Abuse Research: A South African Journal* 11; P Hlophe 'An exploratory study on *ukuthwala* and crime: A perspective of *inqaba kamveliqangi* cultural organisation' Unpublished MSocSci thesis, University of KwaZulu-Natal, 2021, 169; Karimakwenda (n 1); BJ Machaka 'The cultural practice of *ukuthwala* in South Africa' LLM Thesis, Nelson Mandela University, 2019; Mwambene & Sloth Nielsen (n 1); South African Law Reform Commission (SALRC) 'The Practice of *ukuthwala*' Discussion Paper Project 138 (2016); and Moore & Himonga (n 1) 63.

[4] Koyana & Bekker (n 1); Karimakwenda (n 1): L Mwambene & H Kruuse 'The thin edge of the wedge: *ukuthwala*, alienation and consent' (2017) 33 *South African Journal on Human Rights* 25; TW Bennett 'The cultural defence and the custom of *Thwala* in South African Law' (2010) 10 *University of Botswana Law Journal* 3; Moore & Himonga (n 1) 63. See Part 2 infra.

[5] C Himonga & T Nhlapo (eds) *African Customary Law in South Africa* 2 ed (2023) 308. See also S Dlamini & MS Makhaye 'Community policing as a panacea for gender based violence impasse' (2023) 12 *African Journal of Gender, Society and Development* 7 at 22.

[6] J Mkhuseli 'The customary law practice of *ukuthwala*: An antithesis in South African Constitutional Order' LLD thesis, Nelson Mandela University, 2018.

[7] Charlesworth's question becomes relevant: '[D]o legal rights really offer anything to women seeing that their disadvantages are often based on structural injustice and winning a case in court will not change this?' (Charlesworth as cited by R Cook 'Women's international human rights law: The way forward' (1993) 15 *Human Rights Quarterly* 230 at 232. Cook, however, acknowledges that other scholars, such as Adetoun Illumoka, have questioned the rights discourse in Africa, arguing that 'it may not be useful since

fails to take into account the very goal or rationale for the practice itself, that of fostering family relations within the community. It also fails to recognise that the ultimate delivery of *lobolo* that accompanies a successful *ukuthwala* process can alleviate the family's poverty and hardship in the rural areas.[8] Thus, any state approach that fails to include the community in supporting victims and resolving abuses in the context of extreme poverty will fail.[9]

The chapter is divided into six parts, including this introduction. The second part uses the landmark case of *Jezile v S*[10] as a point of departure in understanding *ukuthwala*. This section outlines the circumstances that usually accompany the process and the community's response as a way of highlighting possible areas of support that victims of *ukuthwala* require. The third part outlines African feminist legal theory as a theoretical framework for the fourth part in which we set out and assess the limitations of the current laws and policies. This fourth part not only shows how the policies and laws are structured, it also highlights areas in need of reform so as to make them more responsive to children and women's needs as victims of *ukuthwala*.[11] In the fifth part, we attempt to show how explicit acknowledgement of community goals and concerns about family cohesion is central to any effective response to supporting

the severity of the socio-economic problems faced by women may require a basic needs strategy, rather than a rights strategy'.)

[8] Studies showing the transactional nature of the process. In addition, Anathi's grandmother's concerns regarding the lack of child support and family ties. As it will be discussed later, Anathi, is a pseudonym for the girl in the Engcobo case study below.

[9] This is because the abuse of the practice continues despite individualist responses to the problem as shown by the *Jezile* incarceration. See infra, Part 2. In a recent study, the authors suggest that a girls/women who have been '*ukuthwala-ed*' may be more susceptible to commit crime themselves given the trauma they suffered: see C Agboola, E Kofi Appiah & H Namonde Linonge-Fontebo 'Women's pathways into crime and incarceration: Insights from South Africa' (2022) 8 *Cogent Social Sciences* 1 at 9.

[10] Jezile v S 2016 (2) SA 62 (WCC).

[11] Taylor Feltham 'Working Paper No. 46: Foundations for Feminist Legal Theory' *Portland State University Economics Working Papers* (2020) 46 https://pdxscholar.library.pdx.edu/econ_workingpapers (accessed 13 January 2025). Feltham refers to Levit & Verchick's observation at 1 that 'feminist legal theory seeks ultimately to incite change. This means that apart from considering "what is" to provide historical context, we shall aspire in the direction of "what ought to be"'. See, in general, N Levit & RRM Verchick *Feminist legal theory: A primer* 2 ed (2016) 12.

the victims of ***ukuthwala***—this being a direct lesson from African feminism. As a result, we give some recommendations on how the state could implement measures which would more effectively deal with the plight of children and women affected by ***ukuthwala***. The sixth part is our conclusion.

2 Contextualising *Ukuthwala* and Its Impact on Victims

In order to assess the adequacy of the laws and policies that seek to protect and support victims of ***ukuthwala,*** we first narrate what happened in the *Jezile* case.[12] This seminal case is often the reference and departure point for many commentators about the practice of ***ukuthwala*** in South Africa.[13] This is shown by the fact that the judgment covered aspects of the practice in detail, which have now come to characterise modern day (abuse of the) practice.[14] These aspects include the age of the child, the involvement of her family and community, the cultural beliefs of the accused, and the conduct against the child—including her trafficking from a rural setting to a metropolitan area. For the purposes of this article, we use a pseudonym for the girl: Anathi.

The 28-year-old accused, along with the Anathi's uncle, arranged that a customary marriage should take place with Anathi, who was 14 years old at the time, in terms of the ***ukuthwala*** custom.[15] The accused, who

[12] *Jezile v S* (n 10).

[13] See, eg, Mwambene & Kruuse (n 4). J Prinsloo & M Ovens 'Ukuthwala as an aberrant traditional practice: The State versus Nvumeleni Jezile 2014 WCD' (2015) 4 *Acta Criminologica* 169; M Jokani, E Knoetze & D Erasmus 'A criminal response to the harmful practices of ***ukuthwala***' (2018) 39 *Obiter* 747 at 760; C Müller-Van der Westhuizen & R Streso 'Ukuthwala—Gebruik of misbruik?' (2018) 15 *Litnet Akademies* 1143; and B Kruger 'Enhancing the criminal justice response to human trafficking in South Africa: Legislation and case law in the spotlight' (2023) 37 *South African Journal of Criminal Justice* 48.

[14] Expert witness opinion in the *Jezile v S* (n 10).

[15] *Jezile v S* (n 10) paras 5–7: Mwambene & Kruuse (n 4) 25 for a discussion of ***ukuthwala*** and the decision of *Jezile*. *Jezile v S* (n 10) paras 70–72. Koyana & Bekker (n 1). See also N Wadesango & O Chabaya 'Violation of women's rights by harmful traditional practices' (2011) 13 *The Anthropologist* 121; Mubangizi (n 2); C Monyane 'Is *Ukuthwala* another form of "forced marriage"?' (2013) 44 *South African Review of Sociology* 64.

worked in Phillipi (an urban township in Cape Town), travelled back to his original community in the rural area of Engcobo in the Eastern Cape Province where Anathi lived. She was duly '*thwala-ed*' by Jezile and his friends, having been informed by a gathering of male members of both their families that she was to be married. She was taken to Jezile's family home in Engcobo. Anathi ostensibly became Jezile's customary wife, following the successful traditional *lobolo* negotiations by both families.[16]

While these processes were in place, Anathi, who appeared desperately unhappy, attempted to escape from Jezile's family home twice. She was unsuccessful on both occasions, with her family returning her to the accused on both occasions.[17] On one occasion, when she was conveyed over 1000 km from her rural home to Phillipi, she suffered assaults and was raped by the accused.[18] Her third escape attempt from the accused was successful, when she managed to reach a local police station in the Cape Town area.[19] The matter first went before the magistrates' court, where Jezile was charged with and convicted of rape, human trafficking, assault, and assault with intent to do grievous bodily harm in terms of South Africa's relevant statutes.[20] As a result, he was sentenced to 22 years' imprisonment.[21] On appeal to the High Court, the appellant argued that the Court had misdirected itself in not taking account of his cultural practice. He essentially argued that he was in a customary marriage with the complainant at the time of the incidents and, as a result, he could not have committed the offences he had been convicted of.[22] While the High Court set aside the assault convictions, it dismissed the appeals related to the rape and human trafficking offences.

Despite its often violent and abusive stance against children, the practice persists in rural communities across South Africa. For example, approximately five years after the *ukuthwala* had taken place, we recorded

[16] *Jezile v S* (n 10) paras 7–9.

[17] *Jezile v S* (n 10) para 10.

[18] *Jezile v S* (n 10) paras 24–25.

[19] *Jezile v S* (n 10) para 26.

[20] See part 4 infra for a discussion of these statutes.

[21] *Jezile v* S (n 10) para 1.

[22] *Jezile v S* (n 10) para 51.

the views of the community where the families lived and where the *ukuthwala* took place in the *Jezile* case.[23] In looking back on the events (at a time when Anathi would have been 19 years old), one of her uncles suggested:

> Mvumeleni (i.e. Jezile) is in jail, Anathi came back from her marriage, she is not back to school, she has two kids after she separated from her marriage.[24] Does the government consider the fact that they have sent someone to jail who is accused of rape whereas its clear it was not rape in the first place, I think she just saw someone better than Mvumeleni ... Now this whole thing has resulted into more problems especially for the old Gogo [Anathi's grandmother] ... This is [a] sad situation, Gogo has to carry all this difficulty, it's not just one grandchild that she is looking after ... Also Anathi's child does not have a birth certificate. He was recently chased out from the school feeding scheme, because the government school feeding scheme does not recognise a child that has no birth certificate. That child does not exist in their programmes. What Anathi did resulted in more problems, not just Mvumeleni, but also burdening the old grandmother.

In a separate interview, Anathi's grandmother questioned Anathi's actions and reflected on the situation as one of her own (i.e. Anathi's) making:

> Anathi stayed with her in-laws [in the rural area] over a month before leaving for Cape Town. Usually if a girl is not happy, then they do not send her back, but in this case, it seems the mother did not speak to the girl, but only the uncle who took her back to Jezile. No-one has to go to jail because of lobolo. If Anathi had told me that she does not like the marriage, I would have advised her not to go back—but she did not speak to me. It is not common that girls are thwalaed without the knowledge of the family, and also before puberty. Anathi now stays with her father's family, and her mother last visited three years ago. Anathi's first child stays with me, and the second child is with her—Anathi has never visited me or her first child. After the Cape Town court case, both Anathi and her mother came back to stay with me, and then Anathi left to stay with her father's family, and workplace, respectively. It's unfair that Jezile is in jail, I

[23] Mwambene & Kruuse (n 4).

[24] Several family members reported that after Anathi returned she had had two children from different men in the community, and was currently living with one of them in another village.

> cannot sleep at night, I think about him, and his parents. Mvumeleni did not do anything out of the ordinary, not something new, for both families it is painful. Now we know, if a man wants to thwala, we will ask him to also ask the girl.

It is important to note that both the uncle and the grandmother felt that Anathi had betrayed her community by not staying in the marriage, despite the obvious abuse of her human rights as protected by international conventions and national laws.[25] The idea—derived from these interviews—that the accused did 'nothing wrong' and that he had the community's support and sympathy, has major implications for the victim's chance of recovering from the experience and for reintegrating into the community.

In the years that have followed the *Jezile* case, researchers have recorded that the practice continues, particularly in the rural areas of two provinces in South Africa: the Eastern Cape (where the *Jezile ukuthwala* took place) and KwaZulu-Natal. In 2017, Statistics South Africa recorded a great number of child marriages generally, noting that the latter province had the highest number of child brides, which exceeded 25 000 in that year.[26] In reflecting on these numbers, non-governmental organisations (NGOs) have suggested that this high number is attributable to *ukuthwala*, and these children are then subjected to domestic violence, premature and undesired pregnancies, and sexual health risks like exposure to sexually transmitted infections including HIV/AIDS.[27] Scholars also recognise that the country's child marriage rates are arguably much higher than reported due to various factors and practices, including *ukuthwala*.[28]

[25] See the discussion of these conventions and laws in part 4 infra.

[26] Statistics South Africa 'Marriages and divorce' (2017) https://www.statssa.gov.za/publications/P0307/P03072017.pdf (accessed 5 July 2023).

[27] For example, see Masiphephe Network *Harmful practices infringing the rights of women and girls: Policy brief* (2021) https://www.masiphephe.org.za/wp-content/uploads/2022/06/Harmful-Practices-Infringe-the-Rights-of-Women-and-Girls_Final-Policy-Brief-.pdf (accessed 16 August 2023).

[28] E le Roux 'Recognising and responding to complex dilemmas: Child marriage in South Africa' in J Grobbelaar & C Jones (eds) *Childhood vulnerabilities in South Africa: Some ethical perspectives* (2020) 163 at 169.

In 2019, the Committee of the United Nations Convention on the Elimination of All Forms of Discrimination Against Women (CEDAW)[29] conducted a confidential inquiry visit in South Africa under article 8 of the Optional Protocol to CEDAW.[30] This inquiry visit took place after the Committee received a complaint by an NGO task force acting on behalf of about 36 South African NGOs. The NGOs raised concerns about South Africa's high levels of domestic violence; its failure to comply with its due diligence obligation to protect women; and grave and systematic violations of the Convention obligations and commitments.[31] In response to these allegations, the Committee found that 'the persistence of harmful traditional and cultural practices such as ***ukuthwala*** (forced marriages of women and girls to older men through abduction)' exacerbated violence against women.[32] They further found that the characterisation of ***ukuthwala*** as a 'consensual practice' belied the lived experience of women and girls. Instead, the Committee suggested that such characterisation undermined the protection of women and children given that there could be no assurance that the child, in particular, had or could give full and informed consent.[33] The Committee also heard from the South African Human Rights Commission and NGOs that, while not a generalised practice, traditional leaders were complicit in the practice and that traditional leaders often justified ***ukuthwala*** and other harmful practices as consensual cultural practices.[34]

[29] This Committee was set up in terms of CEDAW which was adopted by UN General Assembly resolution 34/180 of 18 December 1979.

[30] See the three reports related to this observation: https://tbinternet.ohchr.org/_layouts/15/TreatyBodyExternal/TBSearch.aspx?Lang=en&TreatyID=3&DocTypeCategoryID=7 (accessed 13 January 2025). These reports are recorded as: 'Inquiry concerning South Africa under article 8 of the Optional Protocol to the Convention on the Elimination of All Forms of Discrimination Against Women' 12 May 2021), UN Doc CEDAW/C/ZAF/IR/1 (2021); Observations of South Africa, 17 November 2021, UN Doc CEDAW/C/ZAF/OIR/1 (2021); and Follow-up report submitted by South Africa, 8 June 2022, UN Doc CEDAW/C/ZAF/FIR/1 (2022).

[31] In terms of art 8, the Committee may investigate allegations of grave or systematic violations of the Convention in a state party.

[32] CEDAW/C/ZAF/OIR/1 (n 30).

[33] See CEDAW /C/ZAF/IR/I (n 30) para 35.

[34] CEDAW /C/ZAF/IR/I (n 30) paras 39–41.

These CEDAW findings are consistent with later research, particularly in 2020 and 2022. For example, in 2020, Ziyande and Oscar[35] interviewed older women who had been '*thwala-ed*' in the Mbizana Municipality—a rural area in the Eastern Cape. The researchers were told by a woman who had been '*ukuthwala-ed*' in her youth that '[i]t was against my own will but my father said the marriage was a good thing for both families'. Another victim suggested: 'I knew that my rights were infringed although I was afraid to disappoint my family' and another victim did not want to marry but was told by her family that 'it is my culture'.[36] When asking victims why they did not report the incident, they told the researchers variously that they did not know *ukuthwala* was unlawful or that they knew but did not want to disappoint their families.[37] The persistent theme in this 2020 research was that the community valued the building of networks between families, and that *ukuthwala* was a method to achieve that goal. It is also clear that pressure was put on girls to accept the process, given the family's wishes, and that the lack of consent was not a recent phenomenon, but repeated by older women.[38]

[35] V Ziyanda & MT Oscar '*Ukuthwala* practice: Conflict of Chapter 2 (Bill of Rights) of South African Constitution Act 108 of 1996 and Cultural Practice' (2020) 4 *AJHSSR* 45.

[36] Ziyanda & Oscar (n 35) 49.

[37] For example, the researchers (n 35) recorded the following reflections at 49–50 (internal referencing omitted): 'I was aware of the illegality of the practice but fear to embarrass my family was the only reason that stopped me from reporting the practice to the police'; 'I am from a well-respected family and I was aware that *ukuthwala* practice is not legal anymore but I had to do it for the sake of my family'; 'If I were aware that *ukuthwala* was against the law, I would have reported it to the police because it was against my own will'; 'I did not see any need to report because I was not aware that it was against the law'. One participant explained that: '[Even though I] knew that the *ukuthwala* practice was illegal I did not have the guts to report the matter to the police officials because my father confused me and told me that it was a culture to save family honour'.

[38] This accords with Rice's research in 2014 where she records that most women are aware of their legal recourse, however, the fear of community shaming and reporting their parents to the police far outweighed the experience of an unwanted marriage. See, in general, K Rice '*Ukuthwala* in rural South Africa: Abduction marriage as a site of negotiation about gender, rights and generational authority among the Xhosa' (2014) 40 *Journal of Southern African Studies* 381.

In 2022, Mabizela's research in another community in Kwazulu-Natal, being Bergville,[39] also found that *ukuthwala* was endorsed by the community as a method of fostering family relations. In particular and consistent with the submissions to the CEDAW Committee, Mabizela found that chiefs and traditional leaders endorsed the practice, although the researcher was not clear whether this included explicit lack of consent by the girl or woman.[40]

In this study, *ukuthwala* was constructed as a socially-endorsed practice by community members, including chiefs or traditional leaders—as a result, having people in positions of power endorsing *ukuthwala* functions to silence ordinary people who may be against the *ukuthwala* as practice or particularities of *ukuthwala*.[41]

Given these research findings, we sought an approach to *ukuthwala* that acknowledges the role of the community and the goals behind the practice in an effort to consider meaningful responses to the practice in its context. We believe this approach to be African legal feminism—although we accept the nuances between individuals that use this lens.[42] We also acknowledge the inherent flaws in essentialising theories as 'African' or 'western' as if these theories are defined by immutable truths in these contexts. However, we do this to illustrate the central concerns of women in an African context.[43] We also explicitly call it an African *legal* feminist

[39] See S Mabizela 'Bergville residents' construction of the cultural practice of *ukuthwala*: A discourse analysis' PhD dissertation, University of South Africa, 2002.

[40] These results have been confirmed by several researchers who state that chiefs are not only staunch proponents of *ukuthwala*, they also tend to ignore the seriousness of criminal cases embedded in the practice. See in general A Claassens & Smythe 'Marriage, land and custom: What's law got to do with it?' (2013) *Acta Juridica* 1; WJ Smit 'Rights, violence and the marriage of confusion: Re-emerging bride abduction in South Africa' (2017) 40 *Anthropology Southern Africa* 56; N Karimakwenda '"Today it would be called rape": A historical and contextual examination of forced marriage and violence in the Eastern Cape' 2013 *Acta Juridica* 339; Van der Watt & Ovens (n 3); and H Venganai '(Re)constructing positive cultures to protect girls and women against sexual violence' (2015) 29 *Agenda: Empowering Women for Gender Equity* 145; C Mitchell & Naydene de Lange (eds) 'Interventions to address sexual violence: Transforming violent cultures for and with girls and young women' (2015) 29 *Agenda*.

[41] Mabizela (n 39) 194.

[42] Our focus is on African sub-Saharan thought, but not exclusively.

[43] There is also the challenge of avoiding straw man characterisations of a theory to emphasise the difference between them. We acknowledge this challenge.

approach to emphasise our goal or purpose, that is, to use its insights to reform the law in consultation with the community—as opposed to state-imposed reform.

3 A Theoretical Lens: African Feminist Legal Theory

Commentators agree that African feminist theory emerged as a response to certain western feminist theories[44] that were seen as inadequate in addressing the experiences of African women.[45] As captured by Filomina, African feminism 'lies in its social and humanist thrust, which recognises that unequal power relations can be based not only on gender,[46] but also on race, class, national origin, and other forms of social dimensions'.[47] This focus on intersectionality can be contrasted with general western feminism in that the latter can be fuelled by an 'anti-male ideology' and preoccupied with 'individualistic' gender inequality, as opposed to 'social and humanistic transformation'.[48] Aderinboyo observed that 'many challenges underpinning African legal theory are cultural and social issues that

[44] See, e.g., D Griffiths 'Decoloniality and the (im)possibility of an African feminist philosophy' (2022) 41 *South African Journal of Philosophy* 240; and EK Bayu 'A comparative analysis on the perspectives of African feminism vs Western feminism: Philosophical debate with their criticism and its implication for women's rights in Ethiopia context' (2019) 11 *International Journal of Sociology and Anthropology* 54.

[45] Bayu (n 44); I Dery 'A situated, African understanding of African feminism for men: A Ghanian narrative' (2020) 27 *Gender, Place and Culture* 1745; R Goredema 'African feminism: The African woman's struggle for identity' (2010) 33. Goredema describes African feminism at 33–34 as a 'feminist epistemology and a form of rhetoric that has provided arguments which validate the experience of women of Africa'.

[46] Matlala thus observes that feminist legal theory postulates that gender plays a significant role in our daily lives and is a central component of our existence. R Matlala 'Introducing feminist legal theory as a basis for South African judicial jurisprudence: Insights from *S v Tshabalala*' (2022) 139 *South African Law Journal* 274.

[47] SC Filomina 'African Feminism' in *Routledge Encyclopedia of Philosophy* (2005) https://www.rep.routledge.com/articles/thematic/african-feminism/v-1 (accessed 5 July 2023); Matlala (n 46) 282; NE Dowd 'Masculinities and feminist legal theory' (2008) 23 *Wisconsin Journal of Law, Gender and Society* 201.

[48] Filomina (n 47); N Nkealah '(West) African Feminism and their challenges' (2016) 32 *Journal of Literary Studies* 62.

pertain to, and affect, African women'.[49] Moreover, western feminism has been criticised for its intentional use of the state[50] as the site for solutions to injustices experienced by women.[51] As MacKinnon argues: 'The law is itself a vehicle for gender discrimination in that the law and legal structures actually create and maintain male dominance'.[52] In contrast, Manji argues that 'the thematical work which privileges state law can at best furnish us with only partial accounts of women's experiences'.[53] In addition, Matlala's conceptualisation of the courts' approach to feminist legal theory is also relevant in understanding the opportunities and limitation of the current laws that seek to support *ukuthwala* victims.[54] She points out that scholars, such as Fineman, argue that feminist theory is not anchored in one discipline and that its principles are not expressed in a uniform methodology.[55]

In addition, African feminism is said to differ from western feminism in its description as a concept that is defined by different cultural notions and realities centred on African culture.[56] Western feminism, on the other hand, has been viewed as 'radical and even toxic to marriage which is valued in the African communities as the foundation of family

[49] A Aderinboyo 'African feminism and women's rights in Nigeria' (2020) SSRN: https://ssrn.com/abstract=3683051 or http://dx.doi.org/10.2139/ssrn.3683051 (accessed 13 January 2025).

[50] Feminist legal theory, according to Fineman, takes law as a primary focus, and engages legal issues because the state is central in the feminist reformist agenda. MA Fineman 'Feminist legal theory' (2005) 13 *American University Journal of Gender, Social Policy & the Law* 13.

[51] EW Stulhofer 'Navigating African feminisms: Wangari Maathai as a portrait' *Africa Knows Conference* (2021) https://nomadit.co.uk/conference/africaknows/paper/58023 (accessed 31 July 2023).

[52] MacKinnon as cited by P Scully 'Should we give up on the state? Feminist theory, African gender history and transitional justice' (2009) 9 *African Journal of Conflict Resolution* 29. Scully quotes MacKinnon's observation that 'using the law to address problems of inequality would create new forms of social and political exclusion against women'.

[53] S Manji 'Imagining women's 'legal world': Towards a feminist theory of legal pluralism in Africa' (1999) 8 *Social and Legal Studies* 435.

[54] Matlala (n 46) 281.

[55] Fineman as cited by Matlala (n 46) 281.

[56] See general discussions by A Kabore 'Differentiating African and Western feminisms through room symbolism' (2017) 5 *Linguistic and Literature Review* 408; 'Women's History month: An interpretation of feminism in Africa' *OUPblog* 22 March 2007 https://blog.oup.com/2007/03/womens_history_-2/ (accessed July 2023).

and society'.[57] This leads to most African feminists abandoning the pursuit of feminist values if it is seen to contradict marital values.[58] In this light then, we argue that African cultural values are central in navigating the support structures necessary for victims of *ukuthwala*.[59] While bearing in mind that certain aspects of culture are harmful to women and children, scholars have generally argued for the retention of 'harmless' African values favourable to social cohesion, particularly related to family ties.[60] In other words, scholars in this movement seek to address African women's various situations and needs based on widely accepted, but non-discriminatory customs.[61] This is illustrated by Bowman and Schneider's[62] observations that 'whilst acknowledging that the formulation of legal theory has played an integral role in the development of social change, feminists should be focused on changing practical realities'.[63]

Furthermore, Nkealah argues that the ultimate goal of African feminism is 'to develop indigenous feminist models that aim to speak to feminism from an African cultural perspective, African geopolitical location, and an African ideological viewpoint'.[64] At the very basic foundational values, scholars have also pointed out that the shortcomings of many Western feminist approaches are that they address gender discrimination

[57] Mbiti 1969 and Gatobu 2013 as cited by Stulhofer (n 51). Dery (n 45) observes at 1745 that 'feminism was largely perceived by most men and women as dangerously feminizing and western custom, capable of destabilizing the cultural exceptionalism of Ghana society'; TS Hussen 'Radical possibilities at crossroads of African Feminism and Digital Activia' PhD, University of the Western Cape, 2021, at 4, where the author observes that 'African feminism challenges racist and Western ideas about African norms'.

[58] To that effect, the following recollection of African feminists illustrates how they distance themselves from the male exclusionary Western feminists agenda: Stulhofer (n 51) recounts Mathaai's experience that she 'realized that the family values superseded the quest for equality'; Arndt recounting about Flora Nwapa, a Nigerian Feminist who 'wanted nothing to do with feminism because of its anti-men stance'. See S Arndt 'Perspectives on African feminism: Defining and classifying African-feminist literature' (2002) 17 *Agenda* 31.

[59] Manji (n 53).

[60] Nkealah (n 48); and Mwambene & Sloth-Nielsen (n 1).

[61] Nkealah (n 48); Arndt (n 58).

[62] CG Bowman & EM Schneider 'Feminist legal theory, feminist lawmaking, and the legal profession' (1998) 67 *Fordham Law Review* 249.

[63] Bowman and Schneider (n 62).

[64] Nkealah (n 48) 62.

on an individualistic basis.[65] They further argue that African feminism's emphasis should be on authentic public participation and decision-making by women in contrast to Western feminism, which emphasises individual female autonomy.[66] Given that the persistent abuse of women and children in cultural practices, including *ukuthwala*, rests in community views, it is imperative that any attempt to resolve such abuses should include a more holistic approach that is community-centred.[67] Moreover, African feminism is resistant to the idea of 'gender separation' and instead seeks to establish gender equality through intergender partnerships.[68] This idea is useful in that any solution to the continued practice would need collaboration with men, particularly the traditional leaders of the community.

4 Policies and Legislative Framework on *Ukuthwala*

As set out by the studies above, *ukuthwala* has a number of detrimental effects on young girls and women, leading to human rights violations.[69] Crucial aspects of these effects, as recorded by the research in communities set out above, are largely repeated in the South African Law Reform Commission's work on the practice.[70] The Commission has recorded how victims of *ukuthwala* are often aged between 12 and 15 years old.[71] They often do not consent, or are pressured into *ukuthwala* by family members.

65 OUPblog (n 56).

66 As above.

67 Mwambene & Kruuse (n 4).

68 OUPblog (n 56).

69 South African Law Reform Commission (SALRC) *The Practice of Ukuthwala Report* Project 138 (2017) 1; L Mwambene & R Mgidlana 'Should South Africa criminalise *ukuthwala* leading to forced marriages and child marriages?' (2021) 24 *Potchefstroom Electronic Journal* 1.

70 The SALRC was established by the South African Law Reform Commission Act 19 of 1973. The objects of the Commission are to make recommendations to the legislature and other organs of state regarding the development, improvement, modernisation or reform of the laws of South Africa. Its report on *ukuthwala*, (SALRC *The Practice of Ukuthwala Report* Project 138 (2017)), was initiated in 2014.

71 Koyana & Bekker (n 1) illustrate that girls aged between 12 and 15 are the point of focus. These young girls are forced to get married to grown up men through the traditional practice with the consent of their parents. The researcher discovered that these

They are also sometimes forced into marriages with HIV-positive men. Several young girls in rural areas, fearful of becoming victims of *ukuthwala,* decide to run away from their communities, ending up living in urban areas such as Gauteng and KwaZulu-Natal.[72] Criminal elements associated with *ukuthwala* have placed this cultural tradition under a spotlight due to the violations of a girl child's rights that takes place when this practice is carried out. The economic gains associated with this practice make some families agree to the *ukuthwala* of a child[73] without considering their interests in education, well-being and development.

At the international level, the legal obligation to eliminate all forms of discrimination against women is a fundamental tenet of international human rights instruments.[74] South Africa is a party to several international conventions which prohibit sex and gender as a ground of discrimination, for example, the United Declaration of Human Rights (UDHR)[75]; the International Covenant on Civil and Political Rights (CCPR)[76]; the International Covenant on Economic, Social and Cultural Rights (CSCR)[77]; and the African Charter on Human and Peoples' Rights (ACHPR).[78] It has been argued that ambit of CEDAW, which applies specifically to women only, goes beyond the earlier human rights conventions by addressing the pervasive and systematic nature of discrimination against women.[79] Article 5 of CEDAW, for example, proscribes discrimination on the basis of harmful cultural practices, which, arguably may include *ukuthwala*, or at least the abuse of such practice.

At the national level, our starting point is the Constitution of the Republic of South Africa, 1996 (the Constitution). The Constitution

young girls are used to improve the living conditions of the family by being sold to the older man under the disguise of the traditional practice of *ukuthwala*.

[72] SALRC Project 138 (n 70) 1.

[73] Smit (n 40) 94, 128 and 148.

[74] Cook (n 7) 230.

[75] General Assembly, Resolution A/RES/217 (III), 10 December 1948.

[76] General Assembly Resolution 2200A (XXI), 16 December 1966, art 2(1).

[77] Resolution 2200A (XXI) (n 76) art 2(2).

[78] Adopted June 27, 1981, Organisation of the African Union (now AU) Doc CAB/LEG/67/3 rev. 5, 21 ILM 58 (1982),

[79] Cook (n 7) 239.

allows for the expression of culture.[80] On the face of it then, the practice of *ukuthwala* is constitutionally protected.[81] However, this constitutional protection must be balanced against the general rights of dignity, freedom and equality, with specific rights to be free from all forms of violence, not to be treated in a cruel, inhuman and degrading way and to have freedom of movement.[82] For children, there is an important rider: Section 28 of the Constitution states that 'a child's best interests are of paramount importance in every matter concerning the child'. The South African Children's Act[83] spells out what this paramount importance means in the context of social and cultural practices: Every child has the right not to be subjected to social, cultural, and religious practices which are detrimental to his or her well-being.[84]

South African common-law and delegated legislation support these constitutional provisions. South African common-law includes the crimes of abduction,[85] kidnapping,[86] assault with intent to cause grievous bodily harm, and common assault.[87] The relatively narrow meaning of common-law rape has been repealed with an expansive definition in terms of

[80] See secs 30 and 31 of the Constitution which respectively outline an individual's right to culture and language, and the collective rights of cultural, religious and linguistic communities. Section 185 of the Constitution seeks to further these rights through the creation of a Commission for the Promotion and Protection of the Rights of Cultural, Religious and Linguistic Communities. Cultural rights are also recognised by sec 211(3), which provides for the application of customary law by South African courts.

[81] TW Bennett 'Conflict of laws' in JC Bekker, C Rautenbach & NMI Goolam *Introduction to legal pluralism in South Africa* (2006) 18; and G Devenish *A commentary on the South African Bill of Rights* (1999) 421.

[82] Section 12(1) of the Constitution.

[83] Act 38 of 2005.

[84] As above.

[85] T Oosthuizen & NM Ngema '*Ukuthwala*: Structured for relevance' (2010) *Speculum Juris* 84 at 89. The authors describe the Roman law origins of the crime in Justinian's Digest where the removal or *raptus*, with or without violence, of a woman from the control of her guardian for the purpose of marrying her or having sexual intercourse with her was penalised. For the nuances of guardianship consent and the offence, see JRL Milton *South African criminal law and procedure* Vol 2 3 ed (1996) 554.

[86] JM Burchell *Principles of criminal law* (2006) 767; S Hoctor *Criminal law in South Africa* (2013) 48 and and CR Snyman *Criminal law* 5 ed (2008) 471.

[87] Snyman (n 86) 447, Koyana and Bekker (n 1) 141, Oosthuizen & Ngema (n 86) 92.

Criminal Law (Sexual Offences and Related Matters) Act[88] which is applicable to all forms of sexual penetration without consent.[89] Chapter 3 of the Act deals with sexual offences against children and specifies that intercourse with children under the age of 16 years, even with their consent, is statutory rape. The Act also retains the common-law position that children under 12 years of age cannot consent to sexual acts.[90] Given these provisions, *ukuthwala* will be deemed rape even if the child, subject to the practice, consented provided that she is below the age of 12 years, and statutory rape in respect of consensual sexual intercourse with a minor who is older than 12 years and younger than 16 years of age.[91]

Another important criminal statute in South Africa relevant to *ukuthwala* is the Prevention and Combating of Trafficking in Persons Act (the Act).[92] This was one of the offences in the *Jezile* case discussed above, and appears to be relatively common in case studies given the apartheid legacy which forced labour migration of men to the cities, while families remained in the rural areas.[93] The offence in this instance is that—as part of the *ukuthwala*—women and girls are transported from rural areas—particularly in the Eastern Cape and KwaZulu-Natal to South Africa's urban area in the Western Cape and Gauteng provinces.[94]

In the context of gender equality, the Promotion of Equality and Prevention of Unfair Discrimination Act (PEPUDA)[95] has relevance for the *ukuthwala* context. Section 8 of PEPUDA provides that specialist Equality Courts can hear claims of unfair discrimination which

[88] Act 32 of 2007.

[89] Sec 2(b) of the Act.

[90] Sec 57 of the Act.

[91] Jokani and others (n 13) 760.

[92] Act 7 of 2013.

[93] Vosloo describes this system poignantly: 'The migrant labour system was an historical system, manipulated by capitalist, colonial and apartheid powers as a means of reconciling the conflicting needs for cheap labour in the mines and cities of "white" South Africa, with the desire to restrict black people to rural areas far away from the "white" cities. As part of this system, people (mostly men) were forced to migrate to places of employment but were not permitted to do so with their families or stay permanently, resulting in a system of oscillating migrancy'. See C Vosloo 'Extreme apartheid: The South African system of migrant labour and its hostels' (2020) 34 *Image & Text* 1.

[94] Jokani and others (n 13) 761.

[95] Act 4 of 2000.

include gender-based violence, female genital mutilation, and any practice including traditional, customary, or religious practice which impairs the dignity of women and well-being of the girl child. This means that where an ***ukuthwala*** practice is found to have been abused, it will amount to a violation of rights in terms of this Act.

The challenge with this panoply of laws and conventions is that they still do not represent the deeply-held cultural beliefs of a certain section of the South African population, particularly in rural and poverty-struck areas.[96] This is evident through the continued practice of ***ukuthwala***.[97] It is also evident in the failure of state policies and programmes to curb the practice. Indeed during our visit, Jezile's community members challenged the researchers to stay longer to see for themselves ***ukuthwala*** happening even after the *Jezile* case.[98] Thus, whatever policies exist on paper, they are not adequately implemented or at least are not working.

The reasons for this are complex, but at its most basic level, and as set out by the case study responses set out above, we suggest that communities feel alienated from the laws that regulate them—if they even know about them. There are multiple reasons for this situation. We suggest that, given case study feedback and research, these reasons could be the following:

(a) Existing laws do not reflect the objectives that the community aims to achieve through the practice. These goals may be motivated by cultural beliefs (the fostering of family ties) or because of socio-economic circumstances (poverty).
(b) Existing laws fail to account for the communities' role and support in the victim's ***ukuthwala***. The laws are based on the idea that there is one accused and one victim. South Africa's criminal law is largely based on Roman-Dutch law. While it accommodates the doctrine of common purpose, this type of framework is wholly inadequate to meet the needs of the day.

[96] See Part 2 above, where we discuss the communities' views on the practice, particularly Anathi's grandmother.

[97] See Part 2 above on recent research findings which show that the practice continues.

[98] Focus group discussion with Jezile's family, September 2015 (transcription on record with the researchers).

(c) Attention is paid to the initial offence and conviction—but the backend is not well dealt with, regardless of whether these laws are state or community-centred. This is because actual state-centred support legislation is still in draft form,[99] and any community initiatives are not institutionalised, are informal, and are unlikely to have lasting effect.

The reason given in point (c) is starkly set out in both the SALRC and CEDAW reports. These reports record that, over the course of almost ten years of the SALRC report (2013–2014), and almost five years of the CEDAW report (2019–2022) several promised state-centred and victim-support pieces of legislation have not been passed because they are still in process.[100] Where there has been interaction with the community, it has been informal and passing.[101] Importantly, support for state shelters and NGO-subsidised shelters has been marred by incompetence in the former, and simply failures to subsidise in the latter.[102]

[99] For example, the Prohibition of Forced Marriages and Child Marriages Bill, the Victim Support Services Bill and the Women Empowerment and Gender Equality Bill.

[100] For example, in the SALRC Revised Discussion Paper 138 (Project 138) *The Practice of ukuthwala* (2015) the Commission drafted and recommended the passing of the Prohibition of Forced Marriages and Child Marriages Bill. It is still not in force. Commentators lauded the prohibition in the Bill, but criticised it in its failure to account for victim support: 'the Prohibition Bill provides no details about the protection, support and assistance for survivors and information relating to service providers' (Supplement DAW/DESA Handbook for Legislation on Violence against Women (2011) 12). In the South African government responses to the CEDAW's observation visit and report in 2019, it promised the passing of the Victim Support Services Bill (published in Government Gazette 43528 of 17 July 2020) and the Women Empowerment and Gender Equality Bill (published in Government Gazette 37005 of 6 November 2013). These Bills too have to date not been passed.

[101] See CEDAW and SALRC reports (n 30 and 70) respectively.

[102] See N McCain 'Lack of government funding hampering women's shelters' *News24* 22 August 2022 https://www.news24.com/news24/southafrica/news/lack-of-government-funding-hampering-womens-shelters-20220822 (accessed 31 July 2023). Importantly, the Commission on Gender Equality (a statutory body set up by South Africa's Constitution) reported on the dire state of shelters in South Africa in its report: *Report on Consultative Hearings into the State of Shelters in South Africa* (2020) avttps://static.pmg.org.za/1/CGE_Report_on_Shelters_2019.20.pdf (accessed 13 January 2025).

5 Necessary Structural Changes to Support Victims of *Ukuthwala*

In its current form, and historically, we have described *ukuthwala* as a traditional practice that has been used to justify forced marriages, often involving young girls.[103] While some efforts have been made to address this harmful practice through legal frameworks and policies,[104] an African feminist legal analysis highlights both the progress and the shortcomings in addressing the issues.[105] Feminist legal scholars have highlighted the challenge of balancing cultural relativism with women's rights.[106]

Part of the challenge with the frameworks and policies regarding *ukuthwala* relates to the question of whether it is the practice itself that is problematic or the abuse of it. On the one hand, scholars and most state actors suggest that the original form of *ukuthwala* was 'benign'[107] in nature, even 'romantic' and 'charming'.[108] In this form, scholars suggest that modernity and poverty have tainted the practice, resulting in distortion and abuse. In its original form these scholars argue that the practice was akin to elopement. In terms of this version, the abduction was performative and not real. In this way, couples could use *ukuthwala* to force their families to accept the marriage or to avoid situations where families could not afford the lengthy and costly negotiations leading up to a typical customary marriage.[109] As Karimakwenda starkly sets out: 'The literature paints *ukuthwala* as an innately benevolent practice involving mock abduction, feigned displeasure by the bride and the absence of sexual intercourse during the process'.[110]

103 See also Karikamwenda (n 1).

104 See CEDAW and SALRC reports (n 30 and 70), respectively.

105 H Charlesworth & C Chinkin The boundaries of international law: A feminist analysis (2000).

106 In general, see NH Msuya 'The concept of culture relativism and women's rights in sub-Saharan Africa' (2019) 54 *Journal of Asian and African Studies* 1145.

107 Mwambene & Sloth-Nielsen (n 1).

108 Koyana & Bekker (n 1).

109 Karimakwenda (n 1) 766 reports on this benign form, but falls within the latter scholar group, ie those who suggest the *ukuthwala* has always been tainted by violence. It has also been suggested that this form was used where the girl or woman is pregnant. Cf Koyana & Bekker (n 1).

110 Karimakwenda (n 1) 770.

Karimakwenda and other scholars, including most NGOs, argue that *ukuthwala* has always been characterised by violence and gender inequality, and that any benign version of it may have existed, but it was the exception rather than the rule.[111] While these scholars admit of sparse research of sexual violence of black women in the past, they point out that there is sufficient research to suggest that customary communities accepted and even endorsed coercive (i.e. violent) forms of *ukuthwala* in the past. Disturbingly, they also argue that—in the quest to reinvigorate and affirm African tradition—the state tends to silence any suggestion that 'ancient Africa' endorsed sexual violence, and this is all a recent phenomenon.[112]

Although we sympathise with commentators who suggest that violence is not a recent phenomenon in the practice, we cannot and do not intend to resolve this issue. Instead, we want to acknowledge this history with its debate, but then go beyond it by looking at ways in which policies and frameworks can change the hearts and minds (and pockets) of those communities who practice *ukuthwala* for the ideal and positive reason they practised it in the past, i.e., for familial ties.

As a result, it is important to acknowledge that the effort to protect and affirm cultural practices (viz, that the only problem with *ukuthwala* is its distortion and abuse) can and does overshadow the rights and agency of women.[113] One way to challenge these issues, as highlighted by African feminists, is to focus on the intersectionality of the issue, and highlight how multiple identities and social categories intersect to shape experiences of those involved in the practice.[114] This type of analysis would include looking at factors such as age, gender, race, and socio-economic status

[111] Karimakwenda (n 1).

[112] Karimakwenda (n 1). See, for example, state publications which endorse this approach: Department of Justice and Constitutional Development '*Ukuthwala*' https://www.justice.gov.za/brochure/ukuthwala/ukuthwala.html (accessed 5 July 2023). In this brochure, the state sets out: 'Today, ukuthwala is being practised in different ways from the original tradition, as it is marked by violence and rape'.

[113] N Karimakwenda 'Rethinking ukuthwala, the South African "bride abduction" custom' (12 September 2021) *The Conversation* https://theconversation.com/rethinking-ukuthwala-the-south-african-bride-abduction-custom-165496 (accessed 13 January 2025).

[114] K Crenshaw 'Mapping the margins: Intersectionality, identity politics, and violence against women of color' (1991) 43 *Stanford Law Review* 1241. For insights on intersectionality and *ukuthwala* in particular, see eg, Mabizela (n 39) 89 and D Mabasa 'Ukuthwala: Is it all culturally relative?' (2015) 555 *De Rebus* 28 at 29.

to better understand the unique challenges faced by different individuals and communities.

Another way in which to address the issues is to focus on the importance of access to justice for marginalised individuals.[115] While laws and policies against *ukuthwala* exist in South Africa, we have seen how their effective enforcement can be hindered by factors such as limited resources, cultural relativism, and a lack of awareness. Linked to the experience that the victim in the *Jezile* case had to undergo, it is crucial to ensure that victims have access to legal remedies and support services, and that these services are culturally-sensitive and responsive. We do not wade into the historical/present debate suffice to say that if *ukuthwala* has to remain as a cultural practice, several cultural protective measures would need to be enforced by the community and particularly traditional leaders. Bennett suggests that these measures include the following processes: The bridegroom's family has to convey a message to the family of the woman on the day of the 'kidnapping' or early the next morning; the bridegroom's family is expected to specify what value in livestock or money they are offering to deliver, and by when.[116] Also, it needs to be explicitly recognised that engaging sexually with the woman who is '*ukuthwala*-ed' is absolutely contrary to customary law.[117] As a general proposition, the community—together with their traditional leadership has to be empowered to achieve their ends without harm to those among them. One way, suggested by Dlamini and Makhaye, is to encourage community policing, where law enforcement agencies and communities seek ways to achieve closer cooperation.[118]

While we acknowledge the tension that often arises between cultural relativism and universal human rights when addressing harmful traditional practices such as *ukuthwala*, we suggest that we can respect the positive goals or purposes of the practice (in this case the fostering of family ties) as long as to do so would not violate fundamental human rights. This means engaging in a dialogue that challenges harmful practices without imposing a singular, external viewpoint.

[115] See for example, S Douglas 'Gender equality and justice programming: Equitable access to justice for women' (2006–7) *United Nations Development Programme*.

[116] Koyana & Bekker (n 1).

[117] Bennett (n 4) 7 and 12.

[118] Dlamini & Makhaye (n 5) 22.

In addition, feminist legal theory underscores the importance of policy implementation and education in achieving meaningful change.[119] In this context then, the harmful aspects of *ukuthwala* should be complemented by comprehensive educational programmes that challenge these harmful gender norms, promote gender equality, and raise awareness about the rights of individuals, particularly women and girls.

6 Conclusion

In conclusion, feminist legal analysis of laws and policies seeking to protect victims of *ukuthwala* in South Africa highlights the need to consider a number of factors. These factors include intersectionality; ensuring access to justice; navigating the tension between cultural relativism and human rights; engaging with legal pluralism; and emphasising policy implementation and education. This multifaceted approach is essential for effectively addressing and supporting victims of *ukuthwala* within a complex sociocultural context. Ultimately, we argue that the involvement of the community is central to all this, and meaningful change to the law can only take place where community needs are met in ways other than *ukuthwala*. The fact that living customary law, in general, is flexible and dynamic makes this endeavour all the more possible.

Bibliography

Aderinboyo, A 'African feminism and women's rights in Nigeria' (2020) SSRN: https://ssrn.com/abstract=3683051 or https://doi.org/10.2139/ssrn.3683051 (accessed 13 January 2025)

Agboola, C; Kofi Appiah, CE & Hamonde Linonge-Fontebo, H 'Women's pathways into crime and incarceration: Insights from South Africa' (2022) 8 *Cogent Social Sciences* 1

Amede Obior, L 'Feminist legal theory, human rights, and culture in Africa' in Yacob-Haliso, O and Falola, T (eds) *The Palgrave handbook of African women's studies* (Springer 2021) 171

Arndt, S 'Perspectives on African feminism: Defining and classifying African feminist literature' (2002) *Agenda: Empowering Women for Gender Equity* 31

[119] See in general, L Amede Obior 'Feminist legal theory, human rights, and culture in Africa' in O Yacob-Haliso & T Falola (eds) *The Palgrave handbook of African women's studies* (2021) 171.

Bayu, EK 'A comparative analysis on the perspectives of African feminism vs Western feminism: Philosophical debate with their criticism and its implication for women's rights in Ethiopian context' (2019) 11 *International Journal of Sociology and Anthropology* 54

Bekker, JC; Rautenbach, C & Goolam, NMI *Introduction to legal pluralism in South Africa* (LexisNexis 2006)

Bennett, TW 'Conflict of laws' in Bekker, JC; Rautenbach, C & Goolam, NMI *Introduction to Legal pluralism in South Africa* (LexisNexis 2006) 18

Bennett, TW 'The cultural defence and the custom of *Thwala* in South African Law' (2010) 10 *University of Botswana Law Journal* 3

Bowman, CG & Schneider, EM 'Feminist legal theory, feminist lawmaking, and the legal profession' (1998) 67 *Fordham Law Review* 249

Burchell, JM *Principles of criminal law* (Juta & Company Ltd 2006)

Buthelezi, MW 'The role of traditional leadership in crime prevention in northern KwaZulu- Natal' (2021) 6 *Just Africa* 37

Charlesworth, H & Chinkin, C *The boundaries of international law: A feminist analysis* (Manchester University Press 2000)

Claassens, A & Smythe, D 'Marriage, land and custom: What's law got to do with it?' 2013 *Acta Juridica* 1

Cook, R 'Women's international human rights law: The way forward' (1993) 15 *Human Rights Quarterly* 230

Crenshaw, K 'Mapping the margins: Intersectionality, identity politics, and violence against women of color' (1991) 43 *Stanford Law Review* 1241

Dery, I 'A situated, African understanding of African feminism for men: A Ghanian narrative' (2020) 27 *Gender, Place and Culture* 1745

Devenish, G *A commentary on the South African Bill of Rights* (Butterworths 1999)

Dlamini, S & Makhaye, MS 'Community policing as a panacea for gender based violence impasse' (2023) 12 *African Journal of Gender, Society and Development* 7

Douglas, S 'Gender equality and justice programming: Equitable access to justice for women' (2006–7) *United Nations Development Programme*

Dowd, NE 'Masculinities and feminist legal theory' (2008) 23 *Wisconsin Journal of Law, Gender and Society* 201

Feltham, T 'Working Paper No. 46: Foundations for feminist legal theory' Portland State University Economics Working Papers (2020)

Filomina, SC 'African feminism' in *Routledge Encyclopedia of Philosophy* (Routledge 2005)

Fineman, MA 'Feminist legal theory' (2005) 13 *American University Journal of Gender, Social Policy & the Law* 13

Goredema, R '*African feminism: The African woman's struggle for identity*' (2010) 33

Griffiths, D 'Decoloniality and the (im)possibility of an African feminist philosophy' (2022) 41 *South African Journal of Philosophy* 240

Grobbelaar, J & Jones, C (eds) *Childhood vulnerabilities in South Africa: Some ethical perspectives* (Stellenbosch: African Sun Media 2020)

Himonga, C & Nhlapo, T (eds) *African customary law in South Africa* 2 ed (Oxford University Press: South Africa 2023)

Hlophe, P 'An exploratory study on *ukuthwala* and crime: a perspective of *inqaba kamveliqangi* cultural organisation' (2021) MSocSci thesis, University of KwaZulu-Natal, 2021

Hoctor, S *Criminal law in South Africa* (2013) 48

Hussen, TS 'Radical possibilities at crossroads of African feminism and *digital activia'* PhD, University of the Western Cape, 2021

Jokani, M; Knoetze, E & Erasmus, D 'A criminal response to the harmful practices of *ukuthwala*' (2018) *Obiter* 747

Kabore, A 'Differentiating African and Western feminisms through room symbolism' (2017) 5 *Linguistic and Literature Review* 408

Karimakwenda, N '"Today it would be called rape": A historical and contextual examination of forced marriage and violence in the Eastern Cape' (2013) *Acta Juridica* 339

Karimakwenda, N 'Deconstructing characterisations of rape, marriage, and custom in South Africa' (2020) 63 *African Studies Review* 763

Karimakwenda, N 'Rethinking *ukuthwala,* the South African "bride abduction" custom' *The Conversation* 12 September 2021 https://theconversation.com/rethinking-ukuthwala-the-south-african-bride-abduction-custom-165496 (accessed 13 January 2025)

Kruger, B 'Enhancing the criminal justice response to human trafficking in South Africa: Legislation and case law in the spotlight' (2023) 37 *South African Journal of Criminal Justice* 48

Le Roux, E 'Recognising and responding to complex dilemmas: Child marriage in South Africa' in Grobbelaar, J & Jones, C (eds) *Childhood vulnerabilities in South Africa: Some ethical perspectives* (Stellenbosch: African Sun Media 2020)

Levit, N & Verchick, RRM *Feminist legal theory: A primer* (2 ed) (NYU Press 2016)

Koyana, D & Bekker, JC 'The indomitable ukuthwala custom' (2007) 40 *De Jure* 139

Mabasa, D '*Ukuthwala*: Is it all culturally relative?' (2015) 555 *De Rebus* 28

Mabizela, S 'Bergville residents' construction of the cultural practice of ukuthwala: A discourse analysis' PhD dissertation, University of South Africa, 2022

Machaka, BJ 'The cultural practice of *ukuthwala* in South Africa' LLM Thesis, Nelson Mandela University, 2019

Manji, S 'Imagining women's "legal world": Towards a feminist theory of legal pluralism in Africa' (1999) 8 *Social and Legal Studies* 435

Masiphephe Network *Harmful practices infringing the rights of women and girls: Policy brief* (2021) https://www.masiphephe.org.za/wp-content/uploads/2022/06/Harmful-Practices-Infringe-the-Rights-of-Women-and-Girls_Final-Policy-Brief-.pdf (accessed 13 January 2025)

Matlala, R 'Introducing feminist legal theory as a basis for South African judicial jurisprudence: Insights from *S v Tshabalala*' (2022) 139 *South African Law Journal* 274

McCain, N 'Lack of government funding hampering women's shelters' *News24* 22 August 2022 https://www.news24.com/news24/southafrica/news/lack-of-government-funding-hampering-womens-shelters-20220822 (accessed 13 January 2025)

Milton, JRL *South African criminal law and procedure* Vol 2 3 ed (Juta & Company 1996)

Mkhuseli, J 'The customary law practice of *ukuthwala*: An antithesis in South African constitutional order' LLD thesis, Nelson Mandela University, 2018

Monyane, C 'Is u*kuthwala* another form of "forced marriage"?' (2013) 44 *South African Review of Sociology* 64

Moore, E & Himonga, C 'Living customary law and families in Africa' (2018) *South African Child Gauge* 61

Msuya, NH 'The concept of culture relativism and women's rights in sub-Saharan Africa' (2019) 54 *Journal of Asian and African Studies* 1145

Mubangizi, J 'A South African perspective on the clash between culture and human rights, with particular reference to gender-related cultural practices and traditions' (2012) 13 *Journal of International Women's Studies* 39

Müller-Van der Westhuizen, C & Streso, R 'Ukuthwala – Gebruik of misbruik?' (2018) 15 *Litnet Akademies* 1143

Mwambene, L & Kruuse, H 'The thin edge of the wedge: *Ukuthwala*, alienation and consent' (2017) 33 *South African Journal on Human Rights* 25

Mwambene, L & Mgidlana, R 'Should South Africa criminalise *ukuthwala* leading to forced marriages and child marriages?' (2021) 24 *Potchefstroom Electronic Journal* 1

Mwambene, L & Sloth-Nielsen, J 'Benign accommodation? *Ukuthwala*, "forced marriage" and South African Children's Act' (2011) 11 *African Human Rights Law Journal* 1

Nkealah, N '(West) African feminism and their challenges' (2016) *Journal of Library Studies/Tydskrif vir Literatuurweetenskap* 62

Oosthuizen, T & Ngema, NM '*Ukuthwala*: structured for relevance' (2010) *Speculum Juris* 84

OUPblog 'Women's history month: An interpretation of feminism in Africa' 22 March 2007 https://blog.oup.com/2007/03/womens_history_-2/ (accessed 13 January 2025)

Prinsloo, J & Ovens, M 'Ukuthwala as an aberrant traditional practice: The State versus Nvumeleni Jezile 2014 WCD' (2015) 4 *Acta Criminologica* 169

Rice, K '*Ukuthwala* in rural South Africa: Abduction marriage as a site of negotiation about gender, rights and generational authority among the Xhosa' (2014) 40 *Journal of Southern African Studies* 381

Rice, K 'Understanding *ukuthwala*: Bride abduction in the rural Eastern Cape South Africa' (2018) 77 *African Studies* 394

Scully, P 'Should we give up on the state? Feminist theory, African gender history and transitional justice' (2009) 9 *African Journal of Conflict Resolution* 29

Smit, WJ 'Rights, violence and the marriage of confusion: Re-emerging bride abduction in South Africa' (2017) 40 *Anthropology Southern Africa* 56

Snyman, CR *Criminal Law* 5 ed (LexisNexis 2008)

Stulhofer, EW 'Navigating African feminisms: Wangari Maathai as a portrait' *Africa Knows Conference* (2021) https://nomadit.co.uk/conference/africaknows/paper/58023 (accessed 13 January 2025)

United Nations Entity for Gender Equality and the Empowerment of Women *Handbook for legislation on violence against women* (2012) https://www.unwomen.org/sites/default/files/Headquarters/Attachments/Sections/Library/Publications/2012/12/UNW_Legislation-Handbook%20pdf.pdf (accessed 13 January 2025)

Van der Watt, M & and Ovens, M 'Contextualising the practice of *ukuthwala* in South Africa' (2012) 13 *Child Abuse Research: A South African Journal* 11

Venganai, H '(Re)constructing positive cultures to protect girls and women against sexual violence / Interventions to address sexual violence: Transforming violent cultures for and with girls and young women' (2015) 29 *Agenda* 145

Vosloo, C 'Extreme apartheid: The South African system of migrant labour and its hostels' (2020) 34 *Image and Text* 1

Wadesango, N & Chabaya, O 'Violation of women's rights by harmful traditional practices' (2011) 13 *The Anthropologist* 121

Ziyanda, V & Oscar, MT '*Ukuthwala* practice: Conflict of Chapter 2 (Bill of Rights) of South African Constitution Act 108 of 1996 and Cultural Practice' (2020) 4 *American Journal of Humanities and Social Sciences Research* 45

Acts

Children's Act 38 of 2005

Constitution of the Republic of South Africa, 1996

Criminal Law (Sexual Offences and Related Matters) Act 32 of 2007

Prevention and Combating of Trafficking in Persons Act 7 of 2013
Promotion of Equality and Prevention of Unfair Discrimination Act 4 of 2000
South African Law Reform Commission Act 19 of 1973

Bills

Victim Support Services Bill: Government Gazette 43528 of 17 July 2020
Women Empowerment and Gender Equality Bill: Government Gazette 37005 of 6 November 2013

Commissions

Commission for the Promotion and Protection of the Rights of Cultural, Religious and Linguistic Communities https://nationalgovernment.co.za/units/view/51/commission-for-the-promotion-and-protection-of-the-rights-of-cultural-religious-and-linguistic-communities (accessed 13 January 2025)
Commission for Gender Equality (CGE) *Report on consultative hearings into the state of shelters in South Africa* (2020) https://static.pmg.org.za/1/CGE_Report_on_Shelters_2019.20.pdf (accessed 13 January 2025)
Department of Justice and Constitutional Development '*Ukuthwala*' https://www.justice.gov.za/brochure/ukuthwala/ukuthwala.html (accessed 13 February 2025)
South African Law Reform Commission (SALRC) Revised Discussion Paper 138 (Project 138) *The Practice of ukuthwala* (2015)
South African Law Reform Commission (SALRC) 'The Practice of *ukuthwala*' Discussion Paper Project 138 (2016)
South African Law Reform Commission (SALRC) *The Practice of Ukuthwala Report* Project 138 (2017) 1
Statistics South Africa 'Marriages and divorce' (2017) https://www.statssa.gov.za/publications/P0307/P03072017.pdf (13 January 2025)
'Traditional leaders praised for denouncing *ukuthwala*' *SA Government News Agency* https://www.sanews.gov.za/south-africa/traditional-leaders-praised-denouncing-ukuthwala (accessed 13 January 2025)

Case law

Jezile v S 2016 (2) SA 62 (WCC)

International Treaties (date order)

African Charter on Human and Peoples' Rights (ACHPR), Organisation of the African Union (now AU) adopted 27 June 1981 doc. CAB/LEG/67/3 rev 5, 21 ILM 58 (1982)

Convention on the Elimination of All Forms of Discrimination Against Women (2021) CEDAW/C/ZAF/IR/1

Follow-up report submitted by South Africa (8 June 2022) CEDAW/C/ZAF/FIR/1

International Covenant on Civil and Political Rights (CCPR), 16 December 1966, General Assembly resolution 2200A (XXI)

International Covenant on Economic, Social and Cultural Rights (CSCR), 16 December 1966, General Assembly resolution 2200A (XXI)

Observations of South Africa (17 November 2021) CEDAW/C/ZAF/OIR/1

United Nations Declaration of Human Rights (UNDHR), General Assembly, Resolution A/RES/217 (III), 10 December 1948

United Nations Department of Economic and Social Affairs (DESA) *Handbook for Legislation on Violence against Women* (2011) 12

United Nations Human Rights Treaty Bodies *Inquiry concerning South Africa under article 8 of the Optional Protocol to the Convention on the Elimination of All Forms of Discrimination against Women* (12 May 2021) https://tbinternet.ohchr.org/_layouts/15/TreatyBodyExternal/TBSearch.aspx?Lang=en&TreatyID=3&DocTypeCategoryID=7 (accessed 13 January 2025)

CHAPTER 5

Cultural Relativism Versus Universalism: A Critical Analysis of the *Chinamwari/ Khomba* Practice in Zimbabwe

Linet Sithole and Cowen Dziva

1 Introduction

Different societies over the world have different cultural practices that largely reflect on the values, beliefs, and ways of life lived from generation to generation.[1] More often than not, these varied traditional cultural practices and beliefs by societies are viewed differently by both onlookers and participants, with some viewing them as beneficial to society, while

[1] L Sithole & C Dziva 'Eliminating harmful practices against women in Zimbabwe: Implementing article 5 of the African Women's Protocol' (2019) 19 *African Human Rights Law Journal* 568.

L. Sithole (✉)
Africa University, School of Law, Mutare, Zimbabwe
e-mail: linet.sithole@africau.edu

C. Dziva
Nehanda Centre for Gender and Cultural Studies at Great Zimbabwe University (GZU), Masvingo, Zimbabwe

E. Durojaye et al. (eds.), *Harmful Practices and Human Rights: An International Perspective*, Human Rights Interventions,
https://doi.org/10.1007/978-3-031-90333-5_5

others despising them.[2] Generally, women's rights have always been sacrificed under the pretext of culture, customs, and patriarchy.[3] Rao Arati correctly observed and described the situation as follows:

> No special group has suffered a greater violation of its human rights in the name of culture than women. Regardless of the particular forms it takes in different societies, the concept of culture in the modern state circumscribes women's lives in deeply symbolic as well as immediately real ways.[4]

Chinamwari/khomba is one such practice that is viewed differently in the twenty-first century. In Zimbabwe, the practice is associated with ethnic groups like the Chewa, Mahenye,[5] Lemba, Shangaan, Ngoni, Venda, and Tonga communities. In the *Shona* language, the word *komba* means ripe. Thus, the ceremony is meant to transition girls from childhood to womanhood making them 'ripe' for life and marriage'.[6]

With the practice, young girls of 13 to 16 years, and some newly-married women are sent for initiation schooling outside the villages with women elders. A study by Muzingili and Taruvingane noted that among the Shangani people of Zimbabwe, girls are eligible for the rite once they go for their first menstrual cycle and that happens at approximately 12 to 14 years of age.[7] In most instances, the *chinamwari* rites take place in winter from June up to August when the young girls are less involved

[2] F Viljoen 'An introduction to the Protocol to the African Charter on Human and Peoples' Rights on the Rights of Women in Africa' (2009) 16 *Washington and Lee Journal of Civil Rights and Social Justice* 11.

[3] H Chukwuma *Women's quest for rights: African feminist theory in fiction* (2006).

[4] R Arati 'The politics of gender and culture in international human rights discourse' in J Peters & A Wolper (eds) *Women's rights, human rights: International feminist perspectives* (1995) 167.

[5] M Naidu & W Muchono 'Male perceptions toward the cultural practice of chinamwari/khomba among the Mahenye' (2019) 19 *The Oriental Anthropologist* 25.

[6] S Moyo & N Matanda 'The chinamwari initiation rite in Zimbabwe: Opportunity or threat to the girl child?' (2020) 3 *American Research Journal of Humanities & Social Science (ARJHSS)* 38.

[7] T Muzingili & R Taruvinga 'Culturally-inflicted child rights violation: A case of khomba practice of Shangaan People in Zimbabwe' (2017) 7 *Mgbakoigba: Journal of African Studies* 34 at 39.

in agricultural activities.[8] The ceremonies are often done in years of good harvest to ensure that hunger is not an issue in the camps.[9] Initiates therefore go away from the village in isolation for three months and no relatives are allowed as camps are off limits to outsiders.[10] While at the initiation school, women trainees are taught about married life, especially sexual expertise, to please their husbands during the marriage.[11] Scholars allege that the initiates spend much of their time half naked in the cold weather, and are subjected to corporal punishment as part of the training.[12] During the *chinamwari* teachings, initiates are taught varied subjects such as sex education, proper conduct as a woman, menstrual care, and other life skills. With all these teachings and activities, the girl child is believed to be exposed to womanhood life and the broader roles she is expected to undertake in society.[13] Writing from a Zambian perspective, Talakinu describes the *chinamwari* practice as follows:

> *Chinamwari* like other female initiation rites is a rite of social maturation where a girl is transformed into an adult through a process that legitimises her 'new' gender and sexual roles. What is also clear is that, *chinamwari* teaches a young girl how to internalise her gender and sexual identities through a process of enculturation, because it is through this process that a young woman learns what is culturally acceptable behaviour of what it means to be a woman.[14]

[8] RS Maposa 'Going under the traditional knife: Linking African traditional education and the ethic of identity through Shangani Culture, Zimbabwe' (2008) 2 *Journal of Emerging Trends in Educational Research and Policy Studies* 479.

[9] 'Chinamwari: Old habits die hard' *The Herald* 29 April 2021 https://www.herald.co.zw/chinamwari-old-habits-die-hard-2/ (accessed 31 June 2023).

[10] Maposa (n 8).

[11] C Chikunda, E Marambire & R Makoni 'The impact of khomba – a Shangaan cultural rite of passage – on the formal schooling of girls and on women's space in the Chikombedzi area in Zimbabwe, Indilinga' (2006) 5 *African Journal of Indigenous Knowledge Systems* 145; AK Siachitema 'Interrogating the role of initiation rites in shaping adolescents' sexual behaviour and gender relations in a changing world' (2013). 2013/06/Siachitema_child3_dpaper.pdf (accessed 22 June 2023).

[12] Chikunda and others (n 11); Siachitema (n 11).

[13] Moyo & Matanda (n 6).

[14] CM Talakinu '"I am because of what i know i have": A descriptive analysis of chinamwari in preparing women for womanhood, sexual life and reproduction' (2018) 12 *Africology: The Journal Pan African Studies* 107.

While there have been studies of *chinamwari/khomba* in various communities including the Mahenye, VaRemba, and the Shangaan, the issue of the *khomba* practice has not been probed from a universalist and cultural relativist perspective.[15] The focus on *chinamwari* from a cultural relativist and universalist approach remains piecemeal and tucked in general women and children's rights research.[16] This chapter seeks to add to the human rights theory by showing the discourses around the *khomba* practice from a cultural relativist and modern human rights thinking to illustrate the conflicting positions. We are neither here to provide an empirical account of the experience of this practice, nor resolve the debate, but to mainly show the implications of the two approaches to women's rights.

The chapter uses a qualitative research methodology informed by the review of laws and extant literature on harmful practices, and women's rights. Thus, the writings of universalist and cultural relativist scholars were consulted in coming up with this analysis.

The chapter comprises five sections starting with this introduction. The second section discusses the place of harmful practices in international and national mechanisms. Sections three and four analyse the major expositions of the universalist and cultural relativist approaches, respectively. The final section concludes the chapter and proffers some recommendations for the enhanced protection of women and girls' rights against harmful practices.

2 The Place of Cultural Practices Under International and National Mechanisms

Cultural practices entail shared norms, values, perceptions and traditions of how people routinely behave in a society.[17] Almost every society the world over has specific traditional cultural practices and beliefs, some of which are beneficial to society, while a majority of them are detrimental to

[15] Naidu & Muchono (n 5).

[16] Sithole & Dziva (n 1).

[17] M Frese 'Cultural practices, norms, and values' (2015) 46 *Journal of Cross-Cultural Psychology* 1327.

the enjoyment of rights by girls and women.[18] This explains why several human rights mechanisms seek to eliminate practices that are harmful to society.[19] For instance, the International Covenant on Civil and Political Rights (ICCPR) protects individuals from 'torture or cruel, inhuman or degrading treatment' and arbitrary or unlawful interference with his or her privacy under articles 7 and 17 respectively.[20] Further, article 3 of ICCPR provides for equality of rights between men and women.[21] The Human Rights Committee (HRC), in its General Comment 28,[22] calls for the equal enjoyment of human rights between men and women by taking cognisance of the impact of culture and tradition on women by stating that:

> Inequality in the enjoyment of rights by women throughout the world is deeply embedded in tradition, history and culture, including religious attitudes. The subordinate role of women in some countries is illustrated by the high incidence of prenatal sex selection and abortion of female foetuses.[23]

Similarly, the Convention on the Elimination of Discrimination Against Women (CEDAW), also prohibits discrimination and calls upon states

[18] OHCHR 'Fact Sheet 23: Harmful traditional practices affecting the health of women and children' (August 1995).

[19] UN General Assembly, Convention on the Rights of the Child, United Nations, Treaty Series, vol 1577, p 3, 20 November 1989; UN General Assembly, Universal Declaration of Human Rights, 217 A (III), 10 December 1948; UN General Assembly, International Covenant on Civil and Political Rights, United Nations, Treaty Series, vol 999, p 171, 16 December 1966; UN General Assembly, Convention on the Elimination of All Forms of Discrimination Against Women, United Nations, Treaty Series, vol 1249, p 13, 18 December 1979; Organisation of African Unity (OAU), African Charter on the Rights and Welfare of the Child, 11 July 1990, AU Doc CAB/LEG/24.9/49 (1990); African Union, Protocol to the African Charter on Human and People's Rights on the Rights of Women in Africa, 11 July 2003 (Maputo Protocol).

[20] ICCPR (n 19).

[21] The states parties to the present Covenant undertake to ensure the equal right of men and women to the enjoyment of all civil and political rights set forth in the present Covenant.

[22] UN Human Rights Committee (HRC), CCPR General Comment 28: Article 3 (The Equality of Rights Between Men and Women), 29 March 2000, UN Doc CCPR/C/21/Rev.1/Add.10 (2000).

[23] Para 5.

parties take all appropriate measures, including legislation, to modify or abolish existing laws, regulations, customs, and practices which constitute discrimination against women.[24] CEDAW defines discrimination as:

> [A]ny distinction, exclusion or restriction made based on sex which has the effect or purpose of impairing or nullifying the recognition, enjoyment or exercise by women, irrespective of their marital status, on a basis of equality of men and women, of human rights and fundamental freedoms in the political, economic, social, cultural, civil or any other field.[25]

Although the *khomba/chinamwari* practice or any harmful practice is not explicitly mentioned, it is argued that harmful practices fit within the definition of discrimination against women as outlined in CEDAW. According to Rahman and Toubia, explaining the impact of female genital mutilation (FGM), state that 'it is a practice exclusively directed towards women and girls with the effect of nullifying their enjoyment of fundamental rights'.[26] The *chinamwari/khomba* practice is also directed at women and has the effect of violating their rights. Further, CEDAW General Recommendations 14,[27] 19,[28] and 24[29] acknowledge the severity of the impact and consequences for women and girls subjected to harmful cultural practices and identify these practices as a form of violence against women. The General Recommendations further recommend that states parties should take all the necessary measures to eliminate the harmful practices against women and girls.

The CEDAW Preamble sets the tone of prohibiting cultural practices by stating that 'the role of women in procreation should not be a basis

[24] Art 2(f) of CEDAW.

[25] Art 1.

[26] A Rudman & N Toubia *Female genital mutilation: A guide to laws and policies worldwide* (2001).

[27] UN Committee on the Elimination of Discrimination Against Women (CEDAW), General Recommendation 14: Female circumcision UN Doc A/45/38 (1990).

[28] UN Committee on the Elimination of Discrimination Against Women (CEDAW), General Recommendation 19: Violence against women (1992).

[29] UN Committee on the Elimination of Discrimination Against Women (CEDAW), General Recommendation 24: Article 12 of the Convention (Women and Health), UN Doc A/54/38/Rev.1 (1999).

for discrimination'.[30] The Preamble further emphasises 'that a change in the ***traditional role of men as well as the role of women in society and the family is needed to achieve full equality of men and women***'. This provision thus recognises how detrimental cultural practices by society may be to women's ability to exercise their rights freely. Indeed, cultural practices such as ***ukungena***[31] in South Africa, early child marriages and *chinamwali/khomba* in Zimbabwe, if not abolished or controlled, can cause harm to women and children's rights, particularly their reproductive health, the right to education, and the right to dignity. Upon this realisation, article 5 of CEDAW therefore obligates states to take

> all appropriate measures [to] modify the social and cultural patterns of conduct of men and women, to achieve the elimination of prejudices and customary and all other practices which are based on the idea of the inferiority or the superiority of either of the sexes or on stereotyped roles for men and women.

The Convention of the Rights of the Child (CRC), established the 'best interests of the child' standard in addressing the rights of children.[32] Harmful practices such as *chinamwari* are recognised as a violation of that best interests standard and a violation of other children's rights guaranteed in the CRC.[33] In this regard, article 24(3) mandates states parties

[30] The paragraph provides as follows: 'Bearing in mind the great contribution of women to the welfare of the family and to the development of society, so far not fully recognized, the social significance of maternity and the role of both parents in the family and in the upbringing of children, and aware that the role of women in procreation should not be a basis for discrimination but that the upbringing of children requires a sharing of responsibility between men and women and society as a whole'.

[31] The *ukungena* practice is called levirate unions in English and these occur when the deceased's surviving male relative inherits the widow of the deceased. The inherited widow becomes the wife to the surviving relative of the deceased. See, MJ Maluleke 'Culture, tradition, custom, law and gender equality' (2012) 15 *Potchefstroom Electronic Law Journal* 1.

[32] Art 3 of the CRC.

[33] CEDAW Committee, Joint General Recommendation 31 of the Committee on the Elimination of Discrimination against Women/ General Comment 18 of the Committee on the Rights of the Child on harmful practices, 14 November 2014, UN Doc CEDAW/ C/GC/31-CRC/C/GC/18 (2014); T Kaime 'The Convention on the Rights of the Child and cultural legitimacy of children's rights in South Africa: Some reflections' (2005) 2 The *African Human Rights Law Journal* 223.

'to take all effective and appropriate measures to abolish traditional practices prejudicial to the health of children'. The CRC goes a step further to define harmful practices in its General Comment 13 by providing that these include, but are not limited to:

> Corporal punishment and other cruel or degrading forms of punishment; female genital mutilation; amputations, binding, scarring, burning and branding; violent and degrading initiation rites; force-feeding of girls; fattening; virginity testing (inspecting girls' genitalia); forced marriage and early marriage.[34]

In the regional human rights system, the African Charter on the Rights and Welfare of the Child (ACRWC) imitates the standard established by the CRC, that the 'best interests of the child shall be the primary consideration' by an individual or authority in addressing issues related to children.[35] Furthermore, the ACRWC calls upon states parties to:

> [T]ake all appropriate measures to eliminate harmful social and cultural practices affecting the welfare, dignity, normal growth, and development of the child and in particular: (a) those customs and practices prejudicial to the health or life of the child; and (b) those customs and practices discriminatory to the child on the grounds of sex or other status.[36]

The Protocol to the African Charter on Human and Peoples' Rights on the Rights of Women in Africa (Maputo Protocol) equally prohibits harmful practices against women.[37] It defines harmful practices as 'all behaviour, attitudes and/or practices which negatively affect the fundamental rights of women and girls, such as their right to life, health, dignity, education, and physical integrity'.[38] Article 5 further enjoins states parties to prohibit and condemn all forms of harmful practices which negatively affect the human rights of women and which are contrary to recognised international standards. States therefore have

[34] Para 29 of the CRC General Comment 13.

[35] Art 4(1).

[36] Art 21.

[37] N 19 (n 19).

[38] Art 1(g).

legally binding obligations to put in place measures that prohibit harmful practices.

Apart from international and regional binding human rights treaties, there also exists international and regional conferences and agreements that recognise the need to end harmful practices as well. The Programme of Action of the International Conference on Population and Development (ICPD),[39] for example, considers FGM as 'a violation of basic rights and a major lifelong risk to women's health'.[40] The ICPD Programme of Action urges states to prohibit FGM wherever it exists,[41] and also recognises that 'early marriage and early motherhood can severely curtail educational and employment opportunities and are likely to have a long-term, adverse impact on them and their children's quality of life'.[42] The Platform for Action of the Fourth World Conference on Women in Beijing also calls on states to eliminate violence against women resulting from harmful traditional practices.[43] Furthermore, in adopting the 2030 Agenda for Sustainable Development, states reaffirmed their commitment to 'eliminate all harmful practices, such as child, early and forced marriage, and female genital mutilation by 2030'.[44]

In Zimbabwe, the Constitution provides for cultural rights—however, such participation in cultural life should not be done in a way that is inconsistent with the Declaration of Rights.[45] Further, section 80(3) of the Constitution outlaws cultural practices that infringe on women's rights by providing that 'all laws, customs, traditions and cultural practices that infringe the rights of women conferred by this Constitution are void to the extent of the infringement'.[46] This is a clear guarantee

[39] UN Programme of Action adopted at the International Conference on Population and Development, Cairo, 5-13 September 1994, UN Doc A/CONF.171113/Rev.

[40] ICPD (n 39) para 7.35.

[41] ICPD (n 39) para 4.22.

[42] ICPD (n 39) para 7.41.

[43] Fourth World Conference on Women, Platform for Action (1995) para 232(g).

[44] UN Department of Economic and Social Affairs Sustainable Development, Sustainable Development Goals, SDG 5 Target 3.

[45] Sec 63 provides: 'Every person has the right—(a) to use the language of their choice; and (b) to participate in the cultural life of their choice; but no person exercising these rights may do so in a way that is inconsistent with this Chapter'.

[46] Sec 80(3) of the Constitution.

of human rights against harmful practices. In addition to the Constitution, section 3(1) of the Domestic Violence Act (DVA) outlaws harmful cultural practices and norms that violate the rights of women such as forced or child marriages and the system of child betrothal or the pledging of young women for avenging spirits.[47] Section 3(1) of the DVA is commendable as it extends the definition of domestic violence by clearly including harmful traditional practices as acts of domestic violence. This complies with state obligations under the international and regional instruments prohibiting harmful cultural practices.[48]

3 Universalist Approach to the *Chinamwari/Khomba* Practice

The universalist view of human rights is rooted in western historical notions of human morals and values—it is because of its western origins that it has been described as a '[w]estern construct'[49] advanced within the 1948 United Nations Declaration of Human Rights.[50] Proponents of universality are of the view that the human rights guaranteed in international treaties and conventions should be applied in all countries, and that they must prevail even when they conflict with established cultural

[47] This is the Shona customary practice of compensatory payment in inter-family disputes as well as in the appeasement of avenging deceased spirits. The wronged family seek compensation in the form of a woman (from the murderer's family) when one of their own is killed. A woman is a child bearer, and this is why a woman is used to go and appease the avenging spirit. A woman will go to the bereaved family and be given a husband who she would then bear children with and when a son was born in the event that a man was killed, he will be given the name of that person and the spirit would rest. See N Chivasa '*Kuripa Ngozi* as a conflict resolution model in Shona communities of Zimbabwe: A conceptual analysis' (2019) 11 *Critical African Studies* 159, who argues that '[a]lthough giving up of a virgin girl for purposes of *kuripa ngozi* is a criminal offence in Zimbabwe, it appears many girls and women continue to suffer in silence because the practice is administered at the family level'. This practice violates women's right to control when they can get married and whether or not to have children.

[48] Art 5 of CEDAW and art 5 of the Maputo Protocol.

[49] M Abdullah 'Balancing cultural relativism and universalism in human rights: A case-study of female genital mutilation in Egypt' (2013) *E-International Relations* https://www.e-ir.info/2014/02/09/a-case-study-of-female-genital-mutilation-in-egypt/ (accessed 18 February 2024).

[50] As above.

or religious practices.[51] Universalists firmly believe that human rights and fundamental freedoms are inherent in the nature and dignity of each human being and that there should be a set of basic ethical standards and principles, acceptable to all cultures, religions and political systems.[52] Thus, every person has human rights and should be protected against violations such as those brought by the *chinamwari* practice. The Universalists view *chinamwari* practice as an onslaught on women's rights, and an attempt by cultural groups and its leaders to willingly violate women's rights.[53]

Many human rights experts and proponents of universalism are of the view that harmful practices like the *khomba* practice, should be considered as a violation of international human rights instruments and should be discontinued.[54] Put differently, universalists argue that the *khomba* practice infringes on various women's and children's rights. First, is the right to health, including reproductive health rights as provided for under the UDHR, the ICESCR, the CEDAW, the CRC, and the Maputo Protocol. During the ceremonies, girls are subjected to severe vaginal pain, and urine retention through lessons on elongation of the labia minora, which is a painful process as the initiates have to use force to pull their clitoris.[55] This violates the freedom from torture, inhuman and degrading treatment requirement as provided for in the international,[56] regional and national legislative framework. The Convention against Torture and Other Cruel, Inhuman or Degrading Treatment or Punishment requires states parties,

[51] K Musalo 'When rights and cultures collide' (2015) 2 https://www.scu.edu/ethics/ethics-resources/ethical-decision-making/when-rights-and-cultures-collide/ (accessed 20 February 2024).

[52] N Sybesma-Knol 'The United Nations system for the protection of human rights. What is happening to the principle of universality?' in A Alen and others (eds) *Liberae Cogitationes. Liber amicorum Marc Bossuyt* (2013) 696.

[53] M Badran 'Competing agenda: Feminists, Islam and the state in nineteenth-and-twentieth century Egypt' in D Kandiyoti (eds) *Women, Islam & the state* (1991) 201.

[54] PD Mitchum 'Slapping the hand of cultural relativism: Female genital mutilation, male dominance, and the health as a human rights framework' (2012) 19 *William & Mary Journal of Women and the Law* 600.

[55] L Vincent 'Virginity testing in South Africa: Re-traditioning the post-colony' (2006) 8 *Culture, Health & Sexuality* 17.

[56] Art 37 of the CRC requires states parties to ensure that no child is subjected to torture or other cruel, inhuman or degrading treatment or punishment.

inter alia, to incorporate the crime of torture in their domestic legislation and to punish acts of torture by appropriate penalties; and to undertake a prompt and impartial investigation of any alleged act of torture.[57] Similarly, section 53 of the Constitution of Zimbabwe particularly prohibits torture by providing that 'no person may be subjected to physical or psychological torture or cruel, inhuman or degrading treatment or punishment'.

Anecdotal evidence has it that the activities at initiation schools include training young women on sexual intercourse exercises through dancing or acting in explicit sexual demonstrations without clothes by initiates. This marks a violent and abrupt initiation of the girl child into sexual relations, which may in turn result in increased teen pregnancies and early marriage. Further,

> attending these ceremonies symbolises that one is not a child anymore and therefore can engage in sexual activities. Young girls can then be married at a young age because they are now viewed as 'old people' (after being initiated).[58]

As such the practice exposes young girls to sex issues, and sometimes marriage in violation of their right to decide freely. For young girls, child marriage will affect their freedom, health and well-being, as well as ultimate development. This is further in direct violation of the CRC which enjoins states parties to 'guarantee children the opportunity to develop physically in a healthy and normal way'.[59]

Second, the rights of the child as laid down in the CRC are violated through the *chinamwari* practice as the procedure is done without the consent of the girls. Describing the FGM practice, which has a similar component of lack of consent with *the khomba* practice, Van Gals states that 'the procedure is considered child abuse because the girls have no

[57] UN General Assembly, Convention Against Torture and Other Cruel, Inhuman or Degrading Treatment or Punishment, United Nations, Treaty Series, vol 1465, p 85, 10 December 1984.

[58] AC Muntali & EM Zulu 'The timing and role of initiation rites in preparing young people for adolescence and responsible sexual and reproductive behaviour in Malawi' (2007) 11 *African Journal of Reproductive Health* 150.

[59] R Abusharaf 'Introduction: The custom in question' in RM Abusharaf (eds) *Female circumcision: Multicultural perspectives* (2006) 11.

say in what happens to them as it is forced upon them'.[60] This blatantly violates the best interests of the child principle and the children's right to be heard.

Last, the practice interferes with the right to education and play.[61] As noted earlier, the ceremony requires about three months to be completed. During this time, girls will be under the watch of women elders at the initiation schools, and being taught household duties such as fetching firewood, washing and cooking for the husband. If this time coincides with the schooling calendar, initiates absent themselves from school. The *Herald* newspaper reported incidences in which young girls dropped out of school to attend the rites and also soon after initiation schools, to join early marriages or commercial sex work to maximise expertise gained from the practice.[62] This also expresses acceptance of the idea that education is not necessary for girls because after marriage, they will be subordinates to their husbands on whom they will depend.[63] This leads to a deliberate violation of their right to be in school and to play with fellow children of their age as provided for in articles 28 and 31 of the CRC, respectively.

While the arguments of the universalism approach are bent on human rights protection, they also have limitations in that they ignore the nature of the society in which harmful cultural practices such as the *chinamwari* are practiced. In such societies, the practice is perceived as necessary to preserve morality. Initiates largely resemble the group's true identity, and they are accepted and deemed ready for marriage life. Just like any other controversial practice including the FGM, the *chinamwari* practice is recognised as the accepted path for girls' graduation to adulthood and marriage. Any attempt towards criminalising the *chinamwari* practice might then deny young women from the cultural group a chance to choose this path of graduating to womanhood for acceptance by the wider society. After all, studies have shown that men, particularly those from these cultural groups, expressed preference towards *chinamwari/*

[60] L van Gils 'Cultural relativism and harmful traditional practices: A consideration of the efforts to eradicate FGM' Masters' thesis in International Public Law, Tilburg University, 2010 http://arno.uvt.nl/show.cgi?fid=122074 (accessed 15 July 2023).

[61] Art 28: States parties recognise the right of the child to education, and with a view to achieving this right progressively and on the basis of equal opportunity, they shall in particular, (a) make primary education compulsory and available free to all.

[62] 'Chinamwari: Old habits die hard' (n 9).

[63] Muzingili & Taruvinga (n 7) 39.

khomba women due to their sexual expertise.[64] Many young women and girls in such societies look towards a time when they can be initiated into this practice and be recognised as real women in society.[65] Given a chance, some women would decide not to abandon the traditions they were socialised to accept.[66]

4 Cultural Relativist Approach to the *Chinamwari/Khomba* Practice

Cultural relativists believe that human rights vary from culture to culture.[67] Cultural relativists maintain that an activity perceived as a human rights violation in one nation or society may be acceptable under the prevalent cultural beliefs in another.[68] For this group, human rights only exist when the society perceives them as such. Besides that, human rights are disregarded as rights. In this way, the *chinamwari* practice is viewed as a source of moral right or validity of rules in societies that prioritise and practice harmful practices. With cultural relativism, the universal application of human rights can only be allowed when it is in tandem with the *chinamwari* culture. It is however as a result of these views that some traditional leaders misuse their collective cultural justifications to violate women and girl child's rights in society.

The cultural relativist believes that cultural differences of certain societies cannot be reconciled with the universalists' belief in a universal norm for human rights. Thus, different cultures have different definitions of what constitutes a 'human right'.[69] In the lenses of cultural relativists, universalists are a product of cosmopolitan ideals whose views and aspirations do not represent the cultures of everyone. In essence, cultural relativists view universalism as an approach advanced by westerners in an attempt to propagate their values and norms globally. For Zimbabwe, these ideas are cemented by the fact that the nation was a

[64] Muzingili & Taruvinga (n 7) 40.

[65] Naidu & Muchono (n 5).

[66] As above.

[67] E Hatch *Culture and morality: The reality of values in anthropology* (1983) 3.

[68] J Donnelly *International human rights* (2013) 260.

[69] TE Huggins 'Anti-essentialism, relativism and human rights' (1996) 92 *Harvard Women's Law Journal* 89 at 92.

former colony of England. Permitting international norms to override the dictates of culture and religion violates state sovereignty and interference with national affairs.[70] Hence any attempt to undo native cultural practices such as the *chinamwari* reminds communities of their historical subjugation by the west.

Moreover, cultural relativists argue that the universalists' perspective does not provide a better or more inclusive set of rights that align with different contexts, histories and backgrounds of people.[71] As such cultural relativists believe that religious and cultural societies should not be obliged to follow and accept the international norms imposed on their societies when they are not in tandem with their local cultures. Consequently, this view has seen conflict with international human rights standards that condemn all harmful practices that subjugate young women and girls. Patel also noted that states sometimes support this stance even at international human rights forums such as the UN Universal Periodic Review.[72] As Patel's study revealed, harmful practices were the frequently raised issues noted on UPR state party reviews. In following up with raised issues, observer states took a strict universalist position, asking the concerned government to eliminate those practices. In response, however, many states were defensive and challenged the normative universalism on the grounds of a strict cultural relativist approach and national sovereignty.[73]

From a cultural relativist point of view, it is argued that the *chinamwari* practice is good for several reasons. The first one is to mentor young women about marriage, as they are expected to get married, find a family, and bring joy to their parents. It is based on this mentoring view that lessons taught to young women and girls during the initiation period include lessons meant to equip them to be bedroom masters and do household chores, among other duties. In turn, men who find women trained by the practice are expected to get sexual pleasure and be content

[70] K Musalo *When rights and cultures collide* (2015) https://www.scu.edu/ethics/ethics-resources/ethical-decision-making/when-rights-and-cultures-collide/ (20 February 2024).

[71] Huggins (n 69).

[72] G Patel 'How "universal" is the United Nations' universal periodic review process? An examination from a cultural relativist perspective' PhD Thesis, University of Leicester, 2015 at 75.

[73] As above.

and faithful to their wives. This in turn is believed to reduce infidelity and incidences of HIV/AIDS infections which is often blamed on multiple concurrent sexual partners as men search for sexual pleasure.[74] This has been labelled as 'the male gaze' by radical feminists.[75] The patriarchal ideology and the practice of *chinamwari/khomba* by extension, constructs women in relation to men—women are a canvas on which male desires are projected, hence subverting female agency and power. Mulvey explains as follows:

> The woman then stands in patriarchal culture as a signifier for the male other, bound by a symbolic order in which man can live out his phantasies and obsessions through linguistic command by imposing them on the silent image of a woman still tied to her place as a bearer of meaning, not maker of meaning.[76]

Supporting this position, but arguing from a sex work and pornography perspective, Dworkin posits that sex work and pornography are inherently violent against women because they normalise the sexual dehumanisation of women, *thereby encouraging men to continue regarding women not as fellow human beings but as passive objects of sexual gratification.*[77] This shows that the *khomba* practice is for the satisfaction of men, although it is performed on women, by women.

The second one is the fact that 'it brings unity among men in the community'.[78] From their study on the perceptions of males towards the practice of *chinamwari*, Naidu and Muchono explained this oneness as follows:

> [E]ven though *chinamwari* is done *for* and taught in the context of the female and her body, the men *claim* that it creates a spirit of oneness and respect *among men* in the community. Men who are married to initiates (i.e. women who have undergone the training or initiation) have the opportunity to meet in private and public spaces to discuss community

[74] 'Chinamwari: Old habits die hard' (n 9).

[75] L Mulvey 'Visual pleasure and narrative cinema' in A Dworkin *Pornography: Men possessing women* (1989).

[76] As above.

[77] A Dworkin *Pornography: Men possessing women* (1989).

[78] Naidu & Muchono (n 5).

development issues. If one is married to a non-initiate, one is not involved in decision-making at community level. The narratives of men highlight this.

From these two arguments, the views of radical feminists are proved correct that the patriarchal nature of our African societies is proving to be favouring practices that benefit men more than women.[79] The authors argue that the *chinamwari* practice in this case, although done for the women, is meant to satisfy men. One initiate in *chikombedzi* was quoted as having stated as follows: 'Khomba practice teaches the manhood in the household as women are also taught to be subordinate to her husband at all times'.[80] Women are taught to believe and see marriage as the future of young girls ahead of education and personal development. Thus, they are expected to prepare for it and all the reproductive gender roles that come with it at all costs. According to feminism, this thinking is anti-developmental as it perpetuates gender inequality and the subordination of women to men in society.

Furthermore, *chinamwari/khomba* is believed to be 'part of child socialization and preservation of cultural identity'.[81] By practicing *chinamwari/khomba*, communities believe that it distinguishes them from other cultures or tribes. Some women are 'forced' and end up going through the cultural practice for fear of being stigmatised[82] or not getting suitors to marry them. The practice is highly respected in those communities practicing it such that a woman who has not been initiated commands less respect within the community than an initiated person.[83] Consequently, this might result in exclusion from some community activities. In the same way, Naidu and Muchono concluded that the *chinamwari* cultural practice seemingly stigmatises and discriminates against the non-initiates and those men married to non-initiates, as being 'cowards'.[84] The scholars further noted how men married to *chinamwari* initiates

[79] M Kambarami 'Femininity, sexuality and culture: Patriarchy and female subordination in Zimbabwe' *Understanding Human Sexuality Seminar Series* (2006) 3.

[80] Muzingili & Taruvinga (n 7) 38.

[81] Muzingili & Taruvinga (n 7) 40.

[82] As above.

[83] As above.

[84] As above.

in Chipinge seem to occupy higher (constructed) positions and have a different class/status in the community compared to those married to non-initiates.[85]

5 Conclusion and Recommendations

The chapter presented two distinctly separate standpoints surrounding the *chinamwari* harmful cultural practice debate—the cultural relativism narrative strongly backed by culture to argue that all cultures are valid and *chinamwari* is culturally valid on one hand, and the universalism narrative backed by universal feminists to eradicate harmful cultural practices. Cultural relativism emphasises the sanctity of people's cultural practices, and universalism gives prominence to human dignity which all cultures must protect and promote. In regarding culture as the only source of validity of a moral right or rule, radical cultural relativism undermines the universality of human rights and provides a ground for obscuring the human rights violations of young women and girls in the name of culture. On the other hand, purely following the radical universalism approach in implementing women's and children's rights standards can sound like another form of cultural imperialism of Zimbabwean societies and might, therefore, provoke resistance from the conservative sections of society that undermine the whole human rights systems.

This chapter calls for moving away from the cultural relativism versus universalism dichotomy to a nuanced discussion that largely acknowledges the merits of universalism and the significance of culture in dealing with the *chinamwari* practice and advancing women's and the girl child's rights. The chapter places the international community, government, and non-state actors in human rights particularly women's and children's rights at the heart of addressing the role of culture and universality in the human rights discourse. The stakeholders are therefore implored to ensure that young women and girls are not at the receiving end of suffering from *chinamwari* and other harmful practices while academic debates rage on. The chapter vouches for increased-informed dialogue on the subject within African societies and cultures where all cultures and practices devoid of best human rights standards and obligations are modified to largely cause proper women and child development.

[85] As above.

These debates will largely enlighten conservatives and contribute to the enhanced cultural acceptance of human rights standards and norms. Cultures are not closed entities, with rigid borders, but they can be developed or changed as a result of interaction with external effects or influence.[86] Societies practicing *chinamwari* may also be enlightened by duty bearers on the constitutional position of culture and human rights, responsibilities, and obligations as cultural groups.

Bibliography

Abusharaf, R 'Introduction: The custom in question' in Abusharaf, RM (ed) *Female circumcision: Multicultural perspectives* (Philadelphia: University of Pennsylvania Press 2006)

Arati, R 'The politics of gender and culture in international human rights discourse' in Peters, J & Wolper, A (eds) *Women's rights, human rights: International feminist perspectives* (Routledge: New York 1995)

Bret, LB *Cultural relativism in the face of the west: The plight of women and female children* (Palgrave Macmillan: New York 2007)

Chikunda, C; Marambire, E & Makoni, R 'The impact of khomba – a Shangaan cultural rite of passage – on the formal schooling of girls and on women's space in the Chikombedzi area in Zimbabwe, Indilinga' (2006) 5 *African Journal of Indigenous Knowledge Systems* 145

Chivasa, N '*Kurita Ngozi* as a conflict resolution model in Shona communities of Zimbabwe: A conceptual analysis' (2019) 11 *Critical African Studies* 1

Chukwuma, H *Women's quest for rights: African feminist theory in fiction* (Pearl Publishers 2006)

Cook, RJ 'Gender, health and human rights' (1995) 1 *Women's Health and Human Rights* 253

Donnelly, J *International human rights* (Boulder CO: Westview Press 2013)

Donnelly, J 'Universality' in David, PF (ed) *Encyclopaedia of Human Rights* (Oxford University Press: New York 2009)

Frese, M 'Cultural practices, norms, and values' (2015) 46 *Journal of Cross-Cultural Psychology* 1327

Hatch, E *Culture and morality: The reality of values in anthropology* (Columbia University Press: New York 1983)

Huggins, ET 'Anti-essentialism, relativism and human rights' (1996) 19 *Harvard Women's Law Journal* 95

[86] I Lakatos 'Thoughts on universalism versus cultural relativism, with special attention to women's rights' (2018) 1 *Pécs Journal of International and European Law* 3.

Maluleke, MJ 'Culture, tradition, custom, law and gender equality' (2012) 15 *Potchefstroom Electronic Law Journal* 1

Maposa, RS 'Going under the traditional knife: Linking African traditional education and the ethic of identity through Shangani Culture, Zimbabwe' (2008) 2 *Journal of Emerging Trends in Educational Research and Policy Studies* 6

Moyo, S & Matanda, N 'The chinamwari initiation rite in Zimbabwe: Opportunity or threat to the girl child?' (2020) 3 *American Research Journal of Humanities & Social Science* 38

Muntali, AC & Zulu, EM 'The timing and role of initiation rites in preparing young people for adolescence and responsible sexual and reproductive behaviour in Malawi' (2007) 11 *African Journal of Reproductive Health* 150

Musalo, K *When rights and cultures collide* (Markkula Center for Applied Ethics, Santa Clara University 2015)

Muzingili, T & Taruvinga, R 'Culturally-inflicted child rights violation: A Case of khomba practice of Shangaan People in Zimbabwe' (2017) 7 *Mgbakoigba: Journal of African Studies* 34

Naidu, M & Muchono, W 'Male perceptions toward the cultural practice of Chinamwari/Khomba among the Mahenye' (2019) 19 *The Oriental Anthropologist* 25

Preston, DM 'Slapping the hand of cultural relativism: Female genital mutilation, male dominance, and the health as a human rights framework' (2012) 19 *William & Mary Journal of Women and the Law* 600

Sybesma-Knol, N 'The United Nations System for the protection of human rights: What is happening to the principle of universality?' in Alen, A; Joosten, V; Leysen, R & Verrijdt, W (eds) *Liberae Cogitationes. Liber amicorum Marc Bossuyt* (Cambridge Intersentia 2013)

Talakinu, CM '"I am because of what i know i have": A descriptive analysis of Chinamwari in preparing women for womanhood, sexual life and reproduction' (2018) 12 *Africology: The Journal Pan African Studies* 107

Van Gils, L 'Cultural relativism and harmful traditional practices: A consideration of the efforts to eradicate FGM' Masters' thesis in International Public Law, Tilburg University, 2010 http://arno.uvt.nl/show.cgi?fid=122074 (accessed 15 July 2023)

Vincent, L 'Virginity testing in South Africa: Re-traditioning the post-colony' (2006) 8 *Culture, Health & Sexuality* 17

International treaties and documents

African Charter on Human and Peoples' Rights 1986 (1982) 21 ILM 58

African Charter on the Rights and Welfare of the Child, OAU Doc CAB/LEG/24.9/49 (1990)

Convention on the Elimination of All Forms of Discrimination Against Women (1980) 19 ILM 33

Convention on the Rights of the Child (1989) 28 ILM 1456

International Covenant on Civil and Political Rights 1976 (1967) 6 ILM 368

International Covenant on Economic, Social and Cultural Rights, GA res. 2200A (XXI), UN Doc. A/6316 (1966)

Protocol to the African Charter on Human and Peoples' Rights on the Rights of Women in Africa. Adopted by the 2nd Ordinary Session of the African Union General Assembly in 2003 in Maputo CAB/LEG/66.6 (2003) entered into force 25 November 2005

OHCHR 'Fact Sheet 23: Harmful traditional practices affecting the health of women and children' (August 1995)

Universal Declaration of Human Rights, adopted 10 December 1948, GA Res 217A (III), UN Doc A/810 71 (1948)

UN Human Rights Committee (HRC), CCPR General Comment 28: Article 3 (The Equality of Rights Between Men and Women), 29 March 2000, UN Doc CCPR/C/21/Rev.1/Add.10 (2000)

UN Programme of Action adopted at the International Conference on Population and Development [Cairo, 5–13 September 1994] A/CONF.171113/Rev

CHAPTER 6

The Conundrum of Exchange of Bride Wealth in Customary Marriages: Is It a Harmful Practice?

Patricia Atim P'Odong

1 Background

In Uganda, marriage is an important and cherished aspect of society.[1] A marriage in Uganda's context can be defined as a voluntary legal ceremony between a man and a woman of marriageable age from which they acquire the status of husband and wife, and acquire various matrimonial

[1] Justice Mubiru, in *Solomon Ayiku v Lekuru Ayiko* High Court Divorce Cause 001 of 2015, stated inter alia that, 'marriage still continues to serve valuable social, legal, economic, and institutional functions, and for that reason, the underlying public policy continues to promote marriage and discourage divorce unless the parties strictly comply with the statutory requirements for divorce'.

P. A. P'Odong (✉)
School of Law, Makerere University, Kampala, Uganda
e-mail: patricia.odong@gmail.com

Pretoria, South Africa

Rondebosch, South Africa

E. Durojaye et al. (eds.), *Harmful Practices and Human Rights: An International Perspective*, Human Rights Interventions,
https://doi.org/10.1007/978-3-031-90333-5_6

rights and duties.[2] Indeed, the right of a man and a woman of marriageable age to marry and found a family is guaranteed under article 31 of the Constitution of Uganda, 1995.[3] The family so created is also entitled to protection by both the state and society.[4] Notably, there are only five types of marriages recognised in Uganda: civil and church marriages,[5] the Customary marriage,[6] the Islamic marriage,[7] and the Hindu marriage.[8] Any persons living together as 'husband and wife' but without solemnising any of these forms of marriages in accordance with the law are held to be in cohabitation and enjoy very limited protection of the law.[9] According to the 2024 National Census report, Uganda's population currently stands at 45.9 million people. Of which 50.6% are married; 26.6% cohabiting or living together, while 18.6% have never married and 2.8% is separated or divorced.[10]

Customary marriages[11] are celebrated by most communities in Africa, and often characterised by the exchange of bride wealth or payment of bride price or transfer of bride gifts,[12] including money, livestock, cloth,

[2] Z Nampewo and others *Family and succession law in Uganda* (2020) 44.

[3] Article 31(1) provides that: 'A man and a woman are entitled to marry only if they are each of age of eighteen years and above and are entitled at that age to (a) found a family; (b) to equal rights at and in marriage, during marriage and at its dissolution.'

[4] Objective XIX of the National Objectives and Directive Principles of State Policy (NODPSP) provides that: 'The family is the natural and basic unit of society and is entitled to protection by the society and the State'.

[5] Regulated by the Marriage Act Cap 251.

[6] Regulated by the Customary Marriage (Registration) Act Cap 248.

[7] Regulated by the Marriage and Divorce of Mohammedans Act Cap 252.

[8] Regulated by the Hindu Marriage and Divorce Act Cap 250.

[9] JD Mujuzi 'Presumption of marriage in Uganda' (2020) 34 *International Journal of Law, Policy and the Family* 247 https://academic.oup.com/lawfam/article-abstract/34/3/247/6024926 (accessed 10 June 2023); See *Musa Kigongo v Olive Kigongo* High Court Mics App 551 of 2015; *Friedman Bigala v Lourna Namuwenge* Civil Suit 98 of 2020 [2023]; *Baryamureeba Steven v Kabakonjo & 6 Others* Civil Suit 20 of 2013.

[10] Uganda Bureau of Statistics *National Population and Housing Census Report* (2024) 30 https://www.ubos.org/wp-content/uploads/2024/12/National-Population-and-Housing-Census-2024-Final-Report-Volume-1-Main.pdf (accessed 5 January 2025).

[11] Customary marriage, termed locally as *nyomkwaro* among the Lango/Acholi, *kuhingira* among the Bakiga/Banyankole, and *kwanjula/kukyala* among the Baganda.

[12] The Supreme Court, in *Mifumi (U) Ltd v Attorney General* Constitutional Appeal 2 of 2014 [2015] UGSC 13 (6 August 2015), declared that the exchange of marriage

and foodstuffs, among others.[13] In most of the communities, it is often the male clan heads who determine what constitutes and the amount of the marital gift (bride wealth) that is supposed to be made prior to the customary marriage.[14] The colonial judges perceived this practice of exchange of bride wealth as a mere 'wife purchase' and an uncivilised practice falling short of a marriage.[15] The notion that bride wealth (price) is payment for the wife prevails to date.[16]

Nevertheless, the Constitution of the Republic of Uganda, 1995 does not prohibit the exchange of marital gifts. In fact, it stipulates that the people of Uganda have a right to practice their different culture and customs, provided they are not inconsistent with the Constitution.[17] The exchange of bride wealth or bride price is still an essential pre-requisite in the celebration of a valid customary marriage among the 46 tribes of Uganda.[18] Bride wealth is often given by the bride-groom's family to the bride's family as a symbol of appreciation or as a reward for their efforts in raising a girl worthy of marriage.[19] Being a social norm, the value of the bride wealth varies depending on the family's values, expectations, status,

wealth should be called 'marital gift' rather than 'bride price'. In communities like India, women pay dowry to the man's (prospective groom's) family. In this paper, I will use the phrase 'bride wealth' or 'bride price' interchangeably because these terms are the most commonly used phrases.

[13] W Chan 'Marital transfers and the welfare of women' (2014) 66 *Oxford Economic Papers* 1019; DK Semenya 'The practical guidelines on the impact of mahadi [bride price] on the young Basotho couples prior to marriage' (2014) 70 *Hervormde Teologiese Studies* 1; JA Conteh 'Dowry and bride price' in NA Naples and others *The Wiley Blackwell Encyclopedia of Gender and Sexuality Studies* (2016) https://www.researchgate.net/profile/John-Conteh-2/publication/305348271_Dowry_and_Bride-Price/links/59e11830aca2724cbfdb6fcf/Dowry-and-Bride-Price.pdf (accessed 10 July 2023).

[14] See generally, HG Jacoby 'The economics of polygyny in sub-Saharan Africa: Female productivity and the demand for wives in Cote d'Ivoire' (1995) 103 *Journal of Political Economy* 938.

[15] Sir Robert Hamilton, CJ in Rex v Amkeyo (1917) EALR 7.

[16] D Bishai & S Grossband 'Far above rubies: The association between bride price and extramarital sexual relations in Uganda' Discussion Paper 2982 (2007) https://docs.iza.org/dp2982.pdf (accessed 3 June 2023). The authors contend that their scientific findings reveal that payment of bride price for men's sexual control over their wives, lowers women's rates of infidelity in Uganda, but not that of men.

[17] Arts 2(2), 21, 31, 32, 33, and 37 of the Constitution of Uganda, 1995.

[18] *Mifumi (u) Ltd v Attorney General* Constitutional Appeal 2 of 2014.

[19] Bishai & Grossband (n 17).

and social standing of the bride.[20] This social standing may vary from one community to another but includes aspects like the bride's economic status, level of education, height, beauty marks, and ability to undertake heavy domestic chores, among others.[21]

It is argued that the traditional justification for the practice was to promote a unified relationship between the families of the bride and groom.[22] Ojok suggests that, in the pre-colonial context, customary marriage was the glue that held different societies and communities together.[23] It was both a cultural and political connecting rod. Clans, tribes, and kingdoms intermarried to promote social cohesion, alliances, trade, peace, and harmony, among others.[24] Further, Ojok rightly explains that among the Luo, a key feature of the customary marriage ceremony is bride price/wealth and/or dowry.[25] Offering the bride wealth at the customary wedding represented the loss of a daughter to a family, hence the loss of labour and someone to tend to younger children within the family. A young man, in paying the bride price, would give the bride's family gifts in the form of livestock to replenish labour and to act as a source of food; these are still typically offered as gifts to the bride's family.[26]

Unfortunately, the practice has of recent been highly commercialised, leading to exorbitant demands from the bride's family that not only economically strain the couples but may also perpetuate gender inequalities, reduce autonomy for the women in decision making in the family, and exacerbate the incidences of gender-based violence as a woman

[20] See W Goldschmidt 'The economics of brideprice among the Sebei and in East Africa' (1974) 13 *Ethnology* 313.

[21] RL Trivers 'Parental investment and sexual selection' in B Cambell (ed) *Sexual selection and the descent of man* (1972).

[22] D Ojok 'The socio-legal dynamics of customary marriage in Uganda' (2017) 7 CEPA Policy Series Papers (2017) https://cepa.or.ug/wp-content/uploads/2018/06/The-Socio-Legal-dynamics-of-Customary-Marriage-in-Uganda.pdf (accessed 10 June 2023).

[23] Ojok (n 23) 7.

[24] Ojok (n 23sd) 4.

[25] As above.

[26] As above.

may be perceived as a husband's property.[27] Hence, the conundrum of whether or not the African customary practice of exchange of bride wealth is indeed a harmful traditional practice. If it is not, then must the exchange of bride gifts be decolonised?[28]

Despite these negative ramifications, the customary practice of exchange of bride wealth between families in Uganda when celebrating a customary marriage is still strong and cherished by the communities. In fact, Mujuzi reports that during the deliberations that preceded the adoption of the 1995 Constitution, the Constituent Assembly noted that:

> Due to mass public opinion, there was no need to abolish the practice of bride price but also concluded that such a practice would be against the Constitution if it violated the dignity and welfare of women.[29]

In order to achieve its tripartite obligation to *protect*, *respect* and *fulfil* the fundamental rights of women and girls, Uganda has put in place national legal frameworks (as discussed below) that govern the institution of the family and regulate marriage ceremonies.

In the analysis that follows, I discuss the legal framework governing marriage relations in Uganda, demystifying what amounts to a harmful practice. I explore the customary practice of the exchange of bride wealth and subsequently answer the question of whether the practice amounts to a harmful practice. I also make recommendations that ought to be adopted to restore the practice to a place where it supports and unites rather than tears apart our couples/spouses, families and communities.

[27] C Wendo 'African women denounce bride price' (2004) 363 *The Lancet* 716; UI Esen 'African women, bride price, and AIDS' (2004) 363 *The Lancet* 1734 https://www.thelancet.com/action/showPdf?pii=S0140-6736%2804%2916266-1 (accessed 6 June 2023).

[28] Sylvia Tamale, in *Decolonization and Afro-Feminism*, defines decolonisation as a 'multi-pronged process of liberation from political, economic, and cultural colonization. Removing the anchors of colonialism from the physical, ecological, and mental processes of a nation and its people'. See S Tamale *Decolonization and Afro-Feminism* (2020).

[29] JD Mujuzi 'Bride wealth (price) and the women's marriage—Related rights in Uganda: A historical constitutional perspectives and other developments' (2010) 24 *International Journal for Policy, Law, and Family* 415.

2 Legal Framework Governing Customary Marriages in Uganda and Jurisprudential Developments

2.1 International and Regional Treaties

Uganda is a state party to various international and regional instruments which guarantee a number of rights, including the right of persons of marriageable age to marry and found a family. For instance, article 16 of the Universal Declaration of Human Rights, 1948 (Universal Declaration)[30] explicitly states that:

> (1) Men and women of full age, without any limitation due to race, nationality, or religion, have the right to marry and to found a family. They are entitled to equal rights as to marriage, during marriage, and at its dissolution.
> (2) Marriage shall be entered into only with the free and full consent of the intending spouses.
> (3) The family is the natural and fundamental group unit of society and is entitled to protection by society and the State.

This guarantee is further replicated in article 10 of the International Covenant on Economic, Social and Cultural Rights (ICESCR), article 23 of the International Covenant on Civil and Political Rights (ICCPR),[31] article 16(1)(a)-(c) of the Convention on Elimination of All Forms of Discrimination Against Women (CEDAW),[32] and article 23(1)(a)-(b) of the Convention on the Rights of Persons with Disabilities (CRPD).[33]

[30] UN General Assembly, Universal Declaration of Human Rights, 217 A(III), 10 December 1948.

[31] UN General Assembly, International Covenant on Economic, Social and Cultural Rights, United Nations, Treaty Series, vol 993, p 3, 16 December 1966.

[32] UN General Assembly, Convention on the Elimination of All Forms of Discrimination Against Women, United Nations, Treaty Series, vol 1249, p 13, 18 December 1979.

[33] UN General Assembly, Convention on the Rights of Persons with Disabilities: Resolution adopted by the General Assembly, 24 January 2007, UN Doc A/RES/61/106 (2007), Annex I.

At a regional level, the African Charter on Human and Peoples' Rights (African Charter)[34] also guarantees the right to family and mandates the state to eliminate every discrimination against women and ensure the protection of women and children as stipulated in international conventions and declarations.[35] Commendably, the Protocol to the African Charter on the Rights of Women in Africa (also referred to as the Maputo Protocol)[36] expounds on the right to voluntarily marry and found a family; and emphasises other aspects like encouraging monogamy; recording and registration of all marriages, matrimonial regime; choice to use husband's name, among others.[37]

Notably, all the above instruments protect the right to equality and non-discrimination of women and men in all spheres of life, and enjoin states parties to take all necessary legislative, administrative, or programmatic measures to eliminate any form of discrimination.[38]

Although the international and regional instruments do not explicitly address the practice of exchange of bride price, they laudably establish overarching principles that can inform our understanding of the practice in the context of human rights and equality. These can be summarised into three principles, vide:

1. Consent and Free Choice: The human rights instruments emphasise how crucial free and informed consent is to a successful marriage.[39] They provide that any marriage arrangement should be founded on

[34] Adopted 26 June 1981, OAU Doc CAB/LEG/67/3 Rev 5 (entered into force 21 October 1986).

[35] Art 18(3).

[36] OAU Doc CAB/LEG/66.6 (2003).

[37] Art 6.

[38] Art 2 of the Universal Declaration; art 2(2) of the ICESCR; art 2(1) of the UN General Assembly, International Covenant on Civil and Political Rights, United Nations, Treaty Series, vol 999, p 171, 16 December 1966; arts 1 and 2(b) and UN Human Rights Committee (HRC), ICCPR General Comment 19: Article 23 (The Family) Protection of the Family, the Right to Marriage and Equality of the Spouses, 27 July 1990, paras 4, 5 and 8; CEDAW; art 5 of the CRPD; art 2 of the African Charter; and art 2 of the Maputo Protocol.

[39] *See*, Plan International and ECPAT *Thematic report: Unrecognized sexual abuse and exploitation of children in child,* early and forced marriage (2015) https://www.ecpat.org/wp-content/uploads/legacy/Child%20Marriage_ENG.pdf (accessed 15 January 2025).

the free will and consent of both parties including the exchange of a bride price.
2. Non-Discrimination: The international legal framework provides for non-discrimination and gender equality. Hence, the underlying ideology is that bride price exchange should not support women's subordination or unfair treatment in any way.[40]
3. Elimination of Harmful Practices: Both the Maputo Protocol and CEDAW focus on eliminating harmful practices that violate women's rights.[41] While the two instruments do not particularly address bride price, they seek to ensure that harmful traditional behaviours are eliminated.

Similarly, article 21 of the African Charter on the Rights and the Welfare of the Child (ACRWC) is significant because it speaks particularly to social and cultural practices that are harmful to children. It states that:

> Article 21. Protection against Harmful Social and Cultural Practices:
> States Parties to the present Charter shall take all appropriate measures to eliminate harmful social and cultural practices affecting the welfare, dignity, normal growth, and development of the child and in particular:

(a) Those customs and practices prejudicial to the health or life of the child; and
(b) Those customs and practices discriminatory to the child on the grounds of sex or other status.

> 2. Child marriage and the betrothal of girls and boys shall be prohibited and effective action including legislation, shall be taken to specify

[40] See generally, H Asiimwe 'The changing dynamics, trends and perceptions in the bride price custom in Uganda and the implications—A feminist perspective: A case of Banyakitra ethnic group in Western Uganda' Masters' thesis, Institute of Social Studies, The Hague, The Netherlands, 2013 https://thesis.eur.nl/pub/15309/HAsiimwe_moodledata_temp_turnitintool_111673799._42_1384407653_2029.pdf

[41] Art 17(1) of the Maputo Protocol states that: 'Women shall have the right to live in a positive cultural context and to participate at all levels in the determination of cultural policies.' Art 2(f) of CEDAW enjoins states parties to take all appropriate measures, including legislation to modify or abolish existing laws, regulations, customs and practices which constitute discrimination against women.

the minimum age of marriage to be 18 years and make registration of all marriages in an official registry compulsory.

Therefore, Uganda as a state party to these international and regional human rights instruments is enjoined to realise the obligations therein.

2.2 *National Laws and Policies*

In adherence to her obligation as stipulated in the various international and regional treaties, Uganda has enacted progressive laws to meet the international standard.

2.2.1 The 1995 Constitution

Preserving culture was one of the long-term targets envisaged by the drafters of the 1995 Constitution of Uganda.[42] According to Objective XXIV of the National Objectives and Directive Principles of State Policy, the cultural values of Ugandans will always be protected and promoted and the only requirement for the preservation and promotion of the cultural practices is that they should be consistent with fundamental human rights and freedoms, human dignity, and democracy. Laws, culture, customs, or traditions which are against the dignity, welfare, or interest of women or which undermine their status are prohibited by the Constitution.[43] Article 37 further guarantees the right to culture:

> Every person has a right as applicable to belong to, enjoy, practise, profess, maintain, and promote any culture, cultural institution, language, tradition, creed, or religion in a community with others.

Evidently, the framers of the Constitution intended to protect the institution of the family – with respect to culture.

Specific to the right to marry, article 31 provides that:

> (1) Men and women of the age of eighteen years and above have the right to marry and to found a family and are entitled to equal rights in marriage, during marriage and at its dissolution. ...

[42] Art 37 of the Constitution of Uganda, 1995; also see, *Mifumi (U) Ltd v Attorney General* Constitutional Appeal 2 of 2014 [2015] UGSC 13.

[43] Arts 2(2), 21, 31, 32 and 33.

(3) Marriage shall be entered into with the free consent of the man and woman intending to marry.

Although the Constitution does not expressly provide for the principles that apply particularly to customary marriages, the general provisions discussed above apply to such marriages just like they do to other forms of marriage.

Furthermore, article 32 of the Constitution outlaws all cultural practices that are against the dignity, culture, and welfare of women.[44]

Uganda's Constitution was lauded for being the most progressive on the African continent in protecting women's rights in *Uganda Association of Women Lawyers v Attorney General*.[45] The learned Justice praised the progressive nature of the 1995 Constitution as follows:

> The preamble to the Constitution makes it clear that the framers intended to build a popular and desirable Constitution based on the principles of unity, peace, equality, democracy, freedom, social justice, and progress ...
> It is in substance a colonial relic whereby the traditional patriarchal family elevated the husband as the head of the family and relegated the woman to a subservient role ... Marriage is now viewed as an equal partnership between husband and wife. Still, the old ideas and patterns persist, as do their psychological and economic ramifications. That notwithstanding, women are entitled to full equality in respect of the right to form a family, their position within the functioning family, and upon dissolution of the family so proclaims Article 33(1) ...
> It is well to remember that the rights of women are inalienable, interdependent human rights which are essential in the development of any country and that the paramount purpose of human rights and fundamental freedoms is their enjoyment by all without discrimination ... It is further important to note and appreciate that the 1995 Constitution is the most liberal document in the area of women's rights than any other Constitution South of the Sahara ...

[44] Art 32(2); also see, art 33 specific to the protection of women's rights.

[45] Constitutional Petition 02 of 2003.

2.2.2 The Customary Marriage (Registration) Act (CMRA)[46]

The Act defines customary marriage as a marriage celebrated according to the rites of an African community and one of the parties who is a member of that community, or any marriage celebrated under Part III of this Act.[47] Where the parties belong to different communities, the customary practice of the bride is followed by the groom and his family.[48] The Act also provides for the establishment of marriage districts for the purpose of the registration of customary marriages,[49] the appointment of the registrar of customary marriages,[50] the celebration of customary marriages in any part of Uganda, and the recognition that such marriages are potentially polygamous,[51] the process that has to be followed and the requirements that have to be fulfilled for a customary marriage to be registered,[52] the issue of customary marriage certificates and the registration of such marriages out of time,[53] void customary marriages and the relationship between customary marriages and monogamous or Muslim marriages,[54] and failure to register a customary marriage.[55]

Notably, the CMRA has no explicit provision regarding the exchange of bride wealth (price) hence the reliance on judicial decisions and customary practices.

2.3 Progressive Jurisprudential Developments

Public Interest Litigation (PIL) and judicial activism have been instrumental in transformative jurisprudence and upholding fundamental

[46] Cap 248.

[47] Sec 1.

[48] *Nassanga v Nanyonga* [1977] HCB 318.

[49] Sec 2.

[50] Sec 3.

[51] Sec 4.

[52] Sec 6.

[53] Secs 5, 6 & 10.

[54] Secs 11, 12 & 13.

[55] Sec 20.

human rights.[56] This section provides an analysis of key progressive judicial decisions that have a bearing on the issue of the validity of customary marriage, and exchange of bride wealth, and have contributed significantly to upholding positive customary practices in addition to protecting women's rights.

2.3.1 Alai V Uganda [1967] EA 596

The case was a reference from the Chief Magistrates' Court to the High Court. Alai Bin Siruru (appellant) was charged with adultery under article 150A(1) of the Penal Code Act having been 'caught' having sexual intercourse with Adija Bint Iburahim, who was not considered to be his wife. The complainant contended that they had celebrated a marriage in 1963 and presented a marriage certificate to that effect.

The appellant, on the other hand, swore that Adija was his wife who he had married in 1960. He presented witnesses to the marriage including the second respondent's sister and mother who testified to the fact that the two were legally married under Islamic religious tradition. One of the issues before the Court was whether the appellant and Adija were husband and wife within the definition of section 4 of the Penal Code Act. Sir Udo Udoma held that:

> The learned Chief Magistrate had erred in his interpretation of the provision of the Penal code ... that a narrow construction of the meaning of husband and wife would be discriminatory in that it would close out other forms of marriages that are recognized by law like customary marriages which are recognized in Ugandan legal jurisprudence among other forms of marriages.

2.3.2 Mifumi (U) Ltd v Attorney General (Constitutional Appeal 2 of 2014) [2015] UGSC 13

Mifumi (U) Ltd petitioned the Constitutional Court seeking a declaration that the practice of demanding bride price and its repayment at the conclusion and dissolution of a marriage is unconstitutional. The appellants further contended that the exchange of bride price practiced by several ethnic groups in Uganda was repugnant to article 31(3) of

[56] J Oloka-Onyango 'When courts do politics: Public interest law and litigation in East Africa' (2017) *Cornell Institute for African Development Series* https://www.cambridgescholars.com/resources/pdfs/978-1-4438-9122-6-sample.pdf (accessed 15 June 2023).

the Constitution of Uganda, 1995, which afforded women equal rights and dignity as men, and free consent to marry. They also averred that the custom portrayed women as an article for sale, which amounts to degrading treatment which is inconsistent with and in contradiction with article 24. They asserted that payment of bride price occasions domestic violence and abuse of women and adduced evidence of victims of domestic violence that had been married under customary arrangements.

By a majority of 4-1, the Constitutional Court dismissed the petition. The appellants appealed to the Supreme Court to determine the following issues: (a) Whether bride price promotes inequality in marriage; (b) Whether bride price fetters the free consent of persons intending to marry; and (c) Whether the Constitutional Court erred in failing to declare the payment of bride price unconstitutional.

The Court affirmed that indeed the practice of bride wealth is not solely a creature of customary marriages but a practice that is common in all other forms of marriages. Justice Tumwesigye agreed with the lead judgement in the Constitutional Court to the effect that:

> [The] practice of bride price, the payment of a sum of money or property by the prospective son-in-law to the parents of the prospective bride as a condition precedent to a legal customary marriage, is not barred by the Constitution. It is not per se unconstitutional. The Constitution does not prohibit a voluntary, mutual agreement between a bride and a groom to enter into the bride price arrangement. A man and a woman have the constitutional right to choose the bride price option.

Court was of the view that inequality and wife battery are not peculiar to only customary marriages but also other forms of marriages. The Supreme Court held that the payment of bride price in customary marriage was overrated by the appellants as a significant factor in the promotion of inequality and violence against women. Justice Tumwesigye declared:

> [T]here are many more husbands who give bride price but who do not use it as a justification for inflicting violence and abuse on their wives. Therefore, while acknowledging that there may be some husbands who might use it as a justification to batter and abuse their wives, often used more as a pretext than the actual reason, this cannot constitute sufficient justification for denying the enjoyment and practice of the custom to people who cherish it as is provided for under Article 37 of the Constitution.

The Court stressed that the appellants had failed to tender any evidence to attest to the fact that the women were battered because of the bride price that had been paid. The Court, therefore, concluded that the practice of demanding for bride price could not be the major factor behind domestic violence. The Court however held that the practice of demanding the refund of the bride price upon dissolution of the marriage is unconstitutional.

2.3.3 *Uganda v Nakoupuet (Criminal Case 109 of 2016) [2019] UGHCCRD 14*

The accused was charged with rape of the complainant contrary to the Penal Code Act. The accused contended that the complainant was his wife since he had paid the bride price to her father. He abducted her and raped her with the aid of her brothers. In convicting the accused of rape, Justice Batema called for the abandonment of the backward culture of abduction and rape among the Karamojong which masqueraded as marriage. He stressed that:

> Laws, cultures, or traditions which are against the dignity, welfare, or interest of women or any marginalized group … or which undermine their status, are prohibited by this Constitution … We cannot condone the violation of these constitutional rights … in the name of culture … We have the legal mandate to, and so must, question the rape culture. This is the time to break the culture of silence and condemn this negative culture in the strongest terms possible. The conviction and sentence must send a clear message to the accused person and anyone intending to abduct and rape the women of Uganda that it is a serious capital offence ... the culture of abduction and rape is a form of torture, cruelty, inhuman and degrading treatment which is outlawed under Article 24 the Constitution. Article 44 makes freedom from torture a non-derogable right and Article 32(2) also directly prohibits any type of sex and gender-based violence propped by customs and traditions. Under Article 6 of the Maputo Protocol, Uganda undertook to ensure that women and men enjoy equal rights as equal partners in marriage and also committed itself to enact appropriate laws to guarantee that no marriage shall take place without the free will and full consent of both parties ... It is high time the culture of abduction and rape is abandoned by our people of Karamoja because not only was there nothing positive and worth promoting in the cultural rape but the same is also an infringement of Article 16(1) of CEDAW and Article 31(1) of Uganda's Constitution together with the penal laws intended to protect and enforce the rights.

2.3.4 *Uganda v Yiga Hamidu (Criminal Session 5 of 2002) [2004] UGHCCRD 5*

The accused had made a marriage proposal for the complainant to her father and claimed part-payment of the bride price. The purported marriage ceremony was halted pending HIV/AIDs results since it was suspected that the accused's deceased wife had succumbed to the virus. The accused attempted unsuccessfully to convince the complainant to live with him. He eventually abducted her and raped her with the aid of the co-accused contrary to sections 123 and 124 of the Penal Code Act. Justice Kibuuka-Musoke found the accused guilty of rape and declared that:

> No sane person who regards any woman as his wife would wish to have her exposed to such shame as A1 put the complainant in this case to by inviting two men to hold her while he was having sexual intercourse with her. No husband, worth the name, would leave his bride lying in the dirt on the floor of his bedroom crying and dejected, on the first day of their marriage which normally marks the peak of their love. No husband would lock up his loving bride in his bedroom like a prisoner of war on the first day of their marriage.
>
> That strange conduct, on the part of A1, renders it clear to me that A1 did not believe, deep in his heart, that the complainant was his bride. For after treating her in that savagery manner, he could never hope to have any love from her. His having sex with her at such a time of the day in such a fashion, was a mere release of vengeance upon her having refused to get married to him. He did not care what would follow.
>
> In my humble view, even if it was true that A1 and the complainant had been customarily or otherwise truly married and were, therefore husband and wife, or even if it was true that A1 honestly believed that the complainant was his customarily wedded wife, still the facts and circumstances of this case would render A1 guilty of rape.
>
> It clearly appears to me that the existence of a valid marriage between an accused and complainant or an honest belief that a valid marriage between the two does/can exist in Uganda, no longer constitute a good defence against a charge of rape after the promulgation of the Constitution of the Republic of Uganda, 1995 and provisions in Articles 20, 31, 33 and 273 of the Constitution.
>
> The presumption of consent, even where a man and woman are validly married ... appears to be wiped out by the provisions of the Constitution which provide that the Husband and wife enjoy equal rights in marriage. They enjoy equal human dignity. No activity on the party of any of the

two which is an affront to those rights in relation to the other, can be sustained by a court of law.[57]

2.3.5 *Okello v Akello (Civil Appeal 2019/84) UGHC 186 of 2020*

The respondent (Akello) and the deceased (Benson Ocan) had been married under Langi custom but later separated. After the death of the deceased, the respondent made an application for letters of administration of the estate of her late husband. However, the appellant—the deceased's mother-in-law (Okello)—challenged the grant of the letters of administration and lodged a caveat to that effect.

One of the issues for determination was whether there was a valid marriage between the respondent and the deceased under Langi custom, following only part-payment of Uganda Shillings 200,000 for the marital gift and subsequent failure to pay the full amount. Justice Stephen Mubiru held that:

> It was not demonstrated to the court that there was no valid marriage negotiated, celebrated, and entered into in accordance with the Lango custom. Before, the 1995 Constitution it was trite law that no valid customary marriage was complete unless dowry was fully paid, however, following the promulgation of the 1995 Constitution, the jurisprudence underwent a significant transformation. So to hold that partial payment of the bride price is a ground for nullification of a customary marriage would be repugnant to natural justice, equity, and good conscience, in that it would connote that marriage gifts are a price paid for the bride, in a purchase-and-sale transaction, thus reducing customary marriages to an arrangement of wife purchase. The notions of justice and equality of spouses in marital relations, as dictated by the current legal system, especially under Article 33(6) of the 1995 Constitution that prohibits customs or traditions which are against the dignity, welfare, or interest of women or which undermine their status, militate against a result that elevates marriage gifts to a role that lowers the status of women within the institution of marriage, as a purchase of the groom ... The payment of bride price, dowry, or marriage gift, important as it may be from a ceremonial and ritual point of view, can no longer be regarded as an essential requirement for a valid customary marriage, though it remains an element intrinsically

[57] *Uganda v Yiga Hamidu* (Criminal Session 5 of 2002) [2004] UGHCCRD 5 (9 February 2004).

linked to a customary marriage ... as long as there is an agreement that it will be paid, it needn't be paid in full.

2.4 *My Reflections*

The jurisprudence demonstrates the importance of having a judiciary that is awake to the changing social and economic realities of the people. By its progressive decisions, the courts are applauded for rising up to the mandate bestowed upon them by article 126(1) of the Constitution, which provides that:

> Judicial power is derived from the people and shall be exercised by the courts established under this Constitution in the name of the people, in conformity with the law, and with the values, norms, and aspirations of the people.

The exchange of bride wealth is a cultural norm and aspiration of the people, but does it amount to a harmful traditional practice warranting abolition by the law?

3 Colonialism and the Twist in the Perception of Marital Gifts

Colonialism was not just a political or cultural imposition but at its heart lay the development and export of finance capital.[58] The colonialists and the missionaries perceived African customary practices as archaic and barbaric. The colonial masters not only created a discourse of difference between Europeans and Africans, depicting the race and culture of the former as superior to that of the latter, but also reinvented new notions of differences in the relationship between African 'men' and 'women' through capitalism, religion, law, education, and reconstructed cultures.[59]

The colonialists created new structural drivers of inequities and totally altered the political economy of gender relations between African women

[58] See the detailed discussion in Tamale (n 29).

[59] P Wolfe 'History and imperialism: A century of theory, from Marx to postcolonialism' (1997) 102 *The American Historical Review* 388 https://doi.org/10.2307/2170830 (accessed 21 July 2023).

and men.[60] As a result of their dominion, colonised women were either diminished or erased from important areas of social and public life.[61] They also altered the indigenous gender systems and created a concept of sexuality that focused on the excesses and immorality of African women rather than on the critical role the women played in the African family and community.[62]

Bride price exchange predates colonialism, with roots in pre-colonial African cultures, where it was primarily a symbol of appreciation and respect.[63] However, under colonial rule, bride price evolved into a tool to subjugate and exploit women, further entrenching gender inequality and oppressive social norms. European powers often manipulated and co-opted existing cultural practices, including bride price, to maintain control over African societies.[64]

In African societies, the tradition of bride price was a deeply embedded cultural practice and often considered an essential aspect of marriage. However, the colonialists created a mixture of customary law that was widely different from the pre-colonial customs so as to meet their capitalistic and imperialist goals.[65] In the pre-colonial era, bride price was a gift but today the practice has been overtly affected by colonialist capitalism to the point where the exchange of items is viewed as the sale/purchase of the woman—a notion expressly stated by Sir Robert Hamilton CJ in *Rex v Amkeyo* in 1917.[66]

Even the translation of marital gifts into English is a wrong that was perpetuated by the colonialists. The terms given to the marital gift

[60] See, for instance, J Frémont 'Legal pluralism, customary law and human rights in Francophone African countries' (2009) 40 *Victoria University of Wellington Law Review* 149.

[61] M Torque 'Demystifying the International Criminal Court (ICC) target Africa political rhetoric' (2017) 7 *Open Journal of Political Science* 178.

[62] See generally, S Tamale (ed) *African sexualities: A reader* (2011).

[63] AR Nwabude 'Traditional African (the Igbo) marriage customs and the influence of the Western culture: Marxist approach' (2022) 10 *Open Journal of Social Sciences* 224.

[64] See X Mendez 'Notes towards a decolonial feminist methodology: Revisiting the race/gender matrix' (2005) 5 *Trans-Scripts* 45. Also see, S Wynter 'Unsettling the coloniality of being/power/truth/freedom: Towards the human, after man, its overrepresentation—An argument' (2003) 3 *CR: The New Centennial Review* 257.

[65] See A Theodore *The invention of the White race: The origins of racial oppression in Anglo-America* (1997); and A Mbembe *Critique of Black reason* (2017).

[66] (1917) EALR 7.

exchange do not capture the nuance of the tradition. The imperialists used words like bride price, dowry, and others which eliminate the fact that it is an exchange of a gift between two families and or communities—that was meant to express appreciation and strengthen ties. However, for the sake of this discussion, I will use the words interchangeably but that does not mean that I agree with the description and meaning the words stand for.

4 The Conundrum: Is the Exchange of Bride Wealth in Solemnising a Customary Marriage an Harmful Traditional Practice?

4.1 *Understanding the Concept of Harmful Traditional Practice (HTP)*

As early as 1917, the practice of exchange of bride wealth in celebration of a customary marriage had already attracted a negative connotation. In *Rex v Amkeyo*, the issue before the Court was whether the native customary marriage was a valid marriage, hence evidence could not be adduced from the wife against her husband in accordance with the Evidence Act. Sir Robert Hamilton CJ averred that such a relationship could not be a marriage since there was no free consent ... the marriage was 'inconceivable' among 'civilised' people since the woman was not a free contracting person, the woman was the chattel that was up for sale and the marriage was potentially polygamous. He held that:

> [T]he use of the word marriage to describe the relationship entered into by an African man with a woman of his tribe in the native custom is a misnomer ... I know no word that can correctly describe it [Customary Marriage] 'wife purchase' is not altogether satisfactory, but it comes much nearer to the idea than that of a marriage understood by civilized people.[67]

The CEDAW Committee recommended that Uganda abolishes the customary practice of bride price, among others.[68] Mujjuzi has also

[67] As above.

[68] Committee on the Elimination of Discrimination against Women, Concluding Observations on the Third Periodic Report of Uganda (CEDAW/C/UGA/3) August 2002, paras 152-153 https://www.un.org/womenwatch/daw/cedaw/cedaw25years/content/english/CONCLUDING_COMMENTS/Uganda/Uganda-CO-3.pdf (accessed 26 June 2023).

argued that the Supreme Court addressing their mind to the recommendations of the CEDAW Committee and other progressive laws to which Uganda is privy, ought to have declared the cultural practice of exchange of bride price in celebrating customary marriages unconstitutional.[69]

And yet, the Constituent Assembly debates and public consultations revealed that the customary practice of exchange of bride price is cherished by the vast majority of the populace.[70] Besides, article 37 of the 1995 Constitution guarantees the enjoyment of one's custom. But, such custom must not be inconsistent with the Constitution as stipulated in article 2(2), and if so it is void to the extent of that inconsistency.[71] The legislature and the courts are mandated to pass laws and make decisions respectively, that align with the changing circumstances in society and also meet the aspirations of the Constitution and the people.[72] The Judicature Act (as amended) also permits the application and enforcement of customary law that is not repugnant to natural justice, equity, and good conscience.[73]

In *Bruno Kiwuwa v Juliet Namazi & Ivan Serunkuma*,[74] Justice Remy Kasule observed that a custom is only repugnant to justice and morality if it causes aversion and disgust to the principles of good behaviour and as to what is reasonable and fair. Further, when a custom goes contrary to the rules of behaviour basic to human nature and is contrary to what is morally right and acceptable, then such a custom violates natural justice, equity, and good conscience.

Is the practice of exchange of bride wealth therefore a repugnant custom that amounts to a harmful traditional practice?

The CEDAW Committee defines harmful practices as:

[69] Mujuzi (n 30) 427.

[70] As above.

[71] See art 21 on equality and non-discrimination on any ground including sex, gender, and social standing among others; arts 32(2) and 33(6) that prohibit the application of customs and laws that violate the rights and dignity of women; art 273 permits the modification of any laws existing prior to the adoption of the 1995 Constitution to meet the standards set by the Constitution.

[72] Arts 79 & 126 of the Constitution.

[73] Secs 13-14 Judicature Act, 2006 (as amended).

[74] HCCS 52 of 2006.

> Persistent practices and behaviours that are grounded on discrimination on the basis of sex, gender, age, and other grounds as well as multiple and/or intersecting forms of discrimination that often involve violence and cause physical and/or psychological harm or suffering. The harm that these practices cause to the victims surpasses the immediate physical and mental consequences and often has the purpose or effect of impairing the recognition, enjoyment, and exercise of the human rights and fundamental freedoms of women and children. There is also a negative impact on their dignity, physical, psychosocial, and moral integrity, development, participation, health, educational, economic, and social status.[75]

According to the Committee, to be regarded as harmful, practices should meet the following criteria:

(a) They constitute a denial of the dignity and/or integrity of the individual and a violation of human rights and fundamental freedoms enshrined in the two Conventions—CEDAW and CRC;
(b) They constitute discrimination against women or children and are harmful insofar as they result in negative consequences for them as individuals or groups, including physical, psychological, economic, and social harm and/or violence and limitations on their capacity to participate fully in society or develop and reach their full potential;
(c) They are traditional, re-emerging, or emerging practices that are prescribed and/or kept in place by social norms that perpetuate male dominance and inequality of women and children, based on sex, gender, age, and other intersecting factors;
(d) They are imposed on women and children by family, community members, or society at large, regardless of whether the victim provides, or is able to provide full, free, and informed consent.[76]

Harmful traditional practices, as a form of gender-based violence, are those customs that are known to have negative effects on people's health

[75] See Committee on the Elimination of Discrimination Against Women, Joint General Recommendation/General Comment 31 of the Committee on the Elimination of Discrimination Against Women and 18 of the Committee on the Rights of the Child on harmful practices, 4 November 2014, UN Doc CEDAW/C/GC/31-CRC/C/GC/18 (2014) https://www.equalrightstrust.org/ertdocumentbank/CEDAW%20CRC_GR31%20GC18.pdf (accessed 15 January 2025).

[76] As above.

and to obstruct the goals of equality, political and social rights and the process of economic development.[77] Harmful traditional practices may manifest in different forms, including female genital mutilation, early child marriage, forced marriage, widow inheritance, killing of twin children, forceful abduction for marriage, widowhood rituals, lip plates, forced clitoris elongation, and son preference, among others.[78]

It goes without saying that the main cause of the harmful practices is the patriarchal society from which ideologies of women's inferiority stem. The CEDAW Committee states that the causes of harmful practices are multidimensional and include stereotyped sex and gender-based roles, the presumed superiority or inferiority of either of the sexes, attempts to exert control over the bodies and sexuality of women and girls, social inequalities, and the prevalence of male-dominated power structures.[79]

Despite the positive traditional purpose of exchange of bride wealth between two families of the bride and groom, the commercialisation of the practice today, which is akin to the selling of the bride, diminishes its traditional significance.[80] It now manifests as a tool for the economic exploitation of the groom's family and in some cases commodifying the women/girls.[81] The commercialisation of the practice has also increased incidences of defilement, and early and forced child marriage by parents who seek some financial gain from marrying off their daughters, a key factor in diminishing gender equality between spouses.[82] Decisions about contraception, family planning, and reproductive healthcare are influenced or even determined by the husband without taking into

[77] The Open University 'Adolescent and youth reproductive health Module: 5. Harmful Traditional Practices (HTPs)' https://www.open.edu/openlearncreate/mod/oucontent/view.php?id=66&printable=1 (accessed 8 July 2023).

[78] OHCHR 'Fact Sheet 23: Harmful traditional practices affecting the health of women and children' (23 August 1995) http://www.ohchr.org/Documents/Publications/FactSheet23en.pdf (accessed 15 January 2025).

[79] Joint General Recommendation (n 76).

[80] L Corno & A Voena 'Selling daughters: Age at marriage, income shocks, and bride price tradition' IFS Working Paper W16/08 (2016) https://ifs.org.uk/sites/default/files/output_url_files/WP201608.pdf (accessed 16 January 2025).

[81] G Hague, RK Thiara & A Turner 'Bride-price and its links to domestic violence and poverty in Uganda: A participatory action research study' (2011) 34 *Womens Studies International Forum* 550 https://doi.org/10.1016/j.wsif.2011.06.008

[82] AK Blanc and others 'Negotiating reproductive outcomes in Uganda' (2015) Uganda: Macro International and Institute of Statistics and Applied Economics.

consideration the woman's own needs, desires, and informed choices.[83] Hence, payment of bride wealth may affect a woman's autonomy in the marriage.[84]

Despite these ills, to date, the practice is still highly regarded by the populace as a traditional expression of gratitude from the groom to the bride's parents/family for raising the bride and honouring the groom's proposal to their daughter.[85] Okot argues that the relevance of customary marriage as a cultural and social rite cannot be disputed; if anything, this practice should be deliberately promoted in an era where cultural degeneration avalanche is becoming more unprecedented.[86] The Supreme Court, in *Mifumi v Attorney General* (supra), took judicial notice of the exchange of marital gifts and held that there was nothing wrong with the practice during customary marriage in different communities in Uganda—the only problem being that demanding it at dissolution is unconstitutional. This view had also been adopted in several other cases like *Aggrey Owori v Rosette Tagire*,[87] *Nemezio Ayiiya Pet v Sabina Onzia Ayiiya*,[88] and similarly in *Wango v Dominiko Manano*.[89]

Hence the ball is in our court to practice the culture of exchange of bride price in a manner that does not infringe the standards set in articles 2(2), 21, 31, 32(2), and 33(6) of the 1995 Constitution and other laws discussed above.

[83] M Okioma 'Bride price-paving the way for a killer' Paper presented at the International Conference on bride price and development, 16–18 February 2004, Makerere University, Kampala, Uganda.

[84] The Sub-Commission on Prevention of Discrimination and Protection of Minorities *Report of the second United Nations regional seminar on traditional practices affecting the health of women and children* Colombo, 4–8 July 1994, 28 July 1994, UN Doc E/CN.4/Sub.2/1994/10 (1994).

[85] SJ Tambiah 'Dowry and bride wealth, and the property rights of women in South Asia' in J Goody & S Tambiah (eds) *Bride wealth and dowry* (1993).

[86] D Ojok (n 23) 8.

[87] HCCS 178/2000.

[88] HCCS 8/1973.

[89] (1958) EA 124.

5 Way Forward: Recommendations

5.1 Rename from Bride Wealth/Price to Bride Gifts

This is to reiterate the call by the Supreme Court in *Mifumi (U) Ltd v the Attorney General*, that the term be renamed 'bridal gifts'.[90] The Supreme Court asserted that the practice of exchange in bride wealth or price should be referred to as 'bridal gifts' and not 'bride price' or 'bride wealth' in order to eliminate the idea of commercialisation, and the gifts delivered should not be determined by the bride's family or clansmen but rather left to the decision of the parties marrying. The Marriage Bill, 2017 in the same vein uses the term 'marriage gifts', which can be in form of cash or in kind.[91]

5.2 Adopt By-Laws to Regulate the Practice in the Various Communities

The clan leadership should adopt by-laws to regulate the practice in their respective communities. Some of the examples of by-laws that have been enacted to this effect include: The Local Government (Tororo District) (Regulation of the Exchange of Bridal Gifts) Ordinance 4 of 2009; The Teso Birth, Marriages and Death Law, Legal Notice 252 of 1959; The Bugishu Bride Price Law, Legal Notice 176 of 1960; and the Sebei Bridal Law, Legal Notice 176 of 1960. Most recently, the Nebbi and Acholi Clan leaders have also enacted by-laws to curb early child marriages and regulate bride wealth so as to limit cohabitation and promote customary marriages. Such progressive and positive clan leadership efforts need to be recognised and supported.

Commendably, the proposed Marriage Bill, 2024 recognises the exchange of marriage gifts whether in kind or cash, and prohibits the return of the same upon the termination of the marriage.[92]

[90] *Mifumi (U) Ltd v Attorney General* (Constitutional Appeal 2 of 2014) [2015] UGSC 13.

[91] Clause 15.

[92] See clause 15.

5.3 *Enhance Gender Equality and Human Rights Awareness*

There should be continued legal awareness of the masses so as to enhance knowledge about human rights, women's rights, and gender equality and roles. This will hopefully enhance legal awareness, address the growing incidences of sex, gender-based violence, and gender inequalities fuelled by ignorance, culture, patriarchy, and religion. Human rights and legal awareness will also equip the masses with the information they need to combat any form of harmful cultural practice meted out on them or rights violation.

5.4 *Boost Economic Empowerment Strategies to Combat Poverty*

Poverty is another push factor exposing girls and women to early or forced marriages. Bride wealth is viewed by some families as a source of wealth and an opportunity for the bride's family to get out of poverty. Therefore, the effective implementation of government economic empowerment initiatives like the Youth Livelihood Programme (YLP), Uganda Women Entrepreneurship Programme (UWEP), National Special Disability Grant, Emyooga, and the Parish Development Model (PDM) could potentially improve household incomes, reduce poverty, and the desire for exorbitant bride wealth or even early or forced marriages. This should be coupled with progressive educational policies like the Universal Primary Education (UPE) and Universal Secondary Education (USE) so that children, especially girls, are kept in school longer to avoid dropping out, which also fuels early child marriages.[93]

This should further be buttressed by holding parents accountable and liable for failure to take on their parenting roles and responsibilities towards their children's welfare seriously.

5.5 *Enhance Access to Justice for Women and Girls*

Access to justice remains a critical factor to enable women and girls who have faced any form of abuse to seek redress and hold the perpetrators

[93] J Deng and others 'Returns to education in the marriage market: Bride price and school reform in Egypt' World Bank Policy Research Working Paper 10288 (2023) https://openknowledge.worldbank.org/server/api/core/bitstreams/7b9d0c21-12df-42b6-a57a-b87c63c6e8f6/content (accessed 16 January 2025).

accountable. The judicial system should be gender sensitive and friendly to enable easier access to justice for vulnerable groups including women and girls. The government should also adopt and pass the National Legal Aid Bill so as to provide support to legal aid service providers.

5.6 Promote Public Interest Litigation and Judicial Activism

As demonstrated by the court decisions discussed above, PIL and judicial activities in safeguarding and promoting the rights of women and girls must be underscored. It is through judicial activism that we are able to enforce the various progressive legal frameworks Uganda has ratified and adopted that guarantee fundamental human rights of all persons, including women and girls. Harmful practices, if not outlawed by legislation, must be declared unconstitutional by the courts. Where individuals are unable to enforce their rights, PIL met with judicial activism is the way forward.

6 Conclusion

The jurisprudence and literature confirm that bride wealth is still a significant aspect of celebrating customary marriages in Uganda and cannot be abolished. However, be that as it may, the aspirations of the 1995 Constitution, coupled with the obligations bestowed on both state and non-state actors to uphold fundamental human rights of all persons, including women, leaves no room for perpetuating harmful traditional practices in the name of culture and patriarchy. Therefore, although the practice of exchange of bride wealth is so entrenched in our society in celebration of customary marriage, the practice must be regulated by the state to avoid its negative ramifications on the rights of women and girls. Governments, international organisations, and civil society groups should work together to raise awareness about the harmful consequences of child marriage, advocate for legal reforms, provide support services for vulnerable girls, ensure access to economic initiatives by women, and promote girls' education as a means of empowerment.

Bibliography

Asiimwe, H 'The changing dynamics, trends and perceptions in the bride price custom in Uganda and the implications – A feminist perspective: A case of Banyakitra ethnic group in Western Uganda' Master's thesis, Institute of Social Studies, The Hague, The Netherlands, December 2013 https://thesis.eur.nl/pub/15309/HAsiimwe_moodledata_temp_turnitintool_111673799._42_1384407653_2029.pdf (accessed 16 January 2025)

Bishai, D & Grossband, S 'Far above rubies: The association between bride price and extramarital sexual relations in Uganda' (2007) Discussion Paper 2982 https://docs.iza.org/dp2982.pdf (accessed 16 January 2025)

Blanc, AK; Wolff, B; Gage, AJ; Ezeh, AC; Neema, S & Ssekamatte-Ssebuliba, J *Negotiating reproductive outcomes in Uganda* (Calverton, MD and Kampala, Uganda: Macro International and Institute of Statistics and Applied Economics 1995)

Chan, W 'Marital transfers and the welfare of women' (2014) 66 *Oxford Economic Papers* 1019 http://www.jstor.org/stable/43773045 (accessed 16 January 2025)

Conteh, JA 'Dowry and bride price' in Naples, N; Hoogland, RC; Wickramasinghe, M & Wong, WCA (eds) *The Wiley Blackwell encyclopedia of gender and sexuality studies* (Wiley-Blackwell 2016)

Corno, L & A Voena 'Selling daughters: Age at marriage, income shocks, and bride price tradition' IFS Working Paper W16/08 (2016) https://ifs.org.uk/sites/default/files/output_url_files/WP201608.pdf (accessed 16 January 2025)

Deng, J; Elmallakh, NY; Louis, W; Flabbi, L & Gatti, RV 'Returns to education in the marriage market: Bride price and school reform in Egypt' World Bank Policy Research Working Paper 10288 (2023) https://openknowledge.worldbank.org/server/api/core/bitstreams/7b9d0c21-12df-42b6-a57a-b87c63c6e8f6/content (accessed 16 January 2025)

Frémont, J 'Legal pluralism, customary law and human rights in Francophone African countries' (2009) 40 *Victoria University of Wellington Law Review* 149

Goldschmidt, W 'The economics of bride price among the Sebei and in East Africa' (1974) 13 *Ethnology* 313

Hague, G; Thiara, RK & Turner, A 'Bride-price and its links to domestic violence and poverty in Uganda: A participatory action research study' (2011) 34 *Women's Studies International Forum* 550

Jacoby, HG 'The economics of polygyny in sub-Saharan Africa: Female productivity and the demand for wives in Cote d'Ivoire' (1995) 103 *Journal of Political Economy* 938

Mbembe *A Critique of Black reason* (Durham: Duke University Press 2017)

Mendez, X 'Notes towards a decolonial feminist methodology: Revisiting the race/gender matrix' (2005) 5 *Trans-Scripts* 41

Mujuzi, JD 'Bride wealth (price) and the women's marriage – related rights in Uganda: A historical constitutional perspectives and other developments' (2010) 24 *International Journal for Policy, Law and Family* 414

Mujuzi, JD 'Presumption of marriage in Uganda' (2020) 34 *International Journal of Law, Policy and the Family* 247 https://academic.oup.com/lawfam/article-abstract/34/3/247/6024926 (accessed 16 January 2025)

Nampewo, Z; Atim, P; Musoke, H & Kange, V *Family and succession law in Uganda: International Encyclopedia of Law Series* (Netherlands, Kluwer International Law 2020)

Nwabude, AAR 'Traditional African (the Igbo) marriage customs and the influence of the Western culture: Marxist approach' (2022) 2 *Open Journal of Social Sciences* 224

Ojok, D 'The socio-legal dynamics of customary marriage in Uganda' (2017) 7 CEPA Policy Series Papers Kampala https://cepa.or.ug/wp-content/uploads/2018/06/The-Socio-Legal-dynamics-of-Customary-Marriage-in-Uganda.pdf (accessed 16 January 2025)

Okioma, M 'Bride price – Paving the way for a killer' Paper presented at the International Conference on Brideprice and Development, 16–18 February 2004, Makerere University, Kampala, Uganda

Oloka-Onyango, J *When courts do politics: Public interest law and litigation in East Africa* (Cornell Institute for African Development Series 2017) https://www.cambridgescholars.com/resources/pdfs/978-1-4438-9122-6-sample.pdf (accessed 16 January 2025)

Open University 'Adolescent and youth reproductive health Module: 5. Harmful Traditional Practices (HTPs)' https://www.open.edu/openlearncreate/mod/oucontent/view.php?id=66&printable=1 (accessed 8 July 2023)

Plan International & ECPAT *Thematic report: Unrecognised sexual abuse and exploitation of children in child, early and forced marriage* (2015) https://www.ecpat.org/wp-content/uploads/legacy/Child%20Marriage_ENG.pdf (accessed 16 January 2025)

Semenya, DK 'The practical guidelines on the impact of mahadi [bride price] on the young Basotho couples prior to marriage' (2014) 3 *Hervormde Teologiese Studies* 1

Tamale, S (ed) *African sexualities: A reader* (Oxford: Pambazuka Press 2011)

Tamale, S *Decolonization and Afro-feminism* (Ottawa: Daraja Press 2020)

Tambiah, SJ 'Dowry and bride wealth, and the property rights of women in South Asia' in Goody, J & Tambiah, SJ (eds) *Bride wealth and dowry* (Cambridge University Press 1993)

Theodore, A *The invention of the White race: The origins of racial oppression in Anglo-America* (London & New York: Verso 1997)

Torque, M 'Demystifying the International Criminal Court (ICC) target Africa political rhetoric' (2017) 7 *Open Journal of Political Science* 178

Trivers, RL 'Parental investment and sexual selection' in Cambell, B (ed) *Sexual selection and the descent of man* (Aldine de Gruyter 1972)

Uganda Bureau of Statistics *National Population and Housing Census Report, 2014* (2016) https://unstats.un.org/unsd/demographic-social/census/documents/Uganda/UGA-2014-11.pdf (accessed 16 January 2025)

Umo, IE 'African women, bride price, and AIDS' (2004) 363 *The Lancet* 1734

Voena, A & Corno, L 'Selling daughters: Age at marriage, income shocks, and bride price tradition' IFS Working Paper W16/08 (2016) https://ifs.org.uk/sites/default/files/output_url_files/WP201608.pdf (accessed 16 January 2025)

Wendo, C 'African women denounce bride price' (2004) 363 *The Lancet* 716

Wolfe, P 'History and imperialism: A century of theory, from Marx to postcolonialism' (1997) 102 *The American Historical Review* 388

Wynter, S 'Unsettling the coloniality of being/power/truth/freedom: Towards the human, after man, its overrepresentation—An argument' (2003) 3 CR: The New Centennial Review 257

Acts

Constitution of Uganda, 1995

Customary Marriage (Registration) Act Cap 248

Hindu Marriage and Divorce Act Cap 250

Judicature Act, 2006 (as amended)

Marriage Act Cap 251

Marriage and Divorce of Mohammedans Act Cap 252

Case law

Aggrey Owori v Rosette Tagire HCCS 178/2000

Alai v Uganda [1967] EA 596

Baryamureeba Steven v Kabakonjo Civil Suit 20 of 2013

Bruno Kiwuwa v Juliet Namazi & Ivan Serunkuma HCCS 52 of 2006

Friedman Bigala v Lourna Namuwenge Civil Suit 98 of 2020 [2023]

Mifumi (U) Ltd v Attorney General (Constitutional Appeal 2 of 2014) [2015] UGSC 13 (6 August 2015)

Musa Kigongo v Olive Kigongo High Court Mics App 551 of 2015

Nassanga v Nanyonga [1977] HCB 318

Nemezio Ayiiya Pet v Sabina Onzia Ayiiya HCCS 8/1973

Okello v Akello (Civil Appeal 2019/84) UGHC 186 of 2020

Rex v Amkeyo (1917) EALR 7

Solomon Ayiku v Lekuru Ayiko High Court Divorce Cause 001 of 2015
Uganda v Nakoupuet (Criminal Case 109 of 2016) [2019] UGHCCRD 14
Uganda v Yiga Hamidu (Criminal Session 5 of 2002) [2004] UGHCCRD 5 (9 February 2004)
Wango v Dominiko Manano (1958) EAA 124

International treaties

Committee on the Elimination of Discrimination against Women, Concluding Comments of the Committee on the Elimination of Discrimination against Women: Uganda: Third Periodic Report of Uganda, UN Doc CEDAW/C/UGA/3) (August 2002) https://www.un.org/womenwatch/daw/cedaw/cedaw25years/content/english/CONCLUDING_COMMENTS/Uganda/Uganda-CO-3.pdf (accessed 26 June 2023)
Committee on the Elimination of Discrimination against Women, Concluding Observations on the Third Periodic Report of Uganda (CEDAW/C/UGA/3) August 2002 https://www.un.org/womenwatch/daw/cedaw/cedaw25years/content/english/CONCLUDING_COMMENTS/Uganda/Uganda-CO-3.pdf (accessed 26 June 2023)
Committee on the Elimination of Discrimination Against Women, Joint General Recommendation/General Comment 31 of the Committee on the Elimination of Discrimination Against Women and 18 of the Committee on the Rights of the Child on harmful practices, 4 November 2014, UN Doc CEDAW/C/GC/31-CRC/C/GC/18 (2014) https://www.equalrightstrust.org/ertdocumentbank/CEDAW%20CRC_GR31%20GC18.pdf (accessed 15 January 2025)
Convention on the Elimination of All Forms of Discrimination Against Women, United Nations Treaty Series, vol 1249, p 13, 18 December 1979.
Convention on the Rights of Persons with Disabilities: Resolution adopted by the General Assembly, 24 January 2007, UN Doc A/RES/61/106 (2007)
International Covenant on Economic, Social and Cultural Rights, United Nations, Treaty Series, vol 993, p 3, 16 December 1966
OHCHR 'Fact Sheet 23: Harmful Traditional Practices Affecting the Health of Women and Children' (23 August 1995) http://www.ohchr.org/Documents/Publications/FactSheet23en.pdf (accessed 15 January 2025)
Sub-Commission on Prevention of Discrimination and Protection of Minorities, Report of the second United Nations regional seminar on traditional practices affecting the health of women and children Colombo, 28 July 1994, UN Doc E/CN.4/Sub.2/1994/10 (1994)
Universal Declaration of Human Rights, 217 A(III), 10 December 1948

CHAPTER 7

Tobacco-Related Harms and Gender: An Overview with Perspectives from India

Upendra Bhojani and Pragati B Hebbar

1 Introduction

In this chapter, we start by reiterating what is now widely recognised: that tobacco use, and production, constitute a harmful practice at an individual and societal level. We review the sex-based differences in tobacco risks (consumption and exposure to second-hand smoke), the resultant disease burden, as well as the access to health and social care. We then analyse, in detail, how gender as a social construct is key to understanding

U. Bhojani and P. B. Hebbar: Both authors contributed equally.

U. Bhojani (✉)
Centre for Commercial Determinants of Health, Institute of Public Health, Bengaluru, India
e-mail: upendra@iphindia.org

P. B. Hebbar
Institute of Public Health, Bengaluru, India
e-mail: pragati@iphindia.org

E. Durojaye et al. (eds.), *Harmful Practices and Human Rights: An International Perspective*, Human Rights Interventions,
https://doi.org/10.1007/978-3-031-90333-5_7

these stark sex-based differences. We highlight how tobacco businesses have for a long time considered gender in their market research, product development and marketing campaigns targeted at men and women to boost tobacco sales globally and in India. Such efforts aimed at reaping market benefits have invariably reinforced, often harmful, conventional gender stereotypes around tobacco use. We summarise the available scholarship on gender and tobacco that is very limited, with a dominant Anglo-American focus. We highlight the critique of the available research that despite its usefulness is not sufficient and lacks relevance to explain the gendered nature of tobacco in other societies including India. We then review whether and how the prevailing tobacco control policies and programmes in India address (or fail to address) gender and the way forward for more gender-inclusive and gender-sensitive tobacco control.

2 Tobacco Consumption

Tobacco is one of the major contributing factors for Non-Communicable Diseases (NCDs) globally. Over 1.3 billion people smoke globally. Women account for about 20% of the global smokers.[1] The habit is more prevalent among lower socio-economic groups, and around 80% of them are living in low- and middle-income countries.[2] The absolute number of women smokers is more in developing countries (9%) than in developed countries (22%).[3] Globally smoking prevalence among women is highest in Europe followed by the Americas and the Western Pacific regions, while in several countries of Southeast Asia and Eastern Mediterranean regions women are less likely to smoke due to cultural and religious reasons.[4] In the Western Pacific region being born male is the greatest risk factor for tobacco use.[5] The prevalence of smokeless tobacco use is highest in the

[1] WHO fact sheet 'Women and tobacco use' (2014) https://apps.who.int/iris/bitstream/handle/10665/204209/Fact_Sheet_TFI_2014_EN_15320.pdf?sequence=1 (accessed 24 August 2024).

[2] WHO fact sheet 'Tobacco' (2023) https://www.who.int/news-room/fact-sheets/detail/tobacco (accessed 20 June 2023).

[3] J Mackay & A Amos 'Women and tobacco' (2003) 8 *Respirology* 123.

[4] A Chhabra, S Hussain & S Rashid 'Recent trends of tobacco use in India' (2021) 29 *Journal of Public Health* 27.

[5] M Morrow & S Barraclough 'Tobacco control and gender in Southeast Asia. Part I: Malaysia and the Philippines' (2003) 18 *Health Promotion International* 255.

Southeast Asia region which contributes to 90% of the overall tobacco users globally. Data from 151 countries reveal that 7% of adolescent girls and 12% of boys smoke tobacco and in some countries, the gap between boys and girls is minimal, for example, in Russia, 24% of girls and 27% of boys smoke cigarettes.[6]

In India 28.6% of the adults (about 275 million) use tobacco of which 10.7% is in the form of cigarettes and bidis (accounting for 12% of the world's smokers) while 21.4% is in the form of smokeless tobacco products such as betel quid, gutka/paan masala etc.[7] About 3,4% adults are dual users consuming smoke and smokeless tobacco products.[8] Smoking trends in India among men have shown an overall decline over the last two decades with a significant decline (from 33.4 to 24.3%) during the period of 2005–2009. In the similar period, women smoking has seen a rise from 1.4 to 2.9% and overall, there has been a rising trend over the past two decades.[9]

Smokeless tobacco is the dominant form of tobacco consumption in India. A study found that the prevalence of smokeless tobacco was nearly two times that of smoking in India. Analysis of 2005 data revealed that the proportion of smokeless tobacco users among total tobacco users was 65.8% for men and 88.7% for women, while in 2009 this rose to 74.2% for men and 92.9% for women in the age group of 15–49 years.[10] SLT and other local products' affordability have not reduced despite the government's introduction of GST for tobacco products like cigarettes and bidis because they are not included in this, which is advantageous for individuals who use these products.[11]

[6] Centers for Disease Control and Prevention 'Tobacco use among women' (2011) www.cdc.gov/tobacco/global/gats/countries/wpr/fact_sheets/ (accessed 24 August 2023).

[7] As above.

[8] As above.

[9] S Goel and others 'Smoking trends among women in India: Analysis of nationally representative surveys (1993-2009)' (2014) 3 *South Asian Journal of Cancer* 200.

[10] GK Mini & KR Thankappan 'Switching to smokeless tobacco, the most common smoking cessation method: Results from the Global Adult Tobacco Survey, India' (2016) 136 *Public Health* 172.

[11] N Sharma and others 'Socio-economic status differences in changing affordability of tobacco products from 2011–2012 to 2018–2019 in India' (2023) 25 *Nicotine & Tobacco Research* 709.

Apart from sex-based differences, tobacco use is also shaped by income, location and education among others. Tobacco use is found to be high, in general, among men, those with less of a formal education, those with lower incomes and those residing in rural areas.[12] Indian states with higher per capita Gross Domestic Product such as the states in central and southern India (Delhi, Goa, Maharashtra, Kerala, Tamil Nadu and Karnataka) recorded a very low prevalence of women smoking; while states with low per capita Gross Domestic Product, such as the north-eastern states of Mizoram, Sikkim and Nagaland had a high prevalence of women smoking. Another pattern related to smoking among women is that the prevalence was much higher among those who are illiterate (about 3%) compared to those with more than 10 years of schooling (about 0.05%). This trend can be seen in states with lower female literacy rates when compared to states with high female literacy.[13] The prevalence of tobacco use among women consistently increases with age from 3.7% in the 15–24 age group to 31% among women aged 65 years and above (Table 1).[14]

Furthermore, the tobacco use pattern and the product types vary regionally. Even though the overall tobacco use is higher among men, the prevalence of smokeless tobacco is significantly higher among women

Table 1 Prevalence of tobacco use based on gender and residence as per the National Family Health Survey (India)

Category	*Urban*		*Rural*	
	Men	*Women*	*Men*	*Women*
Prevalence of tobacco use	32.6%	9.0%	47.6%	16.9%
Smoking only	14%	0.7%	15.5%	2.3%
Smokeless only	17.1%	10.7%	26.4%	20%
Dual use of tobacco	6.4%	0.4%	10.5%	1.3%

[12] A Singh & L Ladusingh 'Prevalence and determinants of tobacco use in India: Evidence from recent global adult tobacco survey data' (2014) 9 *PLoS One* e114073.

[13] Mini & Thankappan (n 10).

[14] WHO 'Global adult tobacco survey (GATS 2) India report 2016-17' (2017).

compared to men (31%) especially in the North-East region (33%).[15] While in general, cigarette use prevalence is much higher among men compared to women, the mean number of cigarettes smoked per day is higher for women (about seven per day) compared to men (about 6.1 per day).[16]

3 Exposure to Second-Hand Smoke

Exposure to second-hand smoke is a well-documented health hazard. In 2004, second-hand smoke exposure was estimated to have caused about 0.6 million premature deaths globally, of which 28% were among children. About 64% of the 430 000 adult deaths by second-hand smoke were among women.[17] As per 2019 estimates, 1.3 million out of the total of 8.7 million deaths related to tobacco are among non-smokers exposed to second-hand smoke. The same data indicates that 51 000 children and adolescents die from second-hand smoke exposure each year. Some of the main causes of death due to second-hand smoke exposure are ischemic heart disease, chronic obstructive pulmonary disease, stroke, lower respiratory disease, type 2 diabetes and cancers. Children and infants are most vulnerable when they are exposed to second-hand smoke as they breathe rapidly and their lungs are still developing, and the detrimental effects continue to have negative health impacts in adulthood as well.[18]

As per the Global Adult Tobacco Survey 2016–17 data, 30.2% adults (32.7% men and 17.9% women) were exposed to second-hand smoke at work in India. The exposure was higher in rural areas at 34.3% compared to 25.3% in urban areas. With increase in education, the exposure to second-hand smoke reduced: 40.6% of individuals with no formal schooling were exposed to second-hand smoke compared to 22.3% for those with secondary education and above. Furthermore, about 38.7% adults (38.1% men and 39.3% women) were exposed to second-hand

[15] G Nayak and others 'Gendered pattern and predictors of tobacco use in India: Evidence from the second round of global adult tobacco survey' (2023) 48 *Indian Journal of Community Medicine* 241.

[16] P Mohan, HA Lando & S Panneer 'Assessment of tobacco consumption and control in India' (2018) 9 *Indian Journal of Clinical Medicine* doi:10.1177/1179916118759289.

[17] JM Samet & SY Yoon 'Gender, women, and the tobacco epidemic' (2010) 249.

[18] WHO 'WHO report on the global tobacco epidemic: Protect people from tobacco smoke' (2023).

smoke at home. A similar negative association between education and exposure to second-hand smoke exposure was observed: 49.4% adults with no formal schooling were exposed to second-hand smoke compared to 27.5% of those with secondary education and above.[19]

4 Disease Burden

Recent data indicate that about 2.14 million deaths and about 229.77 million Disability Adjusted Life Years lost among women are attributed to tobacco use including exposure to second-hand smoke.[20,21] In 2019, 9 out of 10 leading causes of death for women were related to tobacco use.[22] China represented the highest absolute number of tobacco-related deaths among women, while proportionally, Montenegro and Denmark represented the highest proportion of tobacco-related deaths among women in 2019.

In India, a nationally representative study estimated a total of about one million adult deaths attributable to tobacco smoking in 2010. It established that tobacco smoking increases risk for all-cause mortality among women (risk ratio = 2) and men (risk ratio = 1.7).[23] For the same year, another study estimated that over 0.36 million deaths (368 127 deaths including, 217 076 deaths among women and 151 051 deaths among men) attributable to the use of smokeless tobacco.[24] It established that smokeless tobacco use increases risk of all-cause mortality among women (relative risk = 1.34) and men (relative risk = 1.17). So, in total, tobacco use possibly accounted for over 1.3 million deaths

[19] WHO (n 14).

[20] Tobacco Atlas 'Worldwide smoking deaths per year' (2022) https://tobaccoatlas.org/challenges/deaths/ (accessed 24 August 2023).

[21] C Murray and others 'Global burden of 87 risk factors in 204 countries and territories, 1990-2019: A systematic analysis for the Global Burden of Disease Study 2019' (2020) 396 *Lancet*.

[22] Tobacconomics 'The importance of tobacco control for women in low- and middle-income countries' (2022) https://tobacconomics.org/blog/the-importance-of-tobacco-control-for-women-in-low-and-middle-income-countries/ (accessed 24 August 2023).

[23] T Sharma & M Khapre 'Exposure of second hand smoke in women and children: A narrative review' (2021) 10 *Journal of Family Medicine and Primary Care* 1804.

[24] DN Sinha and others 'Smokeless tobacco use: A meta-analysis of risk and attributable mortality estimates for India' (2014) 51 *Indian Journal of Cancer*.

in 2010. The relative risk of dying from tobacco use and the absolute number of deaths from smokeless tobacco use are higher among women compared to men. Smokeless tobacco use has been found to contribute to oral cancers and precancers, cardiovascular diseases, preterm birth and stillbirth among women.[25] Another study estimated tobacco attributable mortality at nearly 23.7% (527 500) deaths in men and about 5.7% (83 000) deaths among women based on a cohort study in Mumbai.[26] In case of SLT in 2017, at least 2.5 million DALYs and 90,791 lives were lost attributable to oral, pharyngeal and oesophageal cancer. Estimates from another study indicate over 6 million DALYs and 258 006 lives lost from ischemic heart disease attributable to SLT.[27]Click or tap here to enter text.

Studies have shown that women may be more susceptible to the effects of tobacco use and its long-term ramifications.[28] Women who smoke have a greater risk of developing cervical cancer, lung cancer, osteoporosis and other diseases related to the reproductive system. Beyond the common health effects faced by men and women related to tobacco use, some specific conditions affect women such as female-specific cancers, coronary heart diseases linked with oral contraceptive usage, reproductive phases of menstruation, pregnancy, infertility and menopause being affected.[29]

5 Access to Healthcare Services

Most people are now aware that smoking has some negative effects as a result of ongoing awareness-raising efforts, but their levels of awareness vary, and they lack specific understanding about how gender influences the outcomes. In comparison to their male smoking counterparts, women

[25] LD Goyal and others 'Variations in the patterns of tobacco usage among Indian females—Findings from the global adult tobacco survey India' (2022) 22 *BMC Women's Health*.

[26] GA Mishra and others 'An overview of the tobacco problem in India' (2012) 33 *Indian Journal of Medicine and Paediatric Oncology* 139.

[27] K Siddiqi and others 'Global burden of disease due to smokeless tobacco consumption in adults: An updated analysis of data from 127 countries' (2020) 18 *BMC Medicine*.

[28] SD Rahmanian and others 'Tobacco use and cessation among women: Research and treatment-related issues' (2011) 20 *Journal of Women's Health* 349.

[29] Mackay & Amos (n 3).

frequently exhibit a higher risk of having cardiovascular, reproductive, and psychiatric illnesses, with a specific susceptibility to adverse pregnancy outcomes and malignancies of the breast and cervix.[30] Attempts and the success rate of quitting are also comparably low among females due to a variety of factors, including interactions with sex hormones, potential weight gain, perceived stress and depressive disorders associated with quitting.[31] In the UK, it was seen that women were more likely to use free services that were provided but the success rates are lower than men.[32] Theorists have analysed the role of gender, narrative of excess and will power in shaping the discourse around cessation. Portraying only 'excessive' tobacco use as an issue of moderation is normalised, similarly by putting the onus of quitting on individual willpower and masculinising the virtue of self-control, the industry has profited from such gendered conditioning.[33]

In addition to the negative impact of tobacco use on women's health, there are several critical issues that require immediate attention, including the financial burden, the difficulty in accessing cessation services, the gender and social stigma attached to tobacco use among women, industrial exploitation, wage disparities and the need for more robust and gender-inclusive policies. Due to the availability of products in wide price ranges, people from low economic backgrounds can afford to use tobacco as a daily recreational habit, spending a sizable percentage of their income on it and eventually incurring catastrophic health costs as a result.

The intention to quit the habit is very low, especially among individuals using SLT about 5% compared to 13% for smokers, and the success rate is likewise poor when compared to men; this may be attributed to inadequate awareness-raising efforts, as well as a reluctance on the part of health professionals to enquire about women's tobacco use history.[34] For individuals who are ready to quit, there are several factors that prevent

[30] Sharma & Khapre (n 23).

[31] AM Allen and others 'Women and smoking: The effect of gender on the epidemiology, health effects, and cessation of smoking' (2014) 1 *Current Addiction Reports* 53.

[32] A Amos and others 'Women and tobacco: A call for including gender in tobacco control research, policy and practice' (2012) 21 *Tobacco Control* 236.

[33] C White, JL Oliffee & JL Bottorff 'Tobacco and the invention of quitting: A history of gender, excess and will-power' (2013) 35 *Sociology of Health and Illness* 778.

[34] Mini & Thankappan (n 10).

them from using cessation services, including decision-making, family support, lack of resources and accessibility issues.

6 Gender and Tobacco

As indicated in the earlier section, the sex-disaggregated data reveal stark and consistent differences between men and women, boys and girls, in terms of the risk exposure (use of tobacco and exposure to second-hand smoke), the disease burden as well as access to healthcare and social support. Here, gender as a social construct is an important driver of these differences—related but distinct from biological sex—in terms of how society considers it appropriate for people from different sexes to exhibit certain behaviours and play certain roles in society.[35]

There is very limited research scholarship around the role of gender in tobacco use and much of this comes from Europe and the USA. In general, tobacco use, especially cigarette smoking, has been shown to be associated with the notions of masculinity implying authority, assertiveness and risk-taking. This makes boys and men more vulnerable wherein there remains some degree of social expectation and approval for smoking by men. In contrast, cigarette smoking by girls and women is often met by social disapproval. This, along with wider gender-based differences in resources and power, generally mean that women face a lot more barriers in accessing health and social support in quitting tobacco use and/or managing tobacco-related harms.

6.1 Gender in Marketing of Tobacco Products

The internal documents of large transnational tobacco corporations reveal that the industry recognised the role of gender in tobacco smoking long before public health researchers and advocates started talking about it. The industry employed gender-informed product variants and marketing campaigns to sustain and expand their markets among young

[35] S Hawkes, K Buse & S-Y Yoon 'Gender-responsive tobacco control: Evidence and options for policies and programmes: Report summary' (2018).

people including recruiting women smokers.[36,37] For example, the Phillip Morris & Co used a very popular 'Marlboro Man' campaign to change the perception of the Marlboro brand of filtered cigarettes in the United States.[38] This brand of cigarettes was initially marketed towards women, positioning it as feminine cigarette with a filter (as a response to emerging concerns about health harms of cigarettes) that was 'Mild as May'. Men were hesitant to use this brand even if they were open to use filtered cigarettes given this feminine perception of the brand. The 'Marlboro Man' campaign launched in mid 1950s, and later 'Marlboro Country' campaign made use of a cowboy character that was manly, rugged, independent and heroic to appeal to male smokers.[39] These campaigns were successful in boosting the sales of Marlboro cigarettes making it a popular brand among male smokers.

Similarly, in the latter half of the twentieth century, tobacco companies started targeting women (often young women) by optimising on the changing social norms in the United States incorporating women emancipation messaging into their advertising. These campaigns were aimed to popularise the supposed women brands of cigarettes. The Phillip Morris & Co advertised their Virginia Slim brand using a theme, 'you've come a long way, baby'.[40] RJ Reynolds, a rival of the Phillip Morris, launched a campaign for their Dakota brand appealing to women, with a theme 'Dakota, when smooth comes easy'.[41] Such campaigns targeting women dealt with themes revolving around slimness, glamour, liberation or independence for women.

Analysis of the industry strategies using gender-informed products and advertising suggests that these endeavours ended up reinforcing the conventional and often harmful gender stereotypes for men and women

[36] SE Hill & S Friel '"As long as it comes off as a cigarette ad, not a civil rights message": Gender, inequality and the commercial determinants of health' (2020) 17 *International Journal of Environmental Research and Public Health*.

[37] EM Barbeau, A Leavy-Sperounis & ED Balbach 'Smoking, social class, and gender: What can public health learn from the tobacco industry about disparities in smoking?' (2004) 13 *Tobacco Control* 115.

[38] Hill & Friel (n 36).

[39] Wikipedia 'Marlboro Man' https://en.wikipedia.org/wiki/Marlboro_Man (accessed 24 August 2023).

[40] Hill & Friel (n 36).

[41] Barbeau, Leavy-Sperounis & Balbach (n 37).

wherein men were supposed to be bold and risk-taking, while women were supposed to be slim, glamourous but vulnerable.[42] Interestingly, the idea of women emancipation and empowerment was co-opted by the tobacco industry in the United States in line with the growing liberation struggles and movements by women.[43] The companies were sure not to challenge the dominant social norms but to ride on that wave promoting their brands.[44] This notion is so well captured in an internal industry document written in 1969 wherein Hal Weinstein (a Vice President and Creative Director of an ad agency) shared information about building the Virginia Slim brand, and especially taking the campaign to African American neighbourhoods:

> Frankly we weren't sure, with our theme 'You've come a long way, Baby'—that we could run this advertising in Ebony, but why not? As long as it still comes off as a cigarette ad, not a civil rights message.[45]

In India, we see the cigarette industry playing a similar tune while targeting men. The Vazir Sultan Tobacco promoted its Charminar cigarette brand highlighting the ruggedness it brings and it being the only thing that satisfies a man.[46] Its advertisement campaigns featured men on horseback on rugged terrain (akin to the cowboys of America) competing fiercely to get a pack of Charminar cigarettes. Campaigns used taglines of 'It takes a Charminar to satisfy a man like you' and 'Give me a bike, Give me a highway, Give me my girl, And give me the taste of toasted tobacco'. The Godfrey Phillips India, apart from Marlboro variants, popularised cigarette brands like Cavanders, associating it with men's outdoor adventures with a tagline: 'The bold taste of confidence', and FourSquare

[42] Hill & Friel (n 36).

[43] As above.

[44] As above.

[45] H Weinstein 'Papers from the 690000 A.A.A.A. Region Conventions: How an agency builds a brand—The Virginia Slims story' American Association of Advertising Agencies (1970) https://www.industrydocuments.ucsf.edu/tobacco/docs/#id=jmnb0122 (accessed 17 January 2025).

[46] K Grewal 'Charminar—The 'rugged' cigarettes that promoted toxic masculinity' *ThePrint* 29 September 2019 https://theprint.in/feature/brandma/charminar-the-rugged-cigarettes-that-promoted-toxic-masculinity/298447/ (accessed 17 January 2025).

associating it with young man's appeal to young woman with a tagline: 'The man with the smooth edge'.

Interestingly, with time, advertisement campaigns have appeared wherein men are shown smoking certain cigarette brands and implying that these men enjoy happy relationships with their women partners or friends. It is as if there was a sort of an adaptation to the changing social norms wherein women were increasingly perceived as being partners (even if not equal) of their male counterparts rather than merely subservient to them, especially among urban and higher income strata. The advertisement campaigns also started portraying the use of cigarettes in a family setup. Some of these campaigns were also carefully crafted to draw an analogy between happy couples and the blend of tobacco and a filter in the context of normalising and popularising filtered cigarettes—a misleading response by the cigarette industry to the growing medical concerns around tobacco harm. The ITC's 'Made for each other' campaign for its Wills brand portraying a happy couple—often curated through best matching couple competitions—in various settings (taking a stroll at a beach; reading a Polish joke book; cuddling a dog; under an umbrella in the rain etc.) carried a line 'Filter and tobacco perfectly matched'.[47] The Godfrey Phillips promoted the Red and White brand with a happy couple—woman in red and man in white dress—with a tagline that loosely translates in English as 'a tasteful pair'. Unrelated to the filter in a cigarette, we came across a vintage advertisement of the Panama brand of cigarette produced by Golden Tobacco featuring a happy couple—a man with a cigarette in his hand lifting his smiling partner—with a tagline 'Yours … Forever'. This strategy of the tobacco industry served it well in making filtered cigarettes acceptable while reiterating societal stereotypes of a happy heterosexual couple.

The cigarette companies in India have attempted to target female smokers mainly through product innovations. Major manufacturers came out with slim cigarettes, cigarettes that are smooth, and that smell less! In 2013, the Godfrey Phillips launched their Stellar Slims series that according to the product development lead at the company offers 'full

[47] IA Dutt '40 years ago...and now: 'Made for each other'—A case of perfect insight' *Business Standard* 20 November 2014 https://www.business-standard.com/article/management/40-years-ago-and-now-made-for-each-other-a-case-of-perfect-insight-114111901337_1.html (accessed 17 January 2025).

satisfaction and low nicotine'.[48] ITC, a cigarette major in India, produces Sleek Line Slim cigarettes with a tag 'Honeydew Smooth'. In 2016, ITC came out with a 'low smell' variant within its popular Classic brand of cigarettes. One of the market analysts commented that 'It's a good marketing strategy. Smell has always been a concern, especially for the first-time cigarette smokers and women, considering our social structure'.[49] Apart from Indian manufacturers, a host of brands targeting women are available for purchase online in India including Mond Super Slim cigarettes in various fruit flavours produced by Gulbahar Tobacco (UAE), ESSE Super Slim Light cigarettes by Korea Tobacco & Ginseng Corporation, Marlboro and others.

When it comes to advertising, unlike in the United States, women are rarely the target of such campaigns and are not shown smoking cigarettes. There are however a couple of exceptions we found, especially in colonial India: an advertisement of the Gauhar be Baha brand of cigarette by Bukhsh Ellahie & Co featuring a popular Hindustani Classical singer, Gauhar Jaan, holding a lit cigarette while listening to music[50] and the only other advertisement of the Bombay Special Cigarettes featuring an urban elite woman holding a cigarette stick in one hand and a tin pack of cigarettes in another.[51]

While women routinely appear in cigarette advertisements that seem to target male smokers, they appear as subjects being appealed by or attracted to men smoking a particular brand of cigarette. Alternatively, they often appear to be approving or reaffirming what cigarettes bring to a man. So, we do not see advertising campaigns linking women smoking with themes of women empowerment and freedom like in the United States. In fact, cigarette smoking by women attracts a strong social

[48] 'Godfrey Philips launches slim cigarettes' *Business Standard* 26 February 2013 https://www.business-standard.com/article/companies/godfrey-philips-launches-slim-cigarettes-107020901104_1.html (accessed 17 January 2025).

[49] S Mitra 'ITC launches "low smell" cigarettes' *Mint* 11 April 2016 https://www.livemint.com/Companies/bLaQFhtQVdFe6eevBCcqaI/ITC-launches-low-smell-cigarettes.html (accessed 17 January 2025).

[50] PB Mukharji 'The first cigarette' (2018) https://web.sas.upenn.edu/mukharji/2018/08/09/bukhsh-ellahie-co/ (accessed 17 January 2025).

[51] S Bhura 'The world of vintage tobacco ads in India' *The Week* 26 December 2019 https://www.theweek.in/leisure/society/2019/12/24/Serendipity-Arts-Festival-The-smokescreen-of-vintage-tobacco-ads-in-India.html (accessed 17 January 2025).

disapproval in India. While the industry has avoided using women emancipation and liberation themes in its cigarette advertising in India—and we do discuss some of the possible reasons for this later in this chapter—movies, especially in recent times, have portrayed women smoking often symbolising their rebellion and aspirations.[52]

6.2 Critique of the Limited Available Research on Gender and Tobacco

It is important to bring in a provocative and substantive critique of much of the current research around gender and tobacco put forward by Qian Hui Tan.[53] While attempting to generate a narrative of gender and smoking from the cultural contexts of Asia, she argued that whatever limited research available by then around gender and smoking was largely Anglo-American centric and routinely used dualistic views/categories of gender (masculine-feminine) and tradition (modernity/western influence-tradition). She argued that out-of-context conceptualisation that often ignores bodily experiences of smokers in preference to research-led conceptual abstractions could misinterpret the role of gender in smoking in a particular society. She demonstrates this by showing how the symbolic use of cigarettes by women as 'torches of freedom', linking it with the modernity and women's struggle for liberation, does not explain/inform negative perceptions of women smokers in Asian society.[54] In fact, in line with her observations in some of the Asian countries, studies from India too suggest widespread negative perceptions of women smokers. Especially, smoking by women is perceived to reflect negatively on culture and character of women smokers while smoking by men is perceived to reflect neutrally or at times even positively on these very attributes.[55] Studies have also shown that women in Asian societies as well as in India under report tobacco use (smoking and smokeless forms)

[52] S Krishnan 'Cigarettes under my burkha, a clichéd symbol of empowerment?' *The Quint* 26 July 2017 https://www.thequint.com/entertainment/lipstick-under-my-burkha-cigarettes-women-liberation (accessed 17 January 2025).

[53] QH Tan 'Gender and tobacco in (globalizing) Asia—Exorcizing the ghosts of dualistic thought?' (2011) 5 *Sociology Compass* 1018.

[54] As above.

[55] UM Bhojani, MA Elias & DN 'Adolescents' perceptions about smokers in Karnataka, India' (2011) 11 *BMC Public Health*.

compared to men, especially in presence of a third person (apart from the interviewer) and social desirability seem to be a crucial factor explaining such underreporting by women tobacco users.[56,57]

She also argues that using gender as a binary construct that misses out on plural gender subjectivities and different kinds of masculinities ends up reinforcing often harmful conventional gender stereotypes, something that not only tobacco industry's gender-based marketing but at times even gender-based tobacco control messaging/initiatives have resulted in.[58] In an earlier section, we demonstrated, through tobacco industry product and advertising interventions, how the tobacco industry indeed ended up reinforcing conventional stereotypes of genders in India.

Another important aspect of the critique of the research examining the role of gender in smoking by Qian Hui Tan is that gender is often examined in isolation without understanding how it intersects with other social attributes such as class, ethnicity, etc.[59] We very much relate with her critique and find very little work that explores such intersectionality in our context while there are clear signs implying the need to study such intersections. For example, the data on prevalence of various types of tobacco products indicate a strong relation between income (or household consumption) and the type of tobacco products consumed. Similarly, there is a social perception reflected in popular media/literature and instrumentalised by the cigarette industry in their advertising campaigns associating bidi smoking with backwardness and cigarette smoking as signifying upward movement in a social and economic class. An art historian, in context of the vintage advertisements of cigarettes opined:

> In India, the urbane and elite cigarette smokers stood apart and distanced themselves from birri-smoking villagers. As cigarettes became the insignia of the urban elite and birris *(bidis)* a sign of backwardness, smoking habits

[56] KH Jung-Choi, YH Khang & HJ Cho 'Hidden female smokers in Asia: a comparison of self-reported with cotinine-verified smoking prevalence rates in representative national data from an Asian population' (2012) 21 *Tobacco Control* 536.

[57] PK Singh and others 'Social desirability and under-reporting of smokeless tobacco use among reproductive age women: Evidence from National Family Health Survey' (2022) 19 *SSM Population Health*.

[58] Tan (n 53).

[59] As above.

> became markers of social distinctions and thereby instruments of power of the elite over illiterate farmers and workers.[60]

It is interesting to note that the cigarette industry has recognised the importance of considering various social attributes of smokers in their market segmentation research for several years.[61] For example, in an internal document of 1989, a typical profile of a smoker using the Dakota brand (meant to be marketed to young women) of RJ Reynolds was described as

> an 18-24 year old female who ... primarily exhibits traditionally 'masculine' character traits ... is fairly downscale with a high school education or less and generally has an unskilled job ... she is professionally not ambitious.[62,63]

How a specific tobacco product is perceived may also shape the role gender plays in tobacco use. For example, in India, while smoking cigarettes by urban elite women remains taboo, smoking of bidis by rural women is not that looked down upon. Hence, it is indeed important to explore how gender intersects with other social attributes and product preferences to shape tobacco use.

6.3 *Gender Within a Neoliberal Economic Order*

Beyond the product development and advertisement/marketing campaigns, large businesses shape gender-based roles within the tobacco sector through structural factors and corporate strategies/environments that are beyond marketing. Hill and Friel[64] reviewed literature mapping association between the commercial determinants of health and gender including gender inequalities using the case of harmful commodity industries (tobacco and alcohol). They highlight how the neoliberal

[60] Bhura (n 51).

[61] Barbeau, Leavy-Sperounis & Balbach (n 37).

[62] As above.

[63] Truth Tobacco Industry Documents 'PROJECT VF: Recommended next steps' (1989) https://www.industrydocuments.ucsf.edu/tobacco/docs/#id=zgyl0092 (accessed 17 January 2025).

[64] Hill & Friel (n 36).

economic order itself privileges market-based economically productive roles while devaluing non-market-based roles that often make the core of women's work in many societies—also a case in India—such as domestic work, managing a household, and social and care work at home. This reflects in underemployment of women within the workforce and typically overrepresentation of women within informal and underpaid work. This is especially relevant in India given India is among the major tobacco producers globally. Women and children make up much of the workforce in the manual bidi industry where they roll bidis within homes. It remains precarious work with no social security and a host of occupational hazards. The issues of inadequate and unfair wages as well as exploitation by middlemen contractors are well documented.[65,66] The related issue is of underrepresentation of women within decision-making structures, be it company boardrooms, government offices/committees, and political leadership implying that issues related to women often fail to garner priority and the understanding they deserve. In this line, we discuss underrepresentation of women within public health research and leadership later in this chapter.

6.4 Women in Tobacco Control

The complex picture of gender and tobacco use, harm and access to care has been described in the previous sections of this chapter. The situation in terms of gender and tobacco control is equally complex and understudied and applied in several settings. The lack of women in powerful decision-making spaces, research and practice related to tobacco control and overall health is stark. A look at the list of health ministers at the national level in India reveals that four of the 42 individuals were women, and only one among them occupied the office of the minister for a very short duration of 54 days.[67] Only two of the 13 Director Generals of the Indian Council of Medical Research, the apex body on biomedical

[65] M Arora and others 'The Indian bidi industry: Trends in employment and wage differentials' (2020) 8 *Frontiers Public Health.*

[66] 'Bidi worker: Hard work but low wage' *India Today* 22 December 2014 https://www.indiatoday.in/magazine/economy/story/19780415-bidi-worker-hard-work-but-low-wage-822916-2014-12-22 (accessed 17 January 2025).

[67] Wikipedia 'Ministry of Health and Family Welfare' https://en.wikipedia.org/wiki/Ministry_of_Health_and_Family_Welfare (accessed 28 August 2023).

research in India, were women scholars.[68] Such underrepresentation of women in decision-making spaces related to health research and policy-making undermine their perspectives shaping health research agenda and decisions.

A quick scan of research outputs on PubMed with the keywords of 'tobacco control' and 'India' for the past year (August 2022–2023) provides 61 relevant citations. Of these 32 had women as first author and 22 women were the last authors. In 15 citations, women were both the first and last authors. While there is a fair representation of women researching and publishing about tobacco control in India, there is a need for deepening our understanding of the topic of gender and its ramifications in tobacco control. Some countries have attempted targeted gender-specific programmes; for example Women Against Tobacco Task-force in Hong Kong mobilised women's groups in relation to tobacco cessation programmes.[69] Similarly there are some international networks that attempt to focus on the issue of tobacco use among women and girls such as INWAT (International Network of Women Against Tobacco) that collates evidence and brings together individuals interested in working on the issue.[70]

7 Policy/Regulations

In 2022, more than 71% of the global population or about 5.6 billion people have been covered by at least one of the MPOWER (Monitor tobacco use and prevention policies; Protect people from tobacco smoke; Offer help to quit tobacco use; Warn about the dangers of tobacco; Enforce bans on tobacco advertising, promotion and sponsorship; and Raise taxes on tobacco) measures.[71]

[68] Indian Council of Medical Research 'Former Director Generals' https://www.icmr.gov.in/former-director-generals (accessed 28 August 2023).

[69] G Fernando 'Rethinking tobacco control: The need for gender-responsiveness in tobacco control measures' *UNU IIGH* 31 May 2022 https://iigh.unu.edu/news/news/rethinking-tobacco-control-the-need-for-gender-responsiveness-in-tobacco-control-measures.html (accessed 29 August 2023).

[70] International Network of Women against Tobacco https://inwat.org/about/ (accessed 29 August 2023).

[71] WHO (n 18).

India was one of the early signatories in 2004 to the global public health treaty on tobacco control, the WHO Framework Convention on Tobacco Control (FCTC). The Indian Government enacted the Cigarettes and Other Tobacco Products Act in 2003, which comprehensively encompasses issues related to commerce, production, supply, distribution, and advertisement. Further, in 2007–2008, the National Tobacco Control Programme (NTCP) was launched to structure the tobacco control efforts. The regulatory actions taken by the Government of India are yielding results, as is evident from Global Adult Tobacco Survey-2 (GATS-2, 2016–17) reports; the prevalence has fallen significantly from 34.6% (GATS-1, 2009–10) to 28.6%.[72] Despite that, India remains as the second-highest tobacco product manufacturer and consumer. Despite being a proven measure for tobacco control, the taxation on tobacco products in India has been complex and has evolved along with the national taxation policies. The tax revenue from tobacco products is only 13% of associated health expenditure, around INR1 773.4 billion for persons above 35 years of age, as per the WHO study conducted in 2017.[73]

To date, tobacco control initiatives have primarily been gender-blind and have focused on specific products, such as smoked forms. The voids may be due to the failure in addressing intersectionality in terms of gender, culture, geography, socio-economic circumstances, and also the type of product being used. There are significant differences between the problems experienced by each gender, which are linked to a number of other factors, with women being the most disadvantaged and marginalised group. Due to the disorganised nature of their work, they are not very aware of the policies and legislation currently in place to protect their rights. Unlike lower cadres of workers, the representation of women in decision-making roles and political engagement is minimal in our setting. There is an urgent need to address this so that it can help to include need-based strategies for addressing the gendered effects of tobacco like setting up women-friendly cessation services in accessible areas, alternate livelihood possibilities and financial support for the same. By promoting a

[72] Nayak and others (n 15).

[73] RM John and others 'Economic costs of diseases and deaths attributable to tobacco use in India, 2017-2018' (2021) 23 *Nicotine & Tobacco Research* 294.

participatory approach that involves the target population in need assessment, supporting female researchers in evidence generation, and ensuring representation of women in advocacy planning and policy-making roles can help to overcome the disparities, improve outcomes, and let it be the real torch of freedom and women empowerment.

Tobacco manufacturing companies constantly come up with creative market-securing strategies like 'surrogate marketing' to get around the initiatives for tobacco control from the government. Promotion through social media and other online platforms offers a more extensive and effective way to reach targeted populations, especially the adolescents. In order to address this issue, a revised set of OTT guidelines have been released by Union Health Ministry for regulation of the depiction of Tobacco Products through online platforms and early warning systems—like 'Tobacco Enforcement and Reporting Movement (TERM)' by Vital strategies, a global health organisation—are also in place to report the same.[74] As per COTPA guidelines, there is a permanent ban for a set of harmful tobacco products in India. However, products such as Gutkha and other food items containing tobacco were not covered by this and are instead prohibited as per the Food Safety and Standards (Prohibition and Restrictions on Sales) Regulations 2001, whereas the ban was not successful as the companies introduced two packet forms (all non-tobacco products in one packet with tobacco in a separate packet) that did not fall under the prohibited category. Exploitation of grassroot-level workers is another significant issue specific to the tobacco industry. The majority of them are unorganised as well as unregistered workers who are either self-employed or engaged through contracts with small manufacturing units. Despite the fact that 80% of them are women, there is a significant wage gap between men and women, as seen by the lower average salaries earned by women.[75] In addition to the financial hardship, they also have to deal with major health consequences, including respiratory illnesses such as lung cancer, and issues related to their working posture, but the existing situation makes it difficult for them to switch to alternative options for their livelihood.

[74] Nandita Murukutla and others 'The Tobacco Enforcement Reporting Movement (TERM): An early warning system to track digital tobacco marketing' https://blogs.bmj.com/tc/2022/03/08/the-tobacco-enforcement-reporting-movement-term-an-early-warning-system-to-track-digital-tobacco-marketing/ (accessed 13 July 2023).

[75] Arora and others (n 65).

India is one of the signatories to the Convention on the Elimination of All Forms of Discrimination Against Women (CEDAW) which was signed on 30 July 1980 and ratified on 9 July 1983. CEDAW requires countries to eliminate discrimination against women in all areas and promote equal rights for men and women. Article 12 of the Convention specifically addresses health of girls, adolescents and women suggesting that state parties shall 'place gender perspective at the centre of all policies and programmes' affecting health throughout the lifespan. Several national schemes have been implemented for empowerment of women and improving gender equality in contemporary times in India, such as the Beti Bachao Beti Padhao Scheme (BBBP) for adolescent girls—a multi-ministerial initiative to address low child sex ratio and crimes against girls/women for overall empowerment of girls and women in Indian society; Swachh Bharat, Swachh Vidyalaya—a mission for clean India and clean schools to enhance water, sanitation and hygiene across every school in India; as well as the recent National Education Policy (2020), prioritising gender equity and equitable access to quality education.[76] Despite these progressive policy measures the actual realisation of equal rights for women is yet to be achieved. Women form only 27.4% of the workforce, only 14.39% of seats in our lower hour of Lok Sabha (2019–2024) and 8.8% in the upper house Rajya Sabha (2020) displaying a low representation of women in general and more so in law-making positions.[77]

8 Way Forward

Having outlined various ways in which gender is linked to tobacco, we briefly highlight directions in which we need more actions for gender-inclusive and gender-sensitive tobacco control. We saw that at a structural level, the neoliberal economic order within which businesses function promotes gender inequities keeping women underemployed, underpaid, and underrepresented in decision-making avenues. While there have been

[76] Press Information Bureau 'Measures for gender equality and empowerment of women' (2021) https://pib.gov.in/PressReleseDetailm.aspx?PRID=1779252 (accessed 15 January 2024).

[77] 'Womens rights in India' (2021) https://nhrc.nic.in/sites/default/files/Women%E2%80%99s%20Rights%20in%20India%20complete_compressed.pdf (accessed 25 January 2024).

voices that fundamentally question such an economic system and seek a change, there are also attempts within this overall system to bring more accountability for business, especially for how they impact people and the environment.

The United Nations Guiding Principles on Business and Human Rights, through the three-pillar framework—protect, respect and remedy—define the responsibilities of the state and of businesses in protecting human rights and providing access to effective remediation for business-related human rights abuses.[78] Several governments are operationalising such a framework at national level. In India, it took the form of National Guidelines on Responsible Business Conduct.[79] Under these frameworks, businesses are mandated to make disclosures on their governance practices and how they affect people and the environment. More recently, the regulator in India (Securities and Exchange Board of India) mandated the top 1 000 companies (as per market capitalisation) to file the Business Responsibility and Sustainability Reports in a prescribed format.[80] This format demands companies to make disclosures around environmental, social and governance practices and risks including that for the supply chains. This mechanism has a promise to at least get data and enhance the wellbeing of workers including women workers within tobacco supply chains and factories. However, for now, the tobacco businesses that are often large conglomerates avoid reporting on tobacco businesses. There have been demands to create sector-specific disclosures and treat businesses like tobacco differently than other usual businesses in that tobacco businesses shall not be allowed to advertise themselves as 'responsible' businesses or businesses with high ESG ratings.[81]

Similarly, while tobacco advertisements have been prohibited in India, the industry has found various ways to still promote tobacco products using surrogate products, sponsorships of events, publicity of their

[78] UN 'Guiding principles on business and human rights: Implementing the United Nations "protect, respect and remedy" framework' (2011).

[79] Government of India, Ministry of Corporate Affairs 'National guidelines on responsible business conduct' (2019).

[80] SEBI 'Business responsibility and sustainability reporting by listed entities' (2021) https://www.sebi.gov.in/legal/circulars/may-2021/business-responsibility-and-sustainability-reporting-by-listed-entities_50096.html (accessed 29 August 2023).

[81] Institute of Public Health 'Position paper on Environmental, Social and Governance (ESG) reporting by tobacco companies in India' (2023).

so-called corporate social responsibility activities, portrayal of tobacco through unregulated OTT platforms and through the sheer violations of the prevailing regulations. We need stringent regulations that prevent tobacco advertising, sponsorship and promotion across media/platforms that are well enforced.

As discussed earlier, most policies and programmes aimed at reducing tobacco use are currently gender-blind. This problem is further compounded by very limited research and practically a lack of serious social science information about the gender and tobacco use linkage in India. We need to urgently invest resources in researching how gender and its intersections with other social determinants of health (caste, class, location, religion, work, ethnicity, etc.) shape tobacco use, the resultant burden and access to health and social care for men/boys and women/girls. Such research is crucial to inform gender-sensitive tobacco control policies and programmes. The existing initiatives aimed at providing alternative safe and viable livelihoods to tobacco sector workers, including women beedi workers, need to be strengthened. Initiatives aimed at enhancing gender equity including programmes aimed at health of women and children (e.g., Beti Bachao Beti Padhao movement, maternal and child health initiatives) shall integrate tobacco control-related awareness and support. Unlike the gender-targeted industry campaigns, the inclusion of gender-based messaging and support shall be enabling people and their positive image rather than reinforcing the conventional gender stereotypes.

Acknowledgements We acknowledge Ahalya P Gopi for her research assistance in searching for and sourcing relevant literature and helping us with referencing of the manuscript. We also thank Arushi Thapar of the Institute of Public Health Bengaluru for her help with referencing this manuscript.

Contribution Statement PH drafted sections about background and women in tobacco control apart from ensuring coordination across authors and research assistant. UB drafted a section on gender and tobacco. Both, PH and UB, jointly drafted the way forward section. Both authors read, reviewed, edited and agreed on the final manuscript.

Funding Statement We did not receive any specific funding for this work. Upendra Bhojani and Ahalya P Gopi were supported for their time through the DBT/Wellcome Trust India Alliance fellowships awarded to Upendra

Bhojani (IA/CPHI/17/1/503346; IA/CPHS/22/1/506533). Pragati Hebbar was supported through the DBT/Wellcome Trust India Alliance fellowships awarded to her (IA/CPHE/17/1/503338; IA/CPHI/22/1/506537).

Bibliography

Allen, AM and others 'Women and smoking: The effect of gender on the epidemiology, health effects, and cessation of smoking' (2014) 1 *Current Addiction Reports* 53

Amos, A and others 'Women and tobacco: A call for including gender in tobacco control research, policy and practice' (2012) 21 *Tobacco Control* 236

Arora, M and others 'The Indian bidi industry: Trends in employment and wage differentials' (2020) 8 *Frontiers Public Health*

Barbeau, EM, Leavy-Sperounis, A & Balbach, ED 'Smoking, social class, and gender: What can public health learn from the tobacco industry about disparities in smoking?' (2004) 13 *Tobacco Control* 115

Bhojani, UM and others 'Adolescents' perceptions about smokers in Karnataka, India' (2011) 11 *BMC Public Health*

Bhura, S 'The world of vintage tobacco ads in India' *The Week* 26 December https://www.theweek.in/leisure/society/2019/12/24/Serendipity-Arts-Festival-The-smokescreen-of-vintage-tobacco-ads-in-India.html (accessed 17 January 2025)

'Bidi worker: Hard work but low wage' *India Today* 22 December 2014 https://www.indiatoday.in/magazine/economy/story/19780415-bidi-worker-hard-work-but-low-wage-822916-2014-12-22 (accessed 17 January 2025)

Chhabra, A; Hussain, S & Rashid, S 'Recent trends of tobacco use in India' (2021) 29 *Journal of Public Health* 27

Dutt, IA '40 Years Ago...and now: "Made for each other"- A case of perfect insight' *Business Standard* 20 November 2014 https://www.business-standard.com/article/management/40-years-ago-and-now-made-for-each-other-a-case-of-perfect-insight-114111901337_1.html (accessed 17 January 2025)

Fernando, G 'Rethinking tobacco control: The need for gender-responsiveness in tobacco control measures' *UNU IIGH* 31 May 2022 https://iigh.unu.edu/news/news/rethinking-tobacco-control-the-need-for-gender-responsiveness-in-tobacco-control-measures.html (accessed 29 August 2023)

'Godfrey Philips launches slim cigarettes' *Business Standard* 26 February 2013 https://www.business-standard.com/article/companies/godfrey-philips-launches-slim-cigarettes-107020901104_1.html (accessed 17 January 2025)

Goel, S and others 'Smoking trends among women in India: Analysis of nationally representative surveys (1993–2009)' (2014) 3 *South Asian Journal of Cancer* 200

Government of India, Ministry of Corporate Affairs 'National Guidelines on Responsible Business Conduct' (2019)

Goyal, LD and others 'Variations in the patterns of tobacco usage among Indian females – Findings from the global adult tobacco survey India' (2022) 22 *BMC Women's Health*

Grewal, K 'Charminar – The "rugged" cigarettes that promoted toxic masculinity' *ThePrint* 29 September 2019 https://theprint.in/feature/brandma/charminar-the-rugged-cigarettes-that-promoted-toxic-masculinity/298447/ (accessed 17 January 2025)

Hawkes, S; Buse, K & Yoon, S-Y 'Gender-responsive tobacco control: Evidence and options for policies and programmes report summary' (2018)

Hill, SE & Friel, S '"As long as it comes off as a cigarette ad, not a civil rights message": Gender, inequality and the commercial determinants of health' (2020) 17 *International Journal of Environmental Research and Public Health* https://apps.who.int/iris/bitstream/handle/10665/204209/Fact_Sheet_TFI_2014_EN_15320.pdf?sequence=1 (accessed 24 August 2024)

Indian Council of Medical Research 'Former Director Generals' https://www.icmr.gov.in/former-director-generals (accessed 28 August 2023)

Institute of Public Health 'Position paper on Environmental, Social and Governance (ESG) reporting by tobacco companies in India' (2023)

International Network of Women against Tobacco https://inwat.org/about/ (accessed 29 August 2023)

John, RM and others 'Economic costs of diseases and deaths attributable to tobacco use in India, 2017–2018' (2021) 23 *Nicotine & Tobacco Research* 294

Jung-Choi, KH, Khang, YH & Cho, HJ 'Hidden female smokers in Asia: A comparison of self-reported with cotinine-verified smoking prevalence rates in representative national data from an Asian population' (2012) 21 *Tobacco Control* 536

Krishnan, S 'Cigarettes under my burkha, a clichéd symbol of empowerment?' *The Quint* 26 July 2017 https://www.thequint.com/entertainment/lipstick-under-my-burkha-cigarettes-women-liberation (accessed 17 January 2025)

Mackay, J & Amos, A 'Women and tobacco' (2003) 8 *Respirology* 123

Mini, GK & Thankappan, KR 'Switching to smokeless tobacco, the most common smoking cessation method: Results from the Global Adult Tobacco Survey, India' (2016) 136 *Public Health* 172

Mishra, GA and others 'An overview of the tobacco problem in India' (2012) 33 *Indian Journal of Medicine and Paediatric Oncology* 139

Mitra, S 'ITC launches "low smell" cigarettes' *Mint* 11 April 2016 https://www.livemint.com/Companies/bLaQFhtQVdFe6eevBCcqaI/ITC-launches-low-smell-cigarettes.html (accessed 17 January 2025)

Mohan, P; Lando, HA & Panneer, S 'Assessment of tobacco consumption and control in India' (2018) 9 *Indian Journal of Clinical Medicine* https://doi.org/10.1177/1179916118759289.

Morrow, M & Barraclough, S 'Tobacco control and gender in Southeast Asia. Part I: Malaysia and the Philippines' (2003) 18 *Health Promotion International* 255

Murray, C and others 'Global burden of 87 risk factors in 204 countries and territories, 1990–2019: A systematic analysis for the Global Burden of Disease Study 2019' (2020) 396 *Lancet*

Nayak, G and others 'Gendered pattern and predictors of tobacco use in India: Evidence from the second round of global adult tobacco survey' (2023) 48 *Indian Journal of Community Medicine* 241

Press Information Bureau 'Measures for gender equality and empowerment of women' https://pib.gov.in/PressReleseDetailm.aspx?PRID=1779252 (accessed 15 January 2024)

Rahmanian, SD and others 'Tobacco use and cessation among women: Research and treatment-related issues' (2011) 20 *Journal of Women's Health* 349

Samet, JM & Yoon, SY 'Gender, women, and the tobacco epidemic' (2010) 249

SEBI 'Business responsibility and sustainability reporting by listed entities' https://www.sebi.gov.in/legal/circulars/may-2021/business-responsibility-and-sustainability-reporting-by-listed-entities_50096.html (accessed 29 August 2023)

Sharma, N and others 'Socio-economic status differences in changing affordability of tobacco products from 2011–2012 to 2018–2019 in India' (2023) 25 *Nicotine & Tobacco Research* 709

Sharma, T & Khapre, M 'Exposure of second hand smoke in women and children: A narrative review' (2021) 10 *Journal of Family Medicine and Primary Care* 1804

Siddiqi, K and others 'Global burden of disease due to smokeless tobacco consumption in adults: An updated analysis of data from 127 countries' (2020) 18 *BMC Medicine*

Singh, A & Ladusingh, L 'Prevalence and determinants of tobacco use in India: Evidence from recent global adult tobacco survey data' (2014) 9 *PLoS One* e114073.

Singh, PK and others 'Social desirability and under-reporting of smokeless tobacco use among reproductive age women: Evidence from National Family Health Survey' (2022) 19 *SSM Population Health*

Sinha, DN and others 'Smokeless tobacco use: A meta-analysis of risk and attributable mortality estimates for India' (2014) 51 *Indian Journal of Cancer*

Tan, QH 'Gender and tobacco in (globalizing) Asia – Exorcizing the ghosts of dualistic thought?' (2011) 5(12) *Sociology Compass*

Mukharji, PB 'The first cigarette' (2018) https://web.sas.upenn.edu/mukharji/2018/08/09/bukhsh-ellahie-co/ (accessed 17 January 2025)

Tobacco Atlas 'Worldwide smoking deaths per year' (2022) https://tobaccoatlas.org/challenges/deaths/ (accessed 24 August 2023)

Tobacco Control 'The Tobacco Enforcement Reporting Movement (TERM): An early warning system to track digital tobacco marketing' (2022) https://blogs.bmj.com/tc/2022/03/08/the-tobacco-enforcement-reporting-movement-term-an-early-warning-system-to-track-digital-tobacco-marketing/ (accessed 13 July 2023)

Tobacconomics 'The importance of tobacco control for women in low- and middle-income countries' (2022) https://tobacconomics.org/blog/the-importance-of-tobacco-control-for-women-in-low-and-middle-income-countries/ (accessed 24 August 2023)

'Tobacco use among women' 2011 www.cdc.gov/tobacco/global/gats/countries/wpr/fact_sheets/ (accessed 24 August 2023)

Truth Tobacco Industry Documents 'Project VF: recommended next steps' (1989) https://www.industrydocuments.ucsf.edu/tobacco/docs/#id=zgyl0092 (accessed 17 January 2025)

Weinstein, H 'Papers from the 690000 A.A.A.A. Region Conventions: How an agency builds a brand – The Virginia Slims story' American Association of Advertising Agencies (1970) https://www.industrydocuments.ucsf.edu/tobacco/docs/#id=jmnb0122 (accessed 17 January 2025)

White, C; Oliffee, JL & Bottorff, JL 'Tobacco and the invention of quitting: Aa history of gender, excess and will-power' (2013) 35 *Sociology of Health and Illness* 778

WHO 'Global adult tobacco survey (GATS 2) India report 2016–17' (2017)

WHO fact sheet 'Tobacco' (2023) https://www.who.int/news-room/fact-sheets/detail/tobacco (accessed 20 June 2023)

WHO fact sheet 'Women and tobacco use' (2014)

'WHO report on the global tobacco epidemic: Protect people from tobacco smoke' (2023)

Wikipedia 'Marlboro Man' https://en.wikipedia.org/wiki/Marlboro_Man (accessed 24 August 2023)

Wikipedia 'Ministry of Health and Family Welfare' https://en.wikipedia.org/wiki/Ministry_of_Health_and_Family_Welfare (accessed 28 August 2023)

'Womens rights in India' (2021) https://nhrc.nic.in/sites/default/files/Women%E2%80%99s%20Rights%20in%20India%20complete_compressed.pdf (accessed 25 January 2024)

CHAPTER 8

Child Marriage in the United States: A Human Rights and Feminist Perspective

Susan Weaver and Satang Nabaneh

1 Introduction

Nearly 300,000 minors, under age 18, were legally married in the U.S. between 2000 and 2018.[1]

[1] Unchained At Last 'United States' child marriage problem: Study findings' (2021) https://www.unchainedatlast.org/wp-content/uploads/2021/08/Study-PDF-FINAL-1.pdf (accessed 20 July 2023). See also F Reiss 'Child marriage in the United States: Prevalence and implications' (2021) 69 *Journal of Adolescent Health* S8-S10.

S. Weaver (✉)
Department of Political Science, University of Dayton, Dayton, USA
e-mail: susanweaver.smw@gmail.com

S. Nabaneh
University of Dayton Human Rights Centre, Dayton, USA

Extraordinary Lecturer, Centre for Human Rights, Faculty of Law, University of Pretoria, Pretoria, South Africa

E. Durojaye et al. (eds.), *Harmful Practices and Human Rights: An International Perspective*, Human Rights Interventions,
https://doi.org/10.1007/978-3-031-90333-5_8

Child marriage is a fundamental human rights violation and a harmful practice affecting millions of young girls worldwide, including in the United States (US).[2] According to the United Nations (UN), '[c]hild marriage is any marriage where at least one of the parties is under 18 years of age' and is considered to be a form of forced marriage as often, 'one and/or both parties have not expressed full, free and informed consent' to the union.[3] In 2015, the international community pledged to end child marriage by 2030 under the UN Sustainable Development Goal 5.3,[4] including the US 'along with 193 other countries in a broader mission to achieve gender equality'.[5]

Child marriage has been vehemently condemned by the international community, as it works with the UN to actively work to limit its occurrence worldwide.[6] The global community has articulated a need to address and curtail the practice of child marriage through a number of international human rights instruments. The Universal Declaration of Human Rights (UDHR) adopted in 1948 is a UN General Assembly Resolution, and while not a binding treaty, it has earned the status of customary international law and has served as a basis for subsequent human rights treaties.[7] Articles 16(1) and 16(2) of the Convention on the Elimination of All Forms of Discrimination Against Women (CEDAW)

[2] UNICEF 'Child marriage' https://data.unicef.org/topic/child-protection/child-marriage/ (accessed 20 July 2023).

[3] Office of the United Nations High Commissioner for Human Rights (nd) 'Child and forced marriage, including in humanitarian settings' https://www.ohchr.org/en/women/child-and-forced-marriage-including-humanitarian-settings (accessed 19 January 2025)).

[4] UN Department of Economic and Social Affairs: Sustainable Development 'Goals 5: Achieve gender equality and empower all women and girls—Target 5.3 Eliminate all harmful practices, such as child, early and forced marriage and female genital mutilation' https://sdgs.un.org/goals/goal5#targets_and_indicators (accessed 19 January 2025).

[5] A Jiang & JE Lansford 'State-level legal and sociodemographic correlates of child marriage rates in the United States' (2023) 145 *Children and Youth Services Review* 1. See SDG 'Member states' https://sustainabledevelopment.un.org/memberstates.html (accessed 19 January 2025).

[6] AM Hamilton and others 'Child marriage report: 2022 Report on child marriage in the United States: A national overview of child marriage data and law' (Child USA 2023).

[7] E Warner 'Behind the wedding veil: Child marriage as a form of trafficking in girls' (2004) 12 *Journal of Gender, Social Policy & The Law* 233.

lay out the equal rights to marriage for men and women and that 'marriage shall be entered into only with the free and full consent of the intending parties'.[8]

The UN Convention on Consent to Marriage, Minimum Age for Marriage and Registration of Marriages (Marriage Convention), adopted in 1962, requires member countries to establish a minimum age for marriage. Warner notes that the Marriage Convention was designed to specifically guarantee that 'marriages are the consensual act of knowledgeable adults or near-adults, and in particular to eliminate "child marriages and the betrothal of young girls before the age of puberty"'.[9] Article 1.1 of the Marriage Convention stipulates that marriage must be legally entered into with both parties' free and full consent in the presence of law authorities. Article 2 requires states parties to legislate a minimum age for marriage via domestic policy without establishing or articulating a minimum age specifically.[10]

The Convention on the Elimination of All Forms of Discrimination Against Women (CEDAW) reiterates this requirement, declaring that the marriage of children 'shall have no legal effect'.[11] Article 16(1) requires equal rights to marriage for both men and women, the right to choose a spouse freely, and the right to enter into marriage only with free and full consent. Article 16(2) explicitly states the betrothal and marriage of a child shall have no legal effect, requiring states parties to specify a minimum age for marriage.[12]

In 1990, with the Convention on the Rights of the Child (CRC), the UN defined a child as any person younger than 18, and 'this definition has been adopted to establish quantifiable targets for international development, including child marriage'.[13] However, Warner brings to light the many loopholes present in this provision as the definition of achieving

[8] UN General Assembly, Convention on the Elimination of All Forms of Discrimination Against Women, United Nations, Treaty Series, vol 1249, p 13, 18 December 1979 As above.

[9] Warner (n 7) 249.

[10] As above.

[11] A. Koski & J Heymann 'Child marriage in the United States: How common is the practice, and which children are at greatest risk?' (2018) 50 *Perspectives on Sexual and Reproductive Health* 59.

[12] Warner (n 7).

[13] As above.

'majority' is left to be interpreted by states parties and domestic law, which further complicates, rather than remedies, the issue of setting a minimum age for marriage. A series of provisions apply to the issue of child marriage as they directly address issues known to be consequences of child marriage. Article 2 prohibits discrimination against children, including on the basis of sex. Article 3 stresses that all actions on behalf of children must be in their best interest, making the needs of the child a primary consideration, with protection and care for their wellbeing a priority. Warner provides:

> [A]ll children shall have the right to protection from all forms of physical or mental violence, injury, abuse, maltreatment or exploitation; the right to health; the right to education; the right to protection from abduction, sale or trafficking; the right to rest and leisure, the right to protection from economic exploitation and the right to protection from all forms of exploitation prejudicial to the child's welfare.[14]

Child marriage, as a harmful practice, violates these human rights outlined specifically for children around the globe. Warner critiques the instrumentality of the CRC, '[g]iven all these shortcomings and ambiguities, one cannot look to the CRC as providing a strong framework for prohibiting child marriage, which is unfortunate'.[15]

The General Assembly has adopted numerous resolutions on child marriage.[16] It has acknowledged the necessity of supporting girls and women who have experienced child, early, and forced marriage, along with their children. The Assembly emphasised the importance of eliminating structural barriers that hinder their access to services tailored to their specific needs. The SDGs also call for the elimination of child marriage before the year 2030, though this progress is considered stalled,

[14] Warner (n 7) 252.

[15] Warner (n 7) 253.

[16] See for example, General Assembly Resolutions 74/133 on the rights of the child, 74/134 on the girl child, 74/235 on women in development and 74/126 on improvement of the situation of women and girls in rural areas; and Human Rights Council Resolutions 38/1 and 41/6 on elimination of all forms of discrimination against women and girls; 39/10 on preventable maternal mortality and morbidity and human rights in humanitarian settings; 40/14 on rights of the child: empowering children with disabilities for the enjoyment of their human rights, including through inclusive education; and 41/8 on consequences of child, early and forced marriage.

it is measured by estimating the proportion of women aged 20–24 who were married before age 18.[17]

It is important to note that the US has signed the Marriage Convention, CEDAW and the CRC but has not ratified any of them. Therefore, it is not bound by any of the existing international laws on child marriage. International Conventions rely on states parties to 'enact domestic legislation and adopt other measures to achieve the desired objectives' said parties have promised to address and pursue.[18]

The US State Department has spoken out regularly about addressing child marriage in its foreign policy priorities. In 2016, the

> US State Department's blueprint to empower adolescent girls globally listed reducing child, early, and forced marriage as a key goal, declaring it a clear abuse of human rights that has devastating repercussions on girls' lives, effectively ending their childhoods.[19]

Child marriage is a global concern impacting both human rights and gender equality. Child marriage is recognised globally as a harmful practice that is rooted in gender inequality. The practice flourishes under patriarchal societal structures perpetuating 'the idea that girls are of less value, which leads to their systemic neglect in economic, political, social, legal and educational realms'.[20] Asking where women are and are not in the landscape of marriage in the US is asking feminist questions. The investigation alone rests on the premise that the lives and experiences of young women and marriage need to be taken seriously. In taking them seriously this chapter systematically explores the situation of legal child marriage in the US, the barriers to its prevention, and the ongoing efforts

[17] As above.

[18] Warner (n 7) 247.

[19] F Reiss 'Why can 12-year-olds still get married in the United States?' *The Washington Post* 10 February 2017 https://www.washingtonpost.com/posteverything/wp/2017/02/10/why-does-the-united-states-still-let-12-year-old-girls-get-married/ (accessed 10 May 2023).

[20] Girls not Brides 'Child marriage and gender' https://www.girlsnotbrides.org/learning-resources/child-marriage-gender/; and G Malek, R Arinii & N Bassily 'Patriarchy allows child marriage and female genital mutilation to flourish' *The Guardian* 24 July 2014 (2014) https://www.theguardian.com/global-development/poverty-matters/2014/jul/24/patriarchy-child-marriage-female-genital-mutilation-fgm-feminism (accessed 19 January 2025).

to combat it through legal advocacy and awareness campaigns by both domestic and international non-governmental organisations dedicated to eradicating child marriage and improving gender equality.

Within the US, the marriage of minors remains legal in 37 states.[21] Though most states set the minimum age for marriage at 18, exceptions can be granted in these states under various circumstances, but most commonly with parental consent and some measure of judicial approval. Some states lack an explicitly legislated minimum, below which marriage is prohibited without exception. In 2018, Delaware and New Jersey became the first two states to prohibit the practice entirely, followed by American Samoa and the US Virgin Islands in the same year. Between 2020 and 2024 legislation was passed in 11 other states—Connecticut, Massachusetts, Michigan, Minnesota, New Hampshire, New York, Pennsylvania, Rhode Island, and Vermont—setting the minimum age for marriage at 18.[22] These legislative changes are in large part due to the unwavering advocacy and campaigning of Unchained at Last, the only US non-profit dedicated to ending forced and child marriage in the US through direct services and systems change.[23] Despite the US' commitment to the Sustainable Development Goals (SDGs), particularly goal 5.3, 'the US has done little to address, study or even acknowledge domestic forced [and child] marriage' thus impacting its ability to end this human rights violation by 2030.[24]

This chapter argues that a human rights and feminist examination of child marriage within the context of the US is important. The US is heralded as a 'developed' nation, which leads most to believe harmful practices, such as child marriage, are likely to be rare or wholly non-existent, as it is assumed child marriage practices are associated with countries within the global majority. This chapter outlines the prevalence of child marriage within the US, the lack of knowledge and research on contributing factors, the current age of consent for marriage laws across the states, the challenges to eliminating child marriage in the US, and current strategies underway to decrease and eliminate the practice. It

21 As above.

22 Unchained at Last 'Child Marriage in the US' https://www.unchainedatlast.org/child-marriage-in-the-u-s/ (accessed 23 December 2024).

23 As above.

24 As above.

concludes with a short discussion on the potential avenues for further research and suggestions for moving forward.

2 Prevalence of Child Marriage

2.1 Global Prevalence of Child Marriage

Around the world, rates of child marriage remain high. It is a harmful practice impacting girls and boys, violating their human rights.[25] Research indicates a number of

> factors interact to place a child at risk of marriage, including poverty, the perception that marriage will provide 'protection,' family honor, social norms, customary or religious laws that condone the practice, an inadequate legislative framework and the state of a country's civil registration system.[26]

Though the world has committed to the target of ending child marriage by 2030 with the SDGs, globally, the total number of girls married in childhood is 12 million per year, and without significant progress on addressing the practice, 'more than 100 million additional girls will marry before their 18th birthday by 2030'.[27] Around the world approximately 650 million women and girls alive today were married before they turned 18.[28] Though the practice of child marriage is more common amongst girls, it remains a violation of human rights regardless of sex. UNICEF's global study of men aged 20–24 revealed that 115 million boys and men were married before the age of 18.[29] 'This brings the present-day, worldwide total number of child brides and grooms to about 765 million, 85% of whom are girls and 15% of whom are boys'.[30]

[25] UNICEF 'Child marriage' (Last update 2023) https://data.unicef.org/topic/child-protection/child-marriage/ (accessed 19 January 2025).

[26] As above.

[27] As above.

[28] UNICEF 'Fast facts: 10 facts illustrating why we must #EndChildMarriage' (10 February 2019) https://www.unicef.org/press-releases/fast-facts-10-facts-illustrating-why-we-must-endchildmarriage (accessed 19 January 2025).

[29] UNICEF (n 25).

[30] Hamilton and others (n 6).

Globally child marriage is connected to a variety of factors, including financial, cultural, religious, and other gender inequalities. In many instances it is linked to issues of poverty and a lack of access to educational opportunities.[31] In some cases, it is viewed as the only pathway for girls as they become women and leave their parental homes. Globally, the drivers are complex and interconnected, as evidenced by a meta-synthesis of 12 studies focused on child marriage in the Middle East, Africa, and South Asia, which

> identified six main themes [relating to the incidence of child marriage]: human insecurity and conflict; legal issues; family values and circumstances; religious beliefs; individual circumstances, beliefs, and knowledge; and social norms.[32]

The consequences and implications of child marriage are manifold for child brides and quite different from those of child grooms. For child brides,

> [c]hild marriage often compromises a girl's development by resulting in early pregnancy and social isolation, interrupting her schooling, limiting her opportunities for career and vocational advancement and placing her at risk for domestic violence.[33]

Child grooms similarly are forced to take on adult responsibilities they are likely unprepared for, they may experience early fatherhood, and additional economic pressure in the form of providing for a household, impacting and constraining boy's access to education and opportunities for career advancement.[34] Child marriage effectively cuts short childhood and forces these children to engage their relationships and the world around them in very adult ways.

[31] J Klugman and others 'Voice and agency: Empowering women and girls for shared prosperity' The World Bank (2014).

[32] A Kohno and others 'Investigation of the key factors that influence the girls to enter into child marriage: A meta-synthesis of qualitative evidence' (2020) 15 *PLoSOne* e0235959.

[33] UNICEF (n 25).

[34] As above.

2.2 *US Prevalence of Child Marriage*

Child marriage is often perceived as a problem ailing low- and middle-income countries. Most Americans are unaware the problem exists in the country outside of some religious groups and immigrant communities, who are treated as outliers.[35] However, it remains a pervasive issue and widespread practice across the US, with devastating consequences.

> Between 2000-2018, almost 300 000 children were married in the United States alone. Of those marriages, an estimated 30 000-60 000, or 10-20 per cent, occurred 'at an age or spousal age difference that should have been considered a sex crime' ... approximately 86% of these underage marriages involved girls and 14% involved boys.[36]

Due to age of consent[37] and statutory rape laws across the US, sexual activities with minors, children under a certain age, are criminalised. These laws vary by state, but the purpose is to 'protect children from harms resulting from unequal, manipulative, or predatory relationships',[38] though in most instances, these laws are insufficient to protect against forced marriages.[39]

Statutory rape occurs when sexual activity involves someone below the legal age of consent, regardless of whether it is consensual. Minors lack the legal capacity to give consent. Historically, child marriage was considered a valid legal defence against statutory rape charges in many states. In some states, children are able to legally get married at a younger age than they can legally consent to sex, and some states explicitly exempt sex

[35] DW Lawson and others 'What does the American public know about child marriage?' (2020) 15 *PLoSOne* e0238346. See also NL Syrett *American child bride: A history of minors and marriage in the United States* (2016).

[36] Unchained at Last (n 1). See also P Cassidy & T Turner 'The fight continues to end child marriage in the US' (2021) https://www.unicefusa.org/stories/fight-continues-end-child-marriage-us (accessed 21 July 2023).

[37] J Devendorf Esq 'Criminal defense law' *LawInfo* (19 October 2023) https://www.lawinfo.com/resources/criminal-defense/statutory-rape/age-of-consent.html (accessed 19 January 2025).

[38] Kaya van Roost, Miranda Horn & Alissa Koski 'Child marriage or statutory rape? A comparison of law and practice across the United States' (2022) 70 *Journal of Adolescent Health* S72-S77.

[39] VG Aryama '"I don't": The need for a solution to the child marriage problem in the United States' (2018) 39 *Women's Rights Law Report* 386.

between married persons from their statutory rape laws. 'In these states, the law grants that the same behavior with a child that would be a crime outside of marriage is not a crime within marriage'.[40]

This 'marital defence' previously existed in federal law (18 U.S.C. Section 2243(c)(2)) but was repealed by the Violence Against Women Reauthorization Act of 2022. However, a similar defence surprisingly still exists within the US Military Code (10 U.S.C. Section 920(b)).

In addition, the US Immigration and Nationality Act (INA) lacks a minimum age requirement for spousal or fiancé(e) visa petitions.[41] The US Citizenship and Immigration Services (USCIS) Policy is that the legal validity of a marriage is determined by the law of the place where the marriage was celebrated (place-of-celebration rule). Under this rule, a marriage is valid for immigration purposes under the law of the jurisdiction in which the marriage is performed.[42] However, there is an exception where the marriage would offend the public policy in the US, such as polygamous marriages. Thus, unless an applicant is one of the states that has completely banned child marriage, US citizens, including minors are allowed to petition for visas for foreign spouses or fiancé(e)s, regardless of age. Consequently, even with state laws prohibiting child marriage, the INA could inadvertently encourage such unions, potentially violating the fundamental human rights of children, primarily girls, as recognised by international law.

2.2.1 Cultural, Social, and Economic Factors

The scholarly research on child marriage in the US is minimal, unlike the multitude of research and knowledge on child marriage in middle and low-income countries, where international attention is drawn, and even US Foreign Policy is aimed. The bulk of academic work that does exist really began proliferating after 2018 when activists in the US associated with organisations like Unchained at Last, pushed for legislative change and were successful in Delaware and New Jersey, as well as the work of

[40] As above.

[41] Immigration and Nationality Act, Pub L 82-414, 66 Stat 163 (1952) 9.

[42] See *Matter of Lovo-Lara* 23 I & N Dec 746 (BIA 2005); *Matter of Da Silvam* 15 I & N Dec 778 (BIA 1798).

Tahirih Justice Centre in DC.[43] The existing research spans disciplines from health-related fields of obstetrics and gynaecology; child and adolescent health; social work and children services; and feminist media studies. There seems to be a gap in research from a policy perspective, as most political science research on child marriage is focused on the global south.

Scholars in these fields have started to map the common interrelated or correlated factors at play with US child marriage norms and policies. They examine the intersections of child brides, forced marriage, and intimate partner violence in the US.[44] All reiterate the concerning nature of child marriage and point to the negative consequences associated with this practice, echoing the international community's concerns for increased risk of lower educational attainment, living in poverty, domestic abuse, neglect, mental health, and substance abuse disorders.

US Public Perception of Child Marriage

For many citizens in the global north, the issue of child marriage is perceived to be an issue of lower-income countries, those predominantly in the global south, as one of the notable drivers of child marriage is poverty. Widespread misconceptions about child marriage are not surprising for scholars and activists interested in the domestic response to the issue within the US. Lawson and others in their 2020 research article point to expected misunderstandings of the issue amongst the American public.[45] They point to a 'biased understanding of the topic', noting that

> well-intentioned public awareness campaigns may inadvertently misrepresent the realities of child marriage by presenting extreme scenarios most capable of capturing donor attention. Most notably, [where] child brides are routinely portrayed as extremely young, often prepubescent girls, forcibly married to considerably older men.[46]

[43] See research compiled in Tahirih Justice Centre 'Child marriage poses a serious risk to children' https://www.tahirih.org/pubs/child-marriage-poses-serious-risks-to-children/ (accessed 19 January 2025).

[44] See for example, J McFarlane and others 'Child brides, forced marriage, and partner violence in America: Tip of an Iceberg Revealed' (2016) 127 *Obstetrics and Gynecology* 706.

[45] DW Lawson and others 'What does the American public know about child marriage?' (2020) 15 *PLoSOne* e0238346.

[46] As above.

While no systematic study on these campaigns and their messaging is currently available, the narrative they construct is in contrast to global statistics, worldwide 4% of women aged 20–24 years were first married or in union before age 15, and 19% first married or in union by age 18.[47]

Another facet of mistaken perceptions is the terminology utilised to characterise the issue. As Lawson and others note, 'the term child marriage is rooted in a human rights framework, taking the legal definition of childhood as ending at 18 years', but in popular discourse, the 'term childhood is used inconsistently but generally refers to the period before puberty, after which children become adolescents or teenagers, then adults'.[48] This inconsistency in language and meaning of the term child, compounds the issue of public awareness campaigns exhibiting extreme scenarios, leading the public to falsely assume that child marriage refers specifically to the marriage of especially young girls. International activism on the issue of child marriage presents a moral obligation for intervention as child marriage is categorised as a harmful culturally based practice. This, paired with 'broader ethnocentric misconceptions about low-income countries', positions high-income countries as morally superior despite the fact that child marriage remains legal in most high-income nations.[49]

Through an Amazon Mechanical Turk (MTurk) survey, Lawson and others examine public knowledge of child marriage in the US and ascertain directions of bias. Their survey included questions about the threshold for child marriage, when most child marriages occur, how many states child marriage is legal in, the proportion of women married before 18 in the US, and in which world region child marriage was most common. While not surprising, their results suggest the American public is poorly informed about child marriage, and in line with widespread ignorance about global health issues in general.[50] They found the terminology used to describe the period of childhood adds to the confusion, including terms such as teen marriage, adolescent marriage, and early marriage, which conjures images of young women rather than girl children, who would have a higher degree of autonomy in the decision to marry. The

[47] UNICEF (n 25).

[48] Lawson and others (n 35).

[49] As above.

[50] As above.

majority of the survey respondents believed that child marriage is illegal throughout the majority of the US.

Building on this work, Gupte and Anitha examine media coverage of child and forced marriage in US newspapers in their 2023 article examining gender violence. The increased media attention since the early 2010s, with survivors publicly sharing their experiences and disseminating it via social media platforms, has led to activists pushing for legislative change. News media, in addition to social media, helps the general public understand social issues via the use of simple narratives. The framing of such narratives influences public perceptions and affects public policy discourse.[51] These scholars analyse media framing 'by analysing the language used to construct child/forced marriage in six newspapers'.[52] They found a combination of two framing techniques at work within these newspapers. Where 'episodic framing focused on police and legal cases or individuals and one-off incidences (44%) [and] thematic framing was issue-focused and provided contextual information (56%)'.[53] Overall, the media created awareness of gender violence, influencing how it is perceived by covering state law permitting child marriage in the US, campaigns to implement minimum marriage ages, and the 'efforts of advocacy organisations, survivors, and op-ed writers'.[54] This study illustrated that child marriage is of interest to both liberal and conservative print media, and the coverage helped to advance minimum marriage age legislation.

Drivers of Child Marriage in the US

Unlike the contributing factors to child marriage globally, in the context of the US, little is known or studied about the drivers underpinning child marriage in the US. The associations with poverty, religious and cultural customs, and societal norms associated with global studies of child marriage while present, via anecdotal cases, do not necessarily hold

[51] M Gupte & S Anitha 'Gender violence or tradition?: Media coverage of child/forced marriage in US newspapers' (2024) 24 *Feminist Media Studies* 34.

[52] As above.

[53] As above.

[54] As above.

the same significance they do globally and in low- and middle-income countries.[55] The timing of marriage in the US

> varies according to demographic characteristics, geographic region and other traits. Earlier work has shown that Hispanic women, women from disadvantaged households, and women living in the Southern United States are more likely than others to have married as children.[56]

In the general public discourse, there are two common reasons discussed as potential drivers for the occurrence of marriage at a young age, both are frequently brought up in public and political discussion when the issue of child marriage is raised. The first is the idea of young love, where at least one partner in the relationship is younger than 18, and the couple actively pursues marriage of their own accord, the 'Romeo and Juliet' effect, if you will. The second is when a pregnant teen is counselled to get married to avoid the stigma of unwed motherhood, often called the 'shotgun wedding' situation.[57]

Human Rights Implications

The human rights implications of child marriage in the US are manifold, and in line with the consequences studied globally. On the whole,

> child marriage is associated with a wide range of adverse health and economic outcomes. Marriage often leads to changes in sexual behaviour, and it is therefore unsurprising that early marriage places girls at risk for poor reproductive health outcomes

and a high occurrence of adolescent pregnancies.[58] As observed in developing nations, girls who marry as children in the US achieve lower educational outcomes than their peers when compared to those who do not get married until they are adults. That lower educational attainment

[55] Reiss (n 19).

[56] A Koski & J Heymann 'Child marriage in the United States: How common is the practice, and which children are at greatest risk?' (2018) 50 *Perspectives on sexual and reproductive health* 59.

[57] A Wahi and others 'The lived experience of child marriage in the United States' (2019) 34 *Social Work in Public Health* 201.

[58] As above.

is also linked to poverty, 'girls who marry as children in the United States are much more likely to live in poverty later in life when compared to their peers who delay marriage'.[59] The Committee on the Elimination of Racial Discrimination (CERD) in its latest Concluding Observations on the US, expressed concerns that

> systemic racism, along with intersecting factors such as gender, race, ethnicity, and migration status, have a profound impact on access by women and girls to the full range of sexual and reproductive health services in the State party without discrimination.[60]

A study on American women who were pregnant or within a year of giving birth found a connection between marriage age and mental health. Wherein,

> women younger than age 25 were found to be at a greater risk of experiencing substance abuse, major depressive disorder and postpartum depression especially if they are divorced or widowed compared to women older than 25 years. Delaying marriage after age 25 may be a protective factor in the mental health of women as well.[61]

This study didn't hone in on adolescent pregnancy specifically, so much more research is needed to understand the correlation between child marriage, teen pregnancy, and mental health outcomes.

Another consequence of child marriage in the US is the increased likelihood that the marriage will end in divorce, in a recent study, nearly 25% of 15–17-year-olds married as children were divorced before their 18th birthdays.[62] Additional studies have found

> teenage marriages result in higher divorce rates compared to those who delay marriage past teenage years, and divorcing at an early age also

[59] GB Dahl 'Early teen marriage and future poverty' (2010) 47 *Demography* 689.

[60] Committee on the Elimination of Racial Discrimination, Concluding Observations on the combined tenth to twelfth reports of the United States of America, 21 September 2022, UN Doc CERD/C/USA/CO/10-12 (2022).

[61] Y Le Strat, C Dubertret & B Le Foll 'Child marriage in the United States and its association with mental health in women' (2011) 128 *Pediatrics* 524.

[62] Koski & Heymann (n 56).

> contributes to economic instability and poorer mental health outcomes that is already present in child marriage survivors.[63]

When considered from a policy perspective, in many US states, minors do not have any legal right to file for divorce,

> thus prohibiting a route for married children to escape abusive and/or unhappy relationships legally. To make matters worse, minors are not allowed in domestic violence shelters without an adult's permission, potentially leaving married minors trapped in a legal vice.[64]

The laws concerning consent, statutory rape, emancipation, and marriage seem to overlap and contradict one another in the case of child marriage and still vary across the nation from one state to another. In most states, minors can petition for emancipation, which is a 'court process through which a minor becomes self-supporting, assumes adult responsibility for their welfare, and is no longer under the care of their parents' before they have reached the age of majority, which is 18 for most states.[65] If the minor gets married, they are granted automatic emancipation in most states. For some states, this emancipation is limited and does not come with full adult privileges, and there remain limits on behaviour such as consuming alcohol and voting, though a legal adult, they are unable to do both. It is in this limited emancipation space where access to legal rights for divorce, domestic abuse shelters, etc., seems to reside.

Lived Experience of Child Marriage in the US

A 2019 study on the reasons why children marry in the US, and their experiences within those marriages illuminated a pattern of experience amongst this hidden population. Through semi-structured interviews and online surveys of 21 participants, the child marriage experiences documented were rife with high levels of violence, financial control, and lack of autonomy over reproductive healthcare and choices.[66]

[63] ND Gleen and others 'Later first marriage and marital success' (2010) 39 *Social Science Research* 787.

[64] As above.

[65] J Yeban 'Emancipation of minors' *FindLaw* (11 April 2024).

[66] Wahi and others (n 57).

The results of this study identified three major themes, 'Romeo and Juliet'; 'La La Land'; and 'That was the Expectation', amongst the perspectives of the participants and what led to their marriages as children. The first theme, 'Romeo and Juliet', was characterised by the notion of love and a lack of control or consent to the marriage. Amongst the respondents, there was an 'overall desire to please the adult parent or caregiver' when asked about consenting to the marriage.[67] One of the public presumptions is that child marriages occur because of 'young love' or the 'Romeo and Juliet' effect. The conversation with these participants about the concept of love and consent refuted this public assumption,

> the Romeo and Juliet notion of young love and lust was hard to find in many of the responses—what took its place for qualifications for what the child thought was love versus the reality of what the adult knows..[68]

Those participants who reported marrying without full consent also reported that their education was disrupted as a result of the marriage.

The second theme, 'La La Land', covered the extent to which the adult participants understood as children what entering into marriage meant, especially for those who also became parents as children. There was an overall lack of understanding of what marriage was and an association of marriage with childhood perceptions of 'happily ever after', princesses, and 'make-believe'.[69] Lastly, the third theme, 'That was the Expectation', captured the extent to which there was an expectation based on cultural and family beliefs, to marry at a young age. One of the participants noted there was a cultural expectation to marry a relative and marry at a young age as their mother did. Another noted the intersection between familial beliefs about pregnancy, if one got pregnant, no matter how young, they ought to get married. In some instances, there was a feeling of reluctance on behalf of the family, but the cultural or religious community they were a part of insisted on marriage due to pregnancy or other expectations.[70]

Collectively, most of the participants in this study were divorced before the age of 25, most reported

[67] As above.

[68] As above.

[69] As above.

[70] As above.

> incidents of physical, sexual, or emotional violence, as well as high amount of fiduciary abuse where the spouse took control of finances ... [most] reported having their education affected as a result of disapproval from their spouse or the necessity of being a parent/primary caregiver above education.[71]

The lived experience of child marriage in the US is not congruent with popular hypotheses about why child marriage takes place. Adolescent pregnancy featured highly amongst this small population of individuals, love was not a major factor in most of the experiences, but the pressure of family members was present in most cases, with a lack of consent and understanding consent on behalf of the minor getting married.[72]

3 US Child Marriage Law

Due to the nature of the governing and legal structures within the US, marriage law, and thus the issue of child marriage, falls under the purview of each individual state. Though constitutional restrictions, like the federal right to same-sex marriage and the right to interracial marriage, supersede state marriage law. Despite the clear evidence of the occurrence of child marriage, 'the US government consistently fails to take federal action to confront the problem' as there is no federal law banning child marriage.[73] In August of 2024, the Child Marriage Prevention Act was introduced in the Senate, a body of the US Congress, aiming to close gaps in federal law and end child marriage across the country.[74]

Due to state autonomy over marriage laws, there is a lack of national consensus regarding proper and effective child marriage laws. Thus, the legal framework is uneven and mixed, with some states strongly protecting against child marriage and others maintaining lax laws that ultimately facilitate the practice.[75] In addition to these disparities, the lack of a federal prohibition against child marriage has meant many state laws are rife with legal loopholes, no matter if an age floor for marriage has been

[71] As above.

[72] As above.

[73] Hamilton and others (n 6).

[74] Girls not Brides 'New federal law aims to accelerate action to end child marriage in the U.S.' (2024); and see sec 4990 of the Child Marriage Prevention Act of 2024.

[75] Hamilton and others (n 6).

set at 18, often there are many exceptions to the rule, such as parental consent, judicial approval, lack of official proof of age and residency requirements.[76]

Every state in the US has marriage laws that include common law marriages. Each state is responsible for articulating policies and requirements for the citizens within the state. This includes requirements such as

> getting a marriage license, being of sound mind, and meeting the age of consent as provided by state laws. The age of marriage differs from the age of majority and the age of consent for sexual relations.[77]

To date, 11 states have legislated the minimum marriage age of consent to 18 years old, without exceptions, meaning in these 11 states, minors cannot get married. The remaining 37 states, as well as the District of Columbia and Puerto Rico, allow concessions to their minimum marriage age of consent. For example, under DC laws, individuals aged 16–17 can obtain marriage licenses with consent from one parent or guardian.[78] However, this law lacks provisions to independently assess the child's consent or to screen for potential coercion or harm. The reliance on parental consent overlooks the possibility that such consent may be influenced by undue pressure from the parent or guardian.

Though the age of consent is set at 18 (21 in Mississippi and Puerto Rico),[79] minors are allowed to marry if they meet certain criteria, whether that be parental consent, court order, or minor emancipation. Additionally, a few states stipulate a maximum age gap allowed between a minor getting married and their partner and others stipulate a waiting period or

[76] As above.

[77] (FindLaw, 2023).

[78] DC Code § 46-411 states: 'If any person intending to marry and seeking a license therefore shall be under 18 years of age, and shall not have been previously married, the said Clerk shall not issue such license unless a parent, or, if there be neither father nor mother, the guardian, if there be such, shall consent to such proposed marriage, either personally to the Clerk, or by an instrument in writing attested by a witness and proved to the satisfaction of the Clerk.' See Tahirih Justice Centre 'Child marriage in Washington, DC' (17 September 2024).

[79] As a territory of the United States, Puerto Rico's residents are US Citizens, and subject to US federal laws.

counselling prior to receiving legal permission to marry below the age of 18.

Below, Table 1 captures the current marriage age of consent laws across the 50 states, the District of Columbia, and Puerto Rico as of 29 June 2023. This snapshot comes from FindLaw, a leading provider of online legal information that contains 'free up-to-date, and easily understandable legal information and tools' as well as a lawyer directory with the goal of connecting people with legal issues to the right professionals.

The table above captures the state, the legal age of consent for marriage, the age of marriage with parental consent, court order, or emancipation, the maximum age gap allowed where noted, and the waiting period required where noted. Counselling requirements are denoted by an asterisk in the column of parental consent permissions.

3.1 Challenges and Barriers to Effective Implementation

There are many challenges and barriers to effectively implementing a standard age of consent for marriage across all US states. The decentralised nature of the US legal system, where individual states hold significant authority, presents challenges in addressing issues like child marriage. This lack of federal uniformity can lead to inconsistencies in laws and enforcement across different states. This results in a wide variety of marriage and age of consent laws, rife with exceptions and loopholes, making adherence to a minimum age of marriage inconsistent across the US. In the US, power is shared, diffused, between the Federal Government—consisting of three branches: an executive, a legislature, and a judiciary—and 50 state governments similarly organised to the federal government with three branches.[80]

Though many of the states within the US formally set the minimum age for marriage at 18 years, most allow for at least one form of exception to this rule, which allow minors to marry both other minors as well as non-minors. Some states include age gap rules to those exceptions where there is a maximum age gap allowed between the minor and the other party.

[80] Constitution Annotated 'Intro 7.3 Federalim and the Constitution' https://constitution.congress.gov/browse/essay/intro.7-3/ALDE_00000032/ (accessed 19 January 2025).

Table 1 Marriage age of consent laws by state as of 29 June 2023

State	*Age of consent*	*Parental consent/Minor emancipation*	*Max age gap*	*Waiting period*
Alabama	18	16		
Alaska	18	16	3	
Arizona	18	16	3	
Arkansas	18	17		
California	18	No minimum		30 days
Colorado	18	16	3	
Connecticut[81]	18	NA[82]		
Delaware[83]	18	NA		
Florida	18	17	2	
Georgia	18	17*	4	
Hawaii	18	15		
Idaho	18	16	3	
Illinois	18	16		
Indiana	18	16*	4	15 days
Iowa	18	16		
Kansas	18	16		
Kentucky	18	17		
Louisiana	18	16	3	
Maine	18	16/17**		

(continued)

81 Connecticut passed HB6569 in 2023, Unchained at Last 'Child marriage in Connecticut' https://www.unchainedatlast.org/child-marriage-in-connecticut/ (accessed 19 January 2025).

82 NA means 'not applicable' meaning there are no exceptions for child marriage in this state.

83 Delaware passed HB337 in 2018 Unchained at Last 'Marriage in Delaware' https://www.unchainedatlast.org/child-marriage-in-delaware/ (accessed 19 January 2025).

Table 1 (continued)

State	*Age of consent*	*Parental consent/Minor emancipation*	*Max age gap*	*Waiting period*
Maryland	18	17		
Massachusetts[84]	18	NA		
Michigan[85]	18	16		
Minnesota[86]	18	NA		
Mississippi	21	15f; 17 m		
Missouri	18	16	If > 21 cannot marry anyone < 18	
Montana	18	16*		
Nebraska	19	17		
Nevada	18	17		
New Hampshire[87]	18	16		
New Jersey[88]	18	NA		
New Mexico	18	16; < 16 with court order		
New York[89]	18	NA		
North Carolina	18	16	4	

84 Massachusetts ended child marriage in 2022 through a provision in the state budget, Unchained at Last 'Child marriage in Massachusetts' https://www.unchainedatlast.org/child-marriage-in-massachusetts/ (accessed 19 January 2025).

85 Michigan passed SB209, 212, 213 and 216/HB4924-4296 in 2023, Unchained at Last 'Child marriage in Michigan' https://www.unchainedatlast.org/child-marriage-in-michigan/ (accessed 19 January 2025).

86 Minnesota passed SF1393/HF745 in 2020, Unchained at Last 'Child marriage in Minnesota' https://www.unchainedatlast.org/child-marriage-in-minnesota/ (accessed 19 January 2025).

87 New Hampshire passed SB359 in 2024, Unchained at Last 'Child marriage in New Hampshire' https://www.unchainedatlast.org/child-marriage-in-new-hampshire/ (accessed 19 January 2025).

88 New Jersey passed A865/S427 in 2018, Unchained at Last 'Child marriage in New Jersey' https://www.unchainedatlast.org/child-marriage-in-new-jersey/ (accessed 19 January 2025).

89 New York passed A3891/S3086 in 2021, Unchained at Last 'Child marriage in New York' https://www.unchainedatlast.org/child-marriage-in-new-york/ (accessed 19 January 2025).

State	*Age of consent*	*Parental consent/Minor emancipation*	*Max age gap*	*Waiting period*
North Dakota	18	16		
Ohio	18	17	4	
Oklahoma	18	16; < 16 with court order		
Oregon	18	17		
Pennsylvania[90]	18	NA		
Rhode Island[91]	18	NA		
South Carolina	18	16		
South Dakota	18	16		
Tennessee	18	17	4	
Texas	18	16		
Utah	18	16	7	
Vermont[92]	18	NA		

(continued)

90 Pennsylvania passed HB360/SB81 in 2020, Unchained at Last 'Child marriage in Pennsylvania' https://www.unchainedatlast.org/child-marriage-in-pennsylania/ (accessed 19 January 2025).

91 Rhode Island passed H5387/S398 in 2021, Unchained at Last 'Child marriage in Rhode Island' https://www.unchainedatlast.org/child-marriage-in-rhode-island/ (accessed 19 January 2025).

92 Vermont passed H148 in 2023, Unchained at Last 'Child marriage in Vermont' https://www.unchainedatlast.org/child-marriage-in-vermont/ (accessed 19 January 2025).

Table 1 (continued)

State	*Age of consent*	*Parental consent/Minor emancipation*	*Max age gap*	*Waiting period*
Virginia[93]	18	*Emancipation by court order*		
Washington[94]	18	17		
West Virginia	18	16	4	
Wisconsin	18	16		
Wyoming	18	16		
District of Columbia	18	16		
Puerto Rico	21	18		

93 Virginia passed HB994 in 2024, Unchained at Last 'Child marriage in Virginia' https://www.unchainedatlast.org/child-marriage-in-virginia/ (accessed 19 January 2025).

94 Washington passed HB1455 in 2024, Unchained at Last 'Child marriage in Washington' https://www.unchainedatlast.org/child-marriage-in-washington/ (accessed 19 January 2025).

The most common exception is that of parental consent. As illustrated in Table 1, parental consent is an option in 40 states as well as the District of Columbia and Puerto Rico, bringing the minimum age down to 16 or 17 in most states, with a few outliers. Hawaii's parental consent exception brings the marriage age floor down to 15, and Mississippi brings it down to 15 years of age for females, but 17 years of age for males. New Mexico and Oklahoma allow for marriage under the age of 16 by an order of court. California has no minimum age for marriage with parental consent. Of those states with parental consent exceptions, 12 include an age gap maximum ranging from two to four years, with Utah including a maximum seven-year age gap and Missouri stipulating that anyone over the age of 21 cannot marry anyone younger than 18. Four states require counselling in addition to parental consent, and two require a specified waiting period.

In addition to the exceptions, there are a variety of loopholes that make child marriage easier and more likely in some states.[95] Analysis of the data from the Tahirih Justice Centre's 2021 report analysing the variety of provisions across the states making child marriage easier and more likely, or harder and less likely, illuminated approximately eight loopholes and the number of states where such loopholes exist—listed in Table 2—with the most impact on minors obtaining marriage licenses.[96]

Amongst those loopholes, as of the 2021 report, 47 states lack a requirement for minors to be given information on their rights and resources for domestic violence.[97] In 43 states, waiting periods are not required to issue minors' marriage licenses. In 39 states, there is no maximum age difference threshold in relation to parties entering into marriage. In 34 states, unemancipated minors are not always required to receive judicial approval for marriage. In 37 states, court clerks can issue marriage licenses to out-of-state unemancipated minors. In 35 states, parental consent only requires one parent. In 28 states, official proof of

[95] Jiang & Lansford (n 5).

[96] As above.

[97] Tahirih Justice Centre 'Appendix A: All states and DC, analysis of state laws on minimum marriage age and exceptions permitting marriage under age 18' (2021) https://www.tahirih.org/wp-content/uploads/2021/09/August-2021-50-State-Appendices-withDetailed-Scorecards-on-Features-of-States-Minimum-Marriage-Age-Laws-1.pdf (accessed 19 January 2025). See also Jiang & Lansford (n 5).

Table 2 State child marriage 'loophole' data from Jiang & Lansford (2023)

Loophole	*Number of states as of 2021*
Official proof of age not required	28
Clerks can issue marriage licenses to out-of-state unemancipated minors	37
Parental consent only requires one parent	35
Clerks can approve all marriage licenses	15
There no maximum age difference between parties	39
Un-emancipated minors are not always required to receive judicial approval	34.5
Waiting periods are not required to issue minors' marriage licenses	43.5
Minors are not mandated to be given information on their rights and resources in case of domestic violence	47

age is not required. In 15 states, court clerks, not judges, can approve all marriage licenses.[98]

4 Efforts to Combat US Child Marriage

Where government officials have failed to act and effectively combat child marriage in the US, US-based activist organisations have taken up the call to spread awareness, educate, and lobby state governments to take the issue of child marriage seriously. The issue of child marriage in the US has gained significant attention in recent years, thanks in part to the advocacy efforts of various organisations. Since 2018, nine states have enacted laws establishing the minimum age for marriage at 18, with no exceptions permitted.

4.1 *Unchained at Last*

Unchained at Last is a US-based, 'survivor-led nonprofit organization dedicated to ending forced and child marriage in the United States through direct services and systems change'.[99] Formed in 2011 in the

[98] As above.

[99] Unchained at Last 'Unchained at a glance' (2023) https://www.unchainedatlast.org/unchained-at-a-glance/ (accessed 19 January 2025).

state of New Jersey, the organisation originally set out to expose religious divorce laws in the Orthodox Jewish community, and help women and girls flee arranged/forced marriages. The successful banning of child marriage in nine US states is largely attributed to the tireless work of this organisation and its founder, Fraidy Reiss, a forced marriage survivor turned activist.

The organisation worked to influence New Jersey state law to help domestic violence survivors, introduced a bill to end child marriage in the state of New York, and engaged with the US White House on forced marriage in 2014 and 2015. In 2017, the bill in New Jersey that Unchained assisted with was approved by the legislature only to be later vetoed by the governor. In this same year, however, the movement to end child marriage exploded onto the national stage, gaining momentum with bills introduced in ten additional state legislatures, most of which Unchained helped write.[100] In 2018, Delaware became the first state in the US to end all child marriage without exceptions. Then, the New Jersey legislature passed the bill Unchained at Last wrote and promoted for three years to end child marriage, and it was signed into law, making New Jersey the second US state to end child marriage, both cases were a direct result of the tireless work and advocacy of the organisation.[101]

Since 2018, the organisation has continued to advance the call for ending child marriage, assisting in the writing of bills banning child marriage, and promoting them across the US. Their efforts led to Pennsylvania, Minnesota, and the US Virgin Islands to vote unanimously in favour of legislation banning child marriage without exceptions, and during a global pandemic in 2020.[102] These successes were followed by the successful passing of laws ending child marriage in Rhode Island and New York in 2021. Subsequently, in 2021, Unchained at Last released a groundbreaking study illustrating how

> nearly 300,000 children, a few as young as 10, were legally married in the US between 2000 and 2018. The study also shows some 60,000

[100] Unchained at Last 'History of Unchained' https://www.unchainedatlast.org/history-of-unchained/ (accessed 19 January 2025).

[101] As above.

[102] As above.

marriages since 2000 occurred at an age or spousal difference that should have constituted a sex crime.[103]

In 2022, Massachusetts ended child marriage, followed by Vermont and Connecticut and Michigan in 2023, and Washington, Virginia, and New Hampshire in 2024.

In addition to weighing in on bills related to child marriage and advocating relentlessly for the end of child marriage from one state to the next, Unchained at Last also provides crucial legal and social services for free to assist women, girls, and others in the US escape arranged and forced marriages, and rebuild their lives. The organisation pushes for social, policy, and legal change, leading a growing national movement to eliminate child marriage in every US state and at the federal level.[104]

4.2 *Tahirih Justice Centre*

The Tahirih Justice Centre is a national, non-profit organisation in the United States working to serve women, girls, and all immigrant survivors of gender-based violence. Their work includes providing survivors of gender-based violence with free legal support, and social services to assist them in securing their rights and building stable lives.[105] Additionally, they engage in policy advocacy as well as research-based training and education, leading to a transformative approach to addressing gender-based violence by assisting survivors and simultaneously working to change the systems complicit in the occurrence of violence in the first place.

Forced and child marriage are amongst the many issues the Tahirih Justice Centre works to address by partnering with survivors and help lead the campaign to end child marriage across the United States. In 2011 Tahirih formed the Forced Marriage Working Group in response to the need to bring together those who witness survivors facing barriers

[103] Unchained at Last (n 100).

[104] Unchained at Last (n 99).

[105] Tahirih Justice Centre 'About us' https://www.tahirih.org/about-us/ (accessed 18 December 2024).

to services.[106] Tahirih is currently involved in state-by-state advocacy to end child marriage, by

> testifying in person and submitting written testimony to state legislatures; raising awareness through media engagement and outreach; providing critical insights from [their] direct services experience; and serving as an expert resource on legislative approaches.[107]

Recently, Tahirih Justice Centre, in collaboration with other organisations, is leading the advocacy work under the ambit of the *DC Coalition to End Child Marriage*.[108]

4.3 Girls Not Brides

Girls not Brides is a global civil society network working in partnership with more than 1 400 civil society organisations (CSOs) across 100 countries, all committed to ending child marriage. The network took off in 2011 with an express focus on the harmful practices holding girls and women back. In 2013 it became a private charity registered in England and Wales. Member organisations of the Girls not Brides' network range from small grassroots actors to large international organisations spanning various sectors including health, education, human rights, and humanitarian contexts.[109]

Through National Partnerships in 13 regions, networks work to hold governments accountable to develop, implement, and monitor national strategies to address child marriage; raise public awareness on the harmful impacts of child marriage; engage in information sharing and educating on solutions to address child marriage; and coordinate and support efforts

[106] Tahirih Justice Centre 'Celebrating 10 years of the National Forced Marriage Working Group' https://www.tahirih.org/news/celebrating-10-years-of-the-national-forced-marriage-working-group/ (accessed 18 December 2024).

[107] Tahirih Justice Centre 'Child marriage policy' https://www.tahirih.org/what-we-do/policy-advocacy/child-marriage-policy/ (accessed 18 December 2024).

[108] Tahirih Justice Centre: Forced Marriage Initiative 'DC Coalition to End Child Marriage' https://preventforcedmarriage.org/dc-coalition-to-end-child-marriage/ (accessed 18 December 2024).

[109] Girls not Brides 'Our partnership' https://www.girlsnotbrides.org/our-partnership/ (accessed 18 December 2024).

to engage communities, families, and girls in ending child marriage.[110] In 2012, the US Child Marriage Coalition became Girls not Brides USA, the first Girls not Brides National Partnership, instrumental in pushing forward key policies on child marriage in the US. Girls not Brides USA is comprised of 73 CSO members, including Unchained at Last, combining efforts, expertise and evidence in working to end child marriage in the US.[111]

Girls not Brides USA was successful in the inclusion of child marriage in the 2013 Reauthorisation of the Violence Against Women Act (VAWA), the development of the US Global Strategy to Empower Adolescent Girls, and the inclusion of child marriage in the US Department of State's annual country reports on human rights.[112] Girls not Brides USA continues to engage in efforts to shape US policy on child marriage through the production of policy and technical briefs highlighting strategies and guidance to members of the US government, including lobbying efforts for the Keeping Girls in School Act of 2019, which would work to address barriers, including child marriage, that keep 130 million girls from attending school if enacted.[113]

4.4 *Zonta International*

Zonta International is a global organisation of individuals working to improve the world for women and girls. Their Zonta USA Advocacy Action Centre provides tools for members in the US who are invested in gender equality, and to act to improve the lives of women and girls in the US along a variety of issues, including ending child marriage. They work jointly with UNICEF USA to end child marriage in the US.[114] Zonta provides legislation tracking tools in addition to providing ways for individuals to join and engage in advocacy efforts through letter writing and awareness campaigns.

[110] Girls not Brides 'National partnerships & coalitions' https://www.girlsnotbrides.org/our-partnership/national-partnerships-coalitions/ (accessed 18 December 2024).

[111] As above.

[112] Girls not Brides 'United States' https://www.girlsnotbrides.org/our-partnership/national-partnerships-coalitions/united-states/ (accessed 18 December 2024).

[113] As above.

[114] Zonta International 'Zonta USA Advocacy Action Centre' https://www.votervoice.net/Zonta/home (accessed 18 December 2024).

5 Conclusion

Child marriage is a serious problem affecting millions of young girls worldwide, including in the US. Despite the US' efforts to combat child marriage globally, this practice persists within the country and requires a significant amount of additional research and analysis from a human rights and feminist perspective. Research to date is minimal and is originating in children and social services, as well as health fields, but remains scarce in human rights and policy fields with a focus on child marriage within the US. Since 2018, attention to the issue has increased immensely as the tireless work of activists has found success in lobbying for changes to state marriage laws in nine states. The hope is that the work of organisations like Unchained at Last will continue to have ripple effects throughout the country.

The issue of child marriage is one fraught with issues of misinformation, lack of political will, and power politics. The contemporary relevance of addressing the issue is further complicated by recent changes in federal and state law. The current political climate in the US, with numerous state-level changes to laws governing the reproductive rights of women, reinvigorates the concern for child and forced marriage. As options for contraception and reproductive health become increasingly curtailed, so too does the autonomy of girls and young women in other aspects of their lives.

Concrete steps for moving forward are difficult to define, as the legal situation is quite diverse across the states. What is needed initially is accurate and consistent data collection on the prevalence of child marriage across the country. The tracking of marriages, the issuing of licenses, and the collection of information lack standardisation from state to state. The diffused nature of the legal system as a whole presents the biggest problem for effectively combating child marriage in the US. Agreement to global priorities, via international treaties and the Sustainable Development Goals, indicates at minimum a rhetorical commitment by the US to take child marriage seriously. Those international commitments can be utilised as tools to lobby the US government to practically engage the issue and produce legislation banning child marriage in the US and bring the US in line with international human rights law.

Bibliography

Arthur, M; Earle, A; Raub, A; Vincent, I; Atabay, E; Latz, I & Heymann, J 'Child marriage laws around the world: Minimum marriage age, legal exceptions, and gender disparities' (2018) 39 *Journal of Women, Politics & Policy* 51

Aryama, VG '"I don't": The need for a solution to the child marriage problem in the United States' (2018) 39 *Women's Rights Law Reporter* 386

Cassidy, P & Turner, T 'The fight continues to end child marriage in the US' UNICEF USA: https://www.unicefusa.org/stories/fight-continues-end-child-marriage-us (accessed 19 January 2015)

Committee on the Elimination of Racial Discrimination, Concluding Observations on the combined tenth to twelfth reports of the United States of America, 21 September 2022, UN Doc CERD/C/USA/CO/10–12 (2022)

Congress.gov. 'S.4990 – Child Marriage Prevention Act of 2024' (2024) https://www.congress.gov/bill/118th-congress/senate-bill/4990/text (accessed 19 January 2025)

Dahl, GB 'Early teen marriage and future poverty' (2010) 47 *Demography* 689

FindLaw 'State-by-state marriage "age of consent" laws' (2023) https://www.findlaw.com/family/marriage/state-by-state-marriage-age-of-consent-laws.html (accessed 19 January 2025)

FindLaw 'Emancipation of minors' (2023) https://www.findlaw.com/family/emancipation-of-minors/emancipation-of-minors-basics.html (accessed 19 January 2025)

Furlow, B 'Child marriage in the USA: Persistent but little understood' (2018) 2 *The Lancet Child & Adolescent Health* 849

Girls not Brides 'Child marriage and gender' (2024) https://www.girlsnotbrides.org/learning-resources/child-marriage-gender/ (accessed 19 January 2025)

Girls not Brides 'Child Marriage and the SDGs' (2023) https://www.girlsnotbrides.org/learning-resources/child-marriage-and-sdgs/ (accessed 19 January 2025)Girls not Brides 'National partnerships & coalitions' (2024) https://www.girlsnotbrides.org/our-partnership/national-partnerships-coalitions/ (accessed 19 January 2025)

Girls not Brides 'New federal law aims to accelerate action to end child marriage in the US' https://www.girlsnotbrides.org/articles/new-federal-law-aims-to-accelerate-action-to-end-child-marriage-in-the-us/ (accessed 19 January 2025)

Girls not Brides 'Our partnership' (2024) https://www.girlsnotbrides.org/our-partnership/ (accessed 19 January 2025)

Girls not Brides 'United States' (2024) https://www.girlsnotbrides.org/our-partnership/national-partnerships-coalitions/united-states/ (accessed 19 January 2025)

Glenn, ND; Uecker, JE & Love RWB Jr 'Later first marriage and marital success' (2010) 39 *Social Science Research* 787

Gupte, M & Anitha, S 'Gender violence or tradition? Media coverage of child/forced marriage in US newspapers' (2024) 24 *Feminist Media Studies* 34

Hamilton, V 'The age of marital capacity: Reconsidering civil recognition of adolescent marriage' (2012) 92 *Boston University Law Review* 1817

Hamilton, MA; Schidlow, J; Nixon, C; Bohn, AA & Ortiz, A 'Child marriage report: 2022 report on child marriage in the United States: A national overview of child marriage data and law' (Philadelphia: CHILD USA 2023)

Jiang, A & Lansford, JE 'State-level legal and sociodemographic correlates of child marriage rates in the United States' (2023) 145 *Children and Youth Services Review* https://doi.org/10.1016/j.childyouth.2022.106798 (accessed 19 January 2025)

Ketz, A 'Child marriage is currently legal in 46 states' *News Nation* 21 May 2021 https://www.newsnationnow.com/us-news/child-marriage-is-currently-legal-in-46-states/ (accessed 19 January 2025)

Klugman, J; Hanmer, L; Twigg, S; Hasan, T; McCleary-Sills, J & Santamaria, J 'Voice and agency: Empowering women and girls for shared prosperity' The World Bank (2014) https://doi.org/10.1596/978-1-4648-0359-8 (accessed 19 January 2025)

Kohno, A; Techasrivichien, T; Suguimoto, SP; Dahlui, M; Nik Farid, ND & Nakayama, T 'Investigation of the key factors that influence the girls to enter into child marriage: A meta-synthesis of qualitative evidence' (2020) 15 *PLoSONE* e0235959

Koski, A & Heymann, J 'Child marriage in the United States: How common is the practice, and which children are at greatest risk?' (2018) 50 *Perspectives on Sexual and Reproductive Health* 59

Lawson, DW; Lynes, R; Morris, A & Schaffnit, SB 'What does the American public know about child marriage?' (2020) 15 *PLoSONE* https://doi.org/10.1371/journal.pone.0238346 (accessed 19 January 2025)

Le Strat, Y; Dubertret, C & Le Foll, B 'Child marriage in the United States and its association with mental health in women' (2011) 128 *Pediatrics* 524 https://doi.org/10.1542/peds.2011-0961 (accessed 19 January 2025)

Malek, G; R Arinii & N Bassily 'Patriarchy allows child marriage and female genital mutilation to flourish: Young feminists must help steer the fight against wider issues harming girls including poverty, marginalisation and exclusion' *The Guardian.* 24 July 2014 https://www.theguardian.com/global-development/poverty-matters/2014/jul/24/patriarchy-child-marriage-female-genital-mutilation-fgm-feminism (accessed 19 January 2025)

McFarlane, J; Nava, A; Gilroy, H & Maddoux, J 'Child brides, forced marriage, and partner violence in America: Tip of an iceberg revealed' (2016) 127 *Obstetrics & Gynecology* 706 https://doi.org/10.1097/AOG.0000000000001336 (accessed 19 January 2025)

Office of the United Nations High Commissioner for Human Rights (nd) 'Child and forced marriage, including in humanitarian settings' https://www.ohchr.org/en/women/child-and-forced-marriage-including-humanitarian-settings (accessed 19 January 2025)

Reiss, F 'Child marriage in the United States: Prevalence and implications' (2021) *Journal of Adolescent Health* S8-S10

Reiss, F 'Why can 12-year-olds still get married in the United States?' *The Washington Post* 10 February 2017https://www.washingtonpost.com/posteverything/wp/2017/02/10/why-does-the-united-states-still-let-12-year-old-girls-get-married/ (accessed 19 January 2025)

Syrett, NL *American child bride: A history of minors and marriage in the United States*(Chapel Hill: University of North Carolina Press 2016)

Tahirih Justice Centre 'Appendix A: All states and DC, analysis of state laws on minimum marriage age and exceptions permitting marriage under age 18' (2021) https://www.tahirih.org/wp-content/uploads/2021/09/August-2021-50-State-Appendices-withDetailed-Scorecards-on-Features-of-States-Minimum-Marriage-Age-Laws-1.pdf (accessed 19 January 2025)

Tahirih Justice Centre 'Celebrating 10 years of the National Forced Marriage Working Group' (2021) https://www.tahirih.org/news/celebrating-10-years-of-the-national-forced-marriage-working-group/ (accessed 19 January 2025)

Tahirih Justice Centre 'Child marriage policy' (2024) https://www.tahirih.org/what-we-do/policy-advocacy/child-marriage-policy/ (accessed 19 January 2025)

Tahirih Justice Centre 'Child marriage poses serious risks to children' (2020) https://www.tahirih.org/wp-content/uploads/2020/05/Child-Marriage-Impacts-One-Pager-updated-5.8.-2020-REGULAR-PRINT.pdf (accessed 19 January 2025)

Tahirih Justice Centre 'DC Coalition to end child marriage' (2024) https://preventforcedmarriage.org/dc-coalition-to-end-child-marriage/ (accessed 19 January 2025)

Unchained at Last 'Child marriage in Connecticut' (2024) https://www.unchainedatlast.org/child-marriage-in-connecticut/ (accessed 19 January 2025)

Unchained at Last 'Child marriage in Delaware' (2024) https://www.unchainedatlast.org/child-marriage-in-delaware/ (accessed 19 January 2025)

Unchained at Last 'Child marriage in Massachusetts' (2024) https://www.unchainedatlast.org/child-marriage-in-massachusetts/ (accessed 19 January 2025)

Unchained at Last 'Child marriage in Michigan' (2024) https://www.unchainedatlast.org/child-marriage-in-michigan/ (accessed 19 January 2025)

Unchained at Last 'Child marriage in Minnesota' (2024) https://www.unchainedatlast.org/child-marriage-in-minnesota/ (accessed 19 January 2025)

Unchained at Last 'Child marriage in New Hampshire' (2024) https://www.unchainedatlast.org/child-marriage-in-new-hampshire/ (accessed 19 January 2025)

Unchained at Last 'Child marriage in New Jersey' (2024) https://www.unchainedatlast.org/child-marriage-in-new-jersey/ (accessed 19 January 2025)

Unchained at Last 'Child marriage in New York' (2024) https://www.unchainedatlast.org/child-marriage-in-new-york/ (accessed 19 January 2025)

Unchained at Last 'Child marriage in Pennsylvania' (2024) https://www.unchainedatlast.org/child-marriage-in-pennsylania/ (accessed 19 January 2025)

Unchained at Last 'Child marriage in Rhode Island' (2024) https://www.unchainedatlast.org/child-marriage-in-rhode-island/ (accessed 19 January 2025)

Unchained at Last 'Child marriage in Vermont' (2024) https://www.unchainedatlast.org/child-marriage-in-vermont/ (accessed 19 January 2025)

Unchained at Last 'Child marriage in Virginia' (2024) https://www.unchainedatlast.org/child-marriage-in-virginia/ (accessed 19 July 2025)

Unchained at Last 'Child marriage in Washington' (2024) https://www.unchainedatlast.org/child-marriage-in-washington/ (accessed 19 January 2025)

Unchained at Last 'Child marriage in the US' (2024) https://www.unchainedatlast.org/child-marriage-in-the-u-s/ (accessed 19 January 2025)

Unchained at Last 'History of Unchained' (2023) https://www.unchainedatlast.org/history-of-unchained/ (accessed 19 January 2025)

Unchained at Last 'Unchained at a glance' (2023) https://www.unchainedatlast.org/unchained-at-a-glance/ (accessed 19 January 2025)Unchained at Last 'United States' child marriage problem' (2021)

UNICEF '10 million additional girls at risk of child marriage due to COVID-19' (2021) https://www.unicef.org/press-releases/10-million-additional-girls-risk-child-marriage-due-covid-19 (accessed 19 January 2025)

UNICEF 'Child marriage' (2023) https://data.unicef.org/topic/child-protection/child-marriage/ (accessed 19 January 2025)

UNICEF 'Fast facts: 10 facts illustrating why we must #EndChildMarriage' (2019) https://www.unicef.org/eca/press-releases/fast-facts-10-facts-illustrating-why-we-must-endchildmarriage (accessed 19 January 2025)

UN Department of Economic and Social Affairs: Sustainable Development 'Goals 5: Achieve gender equality and empower all women and girls – Target 5.3 Eliminate all harmful practices, such as child, early and forced marriage and female genital mutilation' https://sdgs.un.org/goals/goal5#targets_and_indicators (accessed 19 January 2025)

UN General Assembly, Convention on Consent to Marriage, Minimum Age for Marriage and Registration of Marriages, 7 November 1962

United Nations General Assembly, Resolution 74/126 on improvement of the situation of women and girls in rural areas, 8 January 2020, UN Doc A/RES/74/126 (2020)

United Nations General Assembly, Resolution 74/133 on the rights of the child, 20 January 2020, UN Doc A/RES/74/133 (2020)
United Nations General Assembly, Resolution 74/134 on the girl child, 20 January 2020, UN Doc A/RES/74/134 (2020)
United Nations General Assembly, Resolution 74/235 on women in development, 23 January 2020, UN Doc A/RES/74/235 (2020)
United Nations Human Rights Council, Resolution 38/1 on the elimination of all forms of discrimination against women and girls, 16 July 2018, UN Doc A/HRC/RES/38/1 (2018)
United Nations Human Rights Council, Resolution 39/10 on preventable maternal mortality and morbidity and human rights in humanitarian settings, 5 October 2018, UN Doc A/HRC/RES/39/10 (2018)
United Nations Human Rights Council, Resolution 40/14 on the rights of the child: Empowering children with disabilities for the enjoyment of their human rights, including through inclusive education, 8 April 2019, UN Doc A/HRC/RES/40/14 (2019)
United Nations Human Rights Council, Resolution 41/6 on the elimination of all forms of discrimination against women and girls, 19 July 2019, UN Doc A/HRC/RES/41/6 (2019)
United Nations Human Rights Council, Resolution 41/8 on consequences of child, early and forced marriage, 19 July 2019, UN Doc A/HRC/RES/41/8 (2019)
UN SDG 'Goal 5 Achieve gender equality and empower all women and girls' (2024) https://sdgs.un.org/goals/goal5#targets_and_indicators (accessed 19 January 2025)
Van Roost, K; Horn, M & Koski, A 'Child marriage or statutory rape? A comparison of law and practice across the United States' (2022) 70 *Journal of Adolescent Health* S72-S77
Wahi, A; Zaleski, KL; Lampe, J; Bevan, P & Koski, A 'The lived experience of child marriage in the United States' (2019) 34 *Social Work in Public Health* 201 https://doi.org/10.1080/19371918.2019.1575312 (accessed 19 January 2025)
Warner, E 'Behind the wedding veil: Child marriage as a form of trafficking in girls' (2004) 12 *Journal of Gender, Social Policy & The Law* 233
Yeban, J 'Emancipation of minors' *FindLaw* (11 April 2024) https://www.findlaw.com/family/emancipation-of-minors.html (accessed 19 January 2025)
Zonta International 'USA Advocacy Action Center' (2024) https://www.votervoice.net/Zonta/home (accessed 19 January 2025)

Acts

DC Code § 46–411

Immigration and Nationality Act, Pub. L. No. 82–414, 66 Stat. 163 (1952)

Case law

Matter of Lovo-Lara 23 I&N Dec. 746 (BIA 2005)
Matter of Da Silvam 15 I & N Dec 778 (BIA 1798)

CHAPTER 9

Intimate Partner Violence, Gender Vulnerability and the Realisation of Women's Fundamental Rights in Australia

Toun Adebanjo

1 Introduction

Call the police, he's going to kill me. He's poured petrol on me.[1]

These were Hannah Clarke's chilling words to a neighbour on the morning of 19 February 2020. Hanna and her three young children were just starting their day when their lives were tragically cut short. Her estranged husband had taken her by surprise, jumping into her car and

[1] Coroners Court of Queensland 'Inquest into the death of Hannah Ashlie Clarke, Aaliyah Anne Baxter, Laianah Grace Baxter, Trey Rowan Charles Baxter and Rowan Charles Baxter' (2022) para 202 https://www.courts.qld.gov.au/_data/assets/pdf_file/0010/723664/cif-hannah-clarke-aaliyah-baxter-laianah-baxter-trey-baxter-and-rowan-baxter.pdf (accessed 31 October 2024).

T. Adebanjo (✉)
LLD UFS; Legal Researcher and Consultant, Maryborough, QLD, Australia
e-mail: toun.adebanjo@gmail.com

E. Durojaye et al. (eds.), *Harmful Practices and Human Rights: An International Perspective*, Human Rights Interventions,
https://doi.org/10.1007/978-3-031-90333-5_9

ordering her to keep driving, but Hannah had instead bravely driven into a neighbour's driveway to get help.[2] The horrific events that followed have been captured thus[3]:

> Suddenly, the car exploded. Windows across the street rattled from the explosion. Hannah and Baxter were consumed by the flames as neighbours desperately attempted to hose down the screaming mother. A thick plume of black smoke could be seen across the neighbourhood. Aaliyah, Laianah and Trey – who were strapped in the car's backseat, perished in the flames.

Hannah is one of the many women in Australia who have tragically lost their lives to Intimate Partner Violence (IPV). Based on trends over several years, IPV is an epidemic in Australia, with the majority of victims being women and girls.[4] Although men can be, and have been known to be victims of IPV, the proportion of female victims outweighs that of men.[5] In *Bropho v Hall*,[6] Mitchell J stated: 'the vulnerability of the victim is generally increased by the difficulty which she (it is usually a she) may have in extricating herself'.[7] Certain categories of women have been identified as having a higher risk of experiencing IPV including younger women, indigenous women, women with long-term health conditions, women lacking social support, those in financial distress, victims of child abuse and previous IPV victims.[8] Although there have been numerous

[2] Coroners Court of Queensland (n 11) para 201.

[3] B Antrobus 'Heroic final act of slain mum Hannah Clarke revealed as horror DV murder explored at inquest' *news.com.au* 2 April 2022 https://www.news.com.au/lifestyle/real-life/news-life/heroic-final-act-of-slain-mum-hannah-clarke-revealed-as-horror-dv-murder-explored-at-inquest/news-story/36c85df4214f6df7f15ab741529103a6 (accessed 31 October 2024).

[4] Bowden (n 9).

[5] This is supported by figures provided in the Australia Bureau of Statistics (ABS) 'Personal safety survey' released in March 2023. In the survey, one in six women had experienced physical or sexual violence from a cohabiting partner, while one in 18 men had experienced the same; Australian Bureau of Statistics (ABS) '2 in 5 Australians have experienced physical or sexual violence: Media release' (15 March 2023) https://www.abs.gov.au/media-centre/media-releases/2-5-australians-have-experienced-physical-or-sexual-violence (accessed 31 October 2024).

[6] (2015) WASC 50.

[7] Para 16.

[8] E Stavrou, S Poynton & D Weatherburn 'Intimate partner violence against women in Australia: Related factors and help-seeking behaviours' (2016) *Contemporary Issues in*

responses at community, state and national levels, IPV remains an issue of immense concern in Australia. It is essential therefore that effective responses be formulated once and for all to address the scourge of IPV in Australia.

The UN Declaration on the Elimination of Violence against Women defines violence against women as follows[9]:

> [A]ny act of gender-based violence that results in, or is likely to result in, physical, sexual, or psychological harm or suffering to women, including threats of such acts, coercion or arbitrary deprivation of liberty, whether occurring in public or in private life.

Violence against women could occur in the family, community or could be perpetrated or condoned by the state.[10] IPV could occur in the form of emotional, verbal, physical, sexual, social, economic, psychological and spiritual abuse.[11] Examples of acts that constitute violence against women include battering, sexual abuse, sexual harassment, rape, including marital rape,[12] female genital mutilation, intimidation at work, school and other places, trafficking in women and forced prostitution.[13]

For millions of women, the threat of violence is right at home,[14] and home turns out to be a place of pain and humiliation.[15] Although

Crime and Justice Number 200 https://bocsar.nsw.gov.au/documents/publications/cjb/cjb151-200/cjb200-report-intimate-partner-violence-against-women-in-australia-2016.pdf (accessed 31 October 2024).

[9] Art 3 of the UN General Assembly, Declaration on the Elimination of Violence against Women, 20 December 1993, UN Doc A/RES/48/104 (1993) https://www.ohchr.org/sites/default/files/eliminationvaw.pdf (accessed 31 October 2024).

[10] Art 2 of the Declaration on the Elimination of Violence against Women (n 19).

[11] National Council to Reduce Violence against Women and Children 'Background paper to Time for Action: The National Council's Plan for Australia to reduce violence against women and their children 2009-2021' (2009) 13-14 https://www.dss.gov.au/sites/default/files/documents/05_2012/background_paper_to_time_for_action.pdf (accessed 31 October 2024).

[12] EG Krug and others (eds) *World report on violence and health* (2002) Foreward https://www.who.int/publication/i/item/9241545615 (accessed 31 October 2024).

[13] Art 2 of the Declaration on the Elimination of Violence against Women (n 19).

[14] Krug and others (n 22).

[15] C Garcia-Moreno and others 'WHO multi-country study on women's health and domestic violence against women: Initial results on prevalence, health outcomes and

family life is private and privacy should be respected, the state nevertheless has a duty to ensure the preservation and protection of vulnerable members of society. The court's submission in *State of Western Australia v Cheeseman*,[16] that the hallmark of IPV was the readiness of many victims to return to or remain in a relationship with their abuser, underscores the recurrence of victim vulnerability.[17] Hence, the victim's return to the abuser must not be used as a yardstick to assess rehabilitation, and an otherwise appropriate penalty against an abuser should not be reduced on the strength of it.[18] The court similarly held in *Gomboc v The State of Western Australia*,[19] that while the appellant's participation in rehabilitation programmes since his incarceration was encouraging, offending such as his must be denounced with severe penalties.[20] The facts of *McCoombe v State of Western Australia*[21] buttress this point. In *McCoombe*, the offender had earlier served a 12-month prison sentence for IPV offences against the same victim, who had promptly taken him back on his release on 23 July 2015.[22] Unfortunately, the offending had resumed and escalated, until 14 September, when she sustained second and third degree burns from boiling water which he poured down her back.[23] To worsen matters, the appellant prevented her from seeking medical treatment until four days later.[24] *R v FBC*[25] also shows the error in equating a resumption of the relationship between the parties to rehabilitation. In this case, the victim had, following an incident of domestic violence while she was pregnant, obtained a Temporary Protection Order (TPO) against the applicant, and a Domestic Violence Order (DVO) four

women's responses' (2005) Foreword, viii, https://apps.who.int/iris/handle/10665/43309 (accessed 31 October 2024).

[16] (2011) WASCA 15.

[17] Para 3.

[18] As above.

[19] (2023) WASCA 115.

[20] Paras 222-223.

[21] (2016) WASCA 227.

[22] Paras 8 & 9.

[23] Paras 9-13.

[24] Para 13.

[25] (2023) QCA 74.

months later.[26] The conditions of the DVO included that the offender be of good behaviour towards the complainant, and not commit domestic violence against her.[27] Although they proceeded to get married a few months later, facts emerged that the offending had continued, and could be traced to around the time the DVO was issued and afterwards.[28]

The courts are enjoined to take into account the need to protect victims in their vulnerable states, and to remove the offender to a place where there is no opportunity to further attack the victim.[29] In sentencing an IPV offender, the courts will take into consideration factors including the severity of the offending, the number of offences, the duration, its impact on the victim or victims, and the number of victims. In *R v FBC*,[30] where the offending had included anal rape, and threats to kill them all while aiming a loaded weapon at the complainant and the couple's young children, the court found that the initial sentence of nine years' imprisonment 'fell within a sound exercise of the sentencing discretion'.[31] In *Gillespie v The State of Western Australia*,[32] the court stressed the need to take into account the nature of the offending and the aggravating features, its persistence, the need for specific and general deterrence and the community's protection. In *McCoombe*, the total effective sentence of 6 years and 2 months was upheld, after duly considering the offending to be in the most serious category of its kind, and the offender's antecedents among other things.[33] In *Gillespie*, where the victim had been 21 weeks pregnant at the time the first set of offences occurred, and where the offender had attempted to pervert the course of justice, he was handed a 4-year sentence.[34]

[26] Para 9(a)-(c).

[27] Para 9(c).

[28] Para 9(e)-(g).

[29] *Bropho* (n 16) para 16.

[30] (2023) QCA 74.

[31] Paras 25 & 32.

[32] (2016) WASCA 216.

[33] Paras 15, 35-36.

[34] Paras 4, 15-16.

The negative effects of domestic violence are manifold. It destroys the lives of victims, mostly women, with a ripple effect on their children, their loved ones and the community as a whole.[35] Apart from the obvious impact on the health and well-being of the victim, there are even more consequences of IPV. The estimated annual cost of violence against women and children is $26 billion.[36] IPV has also been identified as a leading driver of homelessness for women.[37] It has also been known to manifest in a cycle or as part of a pattern, whereby a person exposed to domestic violence early in life goes on to perpetrate this same violence as an adult.[38]

The impact of IPV on the wider community is further illustrated by the facts in *R v EQ*,[39] where the applicant had, in a fit of rage against his spouse, threatened to detonate a bomb at Brisbane International Airport on 2 February 2019.[40] The situation was eventually diffused after a couple of hours during which Australian Federal Police Officers and Queensland Police Service Officers had to be deployed to the airport.[41] Although eventually discovered to be an elaborate hoax, the applicant's actions had caused immense panic and trauma not only to his family but the wider community as a whole.[42] The court noted that the offending had had an enormous impact on the operation of the airport, with operations ceasing for almost three and a half hours, the international terminal building being completely evacuated, and six arriving and nine departing flights being delayed.[43] This translated to more than one million USD

[35] *Bropho* (n 16) para 17.

[36] The Australian Government, Dept of Social Services 'Executive summary: The National Plan to End Violence against Women and Children 2022-2032' 5 https://www.dss.gov.au/system/files/resources/national-plan-executive-summary.pdf (accessed 31 October 2024).

[37] The National Plan (n 46) 17.

[38] *Bropho* (n 16) para 18.

[39] (2021) QCA 257.

[40] Paras 13-16.

[41] Paras 15-19.

[42] Paras 13, 17, 21, 22 & 57.

[43] Para 21 & 57.

in costs, not considering the psychological impact on every person who witnessed the offending or was impacted by it.[44]

States are expected to outrightly condemn violence against women, formulate policies to eliminate violence against women, demonstrate a commitment to eliminating violence against women and provide necessary training for law enforcement and public officials in recognising and supporting survivors of IPV, among other things.[45]

2 Legal Framework on Violence Against Women in Australia

Australia has made efforts to stem the tide of IPV. Laws applicable to domestic violence include the Family Law Act 1975,[46] and the Family Law Legislation Amendment (Family Violence and Other Measures) Act 2011,[47] otherwise known as the Family Violence Act. The Family Law Act covers various issues regarding marriage, family, divorce, the welfare of children and matrimonial causes generally. It was not centred around IPV but had some provisions addressing issues related to domestic violence. The Act defines family violence and Family Violence Order,[48] section 67ZBA provides for an interested party alleging family violence to file a notice to that effect, while section 67ZBB enjoins the court to take prompt action in addressing these allegations. Sections 68N to 67 T (Division II, Part VII) aim to resolve inconsistencies between family violence orders and orders or arrangements providing for a child to spend time with a particular person, to prevent such child's exposure to family violence.[49] The Family Violence Act of 2011 was introduced to amend provisions of the Family Law Act, to offer better protection for persons (including children) at risk of family violence. Schedule 1, Part 1 of the Act significantly introduced new definitions for abuse and family violence. It inserts a broader definition of the term family violence into section 4 AB(1) of the Family Law Act, wherein family violence means: 'Violent,

[44] Paras 13, 21, 22 & 57.

[45] Art 4 of the Declaration on the Elimination of Violence against Women (n 19).

[46] Act 53 of 1975.

[47] Act 189 of 2011.

[48] Secs 1 & 4AB.

[49] Sec 68N.

threatening or other behaviour by a person that coerces or controls a member of the person's family (the family member) or causes the family member to be fearful'.

The Act further introduces a new section 4AB(2), which provides a non-exhaustive list of behaviours that could constitute family violence including assault (as well as sexual assault), stalking, repeated derogatory taunts, wilful damage to property, intentionally causing death or injury to an animal, withholding financial support or denying financial autonomy to a person and deprivation of liberty. The Act also significantly introduces section 67ZBA, which allows an interested party who makes allegations of family violence or risk thereof against a party to proceedings to file a notice of such in the prescribed form. In terms of the new section 67ZBB inserted under schedule 1 of the 2011 Act, the court is required to act promptly in relation to allegations of child abuse or family violence.

Significantly, the National Domestic Violence Order Scheme (NDVOS) came into being on 25 November 2017, ensuring that a DVO made in one state became applicable nationally, and could better protect survivors and their families.[50] The different states subsequently made laws to introduce this principle into their state laws.[51] An order made on or after that date was automatically recognised nationally, while orders made prior to that date could be declared at any time by applying to a court anywhere in Australia.[52]

Australian states have their own domestic violence laws, the major provisions of which are similar. The main objects of these laws are to ensure the safety and protection of victims,[53] to prevent or reduce the incidence of domestic violence,[54] guarantee fundamental rights in line

[50] Australian Government (Attorney-General's Department) 'National Domestic Violence Order Scheme' https://www.ag.gov.au/families-and-marriage/families/family-violence/national-domestic-violence-order-scheme (accessed 30 October 2024).

[51] For example, Victoria introduced The National Domestic Violence Order Scheme Act 2016, while Tasmania enacted the Domestic Violence Orders (National Recognition) Act 2016, while chapter 3A of the Domestic and Family Violence Act 2007 (NT) provides for the national recognition of DVOs.

[52] Australian Government (AG's Dept) (n 60).

[53] Sec 3(1)(a) & 4 (Qld); sec 9 (NSW); sec 6(b) (ACT); sec 5(a) (SA); sec 3 (Tasmania).

[54] Sec 3(1)(b) (Qld); sec 9 (NSW); sec 6(a) (ACT).

with international rights instruments[55] and to hold offenders accountable.[56] Most state laws recognise that IPV is mostly perpetrated by men against women,[57] and that certain persons (such as Aboriginal and Torres Strait Islanders, persons from culturally and linguistically diverse backgrounds, LGBTQ communities, older persons and persons with disabilities) could be adversely affected by domestic violence.[58] They also provide for the courts to issue protection orders for victims (DVOs).[59] The aim of a protection order is to preserve the victim's safety by creating some distance between the alleged offender and victim and placing conditions on future relations.[60] DVOs have been found to be 'modestly effective'.[61] Compliance could be an issue, especially where the parties share children.[62] However, in some cases, they have been known to be ineffective in curbing IPV, with the aggressor still able to attack or cause harm, sometimes fatal, to the victim, even in the face of a subsisting protection order. A potent example of this is the Clarke murders. An inquest into the murder of Hannah Clarke and her children found that at the time of their murders, there was a Police Protection Notice (PPN) and a DVO in place, such that Hannah had felt 'protected and reassured by that order'.[63]

The victim, their guardian or agent or a police officer are usually allowed to apply for a DVO,[64] and the issuing authorities are usually the police and the court, as will be seen from the discussion on state laws below. A DVO imposes restrictions on the defendant, including restrictions on access to the protected person, restriction of access to the premises occupied by the protected person, prohibition of the defendant's

[55] Preamble (Qld); sec 9 (NSW).

[56] Sec 3(1)(c) (Qld); sec 6(c) (ACT).

[57] Preamble (Qld); sec 9(3) (NSW).

[58] Sec 4(d) (Qld); sec 9(3) (NSW).

[59] Sec 16 (NSW); sec 23 (Qld).

[60] RM Stambe & S Meyer 'Police and duty lawyer perceptions of Domestic Violence Protection Order proceedings involving parents: Towards greater system accountability and family-centred decision-making' (2023) 38 *Journal of Family Violence* 1405.

[61] Stambe & Meyer (n 70) 1406.

[62] Stambe & Meyer (n 70) 1410.

[63] Paras 14, 99, 103, 118 Coroners Court of Qld (n 11).

[64] Sec 16 (ACT); sec 13 (Victoria).

access to firearms, and prohibition from stalking the protected person or a person with whom they have a relationship.[65] Standard conditions of a DVO include that the respondent must be of good behaviour towards the victim and any other person named in the order.[66] The law usually allows for DVOs to be varied in the different states.[67]

In Queensland, the applicable law is the Domestic and Family Violence Protection Act 2012. The Preamble to the Act recognises that IPV is a leading cause of homelessness for women and children. Sections 4(2)(e) and 22A give a unique perspective where both parties allege IPV against each other, or where there are indications that both partners are violent towards each other (including for their self-protection), in which case the partner most in need of protection should be identified, and only one protection order should be issued. These provisions are significant, given that some abusers have been known to allege abuse from a victim who is fighting back. The onus is on the court to identify and protect the 'original' victim, taking into consideration such factors as the history of the relationship and IPV, and the nature and severity of the harm caused to each other.[68] The Act gives a broad definition of domestic violence to include unauthorised surveillance using technology—reading a person's SMS messages, monitoring their email or internet browser activity, monitoring their social media account and tracking their movement with a GPS tracking device.[69] Section 9 of the Act recognises 'associated domestic violence' as behaviour recognised as domestic violence but against the victim's child, ward, relative or associate. Under sections 23 and 24, Queensland courts can issue a DVO, or a TPO against an offending partner to protect the victim, and their child, ward, relative or associate. The victim, a person authorised by them, a police officer and a person so authorised under another act (such as under a guardianship or power of

[65] Sec 36 (NSW); secs 38, 39 & 44 (ACT); sec 14 (SA). In Queensland, any weapons license is automatically revoked.

[66] Sec 56 (Qld).

[67] Eg secs 64-71 (NT).

[68] Sec 22A(2).

[69] Sec 8(6).

attorney) can apply for a DVO in Queensland.[70] Non-compliance constitutes an offence for which the offender can be charged.[71] In *R v FBC*, the offending had occurred while the complainant was pregnant with the couple's first child and she had taken out a TPO against the applicant.[72] A DVO was subsequently made on 28 February 2018, after the birth of the couple's child.[73] They got married in August 2018, separated in November 2018 and had their second child in March 2019.[74] The applicant, by his offending (including assault, choking and rape), was in breach of the terms of the DVO which was in place against him. His 9-year sentencing by the District Court of Toowoomba was upheld by the Supreme Court of Queensland.[75]

In New South Wales, the applicable laws are the Crimes (Domestic and Personal Violence) Act 2007,[76] and the Crimes Legislation Amendment (Coercive Control) Act 2022,[77] which amended the above law and the Crimes Act 1900.[78] The objects of the 2007 Act include to ensure the safety of all persons who experience or witness domestic violence, to reduce the incidence of IPV and to enact provisions that are consistent with provisions of international rights instruments such as the UN Declaration on the Elimination of Violence against Women and the UN Convention on the Rights of the Child.[79] The Act recognised that domestic violence occurs in all sectors of the community, and extended beyond physical violence.[80] Section 16 provides for the court to issue an Apprehended Domestic Violence Order to protect a victim of domestic violence and any child involved. Such an order may subsist for a period to be specified by the court, which must be as long as is necessary to protect

[70] Sec 25.

[71] Sec 30(1).

[72] Para 9(b).

[73] Para 9(c).

[74] Para 9(d).

[75] Paras 31-33.

[76] Act 80 of 2007.

[77] Act 65 of 2022.

[78] Act 40 of 1900.

[79] Sec 9.

[80] Sec 9(3).

the victim, or where none is specified, the default period.[81] A new and expansive definition of domestic abuse is also being introduced by the Amendment Act of 2022. Behaviours qualifying as domestic abuse under the new section 6A include violent or threatening behaviour, coercion or control, sexually, verbally or financially abusive behaviour, stalking and intimidation.

The 2022 Amendment Act is particularly relevant, given Australia's steps towards legislating coercive control as an offence. It inserted a new Division 6A into the Crimes Act on abusive behaviours towards intimate partners. It introduced definitions of intimate partner and abusive behaviour into the Crimes Act[82] and criminalised abusive behaviour towards current and former intimate partners.[83] The new section 54I of the Crimes Act introduces a Coercive Control Implementation and Evaluation Taskforce, to include a representative of the Police Force and an expert in the domestic and family violence sector. The task force would, among other things, provide advice and training in relation to the offence of coercive control.

The applicable law in the Australian Capital Territory is the Family Violence Act 2016. The Act aims to give victims quick and inexpensive access to the courts.[84] It defines family violence to include physical, sexual, emotional and economic abuse.[85] Part 3 of the Act provides for the process of taking out a Family Violence Order. Factors to be taken into consideration before the court grants such order include the victim's safety, previous incidents of family violence and the welfare of children involved.[86] Where both a parent and child are victims in the same incident of family violence, the child's application for a protection order may be included in the parent's application.[87] The safety of

[81] Sec 79A. The default period is for 2 years generally, and 1 year in the case of a defendant who is under the age of 18 when the application was first made.

[82] Sec 54C & 54F respectively.

[83] Sched 1.

[84] Sec 7(c).

[85] Sec 8.

[86] Sec 14.

[87] Sec 16A.

the victim and children involved is paramount in determining the conditions of the FVO.[88] However, the court is enjoined to adopt conditions that are the least restrictive of the respondent's rights and freedoms.[89] Section 69 precludes the FVO from listing the home and work address of the protected person, except where the protected person has consented to such an inclusion, the inclusion has become necessary to allow compliance, or the court is satisfied that the respondent already knows the address. The courts may amend or review a protection order as may become necessary.[90] Section 119 provides for the recognition of FVOs from other jurisdictions, including foreign jurisdictions.

The provisions of the laws applicable in the other states are similar to those above. In South Australia, the Intervention Orders (Prevention from Abuse) Act 2009 is applicable. The Act applies to both domestic and non-domestic abuse,[91] but proceedings for intervention against IPV are accorded priority.[92] The order issued is known as an intervention order.[93] Section 6 of the Act lists the grounds for issuing an intervention order as being that it is appropriate to do so, given the circumstances, and it is reasonable to suspect that without an intervention, the defendant will commit an act of abuse against the other person. An order could be in force without an expiry date.[94] The Act significantly makes room for the possibility of the defendant seeking help through an intervention programme.[95] In South Australia, an Intervention Order can be issued by the police or the courts.[96]

The Family Violence Protection Act 2008[97] is applicable in Victoria. It recognises the issuance of a Family Violence Intervention Order to

[88] Sec 36.

[89] Sec 37.

[90] Secs 83-97.

[91] Sec 5(a).

[92] Sec 9.

[93] Sec 3.

[94] Sec 11.

[95] Sec 13.

[96] Sec 18 & 20.

[97] Act 52 of 2008.

protect vulnerable persons in a domestic relationship.[98] The Act authorises the police to give an affected party or parties a measure of protection before the court is able to issue an Intervention Order. This is in the form of a Family Violence Safety Notice (FVSN) which can be issued by a police officer of the rank of Sergeant or higher.[99] The FVSN is taken to be an application for a Family Violence Intervention Order,[100] and it may include any conditions that could be included in an Intervention Order.[101] A respondent in contravention of the safety notice could be arrested without warrant.[102] In terms of sections 14 and 15, a police officer can give directions to, and detain an alleged offender as may the necessary. The Act affirms that behaviour constituting family violence does not need to constitute a criminal offence.[103] Also relevant is The National Domestic Violence Order Scheme Act 2016[104] through which DVOs issued outside Victoria, and international orders, became recognised.

The Family Violence Act 2004 applies in Tasmania. In terms of the Act, a Family Violence Order can be issued against a person who has committed family violence or is likely to do so.[105] Like the Victorian Act, it empowers a police officer of the rank of Sergeant or higher to issue a Family Violence Police Order (FVPO) against a person who has committed or is likely to commit a family violence offence.[106] By empowering the police to issue an FPVO in anticipation of an act of violence, the act offers wider protection by being not just preventive, but reactive as well.

In Western Australia, the applicable laws are the Criminal Code (as amended), the Sentencing Act (as amended), which recognised the serial

[98] Sec 11.

[99] Sec 24-26.

[100] Sec 31.

[101] Sec 29.

[102] Sec 38.

[103] Sec 5(3).

[104] Act 53 of 2016.

[105] Sec 16.

[106] Sec 14(1).

family violence offender.[107] Part 1B of the Restraining Orders Act (as amended) provides for the issue of a Family Violence Restraining Order against a perpetrator of IPV. Section 10A set out objects of Part 1B, which like other states, sought to maximise safety of at-risk persons, reduce incidence of IPV and to hold perpetrators accountable. The state introduced the Family Violence Legislation Reform Act (FVLRA) 2020,[108] which amended laws on IPV. Importantly, it criminalised strangulation and 'persistent family violence', by inserting sections 298 and 300, respectively into the Criminal Code. The rationale for criminalising strangulation was captured by the WA Commissioner for Victims of Crime, Kris Krazlan, who stated: 'Someone putting their hands around your neck is the ultimate act of power in family violence'.[109] Strangulation was recognised as a common assault under the law. However, criminalisation elevated this offence, and if convicted, the offender is liable to 5 years' imprisonment, or 7 if there are aggravating circumstances.[110] Also, in terms of section 300, a person could be charged with 'persistent family violence' if on three or more occasions within a period of 10 years, they engage in a 'prescribed offence',[111] and the penalty is 14 years' imprisonment. In *Gomboc's case*, which was an appeal before the Supreme Court of Western Australia, the appellant was resentenced to nine years and six months for family violence offences.[112] On 29 July, 2022, the appellant had been sentenced in the District Court for 19 domestic violence offences against the victim including two counts of aggravated assault occasioning bodily harm, seven counts of making threats to unlawfully harm and six counts of making threats to unlawfully kill.[113] The trial court had among other things, found the appellant's offending to be 'very

[107] Sec 124E & F. The FVLRA also inserted a definition for 'family violence offence' and 'serial family violence offender' into sec 4(1), among others.

[108] Act 30 of 2020.

[109] Government of Western Australian 'New laws target strangulation, persistent family violence' https://www.wa.gov.au/government/announcements/new-laws-target-strangulation-persistent-family-violence (accessed 31 October 2024).

[110] Sec 6 of the FVLRA 2020.

[111] In terms of sec 299 of the Criminal Code.

[112] Para 224.

[113] Para 3.

entrenched behaviour', and sentenced him to 11 years and 10 months.[114] On appeal, the Supreme Court of WA affirmed that the 'persistent, callous and menacing nature' of the appellant's offending warranted a long term of imprisonment.[115] The court further reaffirmed the declaration of Serial Family Violence Offender against the appellant, and left the Lifetime Family Violence Restraining Order in place.[116]

The applicable laws in the Northern Territory are the Domestic and Family Violence Act 2007 and the Criminal Code.[117] The objects of the Act, similar to those found in the IPV laws of other states, are found in section 3 and include prevention, victim safety and offender accountability. Section 18 empowers an issuing authority (police[118] or the court)[119] to make a DVO against a domestic violence offender. In terms of section 17, domestic violence may be perpetrated by proxy, that is a person who advises or procures another to carry out acts of domestic violence is deemed to have committed such act. The DVO may include a Premise Access Order requiring that the defendant vacate the premises where they live or lived with the affected person, or which restrains them from entering the premises except on certain conditions.[120] The Act also provides for the possibility of an offender being required to attend a rehabilitation programme.[121]

It can be seen from the above that many of the state laws on IPV have similar provisions and cover similar issues. The overriding aim is the prevention of IPV, protection of victims/affected persons, offender accountability and rehabilitation among others.

[114] Paras 4, 7, 145, 147 & 150.

[115] Para 9.

[116] Para 228.

[117] Part IIAA, made applicable via sec 15 of the Act.

[118] Sec 41.

[119] Sec 28.

[120] Sec 22.

[121] Sec 85A & B.

3 IPV in Australia

In March 2019, Dr Preethi Reddy, a Sydney Dentist was murdered by her ex-partner, a fellow dentist. The coroner found that Preethi's killer had taken her life by 'blunt force head injury and stab wound to the neck and back' in his hotel room, moments after she had called her new partner from the hotel bathroom.[122] He had afterwards gone out to get a meal at the food court, bought a giant suitcase to stuff her body in and had obtained help from unsuspecting hotel staff to lift the suitcase, which was placed in Preethi's car.[123] Preethi's body would be found almost 24 hours later, by which time, her murderer had taken his own life by ramming headlong into an oncoming truck, endangering the lives of the truck driver and other road users.[124]

Ms Reddy and her abuser had met in 2014 and started a relationship in which he had been controlling, and which had become on-again-off-again by 2015. She moved on and started seeing someone else in 2018. The ex-partners ran into each other at a dentistry conference in March 2019, and this would set the scene for her murder.[125] Dr Reddy in trying to be compassionate and give him closure had agreed to have dinner with him.[126] Sadly instead, he would rather kill her than see her move on with her life.

Intimate Partner Violence continues to plague Australia, with women disproportionately affected. Between 1 July 2010 and 30 June 2014, there were 152 intimate partner homicides in Australia, which followed an identifiable history of IPV, with about 80% of these murders committed by men, an overwhelming majority of whom had been their victim's

[122] C Sutton 'Preethi Reddy Inquest: Killer's grizzly acts before stuffing ex-lover in suitcase' *news.com.au* 24 June 2020 https://www.news.com.au/national/courts-law/preethi-reddy-inquest-killers-grisly-acts-before-stuffing-exlover-in-suitcase/news-story/370ecee461b0e4ae9a82ade182c025ff (accessed 15 August 2023); N Wolfe 'Dentist Preethi Reddy murdered by ex-boyfriend in another horrific domestic violence incident' *news.com.au* 21 May 2021 https://www.news.com.au/lifestyle/real-life/news-life/dentist-preethi-reddy-murdered-by-exboyfriend-in-another-horrific-domestic-violence-incident/news-story/31e193d7db2c82a0c906e60410b84ffa (accessed 15 August 2023).

[123] Sutton (n 132).

[124] As above.

[125] As above.

[126] Wolfe (n 132).

primary abuser prior to her death.[127] It is significant that of the remaining 20% homicides committed by women, more than two-thirds of these were done in retaliation for abuse suffered in the hands of the men in question.[128] More men killed their current female partners at the time than former female partners, with almost half of murdered former partners being killed within three months of the relationship ending.[129] It is also significant to note that 24% of men who killed their intimate partner had been named as respondents in DVOs at the times of the killings,[130] suggesting that DVOs were not that effective in protecting the women who had relied on them. The ages of these male offenders ranged from 19 to 82 years.[131]

In Cripps' review of 151 Australian coronial court investigations and inquests spanning a 20-year period from 2000 to 2020, the vulnerability of indigenous women to intimate partner homicide was highlighted.[132] Indigenous women are more likely to experience IPV than any other group, with the average rate being eight times more than others.[133] They are 32 times more likely to be hospitalised for assault related injuries.[134] Violence represents 10.9% of the burden of disease for indigenous women.[135] In the study by Cripps, the relationships under review varied from less than a year to over 10 years.[136] A recurring theme, however, was the relationships being characterised by patterns of persistence violence which escalated in severity over time.[137] The particularly

[127] Australian Domestic and Family Violence Death Review Network 'Data Report' (2018) xii https://www.coronerscourt.vic.gov.au/sites/default/files/2018-11/website%2Bversion%2B-%2Badfvdrn_data_report_2018_.pdf (accessed 15 Aug 2023).

[128] ADFVDRN (n 137) xii.

[129] As above.

[130] As above.

[131] ADFVDRN (n 137) 13.

[132] K Cripps 'Indigenous women and intimate partner homicide in Australia: Confronting the impunity of policing failures' (2023) 35 *Current Issues in Criminal Justice* 293 at 293.

[133] Cripps (n 142) 294.

[134] As above.

[135] Australian Government (n 46) 17.

[136] Cripps (n 142) 299.

[137] As above.

violent deaths of indigenous victims of IPV are also notable, with the perpetrators usually continuing with the attack even after the victim was unconscious.[138] Alcohol also played a role in about 70% of the domestic violence killing of indigenous women (with the victim also having used in some cases). Indigenous women also experience delayed responses to their calls for help, be it Triple Zero calls or police response, which had left the coroner wondering in some cases whether the lives of the women in question could have been saved had the response been markedly different.

Male-on-female domestic violence is not isolated to Australia. It is the most common form of IPV the world over. In their 2014 WHO-commissioned study, Garcia-Moreno and others found violence by a male intimate partner to be widespread in all countries in the study.[139] Acts constituting IPV which were under review included physical violence, sexual violence, emotionally abusive acts and controlling behaviours. In some cases, the prevalence of severe physical violence (such as being hit with a fist, kicked, dragged, choked, burnt, threatened with a weapon) was as high as 49% (with majority of women experiencing physical violence more than once), sexual violence was found to have a prevalence of as high as 59% while the prevalence of emotionally abusive acts (including being insulted or made to feel bad about oneself, being humiliated in front of others, intimidation or threats) was as high as 75%, with most having occurred within the preceding 12 months.[140]

3.1 The Intersection of Gender and IPV in Australia

History has shown that there is a strong link between gender and IPV. It has been established over time that women continue to be disproportionately affected by IPV than men.[141] Australian state laws on domestic violence expressly acknowledge this fact.[142] The UN Declaration on the Elimination of Violence against Women recognises violence against women as a manifestation of historically unequal power relations between

[138] As above.

[139] Garcia-Moreno and others (n 25) xii. The study was of 24 000 women in ten diverse countries.

[140] Garcia-Moreno and others (n 25) xii-xiii.

[141] NCRVWC (n 21) 12.

[142] Preamble to the Qld Act.

men and women, and as a social mechanism by which women are forced into a subordinate societal role.[143] Violent behaviour is part of a range of tactics used by the abuser to exercise power and control over their victims.[144] Simply put, abusers see violence as a means of subjugating women, and coerce them into submission. As the Nation Council to Reduce Violence against Women and Children has aptly noted, at the core of IPV is the need to control one's partner through fear.[145]

The term 'coercive control' has received renewed attention in the Australian social space following the murder of vulnerable women including Preethi and Hannah. Coercive control has been identified as a form of domestic abuse involving patterns of behaviour which have the cumulative effect of denying a victim their autonomy and independence.[146] With coercive control, the abuser asserts dominance and control over their victim through repeated patterns of abusive behaviour.[147] Behaviours amounting to coercive control include monitoring the victim's communication, denying them access to their family and friends, and intimidation.[148] It has been identified as the most common risk factor for intimate partner homicide.[149] In New South Wales, it was discovered that 111 of 112 intimate partner homicides in the state between 2008 and 2016 were preceded by coercive control.[150] To support the theory of a compulsion for control, reference can be made

[143] Declaration on the Elimination of Violence Against Women.

[144] NCRVWC (n 21) 13.

[145] As above.

[146] Government of New South Wales 'Criminalising coercive control in New South Wales' https://www.dcj.nsw.gov.au/children-and-families/family-domestic-and-sexual-violence/police--legal-help-and-the-law/criminalising-coercive-control-in-nsw.html (accessed 15 August 2023).

[147] L Chung '"Silent, hidden and deathly pandemic": Coercive control should be made a crime, inquiry finds' *Sydney Morning Herald* 30 June 2021 https://www.smh.com.au/national/nsw/silent-hidden-and-deathly-pandemic-coercive-control-should-be-made-a-crime-inquiry-finds-20210630-p58519.html (accessed 30 October 2024).

[148] As above.

[149] J Topsfield 'Domestic violence victims overwhelmingly back criminalising coercive control' *Sydney Morning Herald* 22 March 2023 https://www.smh.com.au/national/domestic-violence-victims-overwhelmingly-back-criminalising-coercive-control-20230321-p5ctvm.html (accessed 31 October 2024).

[150] Chung (n 157).

to the opinion provided by Hannah Clarke's mother on why her daughter's abuser disliked their eldest child: 'He disliked her out of his three children because she was strong and would stand up'.[151]

Violence against women is both a cause and consequence of gender inequality. Unfortunately, violence against women has been recognised as a manifestation of historically unequal power relations between men and women, and as a social mechanism by which women are forced into a subordinate societal role.[152] An integral part of IPV against women is the subjugation of the women in question, such that they come to accept their abuse or degradation as normal or deserved. Garcia-Moreno and others found women who had experienced abuse to be more accepting of wife-beating, and as many as 20% in some of the countries surveyed believing that women did not have the right to refuse sex under any circumstance.[153]

IPV is a form of discrimination against women. It challenges the notion of equality guaranteed to all. Article 1 of the Convention on the Elimination of all forms of Discrimination Against Women (CEDAW) defines discrimination against women to mean any distinction, exclusion or restriction made on the basis of sex which has the effect or purpose of impairing or nullifying women's enjoyment of their fundamental rights and freedoms.[154] Thus, as the abuse of women is usually by male intimate partners for the purpose of establishing control as males over their victims, it would amount to discrimination. Article 5 of CEDAW enjoins all states parties to modify social and cultural patterns necessary to achieve elimination of prejudices, stereotypes and norms which falsely propagate the inferiority of women over men.

A developing aspect of IPV against women is that perpetuated by an abuser in same-sex relationships where both partners are women. This is an issue that keeps evolving. Although the texture of abuse could differ to that of a male-abuser-and-female-victim intimate relationship being that the dynamic of the historically unequal power relation between men and women is absent, elements necessary for abuse, like the need to control

[151] Antrobus (n 13).

[152] UN Declaration on the Elimination of Violence Against Women.

[153] (n 25) xiii-xiv.

[154] UN General Assembly, Convention on the Elimination of All Forms Discrimination Against Women, 18 December 1979, United Nations, Treaty Series, volume 1249, p 13 https://www.refworld.org/docid/3ae6b3970.html (accessed 1 November 2024).

through fear, would still be present. An abusive female partner in a same-sex relationship can rely on perceived homophobia as a tool of control, such as, for example, threatening to out their partner to friends, family and others, instilling fear in a partner by telling them that they would not get help from law enforcement or the justice system due to homophobia and trying to convince a partner that abuse is normal in same-sex relationships.[155]

3.2 IPV as a Limitation to Fundamental Rights

IPV is a violation of fundamental human rights.[156] Violence against women is a violation of women's fundamental rights, as guaranteed under international human rights instruments.[157] The UN Declaration on the Elimination of Violence against Women provides that women are entitled to the equal enjoyment and protection of all rights and freedoms, be it economic, social, cultural, political or otherwise.[158] Thus, there should be no hindrance to their enjoyment of rights including the right to life, equality, health, liberty and security of the person, equal protection under the law, freedom from discrimination, as well as freedom from torture, cruel, inhuman or degrading treatment.[159] International human rights treaties such as the Universal Declaration of Human Rights (Universal Declaration),[160] CEDAW and the International Covenant on Civil and Political Rights (ICCPR)[161] guarantee these rights and freedoms. Some of these rights as they pertain to women will be discussed in further detail below.

[155] NCRVWC (n 21) 15.

[156] Preamble, Family Violence Protection Act 2008 (Victoria).

[157] Garcia-Moreno and others (n 25).

[158] Art 3 of the Declaration on the Elimination of Violence against Women.

[159] Art 3 of the Declaration on the Elimination of Violence against Women.

[160] UN General Assembly, Universal Declaration of Human Rights, 10 December 1948, 217 A (III) https://www.refworld.org/docid/3ae6b3712c.html (accessed 4 February 2024).

[161] UN General Assembly, International Covenant on Civil and Political Rights, 16 December 1966, United Nations, Treaty Series, vol 999, p 171 https://www.refworld.org/docid/3ae6b3aa0.html (accessed 4 February 2024).

The right to life is sacrosanct. It is a fundamental right to which women, like everyone else are entitled. Article 3 of the Universal Declaration and articles 6 and 9 of ICCPR respectively guarantee the rights to life, liberty and security of the person. Domestic violence is a direct threat to these rights. Many women have had these rights taken away from them at the hands of abusive intimate partners. Many women have had their lives taken by husbands, partners, boyfriends and in some cases, new love interests. In July 2023, a 25-year-old Australian woman and an elderly man who had tried to help her were killed by her boyfriend of four weeks, when he purposely crashed into the car they were travelling in.[162] In some of these cases, the abuse victim's children, family, associates or rescuers become collateral damage or 'victims of circumstance', as was the case with Hannah Clarke's children, and the elderly man who had tried to help the 25-year-old abuse victim above.

IPV takes away any notion of equality from the woman being abused in contradiction to the guarantees under international human rights provisions. Articles 15 and 16 of CEDAW are particularly relevant. They recognise the right to equality for men and women. Article 16 recognises women's rights on a range of issues pertaining to the right to enter into a marriage with their free and full consent, equal rights and responsibilities as parents, right to decide on the number and spacing of children, equal rights to guardianship, adoption of children and equal personal rights as husband and wife, including the right to choose a family name, profession and occupation, and equal rights on ownership, enjoyment and disposition of property. The Universal Declaration also recognises these rights. For instance, article 23 guarantees the right to work and free choice of employment. Many women in abusive relationships are deprived of at least one, usually a combination of rights recognised here. For instance, many are prevented from working by their husband or partner, especially after marriage or with the birth of their children. Many women are also not involved in the running of the family's finances. These take power away from such women, thereby deepening the inequality in these relationships.

[162] J Dye, M Bolton & O Jacques 'Man charged with murder after triple fatal Bruce Highway crash at Federal, Queensland' *ABC News* 25 July 2013 https://www.abc.net.au/news/23-07-25/man-charged-with-murder-after-triple-fatal-bruce-highway-crash/102642668 (accessed 1 November 2024).

IPV violates the right to be free from torture, cruel, inhuman, or degrading treatment and punishment, as guaranteed under article 5 of the Universal Declaration, article 3(h) of the Declaration on the Elimination of Violence against Women, and article 7 of the ICCPR. Many women are slapped, beaten, flogged, tortured, choked by their partners and have accepted this as part of their relationships. Sadly, many victims make excuses and cover up for their abusers. The same is sometimes true for friends and family of the abuser.

Freedom of thought and expression is one of the first fundamental rights to be trampled on in relationships experiencing IPV. This right is guaranteed under article 19 of the Universal Declaration and article 19(1) & (2) of the ICCPR. One of the early signs of abuse in intimate relationships is the silencing of the victim's voice, such that they understand that their thought or opinion does not count, or that they are not allowed to have any. This would precede the inevitable chipping away of the abused woman's self-confidence.

IPV directly impacts women's health and their right to healthcare. This right is recognised under article 12 of CEDAW. Article 3(f) of the Declaration on the Elimination of Violence against Women recognises the right to the highest attainable standard of physical and mental health. IPV is a public health issue which has been associated with up to seven diseases or injuries namely depressive disorders, anxiety, early pregnancy loss, suicide and self-inflicted injuries, homicide and violence, alcohol use disorders, preterm birth and birthweight complications.[163] In 2011, IPV was found to have contributed to more burden of disease than any other risk factor for women aged 25–44 years.[164] In 2014–2015, nearly one in five of the 19 000 hospitalisations due to an assault injury was as a result of IPV.[165]

Sadly, many women globally have experienced and continue to experience significant limitations to their rights and freedoms and have accepted this limitation as the norm. In the words of Nelson Mandela, 'many who

[163] Australian Institute of Health and Welfare *Australia's Health 2018* (2018) 195 https://www.aihw.gov.au/getmedia/7c42913d-295f-4bc9-9c24-4e44eff4a04a/aihw-aus-221.pdf.aspx?inline=true (accessed 1 November 2024).

[164] Ayre and others 'Examination of the burden of disease of intimate partner violence against women in 2011: Final report' ANROWS (2016).

[165] Ayre and others (n 174) 146.

live with violence day in and day out assume that it is an intrinsic part of the human condition'.[166]

The harm caused by violence against women goes beyond the immediate harm caused, to affecting their physical, mental and reproductive health among other things.[167] The physical effects of violence may survive the act itself for a long time, and violence could have a cumulative effect on the sufferer.[168] It has devastating consequences for victims, and witnesses, especially children.[169] For instance, women who had ever experienced IPV were significantly more likely to report poor or very poor health than those who had never experienced it.[170] Ever-abused women (that is, women who had been perpetually abused) are more likely to have problems with walking, pain, dizziness, memory loss and performing daily activities.[171] Women victims of physical or sexual violence in intimate relationships have reported significantly higher levels of emotional distress, and are more likely to be suicidal that non-victims.[172] IPV has been found to pre-empt induced abortion and miscarriage in victims.

3.3 *Australia's Efforts in Addressing IPV*

Intimate partner assaults and deaths are preventable. As highlighted by Cripps, these deaths rarely occur without warning.[173] They are generally preceded by increasing violent or abusive incidents indicating a heightened risk of future harm.[174] Prevention would only be possible however is the systems designed to protect women are actually capable of doing so, and if they follow processes focused on women's safety.

Unfortunately, despite the availability and use of DVOs by victims across the country, women in Australia continue to experience abuse in the hands of their partners. It is also striking that many female victims are

[166] Krug and others (n 22).

[167] Garcia-Moreno and others (n 25) xv.

[168] As above.

[169] Garcia-Moreno and others (n 25) vii.

[170] Garcia-Moreno and others (n 25) xv.

[171] Garcia-Moreno and others (n 25) xv.

[172] Garcia-Moreno and others (n 25) xv.

[173] Cripps (n 142) 294.

[174] As above.

threatened, assaulted or killed while there is a subsisting order of protection against their attacker. A case in point is Christine Rakic who was killed by her ex-husband in July 2023 in Sydney. Even though Christine had taken out an Apprehended DVO against her ex-husband, that did not stop him from violently taking her life.[175] At the time of the murder, the offender was out on bail, charged with common assault over a previous attack on her.[176] Hannah Clarke also had a protection order against her murderous ex-husband. Thus, even with a protection order, there is no guarantee for many women across Australia. These women are just few of several who had protection orders against an abuser but who could not be protected.

Despite numerous initiatives aimed at creating awareness and addressing IPV in Australia, these incidents continue unabated. That suggests that efforts to tackle it are inadequate. It must be said that many individuals and organisations have joined in the fight,[177] usually by creating awareness on the issue. These organisations include the White Ribbon Foundation, and the Red Rose Foundation, which are privately run, and the Domestic Violence Prevention Centre[178] which is government-sponsored.

The Australian Police Force has for a long time come under fire for their unhelpful responses to victims of domestic violence. This has been blown more open in recent times, following the death of a 28-year-old indigenous woman, simply identified as Roberta, at the hands of her domestic abuser. The coroner found that the assault which resulted in Roberta's death was the seventh in less than 2 weeks and had occurred a mere 5 days after the police had warned her to stop calling them.[179] She bled to death in silence over several hours lying beside her attacker. The coroner found that the Northern Territory police did nothing to help Roberta, had been rude and dismissive of her and had failed to follow any of the laid down procedures for domestic violence complaints.[180]

[175] Keoghan (n 10).

[176] As above.

[177] They include The Red Rose Foundation and the White Ribbon Foundation.

[178] Domestic Violence Prevention Centre, Contributing to Change 'Activism' https://domesticviolence.com.au/contributing-to-change/activisim (accessed 22 January 2025).

[179] Cripps (n 142) 294.

[180] As above.

The coroner found that the system as a whole had failed Roberta, from the Triple Zero call taker who had incorrectly classified Roberta's call for help, to her partner's parole officer who should have been aware that he was in parole violation.[181] The coroner found that the police had failed to access the offender's criminal history, failed to appreciate the seriousness of his offending and the risk that he posed, failed to use his electronic monitoring device data to find and arrest him, despite being aware of his recent release from prison on a suspended sentence.[182] It was just a matter of time before he killed her.

Another case highlighting the failure of police to help victims, and their disposition towards victim-blaming was spotlighted by Cripps.[183] The victim in question was an aboriginal female who the officers had concluded was intoxicated, without ever talking to her or questioning witnesses, including the ones who had phoned Triple Zero to report the disturbance as it unfolded.[184] Their conclusion of intoxication was reached based solely on her seeming disheveled appearance, being that she was sitting curbside in only her knickers when the officers arrived.[185] She was seen as 'just a drunk Aboriginal female' prompting their initial decision to place her in protective custody.[186] However, it would later emerge that her abuser had removed her clothes only moments before the officers' arrival, as she fled from him.[187] The officers chose instead to speak with her attacker, who they described as helpful and sober. Shockingly, when what was considered a 'higher priority call' came over the police radio, the officers simply told the abuser to remove the victim from the back of their vehicle, effectively sealing her fate. The attack continued immediately after the officers left, following which she lost

[181] As above.

[182] Australian Associated Press 'Police dismissed complaints of indigenous woman fatally bashed by ex-partner, NT inquest finds' *The Guardian* 15 June 2022 https://www.theguardian.com/australia-news/2022/jun/15/police-dismissed-complaints-of-indigenous-woman-fatally-bashed-by-ex-partner-nt-inquest-finds (accessed 1 November 2024).

[183] Cripps (n 142) 302.

[184] As above.

[185] As above.

[186] As above.

[187] Cripps (n 142).

her life. This was another preventable domestic violence death, with the abysmal attitude of the attending officers acting as a catalyst.

Police officers have also been found to delay investigations and action breaches of DVOs to force the victim to reflect on whether she really wanted to follow through with bringing her attacker to book.[188] They have been known to ask victims whether they really want to proceed with charges, to ultimately discourage these women or make them second guess themselves. Worse still, was the revelation that police had consistently failed to enforce DVOs issued to protect indigenous women.[189] These attitudes are appalling and put victims at risk of further harm.[190]

The Australian Police Force has also been found to be plagued by attitudes which are harmful to victims of domestic violence. Members of the force are members of the larger society and are unfortunately products of that same society. In its 2022 report, the Commission of Inquiry into the Queensland Police Response to Domestic and Family Violence stated as follows[191]:

> The Commission has found clear evidence of a culture where attitudes of misogyny, sexism and racism are allowed to be expressed, and at times acted upon, largely unchecked ... It is hardly surprising that these attitudes are reflected then in the way that those police who hold them respond to victim-survivors. It is a failure of the leadership of the organization that this situation has been allowed to continue over many years unchecked.

It was brought to the fore that some male officers were predatory. Incidents of sexist language and behaviours, sexual harassment, assault and rape by police officers were brought to the knowledge of the Commission.[192] When the person charged with upholding the law exhibits traits which could challenge that law, it becomes a problem. It is necessary to

[188] Cripps (n 142) 304.

[189] Cripps (n 142) 303.

[190] Cripps (n 142) 304.

[191] Queensland Government *A call for change: Commission of Inquiry into Queensland police service responses to domestic and family violence: Report* (2022) https://www.qpsdfvinquiry.qld.gov.au/about/assets/commission-of-inquiry-dpsdfv-report.pdf (accessed 1 November 2024).

[192] Queensland Government (n 201) 16.

provide the force with a reorientation, so that Roberta's experience would not become that of more women in Australia.

The Australian government has continued with its efforts to address IPV. In October 2022, it released *the National Plan to End Violence against Women and Children 2022–2032: Ending gender-based violence in one generation.*[193] The National Plan, expected to be implemented through two 5-year plans, aims to end gender violence in one generation.[194] It recognises that ending violence against women and children cannot be achieved by the government alone, but rather, as a joint national effort.[195] The National Plan puts a national policy framework in place to aid government, policymakers, workplaces, relevant organisations and other stakeholders in addressing, preventing and responding to gender-based violence in Australia.[196] It aims to advance gender equality in Australia, breach the gap and provide necessary support for survivors to land on their feet.[197]

The National Plan proposes the active engagement of different sectors. For the health sector, the Plan proposes the delivery of trauma-informed and accessible health services, support for survivors with respect to short and long-term physical and mental health.[198] The Plan challenges the media to address gender inequality, challenge gender stereotypes and work to end the disrespect of women, promote perpetrator accountability and work to eradicate victim-blaming, as well as raise awareness on the availability of survivor support services.[199] Schools are enjoined to integrate intervention initiatives to prevent and respond appropriately to gender-based violence, educate young people on respectful behaviours, and to recognise young people as victim-survivors and meet their safety needs.[200] It proposes that the justice system among other things, provide timely, survivor-centred responses, hold perpetrators to account and

[193] Australian Govt (n 46).

[194] Australian Govt (n 46) 14.

[195] Australian Govt (n 46) 29.

[196] Australian Govt (n 46) 19.

[197] Australian Govt (n 46) 20.

[198] Australian Govt (n 46) 29.

[199] As above.

[200] As above.

recognise young victims of violence as victim-survivors, and make decisions that are in their best interests.[201] The community is also enjoined to integrate prevention of gender-based violence in every aspect, support gender equality and respond to survivors with compassion.[202]

Australian states like New South Wales and Queensland have been vocal about criminalising coercive control. New South Wales has recently introduced the Crimes Legislation Amendment (Coercive Control) Act 2022[203] criminalising coercive control. The Act establishes an Implementation and Evaluation Taskforce on coercive control to consult with stakeholders and provide advice in relation to the offence of coercive control.[204] The move to criminalise coercive control in Australia has received an overwhelming level of support from victims of domestic violence.[205] In spite of this, however, states like Victoria do not have plans to introduce a law criminalising coercive control, given that the state's Family Violence Protection Act already covers coercive behaviour in its definition of family violence.[206] Some experts also submit that there is little evidence to support the impact of criminalisation.[207]

Australian state governments are also working to support women and children affected by IPV. Individuals whose lives have been affected by domestic violence are also working independently or with the government to make a difference. For instance, Nithya Reddy, Preethi's sister has been advocating for support for victims of IPV, including fighting for a domestic violence trauma recovery centre in the Illawara region of New South Wales.[208] The rationale for a trauma centre is that it would help women recognise the signs and dangers of coercive control, and help to reduce IPV and the number of women killed as a result.[209]

Garcia-Moreno and others recommend a two-pronged approach at national level namely strengthening national commitment and action and

[201] As above.

[202] As above.

[203] Act 65 of 2022.

[204] Section 54I(3).

[205] Topsfield (n 159).

[206] As above.

[207] As above.

[208] Wolfe (n 132).

[209] As above.

promoting primary prevention.[210] To strengthen national commitment, they recommend promoting gender equality and women's rights, establishing and monitoring national action plans to address violence against women, including IPV, enlist the help of social, political and religious leaders in speaking out against violence against women and invest in data collection on the subject.[211] In promoting primary prevention, they recommend that states develop, implement and monitor programmes for the primary prevention of IPV such as public awareness creation and prioritising prevention of sexual abuse of young people.[212]

4 Challenges and the Way Forward

At the core of the persistence of IPV are factors such as fear, stigma, shame and powerlessness which hinder the victim from seeking help.[213] Many victims associate speaking up and seeking help with a loss of their privacy, loss of their sense of dignity and a sign of weakness.[214] The loss of privacy becomes a pertinent issue for women in regional or small communities where most people are connected and news travels fast. For instance, a woman could be more reluctant to seek help if the healthcare workers available are persons known to her. Thus, victims of IPV in regional Australia could be at risk of staying in violent relationships, thereby further exposing themselves to severe harm, arising from fear and the stigma attached. One way of tackling this is by scaling up awareness on IPV and the urgency and benefits of seeking help. It is essential that the shame is taken away from survivors.

Many female victims of IPV are unaware that they are experiencing it. This would be especially true for women from backgrounds where it is cultural for women to assume a submissive role in relationships. Such women might be unable to identify abusive behaviour or set boundaries as to what constitutes abuse. Many erroneously believe that traits like extreme jealousy, possessiveness and control are signs of love. Many victims and their loved ones cannot quite define the abuse but would

210 Garcia-Moreno and others (n 25) xvii.

211 As above.

212 As above.

213 NCRVWC (n 21) 16.

214 As above.

usually feel like they are walking on eggshells around the abuser.[215] It is important to educate women and girls on healthy boundaries. This can be done in the form of awareness campaigns via television, radio and newsprint jingles. IPV prevention and awareness can also be developed and incorporated into the Australian school curriculum as appropriate. This ensures that it is taught to young people early to prevent them being victims and to help in identifying if family members are victims of IPV, and encouraging such family members to speak up, or speaking up on their behalf.

Another problem is the reluctance or unwillingness of people outside the abusive relationship to interfere, sometimes based on the belief that the relationship and its issues are personal to the parties involved, or out of fear of being labelled as intrusive, or believing that the abuse is nothing more than a 'lovers' tiff', or not feeling compelled to interfere. For instance, in one of the cases discussed above, the police noted the reluctance of witnesses to speak to officers, despite being aware of the facts of the case, including the gruesome murder of three innocent people.[216] It was also confronting to note that acquaintances of Hannah's murderous husband were quick to leap to his defence or make excuses for him as the story broke. Also, immediately following the suicide of Preethi Reddy's killer, his workplace had put up posts celebrating his life and person.[217] Although it must be pointed out that these posts were put up before the horrific facts behind his death emerged, the reaction of his work colleagues suggest that he was held in high regard. This narrative must be changed as a matter of urgency. The words of Members of the Independent Collective of Survivors, as published in the *National Plan* particularly resonate here[218]:

> Discard the intuition that just because you know someone, they could not possibly hurt or abuse another. The people who use violence and abuse against their families, partners, children, colleagues, friends or dates are people you already know. People you like. People you love.

[215] Antrobus (n 13).

[216] Dye and others (n 172).

[217] Wolfe (n 132).

[218] (n 46) 9.

A reorientation is necessary by educating the citizenry on the importance of looking out for one another. This is a civic duty that everyone owes to the community. Attaching criminality to failure to report or cooperate when required could change the narrative. Introducing a fine or punishment could also address this problem.

Closely following the above problem is the culture of victim-blaming. The American Psychological Association describes victim-blaming as a social psychological phenomenon where people assign blame to the victim of a trauma or tragedy as a way of coping with the occurrence of that trauma or tragedy.[219] Examples of victim-blaming include saying a rape victim caused their rape by their mode of dressing, and saying a victim of domestic violence must have provoked their abuser before the attack. Victim-blaming is counter-intuitive, counter-productive and further drives victims of IPV underground. A re-orientation is also necessary in this regard. Creating awareness and educating the community will be helpful here.

One of the most jarring conclusions in the face of Australia's IPV crisis is the inadequacy of police intervention. For example, there have been many reviews of Queensland Police Service (QPS) response to IPV, which have persistently identified issues including failure to act in accordance with legislation and procedures, to appropriately assess risk, to pursue criminal charges and identify the person most in need of protection (all of which applied in Roberta's case).[220] Unfortunately, these system failures have remained in place.[221] These issues must be addressed urgently. In contrast, examples were given of situations where officers had engaged with victims' complaints in an effective, timely and professional manner, resulting in a significant difference to the victim's safety and willingness to further engage with the police.[222] Sweeping changes have been recommended to police response. These include the trialling of what has been called a 'multidisciplinary police station' which will be equipped to provide additional support services including housing and child safety.[223]

[219] American Psychological Association *Dictionary of Psychology* 'Blaming the victim', https://dictionary.apa.org/blaming-the-victim (accessed 1 November 2024).

[220] QG (n 201) 14.

[221] As above.

[222] As above.

[223] Antrobus (n 13).

A comprehensive health sector response will be beneficial in addressing violence against women.[224] The international community has recognised the interconnectivity of health and gender equality, as evidenced, for example, by the UN Sustainable Development Goal number five, which aims to achieve gender equality and empower women and girls.[225] A rationale given by Gro Harlem Brundtland, former WHO Director is particularly jarring: she questions the sense in saving children from childhood diseases, only to lose them when caught in the crosshairs of IPV.[226] The Australian health sector can and must play a pivotal role in the fight against IPV. Healthcare workers can help in identifying and arresting abuse early, providing support and treatment for victims and referring them for appropriate care.[227]

5 Conclusion

The chapter has extensively examined the issue of IPV in Australia, using a few of its many cases of IPV to depict the harm caused by IPV to women in Australia, their children and families. The chapter has also shed light on the categories of women in Australia who are even more vulnerable, such are younger women, indigenous women, immigrant women, aged women and women with physical and intellectual disabilities. It traced the history of IPV in the country, and the current regime for the protection of women from IPV and the prevention of violence against women. The chapter has established a strong link between gender and IPV, showing that the need to subjugate women is at the root of violence against women. It also shed light on IPV as a limitation to women's rights and freedoms as guaranteed under international treaties, including the right to life, the right to health, the right to liberty, freedom of association as well as freedom from torture, cruel and degrading treatment.

The chapter has also examined Australia's efforts in addressing IPV against women, highlighting the country's successes, with its numerous IPV awareness and prevention initiatives, including the establishment of Domestic Violence Prevention Centres, the availability to victims

[224] Garcia-Moreno and others (n 25) vii.

[225] Available at https://sdgs.un.org/goals/goal5 (accessed 31 October 2024).

[226] Krug and others (n 22).

[227] Garcia-Moreno and others (n 25) vii.

of Domestic Violence Protection Orders against alleged abusers. The chapter also considered the shortcomings in Australia's IPV prevention efforts, the most glaring one being that in spite of all the huge efforts and resources which have gone into addressing IPV in the country, it has continued unabated in Australia, with alarming statistics to boot. Further issues identified with the current regime include the inadequate training and support provided for law enforcement and healthcare workers to identify or help victims of IPV. Recommendations were then made to address these gaps, such as scaling up awareness campaigns on IPV and issues surrounding it, such as what constitutes healthy boundaries, forms of IPV, dangers, prevention and ways of identifying it, and providing adequate training for healthcare practitioners to include recognition of signs of IPV and the provision of appropriate care for survivors.

Bibliography

American Psychological Association *Dictionary of Psychology* 'Blaming the victim' https://dictionary.apa.org/blaming-the-victim (accessed 31 October 2024)

Antrobus, B 'Heroic final act of slain mum Hannah Clarke revealed as horror DV murder explored at inquest' *news.com.au* 2 April 2022 https://www.news.com.au/lifestyle/real-life/news-life/heroic-final-act-of-slain-mum-hannah-clarke-revealed-as-horror-dv-murder-explored-at-inquest/news-story/36c85df4214f6df7f15ab741529103a6 (accessed 31 October 2024)

Australian Associated Press 'Police dismissed complaints of indigenous woman fatally bashed by ex-partner, NT inquest finds' *The Guardian* 15 June 2022 https://www.theguardian.com/australia-news/2022/jun/15/police-dismissed-complaints-of-indigenous-woman-fatally-bashed-by-ex-partner-nt-inquest-finds (accessed 31 October 2024)

Australian Bureau of Statistics 'Personal safety survey' (2021–22) https://www.abs.gov.au/statistics/people/crime-and-justice/personal-safety-australia/latest-release (accessed 31 October 2024)

Australian Bureau of Statistics '2 in 5 Australians have experienced physical or sexual violence' (15 March 2023) https://www.abs.gov.au/media-centre/media-releases/2-5-australians-have-experienced-physical-or-sexual-violence (accessed 31 October 2024)

Australian Domestic and Family Violence Death Review Network 'Data Report' (2018) https://www.coronerscourt.vic.gov.au/sites/default/files/2018-11/website%2Bversion%2B-%2Badfvdrn_data_report_2018_.pdf (accessed 31 October 2024)

Australian Government, National Plan to Reduce Violence against Women and their Children 'Useful statistics' available at https://www.plan4womenssafety.dss.gov.au/resources/useful-statistics/

Australian Government (Attorney-General's Department) 'National Domestic Violence Order Scheme' https://www.ag.gov.au/families-and-marriage/families/family-violence/national-domestic-violence-order-scheme (accessed 31 October 2024)

Australian Institute of Health and Welfare *Australia's Health 2018* (2018) https://www.aihw.gov.au/getmedia/7c42913d-295f-4bc9-9c24-4e44eff4a04a/aihw-aus-221.pdf.aspx?inline=true (accessed 31 October 2024)

Australian Institute of Health and Welfare 'Family, domestic and sexual violence' https://www.aihw.gov.au/family-domestic-and-sexual-violence (accessed 31 October 2024)

Australian Institute of Health and Welfare 'Family, domestic and sexual violence: Intimate partner violence' https://www.aihw.gov.au/family-domestic-and-sexual-violence/types-of-violence/intimate-partner-violence (accessed 31 October 2024)

Ayre, J; On, ML; Webster, K; Gourley, K & Moon, L 'Examination of the burden of disease of intimate partner violence against women in 2011: Final report' ANROWS (Sydney ANROWS 2016)

Bowden, T 'Thirty-one women killed in Australia in 15 weeks renews calls for action' *Australian Broadcasting Corporation News* 13 April 2015 https://www.abc.net.au/news/2015-04-13/thirty-one-women-killed-in-australia-in-15-weeks/6390072 (accessed 31 October 2024)

Chung, L '"Silent, hidden and deathly pandemic": Coercive control should be made a crime, inquiry finds' *Sydney Morning Herald* 30 June 2021 https://www.smh.com.au/national/nsw/silent-hidden-and-deathly-pandemic-coercive-control-should-be-made-a-crime-inquiry-finds-20210630-p58519.html (accessed 31 October 2024)

Coroners Court of Queensland 'Inquest into the death of Hannah Ashlie Clarke, Aaliyah Anne Baxter, Laianah Grace Baxter, Trey Rowan Charles Baxter and Rowan Charles Baxter' (2022) https://www.courts.qld.gov.au/_data/assets/pdf_file/0010/723664/cif-hannah-clarke-aaliyah-baxter-laianah-baxter-trey-baxter-and-rowan-baxter.pdf (accessed 31 October 2024)

Cripps, K 'Indigenous women and intimate partner homicide in Australia: Confronting the impunity of policing failures' (2023) 35 *Current Issues in Criminal Justice* 293

Dye, J; Bolton, M & Jacques, O 'Man charged with murder after triple fatal Bruce Highway crash at Federal, Queensland' *ABC News, Sunshine Coast (Australia)* 25 July 2013 https://www.abc.net.au/news/23-07-25/man-charged-with-murder-after-triple-fatal-bruce-highway-crash/102642668 (accessed 31 October 2024)

Garcia-Moreno, C; Jansen, HAFM; Ellsberg, M; Heise, L & Watts, C 'WHO multi-country study on women's health and domestic violence against women: Initial results on prevalence, health outcomes and women's responses' (WHO 2005)

Government of Western Australian 'New laws target strangulation, persistent family violence' https://www.wa.gov.au/government/announcements/new-laws-target-strangulation-persistent-family-violence (accessed 31 October 2024)

Keoghan, S 'Slain Sydney woman took out AVO against ex-husband' *Sydney Morning Herald* 12 July 2023 https://www.smh.com.au/national/nsw/man-under-police-guard-after-woman-found-dead-in-sydney-s-west-20230712-p5dnl2.html (accessed 31 October 2024)

Krug, EG; Dahlberg, LL; Mercy, JA; Zwi, AB & Lozanoand, R (eds) *World report on violence and health* (WHO: Geneva 2002) https://www.who.int/publication/i/item/9241545615 (accessed 31 October 2024)

National Council to Reduce Violence against Women and Children *Background paper to time for action: The National Council's Plan for Australia to Reduce Violence Against Women and their Children 2009–2021* (2009) https://www.dss.gov.au/sites/default/files/documents/05_2012/background_paper_to_time_for_action.pdf (accessed 31 October 2024)

Queensland Government *A call for change: Commission of Inquiry into Queensland police service response to domestic violence* (2022) https://www.qpsdfvinquiry.qld.gov.au/about/assets/commission-of-inquiry-dpsdfv-report.pdf (accessed 31 October 2024)

Stambe, RM & Meyer, S 'Police and duty lawyer perceptions of Domestic Violence Protection Order proceedings involving parents: Towards greater system accountability and family-centred decision-making' (2023) 38 *Journal of Family Violence* 1405

Stavrou, E; Poynton, S & D Weatherburn 'Intimate partner violence against women in Australia: related factors and help-seeking behaviours' (2016) *Contemporary Issues in Crime and Justice* Number 200https://bocsar.nsw.gov.au/documents/publications/cjb/cjb151-200/cjb200-report-intimate-partner-violence-against-women-in-australia-2016.pdf

Sutton, C 'Preethi Reddy Inquest: Killer's grizzly acts before stuffing ex-lover in suitcase' *news.com.au* 24 June 2020 https://www.news.com.au/national/courts-law/preethi-reddy-inquest-killers-grisly-acts-before-stuffing-exlover-in-suitcase/news-story/370ecee461b0e4ae9a82ade182c025ff (accessed 31 October 2024)

The Australian Government, Department of Social Services *The National Plan to End Violence against Women and Children 2022–2032: Ending gender-based violence in one generation* https://www.dss.gov.au/sites/default/files/documents/12_2023/national-plan-executive-summary.pdf (accessed 31 October 2024)

Topsfield, J 'Domestic violence victims overwhelmingly back criminalising coercive control' *Sydney Morning Herald* 22 March 2023 https://www.smh.com.au/national/domestic-violence-victims-overwhelmingly-back-criminalising-coercive-control-20230321-p5ctvm.html (accessed 31 October 2024)

UN *Universal Declaration of Human Rights* illustrated edition (2015) https://www.un.org/en/udhrbook/pdf/udhr_booklet_en_web.pdf (accessed 12 May 2023)

Wolfe, N 'Dentist Preethi Reddy murdered by ex-boyfriend in another horrific domestic violence incident' *news.com.au* 21 May 2021 https://www.news.com.au/lifestyle/real-life/news-life/dentist-preethi-reddy-murdered-by-exboyfriend-in-another-horrific-domestic-violence-incident/news-story/31e193d7db2c82a0c906e60410b84ffa (accessed 31 October 2024)

Case law

Bropho v Hall (2015) WASC 50
Gillespie v the State of Western Australia (2016) WASCA 216
Gomboc v the State of Western Australia (2023) WASCA 115
McCoombe v State of Western Australia (2016) WASCA 227
R v EQ (2021) QCA 257
R v FBC (2023) QCA 74
State of Western Australia v Cheeseman (2011) WASCA 15

Legislation

The Crimes Act 40 of 1900 (NSW)
The Crimes (Domestic and Personal Violence) Act 80 of 2007 (NSW)
The Crimes Legislation Amendment (Coercive Control) Act 65 of 2022 (NSW)
The Criminal Code Act 1983 (Northern Territory)
The Criminal Code Act 1924 (Tasmania)
The Domestic and Family Violence Act 34 of 2007 (Northern Territory)
The Domestic and Family Violence Protection Act 5 of 2012 (Queensland)
The Family Law Act 1975, Act 53 of 1975
The Family Law Legislation Amendment (Family Violence and Other Measures) Act 189 of 2011
The Family Violence Act 67 of 2004 (Tasmania)
The Family Violence Act 2016 (Australian Capital Territory)

The Family Violence Legislation Reform Act 30 of 2020 (Western Australia)
The Family Violence Protection Act 52 of 2008 (Victoria)
The Intervention Orders (Prevention from Abuse) Act 2009 (South Australia)
The National Domestic Violence Order Scheme Act 53 of 2016
The Restraining Orders Act 47 of 2019 (as amended) (Tasmania)
The Sentencing Act 59 of 1997 (as amended) (Tasmania)

UN Instruments

International Covenant on Civil and Political Rights UN General Assembly, 16 December 1966, United Nations, Treaty Series, vol 999, p 171

United Nations Declaration on the Elimination of Violence Against Women, Proclaimed by General Assembly Resolution 48/104 of 20 Dec 1993

UN General Assembly, Convention on the Rights of the Child, United Nations, Treaty Series, vol 1577, p 3, 20 November 1989

General Assembly and Convention on the Elimination of All Forms Discrimination Against Women, 18, December 1979.UN General Assembly, Convention on the Elimination of All Forms Discrimination Against Women, 18 December 1979, United Nations, Treaty Series, volume 1249, p 13

UN General Assembly, Declaration on the Elimination of Violence against Women, 20 December 1993, UN Doc A/RES/48/104 (1993)

Universal Declaration of Human Rights, UN General Assembly, 10 December 1948, 217 A (III)

CHAPTER 10

The Protection of Human Trafficking Victims in the UK: The Role of the Palermo Protocol and State Obligations in the International Law

Linimose N. Anyiwe and Eghosa O. Ekhator

1 Introduction

Since the problem of trafficking in human beings (THB) has both a domestic and an international dimension, international law can be a powerful tool for combatting human trafficking and consequently

L. N. Anyiwe
School of Law, York St John University, York, UK

E. O. Ekhator (✉)
School of Law and Social Sciences, University of Derby, Derby, UK
e-mail: e.ekhator@derby.ac.uk

E. Durojaye et al. (eds.), *Harmful Practices and Human Rights: An International Perspective*, Human Rights Interventions,
https://doi.org/10.1007/978-3-031-90333-5_10

preventing prosecution of victims of trafficking.[1] Prevention of prosecution of victims of trafficking may be improved through proper identification and prevention measures by states.[2] On the other hand, the values and beliefs held by members of a community are often reflected by their traditional cultural practices.[3] These cultural practices may have been ongoing for long periods, spanning decades, and sometimes passed on from one generation to another. It can be argued that cultural practices and beliefs present two distinct perspectives, each carrying both beneficial and detrimental implications.[4] Some practices or norms are favourable

[1] Generally, see the United Nations Office on Drugs and Crime (UNODC) 'Global report on trafficking in persons' (2022) 7 https://www.unodc.org/unodc/data-and-analysis/glotip.html (accessed 28 October 2024), which states that: 'For the first time in the 20 years that the United Nations Office on Drugs and Crime (UNODC) has collected data on trafficking in persons, we registered a decrease in 2020 in the number of victims detected globally.' Also, see G Kane 'State empowered entities as sites of progress for international anti-trafficking law and policy?' (2023) 5 *Frontiers in Human Dynamics* 1. Furthermore, in February 2021, the European Court of Human Rights in *VCL & AN v The United Kingdom* (Applications 77587/12 and 74603/12), held that the United Kingdom had violated arts 4 and 6 of 'the Convention for the Protection of Human Rights and Fundamental Freedoms following the prosecution of two children who had been the victims of trafficking': S Neves & G Stewart '*V.C.L and A.N v The United Kingdom*: A positive step forward for victims of modern day slavery' Youth Justice League Centre https://yjlc.uk/resources/legal-updates/vcl-and-v-united-kingdom-positive-step-forward-victims-modern-day-slavery (accessed 28 October 2024).

[2] The non-punishment or non-prosecution principle is the precept that states that 'trafficked persons should not be subject to arrest, charge, detention, prosecution, or be penalised or otherwise punished for illegal conduct that they committed as a direct consequence of being trafficked'. This principle or tenet was established in 2002 by the Office of the United Nations High Commissioner for Human Rights. Generally, see International Bar Association (IBA) 'IBA and BIICL launch new report exploring the global implementation non-punishment principle for human trafficking victims' (30 November 2023) https://www.ibanet.org/IBA-and-BIICL-launch-new-report-exploring-the-global-implementation-of-non-punishment-principle-for-human-trafficking-victims (accessed 28 October 2024).

[3] Generally, see E Le Roux, BE Bartelink & S Palm 'What is the harm in "harmful traditional practices"?' *Policy Brief* (November 2017) https://www.gov.uk/research-for-development-outputs/what-is-the-harm-in-harmful-traditional-practices (accessed 28 October 2024).

[4] Also, see B Bartelink & E le Roux with W Levinga 'Harmful traditional practices in the context of faith: A literature review' Part of the UK Government-funded 'Working effectively with faith leaders to challenge harmful traditional practices' Research report (2017) https://prevention-collaborative.org/wp-content/uploads/2021/08/Bartelink_2017_Harmful_practices_context_of_faith.pdf (accessed 28 October 2024).

to all members, while others are detrimental to a specific group such as women and children.[5] Some examples of harmful traditional practices (HTPs) include traditional oath-taking; early marriage; early pregnancy; son preference and its implications for the status of the girl child; female genital mutilation (FGM); forced feeding of women and children; female infanticide; dowry price; traditional birth practices and nutritional taboos during pregnancy; and the various practices or taboos which prevent women and females from controlling their own fertility.[6] Many of these HTPs violate the human rights of women under many domestic and international legal frameworks.

Although many of these practices violate international human rights law and are usually harmful; these practices endure, and they are not queried by the members of the community.[7] They become a norm, the predictable standard for everyday life to a social group and 'may take on an aura of morality in the eyes of those practising them'.[8] Sometimes the perpetrators of these HTPs may argue that the offending acts are being executed with the best intentions for the recipients.[9] However, the United Nations Human Rights Office contends that some of these harmful practices may have been performed for the benefit of males, or the leading male figure in the lives of the women and children experiencing abusive situations.[10] Furthermore, in many parts of

[5] Le Roux, Bartelink & S Palm (n 3). Generally, see BA Haruna & AM Yusuf 'The role of Nigeria Courts in protecting women and children against harmful traditional practices' in A Onuora-Oguno (ed) *Promoting efficiency in jurisprudence and constitutional development in Africa* (2022) 149. Furthermore, there have been divergent academic debates regarding use of the term 'harmful traditional practices' by scholars. Some scholars and stakeholders have argued that the term should be replaced with different terms such as 'violence against women' or 'gender-based violence'. Generally, see Le Roux, Bartelink & Palm (n 3). Notwithstanding the valid criticisms of the term, this chapter uses traditional harmful practices because the chapter also focuses on analysis of traditional oath-taking.

[6] United Nations Office of the High Commissioner for Human Rights (OHCHR) Fact Sheet 23 'Harmful traditional practices affecting the health of women and children' (August 1995).

[7] As above.

[8] As above.

[9] Generally, see B Bartelink & E le Roux, 'What is in a name? Identifying the harm in "harmful traditional practices"' in O Wilkinson, & K Kraft (eds) *International development and local faith actors: Ideological and cultural encounters* (2020) 207.

[10] OHCHR (n 6).

the world, some of these obnoxious cultural or traditional practices have been prohibited by law. For example, several customary laws and practices infringe on the human rights of women (and vulnerable members of the society), thereby restricting access to justice for the vulnerable and marginalised groups in Nigeria including women and children.[11] However, in recent times there have been legislative and judicial interventions upending some of these discriminatory customary practices in Nigeria. For example, the Nigerian judiciary (including the Supreme Court) has recently become an activist, and some relatively recent judgments have been used to nullify several of these discriminatory practices against women in Nigeria.[12]

Furthermore, in many Western countries, similar laws have been enacted, and these laws arguably have changed the traditional or societal outlook of some members of the African immigrant communities in the West. Hence, Igwe in a study focusing on domestic violence law and enforcement amongst the African immigrant community in Ireland states that all the participants in his study acknowledged a change in their attitudes towards domestic violence since moving to Ireland.[13] Igwe further alludes in his study that this also 'revealed that domestic violence awareness campaign in Ireland, as well as law and its effective enforcement, contributed in increasing the participants' knowledge and understanding of domestic violence'.[14] Hence, law can be a tool of social engineering and changing the traditional outlook on societal issues in different parts of the world. This is against the backdrop of Target 5.3 of the Sustainable Development Goals which aims to end harmful practices by 2030.

Also, in many societies, the structural and societal changes required to eliminate gender inequality are inhibited by the political and economic relegation of women by men (and in some cases, the society at large). Hence, some African societies are fundamentally patriarchal. In addition,

[11] EO Ekhator 'Protection and promotion of women's rights in Nigeria: Constraints and prospects' in M Addaney (ed) *Women and minority rights law: African approaches and perspectives to inclusive development* (2019) 17.

[12] JN Ezeilo 'Rethinking women and customary inheritance in Nigeria' (2021) 47 *Commonwealth Law Bulletin* 706.

[13] BO Igwe 'The impact of domestic violence legal regulation and enforcement among Nigerian immigrants in Ireland' PhD thesis, National University of Ireland, Maynooth, 2018.

[14] Igwe (n 13) v.

female sexual control by men may perpetuate the belief that women are inferior to men.[15] An equitable society can only be attained if the fundamental human rights of everyone including women and children, are acknowledged, and upheld. Just as the international community has become aware of the need to achieve equality amongst the sexes, global awareness needs to be promoted to mitigate the continued denial and violation of the human rights of vulnerable social groups.

Furthermore, there have been some developments or pronouncements by the African Union (AU) and its institutions in the fight against human trafficking in Africa. Some of the AU instruments that can be used to tackle the scourge of human trafficking include the African Charter on Human and Peoples' Rights,[16] the African Charter on the Rights and Welfare of the Child[17] and the Protocol to the African Charter on Human and Peoples' Rights on the Rights of Women in Africa (Maputo Protocol).[18] Furthermore, the African Charter on Human and Peoples' Rights and some AU mechanisms are said to render support to the United Nations Protocol to Prevent, Suppress, and Punish Trafficking in Persons, Especially Women and Children (Palermo Protocol)[19] in Africa. For example, article 4(2)(g) of the Maputo Protocol enjoins African states to 'prevent and condemn trafficking in women, prosecute the perpetrators of

[15] OHCHR (n 6).

[16] 16 Organisation of African Unity (OAU), African Charter on Human and Peoples' Rights (Banjul Charter), CAB/LEG/67/3 rev 5, 21 ILM 58 (1982), 27 June 1981.

[17] Organisation of African Unity (OAU), African Charter on the Rights and Welfare of the Child, CAB/LEG/24.9/49 (1990), 11 July 1990.

[18] African Union, Protocol to the African Charter on Human and People's Rights on the Rights of Women in Africa, African Union, 11 July 2003. PS Karenga *West African model to address human trafficking* 1st ed (2022) 27–28. Furthermore, the proposed African Court of Justice and Human Rights has created the offence of human trafficking. However, the court is yet to be operational. For in-depth analysis of the utility of the proposed African Court of Justice and Human Rights as a tool in tackling the scourge of human trafficking in Africa, see T Obokata 'Human trafficking in Africa: Opportunities and challenges for the African Court of Justice and Human Rights' in CC Jalloh, KM Clarke & VO Nmehielle (eds) *The African Court of Justice and human and peoples' rights in context: Development and challenges* (2019) 529.

[19] UN General Assembly, Protocol to Prevent, Suppress and Punish Trafficking in Persons Especially Women and Children, Supplementing the United Nations Convention against Transnational Organized Crime, 15 November 2000, UN Doc A/RES/55/2555/25 (2000) (Palermo Protocol).

such trafficking and protect those women most at risk'.[20] This provision gives fillip to the Palermo Protocol and should be read in tandem with it.[21] Furthermore, at the 44th Ordinary Session of the African Commission on Human and Peoples' Rights held in Abuja, Federal Republic of Nigeria, 2008, when the Resolution on Combatting Human Trafficking in Africa was adopted, members were called upon to frown on human trafficking and harmful practices (cultural, traditional or religious), including child fostering that perpetuates abuse and exploitation, and apprenticeship.[22] In addition, the African Union Commission Initiative against Trafficking (AU. COMMIT) enjoins states to ratify the Palermo Protocol via the Ouagadougou Action Plan to Combat Trafficking in Persons in November 2006.[23]

At the sub-regional level, in 2001, a pronouncement on the Economic Community of West African States Declaration on the Fight against Trafficking in Persons was framed and this also condemned human trafficking.[24] Furthermore, all West African countries have ratified the Palermo Protocol.[25] Arguably, notwithstanding the avalanche of laws and mechanisms prohibiting human trafficking at domestic, sub-regional, regional and international levels in Africa, human trafficking still remain a major issue in many African countries.

[20] Furthermore, art 29 of the African Charter on the Rights and Welfare of the Child enjoins states parties to develop suitable measures to prevent the trafficking of children.

[21] Generally, see R Nekura 'The rights to life, integrity and security of the person' in A Rudman, CN Musembi & TM Makunya (eds) *The Protocol to the African Charter on Human and Peoples' Rights on the Rights of Women in Africa: A commentary* (2023).

[22] African Centre for Democracy and Human Rights Studies 'Resolution on Combating Human Trafficking in Africa' (2008) https://www.acdhrs.org/2008/11/resolution-on-combating-human-trafficking-in-africa/#:~:text=Ratify%20the%20Palermo%20Protocol%20and,combating%20all%20forms%20of%20trafficking (accessed 28 October 2024).

[23] Karenga (n 18) 27.

[24] Also, see Karenga (n 18) 27.

[25] D Ogunniyi & O Idowu 'Human trafficking in West Africa: An implementation assessment of international and regional normative standards' (2022) 19 *The Age of Human Rights Journal* 165.

1.1 Prevalent Forms of HTPs: Focus on FGM

HTPs are often borne out of cultural/community pressure. They may have been firmly and deeply rooted in the structure of a community, thereby becoming a way of life for the social group of individuals concerned. HTPs are forms of violence that have been committed, primarily against women, girls, and children, in certain social groups and communities for so long (spanning decades and generations) that they are considered, or presented by perpetrators, as part of an accepted cultural practice.[26] The most common forms of harmful practices are forced or early marriage, honour-based violence, and female genital mutilation (FGM).[27] Other lesser-known types of harmful practices include bride kidnapping, acid attacks, son preference, breast ironing, and spirit possession.[28] This section of the chapter focuses on FGM as it is one of the more prevalent forms of HTPs experienced by African immigrant communities in the UK.

1.2 Communities at Risk of FGM in the UK

African immigrant communities in the UK that are most at risk of FGM include: Nigerians, Ethiopians, Egyptians, Eritreans, Sierra Leoneans, Somalis, Kenyans, and Sudanese.[29] Conversely, women from non-African communities that are at risk of FGM include Pakistani and Indian women (Muslim Bohra Community); and Indonesian, Malaysian, Yemini and Kurdish women (Iraqi, Turkish and Iranian countries of origin).[30]

[26] Wirral Safeguarding Children Partnership 'Harmful practices' https://www.wirralsafeguarding.co.uk/harmful-practices/ (accessed 29 January 2024). Also, see G Gangoli and others 'Perception and barriers: Reporting female genital mutilation' (2018) 10 *Journal of Aggression, Conflict and Peace Research* 251.

[27] Wirral (n 26).

[28] As above.

[29] United Nations Population Fund (UNFPA) 'Female genital mutilation (FGM) frequently asked questions' (February 2022) https://www.unfpa.org/resources/female-genital-mutilation-fgm-frequently-asked-questions (accessed 28 October 2024). For the situation in Nigeria, see H Hamma 'SDG 3 and maternal health rights: A biosocial approach to ending the VVF scourge in Northern Nigeria' in E Ekhator, S Miller & E Igbinosa (eds) *Implementing the Sustainable Development Goals in Nigeria: Barriers, prospects and strategies* (2021).

[30] Merseyside Protecting Vulnerable People: Harmful Offices Group 'Pan Merseyside Female Genital Mutilation (FGM) Protocol' Version 2 (2019) 7.

Females in African Immigrant communities in the UK may experience severe harm because they have undergone the procedure of FGM.[31] FGM adds no health benefits to the recipient female, rather it causes harm to women and girls in diverse ways.[32] Firstly, the procedure involves the removal of healthy female genital tissue, leading to long-term damage of the female's normal genital tissue.[33] Secondly, FGM results in long-term health complications and interferes with the natural functions of girls and women's bodies.[34]

Many women from African immigrant communities are unaware of the relationship between FGM and its health consequences. Health impact complications are common and may lead to the eventual death of the victim.[35] These complications range from difficulties during childbirth, inadequate sexual health, and painful coitus/pain during sexual intercourse. The complications may be experienced soon after FGM has occurred or many years after the mutilation has been carried out.[36] The number of females who die due to FGM is unknown. However, the highest infant mortality and maternal rates are in FGM-practicing regions.[37] For example, in some parts of Sudan where antibiotics are unavailable, it is estimated that one-third of females who have undergone FGM have passed away.[38]

Further, immediate physical problems associated with the procedure of FGM consist of urine retention due to swelling and blockage of the urethra; fracture, or dislocation of genital organs due to restricted flow

[31] Generally, see United Kingdom 'Guidance on female genital mutilation (FGM): Migrant health guide' (31 August 2014, last updated 13 September 2021) https://www.gov.uk/guidance/female-genital-mutilation-fgm-migrant-health-guide (accessed 28 October 2024). Also see PE Oamen & A Storey *Nigeria Universal Periodic Review: Stakeholder submission on female genital mutilation* Project Report, Birmingham City University (2023).

[32] World Health Organisation (WHO) 'Female genital mutilation' (31 January 2023) https://www.who.int/news-room/fact-sheets/detail/female-genital-mutilation (accessed 28 October 2024).

[33] As above.

[34] As above.

[35] Merseyside (n 30).

[36] WHO (n 32).

[37] Generally, see WHO (n 32).

[38] Merseyside (n 30).

of urine; damage to other organs; injury to adjacent tissue; and haemorrhage and/or intense pain that may lead to shock during and after the procedure.[39] Haemorrhage of the female external genital organs if left unattended without adequate medical care, may result in death, anaemia, or wound infection including tetanus.[40] Tetanus is lethal in 50–60% of cases.[41]

1.3 Criminal Legislation on FGM in the UK

FGM is illegal in the UK and has been a criminal offence since 1985, when the Prohibition of Female Circumcision Act 1985 was enacted. The Act was repealed by the Female Genital Mutilation Act 2003, which closed a gap which previously enabled perpetrators to transport victims outside the jurisdiction of the UK for purposes of FGM. The Female Genital Mutilation Act strengthened existing law to make it an offence to arrange for a child to be taken abroad for FGM, and for UK nationals or permanent UK residents to undertake, procure, counsel, or abet FGM abroad, even in countries where the practice is legal.[42] The Serious Crime Act 2015 extends this protection to girls under the age of 18 who are habitually resident in the UK or on short temporary stays such as students and refugees.[43] The Serious Crime Act also provides for the offence of failing to protect a girl child from FGM. If an offence of FGM is committed against a girl under the age of 16, each person who is responsible for the girl at the time of the FGM occurred will be held liable for the offence.[44] The 2015 Act also enables the high court or family courts to make an FGM Protection Order for individuals who are victims or at risk of FGM (similar to forced marriage protection orders). Victims, relevant third parties (including local authorities), or those at risk, can apply for the orders which set restrictions to protect an individual.

[39] As above.

[40] Greater Manchester Safeguarding 'Female Genital Mutilation Multi-Agency Protocol' https://greatermanchesterscb.proceduresonline.com/chapters/p_fgm.html (accessed 28 October 2024).

[41] As above.

[42] Sec 1 of the Female Genital Mutilation Act 2003.

[43] Sec 70 of the Serious Crime Act 2015.

[44] As above.

1.4 The Nexus Between Human Trafficking and HTPs

Human trafficking victims in the UK may have experienced some HTPs either prior to, during, or after undergoing an exploitative situation.[45] In some instances, tradition or cultural norms may worsen human trafficking in African immigrant communities. This is because, immigrants/emigrants and their descendants who live outside their country of birth or ancestry, either on a temporary or permanent basis, may still maintain ties to their respective countries of origin.[46]

Article 3(a) of the Palermo Protocol defines trafficking in persons as:

> [T]he recruitment, transportation, transfer, harbouring or receipt of persons, by means of the threat or use of force or other forms of coercion, of abduction, of fraud, of deception, of the abuse of power or of a position of vulnerability or of the giving or receiving of payments or benefits to achieve the consent of a person having control over another person, for the purpose of exploitation.

The next section of this chapter focuses on the nexus between human trafficking and HTPs which is assessed using the practice of traditional oath-taking to illustrate the ties that individuals may hold to their countries of origin.

1.5 The Role of Traditional Oath-Taking in Human Trafficking Networks in Some African Communities

It should be noted that traditional oath-taking, or juju practice is not necessarily evil or sinister. For example, traditional oath-taking is a recognised feature of customary arbitration in Nigeria, and this has been

[45] Generally, see International Organisation for Migration (IOM) 'Addressing Human Trafficking and exploitation in times of crisis: Evidence and recommendations for further action to protect vulnerable and mobile populations' (December 2015) https://www.antislaverycommissioner.co.uk/media/1068/addressing_human_trafficking_dec2015.pdf (accessed 28 October 2024).

[46] DR Agunias & K Newland 'Developing a road map for engaging diasporas in development: A handbook for policymakers and practitioners in home and host countries' International Organization for Migration (IOM) and Migration Policy Institute (MPI) (2012) 13. Furthermore, in many Nigerian communities, traditional oath-taking remains an integral part of dispute resolution processes.

recognised by the Nigerian Supreme Court in a plethora of cases.[47] However, the practice of traditional oath-taking, or juju has been abused by many traffickers as a means of silencing or subjugating trafficking victims of Nigerian (African) heritage within and outside the shores of Nigeria.[48] Thus, traditional oath-taking or juju can be used as one of the means by traffickers to control their victims.[49]

Traffickers are also known to use 'juju' or voodoo practices to coerce and compel their victims to carry out their instructions in an exploitative situation.[50] This practice is prevalent in several West African countries including Benin, Ghana, Niger, and Nigeria where the traditional belief in juju and the impact on human life is strong.[51] This belief remains prevalent amongst some sections of African immigrant communities in the UK. Thus, Nigerian organised crime rings that engage in trafficking in persons operate as a business model and control the victims that they have recruited through ritual bondage.[52] Prior to their departure to Europe and the UK, the traffickers who are sponsoring the trip, may force the victims to participate in a religious ceremony.[53] At this ceremony, they are forced to swear traditional oaths to a particular deity in a shrine

[47] Generally, see ES Nwauche 'State response to outcomes of traditional justice resolution mechanisms in Commonwealth Africa: Customary arbitration in Nigeria and Ghana' (2022) 4 *Journal of Commonwealth Law* 73.

[48] Generally, see M Ikeora 'The role of African traditional religion and "Juju" in human trafficking: Implications for anti-trafficking' (2016) 17 *Journal of International Women's Studies* 1.

[49] Generally, see M Van der Watt & B Kruger 'Breaking bondages: Control methods, "Juju," and human trafficking' in J Winterdyk & J Jones (eds) *The Palgrave international handbook of human trafficking* (Palgrave MacMillan 2020) 935.

[50] According to A Chisholm and others 'Rituals as a control mechanism in human trafficking: Systematic review and thematic synthesis of qualitative literature' (2022) *Journal of Human Trafficking* 1, 'juju' is 'a traditional belief system, as practiced mainly in West Africa'. Other terms for the phenomenon or practice of juju include witchcraft, voodoo, and spirits amongst others.

[51] Karenga (n 18). Also, see T Kelley 'Truth or consequences (the deadly kind): Oath swearing in Nigerien customary law' 47 *North Carolina Journal of International Law* 331.

[52] E Apard and others 'Religious, social and criminal groups in trafficking of Nigerian girls and women' ECPAT France (2019).

[53] Generally, see AW Dunkerley 'Exploring the use of juju in Nigerian human trafficking networks: Considerations for criminal investigators' (2018) 19 *Police Practice and Research* 83.

before a juju priest is called upon to enforce the agreement; they are then compelled to sign to pay back the debt.[54]

Traditional oaths directly tie women with the spirits from whom retaliation is expected if the agreement is breached. Women are persuaded that untold misfortune including terminal illness, mental health disorders, and death will befall themselves or their families if they are unable to repay their debt.[55] Further, breaking the oath is viewed as an act of dishonour that reflects badly upon the women's families. By accepting the oath, they have been coerced to accept the situation of exploitation.

In many parts of Nigeria (and amongst Nigerian immigrant communities in the West), traditional oaths have been used to silence some victims of modern-day slavery and human trafficking.[56] Hence, to stop this practice, in 2018 the Oba of Benin Ewuare II (who is the major traditional authority in that part of Nigeria) overturned any traditional 'oaths undertaken by victims of human trafficking'.[57] Different stakeholders have contended that this action by the Oba of Benin will perhaps prevent traditional oaths from being used as a means of silencing modern slavery and human trafficking victims in Edo State of Nigeria.[58]

Furthermore, traditional oath-taking and similar cultural practices have impacted lawsuits or cases involving victims and traffickers in several countries.[59] Thus, there is now a growing awareness by courts in Western countries (and African countries) on the possible impact of traditional oath-taking or juju as a control mechanism on the victims of trafficking.[60]

[54] As above.

[55] AD Garcia 'Trafficking, ritual oaths and criminal investigations' *Forced Migration Review* 64 (June 2020) at 50.

[56] SO Oyakhire 'Expanding the scope of "appropriate measures": Do traditional institutions play a role in facilitating the protection of witnesses of trafficking in persons?' (2019) 6 *Journal of Comparative Law in Africa* 80.

[57] A Baker 'An ancient curse kept Nigerian women bound to sex slavery. Now, it's been reversed' *Time* 17 April 2018 https://time.com/longform/juju-curse-nigeria-sex-slavery-europe/ (accessed 28 October 2024).

[58] As above.

[59] Generally, see R Gershuni 'The interface between trafficking in persons and culture' in R Piotrowicz and others (eds) *Routledge handbook of human trafficking* (2017) 366. Also, see OO Ogwezzy 'The legal impact of voodoo and other control mechanisms on human trafficking in Nigeria' (2023) 3 *Redeemer's University Nigeria, Journal of Jurisprudence & International Law* 234.

[60] Generally, see Gershuni (n 59) for analysis of some of these cases.

On the other hand, there have been a plethora of cases (in Nigeria and abroad), where due to the fear of juju or traditional oath, victims are reluctant to give evidence in criminal trials instituted against their traffickers.[61] However, courts have become creative in surmounting this hurdle. For example, courts have relied on evidence given by anthropologists and experts on traditional oaths or juju, and this has helped the courts to understand why some victims are reluctant to give evidence. Also, expert evidence enables the court to understand the unequal power dynamics between the victims and traffickers, and hence this amongst other reasons enables the courts to convict the suspected traffickers in such cases.[62] The next section focuses on African feminist scholarship or perspectives on HTPs.

1.6 African Feminist Scholarship and HTPs

This section of the chapter relies on African feminist scholarship for its theoretical discussion.[63] African feminist scholarship is neglected in the mainstream feminist scholarship on gender rights (including traditional or harmful practices).[64] There appears to be an overwhelming reliance on Western (liberal) feminist conceptualisations in this sphere.[65]

[61] Generally, see Gershuni (n 59); Ogwezzy (n 59).

[62] As above.

[63] For the evolution of African feminist scholarship, see AA Coetzee 'African feminism as decolonising force: A philosophical exploration of the work of Oyeronke Oyewumi' PhD thesis, Stellenbosch University, 2017 at 4–8. It should be noted that Western liberal feminist theories are valid and appropriate, but we opted to contextualise our analysis via African feminist scholarship in this chapter.

[64] Generally, see O Oyěwùmí 'Conceptualising gender: Eurocentric foundations of feminist concepts and the challenge of African epistemologies' in S Arnfred, B Bakare-Yusuf & EW Kisiang'ani (eds) *African gender scholarship: Concepts, methodologies and paradigms* (2004); S Tamale 'The right to culture and the culture of rights: A critical perspective on women's sexual rights in Africa' (2008) 16 *Feminist Legal Studies* 47; A Gouws 'Theorizing feminism from the South: Knowledge production through South Africa's Feminist Journal AGENDA' (2022) 23 *Journal of International Women's Studies* 57. For some criticisms of Oyěwùmí's works, see B Bakare-Yusuf '"Yoruba's don't do gender": A critical review of Oyeronke Oyewumi's *The invention of women: Making an African sense of western gender discourses*' in S Arnfred, B Bakare-Yusuf & EW Kisiang'ani *African gender scholarship: Concepts, methodologies, and paradigms* (2004) CODESRIA 1.

[65] However, see Oyěwùmí (n 64); AA Coetzee 'Woman, time and the incommunicability of non-Western worlds: Understanding the role of gender in the colonial denial of

Scholars have argued that mainstream Western conceptualisations tend to view customs or culture in Africa via a negative lens and as a barrier to successful legal reform.[66] Notwithstanding, the prevalence of some discriminatory African cultural or traditional norms, customs can also be used as emancipatory means in Africa (including African immigrant communities in the West).[67] Hence, in the Nigerian context, Byron argues that customary arbitration can enhance access to justice for many people living in rural areas in Nigeria.[68] Byron gave the example of the Women's Law Clinic (which is a dedicated Law Clinic) based at the Faculty of Law, University of Ibadan, Nigeria which caters to poor women in that part of Nigeria.[69] The Women's Law Clinic relies on customary arbitration as one of the methods of resolving disputes amongst parties at the Law Clinic.[70]

Therefore, the contemporary approach to the study of women and gender in Africa (including African immigrant societies in the West) is arguably contextualised via African feminist scholarship rather than reliance on global north or Western feminist theories or scholarship.[71]

Customs reflect the times, and, in some societies, HTPs are being gradually eased out even though there appears to be an increase in the statistics regarding HTPs. African feminist scholars contend that women have an invaluable role to play in impacting positively on societal or cultural changes.[72] Here, the contention is that in many pre-colonial African societies' women were active players or decision-makers in the

coevalness' (2021) 22 *Feminist Theory* 465; NH Msuya 'Advocating positive traditional culture to eradicate harmful aspects of traditional culture for gender equality in Africa' (2020) 41 *Obiter* 45.

[66] Generally, see Tamale (n 64).

[67] Also, see Tamale (n 64).

[68] IP Byron 'Customary arbitration as a tool for ensuring access to justice for women in Nigeria: A case study of the women's law clinic' (2017) 11 *Ife Juris Review* 41.

[69] As above.

[70] As above.

[71] However, see JI Uduji, EN Okolo-Obasi & SA Asongu 'Oil extraction and gender equality for social equity: The role of corporate social responsibility in Nigeria's coastal communities' (2023) 81 *Resources Policy* 103346.

[72] According to Tamale (n 64) 49, 'there are many cultural norms and values that are rights-supportive, egalitarian and uplifting; many aspects of "African culture" promote and reinforce women's rights'.

communities.[73] This is contrary to Western feminist scholarship or views that women were not active players in pre-colonial African societies. Thus, notwithstanding the plethora of HTPs, women arguably have the agency to upturn some of these practices in Africa.[74] Furthermore, several relevant stakeholders including civil society groups are playing a major role in the reduction of HTPs by engaging in outreach, educational and sensitisation activities.[75]

Unfortunately, the patriarchal nature of many modern African societies/states is a major stumbling block in this regard. Furthermore, even though cultural rights are recognised in a plethora of international mechanisms, culture or traditional norms which violate human rights are illegal and must be jettisoned.[76]

Accordingly, efforts to eliminate HTPs have not been successful in Africa and amongst many African immigrant communities in the West. For example, the acceptance of traditional oath by victims, although due to duress indicates that any criminal activity which a victim of human trafficking undertakes because of their exploitative situation, may result in criminal prosecution. This is where the non-prosecution principle may be relevant to protect the victim of human trafficking who has also

[73] Oyěwùmí (n 64); Msuya (n 65); II Oronsaye-Agunloye 'Gender politics in historiography: Precolonial Benin' in U Usuanlele (ed) *Benin studies under the scalpel: Essays in honour of Dr Ekhaguosa Aisien* (2020) 71 states that: 'Research has shown that precolonial African woman exercised a considerable amount of autonomy'.

[74] Also, see Msuya (n 65) 45; UN Women 'Traditional leaders across Africa move the needle against child marriage and FGM' (15 November 2018) https://www.unwomen.org/en/news/stories/2018/11/feature-traditional-leaders-across-africa-against-child-marriage-and-fgm (accessed 28 October 2024).

[75] G Gillespie 'FGC? FGM? Female circumcision? Why language matters in helping communities abandon harmful practices' Tostan International (2015) https://tostan.org/fgc-fgm-female-circumcision-why-language-matters-helping-communities-abandon-harmful-practices/ (accessed 28 October 2024). According to R Duivenbode & A Padela 'Female genital cutting (FGC) and the cultural boundaries of medical practice' (2019) 19 *The American Journal of Bioethics* 4: 'Tostan International – an African organization that has led one of the most successful FGC reduction campaigns worldwide.'

[76] For example, the Convention on the Elimination of All Forms of Discrimination Against Women (CEDAW) obligates states parties to 'pursue by all appropriate means and without delay a policy of eliminating discrimination against women'. Generally, see JM Mbaku 'International human rights law and the tyranny of harmful customary and traditional practices on women in Africa' (2021) 52 *California Western International Law Journal* 1.

experienced harmful practice because they are from an African immigrant community in the UK. Further discussion on the non-prosecution principle and its relevance in protecting victims of human trafficking is examined in this chapter. The next section focuses on how international law can be used as a tool to combat the scourge of human trafficking with a focus on the Palermo Protocol.

2 International Law as a Tool for Combatting Human Trafficking

Since the problem of THB has both a domestic and an international dimension, international law can be a powerful tool for combatting human trafficking and consequently preventing prosecution of victims of trafficking. Victims of human trafficking who are African immigrants that are resident in the UK and have experienced harmful practices, may look to international law for legal recourse where possible. In this regard, the prevention of prosecution of victims of trafficking may be improved through proper identification and prevention measures by states. A prominent international law instrument that provides a legal structure on how to define, prevent, and prosecute human trafficking is the Palermo Protocol.[77] The United Nations Office on Drugs and Crime (UNODC) created this instrument which has promoted the combatting of human trafficking in international law.[78] Hence, the Palermo Protocol 'is the only international legal instrument addressing human trafficking as a crime'.[79]

The offence of human trafficking can occur within and outside the borders of one state and one legal system. When trafficking takes place within a state, the government of that state may tackle the issue efficiently within its borders. However, when any element of the process relates to a

[77] For extensive analysis of some of the weaknesses of the Palermo Protocol, see S Scarpa 'UN Palermo trafficking protocol eighteen years on: A critique' in J Winterdyk & J Jones (eds) *The Palgrave international handbook of human trafficking* (2020) 623; J Jones 'Is it time to open a conversation about a New United Nations Treaty to fight human trafficking that focuses on victim protection and human rights?' in J Winterdyk & J Jones (eds) *The Palgrave international handbook of human trafficking* (2020) 1803.

[78] UNODC 'United Nations Convention against Transnational Organized Crime and the Protocols thereto: Status of ratification' https://www.unodc.org/unodc/en/organized-crime/intro/UNTOC.html (accessed 28 October 2024).

[79] Jones (n 77) 1804.

foreign state, the process of protecting the victim can become a little more complicated. For example, when the victim is temporarily crossing from one state to another during their trafficking experience, the state's control over the foreign national's circumstance may become legally limited. This situation makes THB a global issue and indicates the need for international as well as domestic legal regulations to protect victims of human trafficking.

The Palermo Protocol offers some guidance aimed at a better understanding of the offence of trafficking. In particular, the definition of trafficking in the Palermo Protocol has been adopted wholly or in part by the Council of Europe (CoE) Convention, EU Directive, and Modern Slavery Act (MSA) 2015 which all deal with the non-prosecution of victims of human trafficking.[80] Trafficking is deemed to have occurred following the recruitment, transportation, transfer, harbouring, or receipt of persons, by means of threat or use of force or other forms of coercion, abduction, fraud, deception, the abuse of power or of a position of vulnerability for the purpose of exploitation.[81] The Protocol also requires states to establish criminal liability for human trafficking and to assist and protect victims of human trafficking.[82]

[80] Council of Europe, Council of Europe Convention on Action Against Trafficking in Human Beings, CETS 197, 16 May 2005, arts 26 and 12 deal with assistance to victims of trafficking; European Union Directive 2011/36 on Preventing and Combating Trafficking in Human Beings and Protecting its Victims [2011] OJ L101/1, art 8; and Modern Slavery Act 2015, sec 45. According to the House of Commons Home Affairs Committee 'Human trafficking: First Report of Session 2023–24' (8 December 2023) https://publications.parliament.uk/pa/cm5804/cmselect/cmhaff/124/report.html at 40 (accessed 28 October 2024). 'The non-punishment principle is outlined in section 45 of the Modern Slavery Act 2015 and introduces a defence for victims of modern slavery and human trafficking, including children, who are compelled to commit criminal offences as a result of their exploitation.' However, recent developments in the UK are said to undermine the localisation of non-prosecution principle in the UK legal frameworks. For example, provisions of the Nationality and Borders Act 2022 and the Illegal Migration Act 2023 goes against the tenor of the non-prosecution principle. Generally, see J Haynes 'Human trafficking: Iconic victims, folk devils and the Nationality and Borders Act 2022' (2023) 86 *Modern Law Review* 1232; Marija Jovanović & Maayan Niezna 'Non-punishment of victims/survivors of human trafficking in practice: A case study of the United Kingdom' (September 2023, Council of Europe) https://rm.coe.int/non-punishment-of-victims-survivors-of-human-trafficking-in-practice-a/1680ac86f4 (accessed 28 October 2024).

[81] Art 3(a) of the Palermo Protocol.

[82] Arts 5 and 6 of the Palermo Protocol.

However, states' obligations regarding the protection of victims of THB are not properly explained and leave the interpretation of state responsibilities to the discretion of authorities. For instance, states are required to protect the privacy and identity of victims of human trafficking, including making legal proceedings confidential in appropriate cases and to the extent possible under their domestic law.[83] This provision does not create a strong incentive for states to implement the protection measure; it appears to be persuasive rather than an obligatory requirement. Other instruments such as the CoE Convention, EU directive, and the MSA, impose higher standards of protection. They promote a more human rights-centred approach to THB than the Palermo Protocol which possesses a criminal justice approach.[84]

Whereas there are relevant policies and provisions which uphold the non-prosecution of victims of THB for criminal offences committed as a direct consequence of their trafficking status, there have been instances where the protection system in place has been unable to safeguard these individuals. For example, the system has not worked properly in cases where the competent authority has failed to recognise a person as a victim of trafficking or where the state has failed to carry out an adequate investigation to determine whether a person has been trafficked or not.[85] There have also been situations where the trafficked individual has been prosecuted against the public interest and an order has been given for them to be returned to their home country where they are at risk of re-trafficking and re-victimisation.[86] Consequently, the question arises: why are victims of THB being prosecuted, when there are mechanisms in place to prevent prosecution? Unfulfilled state obligations have been determined to be

[83] Arts 6(1) of the Palermo Protocol.

[84] I Atak & JC Simeon 'Human trafficking: Mapping the legal boundaries of international refugee law and criminal justice' (2014) 12 JICJ 1019 at 1024.

[85] *LM, DG and MB* in *R v LM & Ors* [2010] EWCA Crim 2327, para 29; *Rantsev v Cyprus & Russia* App 25965/04 [2010] 51 EHRR 1.

[86] *HD (Trafficked Women)* CG [2016] UKUT454 (IAC), para 1; *Marian v Regional Prosecutor's Office of Ruse, Bulgaria* [2019] EWHC 602 (Admin). Hence, S Demeke 'A human rights-based approach for effective criminal justice response to human trafficking' (2024) 9 *Journal of International Humanitarian Action* 1 argues that: 'For long, the obvious and perhaps the most visible practice to deal with cases of trafficking has been employing a criminal justice approach where the focus largely lies on the persecution [prosecution] of the criminal instead of the protection of the survivors.'

one of the main reasons why victims of THB are prosecuted for their involvement in illegal activities.

2.1 Unfulfilled State Obligations

It is essential to consider the role of unfulfilled state obligations in the discussion of non-prosecution of victims of human trafficking. This is because unfulfilled state obligations have been recognised as one of the factors that contribute to the prosecution of victims of THB. The non-prosecution principle is contingent on the premise that victims of THB who have committed criminal offences as a direct consequence of their trafficking status, should be absolved of criminal liability and provided immunity from prosecution. Defence lawyers and prosecutors are urged to make proper enquiries in criminal cases involving individuals who may be victims of THB.[87] Where there is credible suspicion that a person has been trafficked, states have a positive obligation to further investigate human trafficking cases. The state is obliged to identify victims of THB, and to ensure that trained and qualified individuals are involved in the process of victim identification including children.[88] In addition, a duty is imposed on member states to investigate or prosecute offences in human trafficking cases even when a victim has withdrawn his or her statement; and irrespective of any report by the victim.[89] The provisions discussed above are directly relevant to member states of the CoE Convention and EU Directive. Specifically, it relates to states that are signatories to the respective instruments. It is expected that those states that are not bound by the EU Directive or CoE Convention, may focus on their own domestic laws as a guide, to determine the best course of action in human trafficking cases. A La Strada International report also discusses the possibility of partially criminalising the 'knowing use' of services of trafficked persons into their criminal codes.[90] The mental element (*mens*

[87] *R v O* [2008] EWCA Crim 2835, para 15.

[88] Convention on Action Against Trafficking in Human Beings (n 80) art 10.

[89] European Union Directive 2011/36 on Preventing and Combating Trafficking in Human Beings and Protecting its Victims [2011] OJ L101/1, art 9.

[90] La Strada International 'The impact of criminalising the "knowing use" on human trafficking' Policy Paper (December 2022) 5 https://documentation.lastradainternational.org/doc-center/3476/policy-paper%C2%A0the-impact-of-criminalising%C2%A0the-%E2%80%98knowing-use%E2%80%99-on-human-trafficking (accessed 28 October 2023).

rea) required by national provisions is that the user/offender 'knew' the person was a victim of human trafficking or 'should have known' and proceeds to exploit the vulnerable individual. Currently, two-thirds of EU member states have introduced this partial criminalisation and its adoption by more member states may indicate that investigation and prosecution rates of human trafficking offences may be improved.[91]

States are obliged to criminalise any or all acts of human trafficking, especially those affecting women and children.[92] Some states that are reluctant to accept responsibility for trafficking situations, may argue that the primary wrong has been committed by private individuals and not by the state itself in order to be absolved wholly or in part of blame.[93] The Office of the High Commissioner for Human Rights (OHCHR) argues that although determining the responsibility of states may be difficult, there are general duties that they are accountable for.[94] States are unable to avoid taking responsibility for the acts of private persons when there is evidence that they could have prevented a negative outcome (for example, prosecuting a credible victim of trafficking) from occurring. This implies that, the source of responsibility in cases of this nature is not the act itself but the state's failure to take adequate measures of prevention in conformity with the prescribed standard.[95] The prescribed standard in the United Kingdom includes observing the 4Ps in the process of upholding state obligations.[96] The 4Ps consists of a strategy to: Pursue (pursue perpetrators of human trafficking and modern slavery crimes); Prevent (prevent individuals from engaging in trafficking activities); Protect (strengthen safeguards against human trafficking and modern slavery by protecting vulnerable people from exploitation); and Prepare (reduce the harm caused by trafficking crimes through improved

[91] As above.

[92] CoE Convention and EU Directive (n 80).

[93] United Nations Human Rights, Office of the High Commissioner, Fact Sheet 36: Human rights and human trafficking (2014) 11 https://www.ohchr.org/en/publications/fact-sheets/fact-sheet-no-36-human-rights-and-human-trafficking (accessed 28 October 2024).

[94] As above.

[95] As above.

[96] HM Government 'Modern slavery strategy' (2014) https://www.gov.uk/government/uploads/system/uploads/attachment_data/file/383764/Modern_Slavery_Strategy_FINAL_DEC2015.pdf (accessed 28 October 2024).

victim identification and enhanced protection and support).[97] The 4Ps complement each other and are best implemented collectively. To obtain a better understanding of the role states play in reducing the offence of human trafficking and promoting immunity from prosecution for victims, it is pertinent to examine the obligations.

This chapter will primarily focus on two obligations—the obligation to prevent human trafficking and the obligation to protect victims of trafficking. The reason for focusing on these areas is to uphold the aims of this chapter. One of the aims of this chapter is to consider ways of promoting immunity from prosecution for victims of human trafficking. Hence, using a victim-centred approach, the goal is to foster greater immunity from prosecution for victims of human trafficking.

2.2 Obligation to Prevent Human Trafficking

An important obligation that states are expected to adhere to is the prevention of the offence of THB. Countries that are signatories to the Palermo Protocol are under an obligation to prevent and combat trafficking in persons and protect victims of THB from re-victimisation.[98] They are also expected to co-operate with the non-governmental/civil sector society and endeavour to strengthen measures to alleviate major causes of trafficking such as poverty and under development.[99] Obokata has shown that the nature and extent of the obligations in article 9 of the Palermo Protocol is dependent on whether a state is an origin or destination location.[100] Regarding states of origin, the pertinent obligation is preventing citizens from being trafficked or re-victimised. Specifically, push and pull factors are considered by the state. The push factors of the offence of THB consist of humanitarian crises, poverty and gender/racial discrimination and these are predominantly assessed in relation to the state of origin of the trafficked victim.[101] The pull factors are the

[97] As above.

[98] Art 9(1)(a) and (b) of the Palermo Protocol.

[99] Art 9(4) of the Palermo Protocol.

[100] T Obokata 'Implementing international law on human trafficking: Case studies of the United Kingdom and Ireland' (2015) 2 *State Practice and International Law Journal* 85 at 91.

[101] As above.

things that appeal to trafficked victims including the demand for trafficked people; and this is often determined by the states of destination.[102]

2.3 *The Role of Destination Countries in Fulfilling the Obligation to Prevent Human Trafficking*

Destination countries are states that attract victims and/or traffickers due to their wealth, demand for workers, and favourable circumstances for a better life. A state can become a destination country where a multitude of individuals transmigrate from nearby countries or countries sharing common borders. Situations of THB entail not only nearby countries but also involve faraway locations, and transit across several country borders. Sometimes passage may comprise simultaneous crossing over land and sea.

In a report by Joy Ezeilo, the former Special Rapporteur on trafficking in persons, especially women and children, on her mission to Italy, observed that the country's geographical location and extended coastline made it a destination and transit country for victims of trafficking.[103] Ezeilo's findings also indicated that anti-trafficking efforts in Italy mainly focused on trafficking for sexual exploitation. In most of these cases, the victims were women and girls from Nigeria and Eastern Europe, mainly Bulgaria, Hungary, Romania, and Ukraine who were forced to engage in street prostitution.[104] According to some scholars and stakeholders, victims from Edo State in Nigeria, particularly from Benin City, constituted a considerable proportion of the persons trafficked for sexual exploitation.[105] The victims informed the Special Rapporteur that they

[102] As above.

[103] JN Ezeilo 'Report of the Special Rapporteur on trafficking in persons, especially women and children, on her mission to Italy' United Nations General Assembly A/HRC/26/37/Add.4, 5 (2014).

[104] As above.

[105] Also, see A Ohonba & K Agbontaen-Eghafona 'Transnational remittances from human trafficking and the changing socio-economic status of women in Benin City, Edo State Nigeria' (2019) 48 *Women's Studies* 531; C Olufade 'Sustenance of sex trafficking in Edo State: The combined effect of oath taking, transnational silence and migration imaginaries on trafficked women in Edo State' (2019). According to the UK government, 'Historically, many women trafficked to Europe, including the UK, were from Edo state, in southern Nigeria. However, they are increasingly also trafficked from other parts of the country. Women may be lured by the promise of false job offers or education in Europe

had paid their traffickers sums which ranged from 30,000 to 60,000 euros to be transported to Europe.[106]

Most trafficked victims migrate from underdeveloped countries to seemingly prosperous countries, seeking economic and financial advancement. Consequently, a great deal of research has focused on the responsibilities of destination countries. Principal amongst these studies is Mandel's examination of trafficking in the UK and Israel. Mandel observes that well-developed and flourishing countries of the world often have a high demand for workers.[107] Thus, a great number of trafficked victims are brought into destination countries through international trade channels to fulfil this immense need for workers' demand. Conversely, it may also be argued that while the destination countries appear to have an extensive requirement for workers, they have also seen the greatest success in rehabilitating victims, enforcing and implementing legislation and prosecuting traffickers.[108] Seideman suggests that destination nations have the greatest legislative success against trafficking primarily because they have the financial resources to create effective legislation.[109] They are able to develop adequate laws because they possess a substantial mechanism that aids in advancing their law-making motives. In comparison, impoverished countries that supply trafficked victims may lack the legislative and financial competence to construct efficient anti-trafficking legislation.[110]

From the argument by Mandel and Seideman discussed above, it may be deduced that source nations/developing countries are otherwise preoccupied with dealing with their everyday challenges in administering government policies. Therefore, they are unable to focus on the proper

and/or manipulated through traditional beliefs (juju)'; UK Government 'Country policy and information note: Trafficking of women Nigeria' (April 2022) (accessible version) (updated 12 August 2022) https://www.gov.uk/government/publications/nigeria-country-policy-and-information-notes/country-policy-and-information-note-trafficking-of-women-nigeria-april-2022-accessible-version (accessed 28 October 2024).

[106] Ezeilo (n 103).

[107] JW Mandel 'Out of sight, out of mind: The lax and underutilized prosecution of sex trafficking in the United Kingdom and Israel' (2012) 21 *Tulane Journal. of International & Comparative Law* 206.

[108] As above.

[109] CA Seideman 'The Palermo Protocol: Why it has been ineffective in reducing human sex trafficking' (2015) 9 *Global Tides* 5.

[110] As above.

implementation of human trafficking policies. This also implies, that developing countries that are not able to institute the change in legislation, will also not be in good stead to ensure that the non-prosecution principle is applied correctly to a victim's case. From the foregoing, one may consider what role the underdeveloped/source countries play in protecting victims of human trafficking and promoting the application of the non-prosecution principle to a victim's circumstance. Since source countries are considered to lack the means to develop important anti-trafficking laws to protect victims of human trafficking, should these countries be exempt from upholding their state obligations?

This raises the question of whether the issue is strictly one of inadequate legislative enactment? It may be contended that the problem is not solely limited to legislative lack thereof, but there are also challenges linked to defective implementation of legislation and/or a lack of political will to enforce the available laws. Notably on the African continent, Nigeria was one of the first countries to pass the then most comprehensive anti-trafficking law which has inspired other countries over the years.[111] Similarly, the Southern African Development Community (SADC) member states also implemented a 10-year SADC Plan of Action to combat human trafficking.[112]

Dempsey and colleagues hold the notion that granting countries any form of privilege or exclusion from upholding their state responsibility, will further encourage them to have non-compliant legislation.[113] They

[111] National Action Plan on Human Trafficking in Nigeria (2009–2012) now updated to the 2022–2026 Plan. Generally, see O Nnamuchi and others 'The trafficking of women in Nigeria: Is there a role for human rights?' (2022) 44 *Human Rights Quarterly* 806. On the other hand, according to MM Okorie & U Okeja 'Prosecuting human traffickers in Nigeria: Victim-witnessing and community-oriented challenges' (2024) *Trends in Organized Crime* https://doi.org/10.1007/s12117-024-09548-y (accessed 23 January 2025) in Nigeria 'antitrafficking structures and institutions are under resourced'.

[112] SADC Strategic Plan of Action on Combating Trafficking in Persons, especially Women and Children (2009–2019). Generally, see CH Vhumbunu 'Combating human trafficking in the Southern African Development Community: Strategies, challenges, and opportunities' (2020) 42 *The Strategic Review for Southern Africa* 179, for analysis of the SADC Strategic Plan of Action on Combating Trafficking in Persons, especially Women and Children (2009–2019).

[113] MM Dempsey, C Hoyle & M Bosworth 'Defining sex trafficking in international and domestic law: Mind the gaps' (2012) 26 *Emory International Law Review* 137 at 157.

argue that countries can simply adopt verbatim the definition of trafficking in article 3 of the Palermo Protocol.[114] This direct adoption would imply that there is no further excuse for the states lacking proper laws to continue using their non-compliant anti-trafficking legislation. Importantly, it would also require very little technical expertise to employ the precise wording of the instrument into a state party's domestic criminal code.[115]

2.4 *Obligation to Protect Victims of Human Trafficking*

Protection of victims of THB should be regarded as a key area of focus for states. It is worthwhile to note that protection obligations are not legally binding or legally enforceable on states. Protection obligations are not legally binding on states because each state may exercise discretion and independent judgement to choose whether to apply international law or domestic law to a victim's case. This has resulted in conflicting measures being taken depending on state preference and capacity. Hence, gaps have been created in implementation depending on where the victims were identified.[116] Some states such as Thailand, Jamaica, and Ghana have specific legislative provisions on protection which include vocational training, compensation, establishment of care centres and a victims' fund.[117] The Palermo Protocol establishes the importance of protecting a victim's privacy, assistance during criminal proceedings, and protection of the physical and mental well-being of victims, as well as the possibility of arranging temporary or permanent residence.[118] This is helpful to encourage victims to recover from their trafficking circumstances and decide whether to co-operate with law enforcement authorities to prosecute their traffickers or not.

Although the protection measures evaluated in articles 2, 6, and 7 of the Palermo Protocol seem reasonable in theory, in practice, the obligation to protect victims under international law is uncertain in terms of applicability. For example, an evaluation of the phrases 'shall endeavour

[114] Dempsey, Hoyle & Bosworth (n 113).

[115] As above.

[116] Obokata (n 100) 90.

[117] As above.

[118] Art 7 of the Palermo Protocol.

to provide', 'shall consider implementing measures,' and 'to the extent possible' imply that states will not be held accountable under international law even if they do not/cannot act.[119] In essence, states are only required to consider implementing protection measures. During the drafting stage of the Palermo Protocol, international organisations including the International Labour Organization (ILO) emphasised the requirement for a more encompassing provision that would comprise additional measures such as protection against reprisal of victims from traffickers and access to embassies.[120] Obokata argues that the retention of this language illustrates that states are reluctant to be legally bound by the obligations.[121] Developing states in particular have expressed concerns that they may not have enough resources to provide requisite protection to victims.[122]

The only strict obligation which contains the words 'shall ensure' refers to assistance during criminal investigation and proceedings.[123] This gives the impression that victims are merely tools to be used for criminal justice without taking into consideration their personal well-being. This practice undermines the key aim of the Palermo Protocol outlined in article 2, and further alienates victims who are already unwilling to approach the authorities due to enforcement action against them and fear of reprisal by traffickers. States such as Serbia, Croatia, and Italy have set a worthy precedent by providing protection to victims without requiring them to participate in trafficking cases.[124] This approach should be taken by all states to illustrate their commitment to protect the human rights of trafficked victims.

[119] Arts 6 and 7 of the Palermo Protocol.

[120] UNODC *Travaux Préparatoires of the Negotiations for the Elaboration of the United Nations Convention Against Transnational Organised Crime and Protocols Thereto* (2006) 366.

[121] Obokata (n 100).

[122] UNODC (n 120) 366.

[123] Art 6(2) of the Palermo Protocol.

[124] Obokata (n 100).

3 Victim Status, a Guide to Promote Improved Understanding of State Obligations

Improving immunity from prosecution for victims of human trafficking is contingent on the state fulfilling its obligation to pursue, prevent, protect, and prepare incentives aimed at reducing the offence of THB. It has been established that unfulfilled state obligations are one of the factors that result in the prosecution of victims of human trafficking. It is advantageous at this point to assess victim status, as a guide to promote further understanding of state obligations and how it affects the non-prosecution of victims.

The examination of victim status is often veiled in different mistaken assumptions and fictitious beliefs. Victims are often portrayed as inactive individuals whose arrival in a destination country was involuntary and occurred solely from coercion by the trafficker. They are assumed to be predominantly women and girls, from a poor background and have a low level of education, Skrikantiah refers to this type of victim as the iconic victim.[125] Vijeyarasa proceeds to dispel these myths by asserting that the four assumptions of a victim: the involuntary victim, the poor victim, the uneducated victim, and the female victim, are often unrealistic views of the typical victim of human trafficking.[126] Hence, the pure victim representation of an innocent, helpless individual is impractical in explaining the different patterns in trafficking situations.

For the first assumption, the involuntary victim is perceived to have been coerced and kidnapped, but often this individual may only be deceived as to the nature or conditions of work, but on arrival at their destination they may employ some level of autonomous decision making in accepting the terms of their new condition.[127] Vijeyarasa also presents an alternative model to the educated victim, and argues that education and trafficking are directly related.[128] Thus, the more educated a person, the more likely it is they migrate and the more exposed they are to

[125] J Srikantiah 'Perfect victims and real survivors: The iconic victim in domestic human trafficking law' (2007) 87 *Boston University Law Review* 157 at 187.

[126] R Vijeyarasa *Sex, slavery and the trafficked woman: Myths and misconceptions about trafficking and its victims* 1st ed (2015) 9.

[127] Vijeyarasa (n 126) 96.

[128] Vijeyarasa (n 126) 112.

exploitation and trafficking.[129] This challenges the assumption that most trafficking victims lack or possess only limited autonomy as a result of low educational attainment. On the contrary it appears higher levels of education may lead to human trafficking situations.[130]

In relation to the third myth, although in general terms, there is some truth to the female victim model, the non-gendering of male victims is a challenge in trafficking cases. The perception in many countries including Ghana is that trafficking mainly relates to children and in some cases the sexual exploitation of adult women, whereas exploited migrants are often men.[131] Human trafficking is not gender or age specific (victims are male and female, including children, women, and men). Hence, there are differences in terms of the extent to which male victims of trafficking are recognised in different countries. Further empirical research on male victims, along with a more nuanced analysis of their trafficking experiences, is warranted.[132] Regarding the last myth of the poor victim of trafficking, Vijeyarasa's findings suggest that the pursuit of improved economic and social circumstances may lead to trafficking situations rather than the need to address extreme hunger or desperation.[133]

An analysis of Vijeyarasa's arguments demonstrates that the experiences of trafficked victims are diverse, and their accounts of exploitation may seem inconsistent. Rijken further illustrates this point by observing that in labour exploitation cases, for example, victims do not perceive that their trafficker has done anything wrong by exploiting them.[134] They often assume that it is logical to be treated differently from the host country's citizens.[135] This observation implies that individuals who have been trafficked do not consider themselves to be victims. There seems to be a discrepancy between how the authorities view victims and how

[129] As above.

[130] Vijeyarasa (n 126).

[131] Vijeyarasa (n 126) 160.

[132] However, see E Njoku and others 'Sex trafficking and sex-for-food/money: Terrorism and conflict-related sexual violence against men in the Lake Chad region' (2022) 22 *Conflict, Security & Development* 79.

[133] Vijeyarasa (n 126) 131.

[134] C Rijken 'Challenges and pitfalls in combatting THB for labour exploitation' in C Rijken (ed) *Combating trafficking in human beings for labour exploitation* 1st ed (2011) 413.

[135] Rijken (n 134) 414.

victims view themselves. Rijken contends that victims think it is justified that they do not receive the same rights as workers from the host country.[136] Accordingly, when they are discovered by the authorities, they do not want to leave their trafficking situation. But may want to continue working for their trafficker who is also their employer, in hopes that they will be paid what they are owed.[137]

Elliot argues that despite the UK being one of the main destination states for victims of human trafficking, it has consistently performed inadequately in securing victims' rights and providing assistance and support to them.[138] One reason for this may be that the approach to human trafficking cases is not from a victim-centred viewpoint.[139] A victim-centred approach would take into account the effect trafficking and any subsequent exploitation may have on the victim and provide support and rehabilitation for them. Therefore, the drafting and enactment of any legislation dealing with trafficking must cover the protection of victims as well as the prohibition, prosecution, and punishment of traffickers.[140] Legislation that deals with only some of these aspects must be complemented by others to address the gap. Arguably, the CoE Convention, EU Directive and the MSA, are well-suited for this purpose. These three instruments complement each other, and when there are disparities in definition or application of legal principle the MSA may be helpful to clarify the provisions in the CoE Convention and EU Directive. The UNODC Model Law against Trafficking in Persons is also useful to provide guidance on any difficulties encountered in applying the non-prosecution principle.[141] The model law has been developed to assist states parties with the implementation of the Palermo Protocol. The model law suggests the inclusion of a provision on the non-prosecution of victims of THB in domestic law.[142]

[136] As above.

[137] As above.

[138] J Elliot *The role of consent in human trafficking* 1st ed (2014) 163.

[139] As above.

[140] Elliot (n 138) 161.

[141] United Nations Office on Drugs and Crime, Model Law against Trafficking in Persons (2009).

[142] Art 10 of the Model Law against Trafficking in Persons.

Victims are persons who have individually or collectively suffered harm, including physical or mental injury, substantial impairment of their fundamental rights, economic loss, or emotional suffering through acts or omissions that are in violation of criminal laws operating within member states, including those laws prohibiting criminal abuse of power.[143] It is important to also point out that a person is considered to be a victim of trafficking if the intention behind their movement and recruitment was exploitation, even if the actual exploitation did not occur.[144] The definition of a victim of trafficking in the Palermo Protocol makes it clear that trafficking occurs once certain acts are carried out for the purpose of exploitation. Hence, it is the purpose, which is the main factor, rather than whether exploitation is present or not. This consideration is relevant for instance in cases of child trafficking where the children are stopped at the port of entry or where there has been a police raid before actual exploitation has taken place.[145] In addition, even if the UK was able to intervene and had successfully prevented exploitation from occurring, victims may have experienced some trauma enroute to the UK, or in their home country and may still be in need of support.[146] In all UK referrals, the Competent Authority (bodies within the UK Modern Slavery Human Trafficking Unit (MSHTU) and the UK Visas and Immigration (UKVI)) is embodied with the task of determining whether a person is a victim of human trafficking or not.[147] In England and Wales, if it is found that a person is not a victim of trafficking, the Competent Authority is required to go a step further and examine whether they are the victim of another

[143] United Nations Human Rights Office of the High Commissioner 'Declaration of basic principles of justice for victims of crime and abuse of power' Adopted by General Assembly resolution 40/34 of 29 November 1985 http://www.ohchr.org/EN/ProfessionalInterest/Pages/VictimsOfCrimeAndAbuseOfPower.aspx (accessed 28 October 2024).

[144] Art 3 of the Palermo Protocol.

[145] L Hooper & K Thomson 'Victims of trafficking and the law session: Victims of trafficking – Immigration law' http://www.airecentre.org/data/files/Comic_Relief_Materials/Glasgow/7_-_Immigration_Materials.pdf (accessed 28 October 2024).

[146] As above.

[147] Generally, see UK Government 'National referral mechanism guidance: Adult (England and Wales)' (Update 21 September 2023) https://www.gov.uk/government/publications/human-trafficking-victims-referral-and-assessment-forms/guidance-on-the-national-referral-mechanism-for-potential-adult-victims-of-modern-slavery-england-and-wales (accessed 28 October 2024).

form of modern slavery, which includes slavery, servitude, and forced or compulsory labour.[148]

Since April 2019, the Single Competent Authority (SCA) has replaced the previous Competent Authority comprised of the MSHTU and UKVI. The current SCA's functions and responsibilities are predominantly the same as the previous Competent Authority. For example, trained specialists in the SCA make decisions about who is recognised as a victim of human trafficking/modern slavery and make decisions on all NRM cases.[149] The SCA makes these decisions on NRM cases regardless of immigration or nationality status of the victim. These were some of the main functions performed by the former Competent Authority comprised of the MSHTU and UKVI.

4 Conclusion

The assessment of state obligations, such as the obligation to prevent human trafficking, and protect victims of trafficking illustrates the role of destination states and origin/source states. States are expected to structure administrative and legislative policies to deter the crime of human trafficking. The state has human rights obligations towards people who have been trafficked or who are at risk of being trafficked in the future. Improving immunity from prosecution for victims of human trafficking is contingent on the state fulfilling its obligation to pursue, prevent, protect, and prepare incentives aimed at reducing the offence of THB. Even though the UK is one of the main destination states for victims of human trafficking, it has consistently performed inadequately in securing victims' rights and aiding support to them.

A foremost reason for the inadequate protection of victim's rights is linked to the existence of HTPs amongst some African immigrant communities within the UK. HTPs are often borne out of cultural/ community pressure. They may have been firmly and deeply rooted into

[148] Home Office 'Victims of modern slavery – Competent authority guidance' (Home Office 21 March 2016) https://www.gov.uk/government/uploads/system/uploads/attachment_data/file/509596/Victims-of-modern-slavery-competent-authority-guidance-v3.0.pdf (accessed 28 October 2024).

[149] Home Office 'Victims of Modern Slavery – Competent authority guidance' (Home Office 29 April 2019, Version 7.0) https://www.safeguardingchildren.co.uk/wp-content/uploads/2019/09/victims-of-modern-day-slavery-competent-authroity-guidance.pdf (accessed 28 October 2024).

the structure of a community, thereby becoming a way of life for the social group of individuals concerned. HTPs are forms of violence which have been committed, primarily against women, girls, and children, in certain social groups and communities for so long (spanning decades and generations), that they are considered, or presented by perpetrators, as part of an accepted cultural practice. The most common forms of harmful practices are forced or early marriage, honour-based violence, and female genital mutilation (FGM). Other less-known types of harmful practices include bride kidnapping, acid attacks, son preference, breast ironing, and spirit possession.

Some human trafficking victims in the UK may have experienced some HTPs either prior to, during, or after undergoing an exploitative situation. In some instances, tradition, culture, or norms may worsen human trafficking in African immigrant communities. This arises because immigrants, emigrants, and their descendants residing outside their country of birth or ancestry—whether temporarily or permanently—often maintain strong ties to their country of origin. The definition of a victim of trafficking in the Palermo Protocol makes it clear that trafficking occurs once certain acts are carried out for the purpose of exploitation. Hence, it is the purpose, which is the main factor, rather than whether exploitation is present or not.

Unfulfilled state obligations and inadequate victim status attainment are two of the main reasons that victims of trafficking are prosecuted for criminal activities carried out during their trafficking circumstances. The UK is obligated not to prosecute victims of trafficking for offences they have been coerced or forced to commit because of their trafficked status. However, a trafficked person does not obtain automatic immunity from prosecution, neither do they have a substantive defence because of their status as victims of trafficking alone. Nonetheless, culpability may be significantly diminished when the evidence points to the fact that the exploited victim was forced by an individual or a group of individuals to carry out the illegal acts. When a victim is prosecuted for offences that have occurred as a direct consequence of their trafficking situation, they can appeal the court's decision based on abuse of process and have their conviction quashed.

In assessing victim status all that is required is substantial evidence that points to the fact that a person was exploited and is a credible victim of THB. However, a simplistic view of a victim as blameless is flawed because it does not consider trafficked victims who have displayed some agency or acted as co-conspirators in their trafficking situation. Hence, it is useful to point out that there is no typical victim of trafficking. They are not all naive, simple people who are tricked. Educated individuals with high social status may also become victims of trafficking because of their desire to earn a living. Significantly, individuals who have been trafficked seldom perceive themselves as victims. Owing to shame stemming from exploitation or fear of retribution, individuals identified by governmental bodies and NGOs often exhibit reluctance in acknowledging their status as trafficking victims. A strengthened approach to victim treatment and protection is essential to facilitate the improved implementation of state obligations.

Bibliography

African Centre for Democracy and Human Rights Studies 'Resolution on Combating Human Trafficking in Africa' (2008) https://www.acdhrs.org/2008/11/resolution-on-combating-human-trafficking-in-africa/#:~:text=Ratify%20the%20Palermo%20Protocol%20and,combating%20all%20forms%20of%20trafficking (accessed 28 October 2024)

Agunias, DR & Newland, K 'Developing a road map for engaging diasporas in development: A handbook for policymakers and practitioners in home and host countries' International Organization for Migration (IOM) and Migration Policy Institute (MPI) (2012)

Apard, E; Chiossone, E; Diagboya, P; Jeannerod, A; Lavaud-Legendre, B; Olufade, C; Plessard, C & Panata, S 'Religious, social and criminal groups in trafficking of Nigerian girls and women' ECPAT France (2019)

Atak, I & Simeon, JC 'Human trafficking: Mapping the legal boundaries of international refugee law and criminal justice' (2014) 12 *Journal of International Criminal Justice* 1019

Bakare-Yusuf, B '"Yoruba's don't do gender": A critical review of Oyeronke Oyewumi's *The invention of women: Making an African sense of western gender discourses*' in Arnfred, S; Bakare-Yusuf, B & Kisiang'ani, EW *African gender scholarship: Concepts, methodologies, and paradigms* (CODESRIA 2004)

Baker, A 'An ancient curse kept Nigerian women bound to sex slavery. Now, it's been reversed' *Time* 17 April 2018 https://time.com/longform/juju-curse-nigeria-sex-slavery-europe/ (accessed 28 October 2024)

Bartelink, B & Le Roux, E 'What is in a name? Identifying the harm in "harmful traditional practices"' in Wilkinson, O & Kraft, K (eds) *International development and local faith actors: Ideological and cultural encounters* (2020)

Bartelink, B & Dr Le Roux, E with Levinga, W 'Harmful traditional practices in the context of faith: A literature review' Part of the UK Government-funded 'Working effectively with faith leaders to challenge harmful traditional practices' Research report (2017) https://prevention-collaborative.org/wp-content/uploads/2021/08/Bartelink_2017_Harmful_practices_context_of_faith.pdf (accessed 28 October 2024)

Byron, IP 'Customary arbitration as a tool for ensuring access to justice for women in Nigeria: A case study of the women's law clinic' (2017) 11 *Ife Juris Review* 41

Chisholm, A; Mark, I; Unigwe, S & Katonaet, C 'Rituals as a control mechanism in human trafficking: Systematic review and thematic synthesis of qualitative literature' (2022) *Journal of Human Trafficking* 1

Coetzee, AA 'African feminism as decolonising force: A philosophical exploration of the work of Oyeronke Oyewumi' PhD thesis, Stellenbosch University, 2017

Coetzee, AA 'Woman, time and the incommunicability of non-Western worlds: Understanding the role of gender in the colonial denial of coevalness' (2021) 22 *Feminist Theory* 465

Demeke, S 'A human rights-based approach for effective criminal justice response to human trafficking' (2024) 9 *Journal of International Humanitarian Action* 1

Dempsey, MM; Hoyle, C & Bosworth, M 'Defining sex trafficking in international and domestic law: Mind the gaps' (2012) 26 *Emory International Law Review* 137

Duivenbode, R & Padela, A 'Female genital cutting (FGC) and the cultural boundaries of medical practice' (2019) 19 *The American Journal of Bioethics* 4

Dunkerley, AW 'Exploring the use of juju in Nigerian human trafficking networks: Considerations for criminal investigators' (2018) 19 *Police Practice and Research* 83

Ekhator, EO 'Protection and promotion of women's rights in Nigeria: Constraints and prospects' in M Addaney (ed) *Women and minority rights law: African approaches and perspectives to inclusive development* (ElevenPub 2019)

J Elliot *The role of consent in human trafficking* 1st ed (Routledge 2014)

Ezeilo, JN 'Report of the Special Rapporteur on trafficking in persons, especially women and children, on her mission to Italy' United Nations General Assembly A/HRC/26/37/Add.4, 5 (2014)

Ezeilo, JN 'Rethinking women and customary inheritance in Nigeria' (2021) 47 *Commonwealth Law Bulletin* 706

Gangoli, G; Gill, A; Mulvihill, N & Hester, M 'Perception and barriers: Reporting female genital mutilation' (2018) 10 *Journal of Aggression, Conflict and Peace Research* 251

Garcia, AD 'Trafficking, ritual oaths and criminal investigations' *Forced Migration Review* 64 (June 2020)

Gershuni, R 'The interface between trafficking in persons and culture' in Piotrowicz, R; Rijken, C & Uhl, B (eds) *Routledge handbook of human trafficking* (2017) 366

Gillespie, G 'FGC? FGM? Female circumcision? Why language matters in helping communities abandon harmful practices' Tostan International (2015) https://tostan.org/fgc-fgm-female-circumcision-why-language-matters-helping-communities-abandon-harmful-practices/ (accessed 28 October 2024)

Gouws, A 'Theorizing feminism from the South: Knowledge production through South Africa's Feminist Journal AGENDA' (2022) 23 *Journal of International Women's Studies* 57

Greater Manchester Safeguarding 'Female Genital Mutilation Multi-Agency Protocol' https://greatermanchesterscb.proceduresonline.com/chapters/p_fgm.html (accessed 28 October 2024)

Hamma, H 'SDG 3 and maternal health rights: A biosocial approach to ending the VVF scourge in Northern Nigeria' in Ekhator, E; Miller, S & Igbinosa, E (eds) *Implementing the Sustainable Development Goals in Nigeria: Barriers, prospects and strategies* (Routledge 2021)

Haruna, BA & Yusuf, AM 'The role of Nigeria Courts in protecting women and children against harmful traditional practices' in Onuora-Oguno, A (ed) *Promoting efficiency in jurisprudence and constitutional development in Africa* (Palgrave Macmillan 2022)

Haynes, J 'Human trafficking: Iconic victims, folk devils and the Nationality and Borders Act 2022' (2023) 86 *Modern Law Review* 1232

HM Government 'Modern slavery strategy' (2014) https://www.gov.uk/government/uploads/system/uploads/attachment_data/file/383764/Modern_Slavery_Strategy_FINAL_DEC2015.pdf (accessed 28 October 2024)

Hooper, L & Thomson, K 'Victims of trafficking and the law session: Victims of trafficking – Immigration law' http://www.airecentre.org/data/files/Comic_Relief_Materials/Glasgow/7_-_Immigration_Materials.pdf (accessed 28 October 2024)

House of Commons Home Affairs Committee 'Human trafficking: First Report of Session 2023–24' (8 December 2023) https://publications.parliament.uk/pa/cm5804/cmselect/cmhaff/124/report.html at 40 (accessed 28 October 2024)

Igwe, BO 'The impact of domestic violence legal regulation and enforcement among Nigerian immigrants in Ireland' PhD thesis, National University of Ireland, Maynooth, 2018

Ikeora, M 'The role of African traditional religion and "Juju" in human trafficking: Implications for anti-trafficking' (2016) 17 *Journal of International Women's Studies* 1

International Bar Association (IBA) 'IBA and BIICL launch new report exploring the global implementation non-punishment principle for human trafficking victims' (30 November 2023) https://www.ibanet.org/IBA-and-BIICL-launch-new-report-exploring-the-global-implementation-of-non-punishment-principle-for-human-trafficking-victims (accessed 28 October 2024)

International Organisation for Migration (IOM) 'Addressing human trafficking and exploitation in times of crisis: Evidence and recommendations for further action to protect vulnerable and mobile populations' (December 2015) https://www.antislaverycommissioner.co.uk/media/1068/addressing_human_trafficking_dec2015.pdf (accessed 28 October 2024)

Jones, J 'Is it time to open a conversation about a New United Nations Treaty to fight human trafficking that focuses on victim protection and human rights?' in Winterdyk, J & Jones, J (eds) *The Palgrave international handbook of human trafficking* (Palgrave Macmillan 2020) 1803

Jovanović, M & Niezna, M 'Non-punishment of victims/survivors of human trafficking in practice: A case study of the United Kingdom' (September 2023, Council of Europe) https://rm.coe.int/non-punishment-of-victims-survivors-of-human-trafficking-in-practice-a/1680ac86f4 (accessed 28 October 2024)

Kane, G 'State empowered entities as sites of progress for international anti-trafficking law and policy?' (2023) 5 *Frontiers in Human Dynamics* 1

Karenga, PS *West African model to address human trafficking* 1st ed (Springer 2022)

Kelley, T 'Truth or consequences (the deadly kind): Oath swearing in Nigerien customary law' 47 *North Carolina Journal of International Law* 331

La Strada International 'The impact of criminalising the "knowing use" on human trafficking' Policy Paper (December 2022) 5 https://documentation.lastradainternational.org/doc-center/3476/policy-paper%C2%A0the-impact-of-criminalising%C2%A0the-%E2%80%98knowing-use%E2%80%99-on-human-trafficking (accessed 28 October 2023)

Le Roux, E; Bartelink, BE & Palm, S 'What is the harm in "harmful traditional practices"?' Policy Brief (November 2017) https://www.gov.uk/research-for-development-outputs/what-is-the-harm-in-harmful-traditional-practices (accessed 28 October 2024)

Mandel, JW 'Out of sight, out of mind: The lax and underutilized prosecution of sex trafficking in the United Kingdom and Israel' (2012) 21 *Tulane Journal. of International & Comparative Law* 206

Mbaku, JM 'International human rights law and the tyranny of harmful customary and traditional practices on women in Africa' (2021) 52 *California Western International Law Journal* 1

Merseyside Protecting Vulnerable People: Harmful Offices Group 'Pan Merseyside Female Genital Mutilation (FGM) Protocol' Version 2 (2019) 7

Msuya, NH 'Advocating positive traditional culture to eradicate harmful aspects of traditional culture for gender equality in Africa' (2020) 41 *Obiter* 45

Nekura, R 'The rights to life, integrity and security of the person' in Rudman, Musembi, CN & Makunyaand, TM (eds) *The Protocol to the African Charter on Human and Peoples' Rights on the Rights of Women in Africa: A commentary* (PULP 2023)

Neves, S & Stewart, G '*V.C.L and A.N v The United Kingdom*: A positive step forward for victims of modern day slavery' Youth Justice League Centre https://yjlc.uk/resources/legal-updates/vcl-and-v-united-kingdom-positive-step-forward-victims-modern-day-slavery (accessed 28 October 2024)

Njoku, E; Akintayo, J & Mohammed, I 'Sex trafficking and sex-for-food/money: Terrorism and conflict-related sexual violence against men in the Lake Chad region' (2022) 22 *Conflict, Security & Development* 79

Nnamuchi, O; Ezeilo, J; Obuka, U; Ilodigwe, M; Ike, C & Obi-Ochiabutor, C 'The trafficking of women in Nigeria: Is there a role for human rights?' (2022) 44 *Human Rights Quarterly* 806

Nwauche, ES 'State response to outcomes of traditional justice resolution mechanisms in Commonwealth Africa: Customary arbitration in Nigeria and Ghana' (2022) 4 *Journal of Commonwealth Law* 73

Oamen, PE; Storey, A; Nazir, A & Yorke, J *Nigeria Universal Periodic Review: Stakeholder submission on female genital mutilation* Project Report, Birmingham City University (2023)

Obokata, T 'Human trafficking in Africa: Opportunities and challenges for the African Court of Justice and Human Rights' in Jalloh, CC; Clarke, KM & Nmehielle, VO (eds) *The African Court of Justice and human and peoples' rights in context: Development and challenges* (Cambridge University Press 2019) 529

Obokata, T 'Implementing international law on human trafficking: Case studies of the United Kingdom and Ireland' (2015) 2 *State Practice and International Law Journal* 85

Ogunniyi, D & Idowu, O 'Human trafficking in West Africa: An implementation assessment of international and regional normative standards' (2022) 19 *The Age of Human Rights Journal* 165

Ogwezzy, OO 'The legal impact of voodoo and other control mechanisms on human trafficking in Nigeria' (2023) 3 *Redeemer's University Nigeria, Journal of Jurisprudence & International Law* 234

Ohonba, A & Agbontaen-Eghafona, K 'Transnational remittances from human trafficking and the changing socio-economic status of women in Benin City, Edo State Nigeria' (2019) 48 *Women's Studies* 531

Okorie, MM & Okeja, U 'Prosecuting human traffickers in Nigeria: Victim-witnessing and community-oriented challenges' (2024) Trends in Organized

Crime https://doi.org/10.1007/s12117-024-09548-y (accessed 23 January 2025)

Olufade, C 'Sustenance of sex trafficking in Edo State: The combined effect of oath taking, transnational silence and migration imaginaries on trafficked women in Edo State' (2019)

Oronsaye-Agunloye, II 'Gender politics in historiography: Precolonial Benin' in Usuanlele, U (ed) *Benin studies under the scalpel: Essays in honour of Dr Ekhaguosa Aisien* (2020) 71

Oyakhire, SO 'Expanding the scope of "appropriate measures": Do traditional institutions play a role in facilitating the protection of witnesses of trafficking in persons?' (2019) 6 *Journal of Comparative Law in Africa* 80

Oyěwùmí, O 'Conceptualising gender: Eurocentric foundations of feminist concepts and the challenge of African epistemologies' in Arnfred, S; Bakare-Yusuf, B & Kisiang'ani, EW (eds) *African gender scholarship: Concepts, methodologies and paradigms* (2004)

SADC 'Strategic Plan of Action on Combating Trafficking in Persons, especially Women and Children (2009–2019)'

Scarpa, S 'UN Palermo trafficking protocol eighteen years on: A critique' in Winterdyk, J & Jones, J (eds) *The Palgrave international handbook of human trafficking* (Palgrave Macmillan 2020) 623

Seideman, CA 'The Palermo Protocol: Why it has been ineffective in reducing human sex trafficking' (2015) 9 *Global Tides* 5

Srikantiah, J 'Perfect victims and real survivors: The iconic victim in domestic human trafficking law' (2007) 87 *Boston University Law Review* 157

Tamale, S 'The right to culture and the culture of rights: A critical perspective on women's sexual rights in Africa' (2008) 16 *Feminist Legal Studies* 47

Uduji, JI; Okolo-Obasi, EN & Asongu, SA 'Oil extraction and gender equality for social equity: The role of corporate social responsibility in Nigeria's coastal communities' (2023) 81 *Resources Policy* 103346

UK Government 'Country policy and information note: Trafficking of women Nigeria' (April 2022) (accessible version) (updated 12 August 2022) https://www.gov.uk/government/publications/nigeria-country-policy-and-information-notes/country-policy-and-information-note-trafficking-of-women-nigeria-april-2022-accessible-version (accessed 28 October 2024)

UK Government 'Guidance on female genital mutilation (FGM): Migrant health guide' (31 August 2014, last updated 13 September 2021) https://www.gov.uk/guidance/female-genital-mutilation-fgm-migrant-health-guide (accessed 28 October 2024)

UK Government 'National referral mechanism guidance: Adult (England and Wales)' (Update 21 September 2023) https://www.gov.uk/government/publications/human-trafficking-victims-referral-and-assessment-forms/guidance-on-the-national-referral-mechanism-for-potential-adult-victims-of-modern-slavery-england-and-wales (accessed 28 October 2024)

UK Home Office 'Victims of modern slavery – Competent authority guidance' (21 March 2016) https://www.gov.uk/government/uploads/system/uploads/attachment_data/file/509596/Victims-of-modern-slavery-competent-authority-guidance-v3.0.pdf (accessed 28 October 2024)

UK Home Office 'Victims of modern slavery – Competent authority guidance' (29 April 2019, Version 7.0) https://www.safeguardingchildren.co.uk/wp-content/uploads/2019/09/victims-of-modern-day-slavery-competent-authroity-guidance.pdf (accessed 28 October 2024)

United Nations Human Rights Office of the High Commissioner 'Declaration of basic principles of justice for victims of crime and abuse of power' Adopted by General Assembly Resolution 40/34 of 29 November 1985 http://www.ohchr.org/EN/ProfessionalInterest/Pages/VictimsOfCrimeAndAbuseOfPower.aspx (accessed 28 October 2024)

United Nations Human Rights, Office of the High Commissioner, Fact Sheet 36: Human rights and human trafficking (2014) 11 https://www.ohchr.org/en/publications/fact-sheets/fact-sheet-no-36-human-rights-and-human-trafficking (accessed 28 October 2024)

United Nations Office on Drugs and Crime (UNODC) 'Global Report on Trafficking in Persons' (2022) 7 https://www.unodc.org/unodc/data-and-analysis/glotip.html (accessed 28 October 2024)

United Nations Office of the High Commissioner for Human Rights (OHCHR) Fact Sheet 23 'Harmful traditional practices affecting the health of women and children' (August 1995)

United Nations Population Fund (UNFPA) 'Female genital mutilation (FGM) frequently asked questions' (February 2022) https://www.unfpa.org/resources/female-genital-mutilation-fgm-frequently-asked-questions (accessed 28 October 2024)

UNODC *Travaux Préparatoires of the Negotiations for the Elaboration of the United Nations Convention Against Transnational Organised Crime and Protocols Thereto* (United Nations: New York 2006)

UNODC 'United Nations Convention against Transnational Organized Crime and the Protocols thereto: Status of ratification' United Nations Convention against Transnational Organised Crime https://www.unodc.org/unodc/en/organized-crime/intro/UNTOC.html (accessed 28 October 2024)

UN Women 'Traditional leaders across Africa move the needle against child marriage and FGM' (15 November 2018) https://www.unwomen.org/en/news/stories/2018/11/feature-traditional-leaders-across-africa-against-child-marriage-and-fgm (accessed 28 October 2024)

Van der Watt, M & Kruger, B 'Breaking bondages: Control methods, "Juju," and human trafficking' in J Winterdyk & J Jones (eds) *The Palgrave international handbook of human trafficking* (Palgrave MacMillan 2020) 935

Vhumbunu, CH 'Combating human trafficking in the Southern African Development Community: Strategies, challenges, and opportunities' (2020) 42 *The Strategic Review for Southern Africa* 179

Vijeyarasa, R *Sex, slavery and the trafficked woman: Myths and misconceptions about trafficking and its victims* 1st ed (2015)

Wirral Safeguarding Children Partnership 'Harmful practices' https://www.wirralsafeguarding.co.uk/harmful-practices/ (accessed 29 January 2024)

World Health Organisation (WHO) 'Female genital mutilation' (31 January 2023) https://www.who.int/news-room/fact-sheets/detail/female-genital-mutilation (accessed 28 October 2024)

Case Law

HD (Trafficked Women) CG [2016] UKUT454 (IAC)

LM, DG and MB in R v LM & Ors [2010] EWCA Crim 2327

Marian v Regional Prosecutor's Office of Ruse, Bulgaria [2019] EWHC 602 (Admin)

R v O [2008] EWCA Crim 2835

Rantsev v Cyprus & Russia App 25965/04 [2010] 51 EHRR

VCL & AN v The United Kingdom (Applications 77587/12 and 74603/12)

Legislation

Female Genital Mutilation Act 2003

Illegal Migration Act 2023

Modern Slavery Act 2015

Nationality and Borders Act 2022

Prohibition of Female Circumcision Act 1985

Serious Crime Act 2015

African Human Rights Instruments

African Union, Protocol to the African Charter on Human and People's Rights on the Rights of Women in Africa, African Union, 11 July 2003

Organisation of African Unity (OAU), African Charter on Human and Peoples' Rights (Banjul Charter), CAB/LEG/67/3 rev 5, 21 ILM 58 (1982), 27 June 1981

Organisation of African Unity (OAU), African Charter on the Rights and Welfare of the Child, CAB/LEG/24.9/49 (1990), 11 July 1990

European Human Rights Instruments

Council of Europe, Council of Europe Convention on Action Against Trafficking in Human Beings, CETS 197, 16 May 2005

European Union, Directive 2011/36 on Preventing and Combating Trafficking in Human Beings and Protecting its Victims [2011] OJ L101/1

UN Instruments

UN General Assembly, Protocol to Prevent, Suppress and Punish Trafficking in Persons Especially Women and Children, Supplementing the United Nations Convention against Transnational Organized Crime, 15 November 2000, UN Doc A/RES/55/25 (2000) (Palermo Protocol)

UN General Assembly, United Nations Convention against Transnational Organized Crime: Resolution adopted by the General Assembly, 8 January 2001, UN Doc A/RES/55/25 (2001) https://www.unodc.org/unodc/en/organized-crime/intro/UNTOC.html (accessed 28 October 2024)

United Nations Office on Drugs and Crime, Model Law against Trafficking in Persons (2009)

CHAPTER 11

An African Feminist Analysis of the Impact of Menstrual Taboos in Abrahamic Religions on Women and Girls in Africa

Zainab Monisola Olaitan

1 Introduction

Sexual and reproductive health rights (SRHR) are beginning to gain momentum in the global political agenda following the fallout of the overturning of *Roe v Wade*[1] in the United States,[2] the criminalisation of abortion in most African countries, and societal attitudes towards

[1] *Roe v Wade* 410 US 113 (1973).

[2] P Ryan, K Moloney & L Nancy 'The rights roll-back is gaining momentum' *International Planned Parenthood Federation* (18 July 2024) https://eseaor.ippf.org/blogs/rights-roll-back-gaining-momentum (accessed 05 November 2024).

Z. M. Olaitan (✉)
Centre for International and Defence Policy (CIDP), Queen's University, Kingston, ON, Canada
e-mail: zainab.olaitan@queensu.ca

E. Durojaye et al. (eds.), *Harmful Practices and Human Rights: An International Perspective*, Human Rights Interventions,
https://doi.org/10.1007/978-3-031-90333-5_11

women's rights generally.[3] The increased focus on SRHR includes harmful practices perpetuated around women's sexuality, reproduction and of the girl-child.[4] The wave of the anti-rights narrative in recent times is also contributing to a resurgence in harmful practices, for example, the attempt to repeal the Anti-Female Genital Mutilation (FGM) Bill in the Gambia[5] and the attempt to repeal the Violence Against Persons Prohibition Act (VAPP) in Nigeria.[6] All these raise concerns about the rights of women and girls, particularly their well-being and dignity. While practices like FGM are popularised and receive relevant attention, menstrual taboos are an equally dangerous and harmful practice that women and girls are exposed to. Menstrual taboos have been the subject of numerous research within and outside of Africa,[7] with most investigating the cultural and religious underpinnings of these taboos and how they manifest in society. Specifically on religious menstrual taboos, studies have been done to understand how different religions grapple with menstruation and their perception of it.[8]

In this chapter, I extend the discourse on menstrual taboos to focus on the human rights implications of religious menstrual taboos on women and girls in Africa. This chapter focuses on analysing the rights-based consequences of menstrual taboos and how they affect the well-being and dignity of women and girls in Africa. I use an African feminist lens to unpack the complex forms of oppression that women and girls in Africa

[3] ZM Olaitan & C Isike 'Anti-rights legislations in Africa: Why South Africa must consolidate its commitment to promoting Human Rights' *University of Pretoria* (20 March 2024) https://www.up.ac.za/news/post_3247608-opinion-piece-protecting-the-rights-of-women-in-south-africa-a-call-for-feminist-leadership- (accessed 29 October 2024).

[4] S Nabaneh *Choice and conscience: Lessons from South Africa for a global debate* (2023).

[5] Human Rights Watch 'Gambia: Bill threatens female genital mutilation ban' (19 April 2024) https://www.hrw.org/news/2024/04/19/gambia-bill-threatens-female-genital-mutilation-ban (accessed 6 November 2024).

[6] D Nandini 'Repealing VAPP Act – A knee-jerk move set to undo Nigeria's decade of progress in protecting the vulnerable' *Africa* 17 September 2024 https://www.africa.com/repealing-vapp-act-a-knee-jerk-move-set-to-undo-nigerias-decade-of-progress-in-protecting-the-vulnerable/ (accessed 5 November 2024).

[7] R Montgomery 'A cross-cultural study of menstruation, menstrual taboos and related social variables' (1974) 2 *American Anthropological Association* 137.

[8] MA Guterman, P Mehta & MS Gibbs 'Menstrual taboos among major religions' (2007) 5 *The Internet Journal of Wealth and Societal Politics* 1.

are exposed to because of menstrual taboos and to consolidate the argument on the human rights implication of menstrual taboos. I apply these frames to understand the impact of menstrual taboos on the well-being of women and girls as a means to spur innovative and pragmatic solutions that better protect their rights. I argue that by restricting women's agency and reinforcing the discrimination and exclusion of women and girls, menstrual taboos perpetuate gender inequality and oppression of women and girls in Africa.

This chapter is divided into six substantive sections: the first being this Introduction; the second section provides context on the practice and prevalence of menstrual taboos within Abrahamic religions, considering that most Africans practice one of the three Abrahamic religions (Christianity, Islam, and Judaism).[9] The third section focuses on expounding an African feminist lens to the discourse on harmful practices and menstrual taboos and how these contribute to the systemic oppression of women and girls in Africa. The fourth section engages the impact of menstrual taboos with a focus on the right to non-discrimination, health, information, dignity, and the restriction of women's agency. It analyses how menstrual taboos infringe on the aforementioned rights while applying an African feminist lens. The fifth section examines previous efforts that have been made to address menstrual taboos; it focuses on two major human rights instruments that guarantee women's rights, that is, the Convention on the Elimination of All Forms of Discrimination Against Women (CEDAW)[10] and the Protocol to the African Charter on Human and Peoples' Rights on the Rights of Women in Africa (Maputo Protocol).[11] The sixth and final section explains some of the challenges that impede the effectiveness of these instruments while also proffering relevant recommendations on what can be done to address menstrual taboos.

[9] Pew Research Centre 'Tolerance and Tension: Islam and Christianity in Sub-Saharan Africa' (15 April 2010) https://www.pewresearch.org/religion/2010/04/15/executive-summary-islam-and-christianity-in-sub-saharan-africa/ (accessed 25 October 2024).

[10] UN General Assembly, Convention on the Elimination of All Forms of Discrimination Against Women, United Nations, Treaty Series, vol 1249, p 13, 18 December 1979.

[11] African Union, Protocol to the African Charter on Human and People's Rights on the Rights of Women in Africa, 11 July 2003.

2 Practice and Prevalence of Menstrual Taboos in Abrahamic Religions

The practice and prevalence of menstrual taboos around the world can be traced to most Abrahamic religions, such as Christianity, Islam, and Judaism, although, other tribal religions have traces of menstrual-related taboos. Steinem[12] notes that as religions formed their taboos around menstruation, they included pre-existing biases against women. She asserts the gendered nature of menstrual taboos by humorously stating that 'if men were able to have periods while women could not, menstruation would become an enviable, boast-worthy, masculine event'.[13] However, menstrual taboos were created by religions to further reinforce and exacerbate stereotypes and prejudices against women.

Guterman and others[14] explain that among most religions, there are striking similarities in how menstruation is perceived and viewed. They note that comparable taboos exist across religions and cultures, although Christianity and Islam were influenced by Judaism, and more modern religions were impacted by primitive ones. Some of the obvious recurring taboos across these religions are isolation, exclusion from religious rituals, and abstinence from sexual activity.[15] In their seminal work on menstrual taboos, Guterman and others[16] discuss that exclusion and segregation are at the heart of most religious menstrual taboos. They explain that religions forbid menstruating women from praying in places of worship (synagogues, mosques, etc.). Some have also created the idea of menstrual huts to further consolidate the exclusion of menstruating women from the rest of society.[17] The second theme that characterises menstrual taboos across different religions is the notion of 'impurity' attached to menstruation. While menstruation is not intrinsically impure or unclean as most religions believe, it is considered spiritually impure, dangerous, unclean, or polluted. Menstruating women are left to grapple with the impurity

[12] G Steinem *Outrageous acts and everyday rebellions* (1986).

[13] G Steinem 'If men could menstruate' (2019) 6 *Women's Reproductive Health* 151.

[14] Guterman, Mehta & Gibbs (n 8).

[15] SF Koren 'The menstruant as other in Medieval Judaism and Christianity' (2009) 17 *Nashim: A Journal of Jewish Women's Studies & Gender Issues* Special Issue: Sexuality in Jewish Contexts 33.

[16] Guterman, Mehta & Gibbs (n 8).

[17] As above.

attached to a natural biological process that happens to them due to religious norms. As a result, menstruating women and girls may already feel alone because they are not allowed to enter places of worship or even pray in solitude. Thirdly, abstinence from sexual activity during menstruation is another recurring theme that exists among Abrahamic religions.[18]

To understand the reasoning behind religious menstrual taboos, it is important to engage their perception of menstruation. In Christianity, menstruating women are viewed as harmful, and this perception informs the antiquated taboo that binds most women practicing the religion.[19] The Book of Leviticus[20] regulates Christianity's perception of menstruation as impurity, stating that:

> [W]henever a woman has a discharge and the discharge from her body is blood, she will remain in a state of menstrual pollution for seven days, anyone who touches her will be unclean until evening.

The verse goes further to state that:

> [A]nyone who touches a menstruating woman or touches the places where she slept or sat will be unclean until evening, and that a man who sleeps with her will be unclean for seven days. On the eighth day after her period, women are told to take two turtledoves or two pigeons to a priest as a sacrificial offering to return them to a state of purity after menstruation.[21]

The impurification of menstruation can also be explained by the idea of 'Eve's curse', a punishment for having accepted the forbidden fruit. Phipps[22] argues that the choice to exclude women from positions of power in Christianity was largely influenced by its perception of menstruation and the resulting menstrual taboos. Furthermore, some Christian denominations, such as Orthodox Churches, forbid women from receiving communion when they are menstruating.[23] Additionally,

[18] As above.

[19] W Phipps 'The menstrual taboo in the Judeo-Christian tradition' (1980) 19 *Journal of Religion and Health* 298.

[20] See Book of Leviticus, chap 15 v 19.

[21] See Leviticus, chap 15, v 19–25.

[22] Phipps (n 19).

[23] As above.

Catholics believe that a woman should not have sex during her menstruation, which is also a result of menstrual taboos.[24] Ruether[25] explains that Catholic canon law prohibits women and girls from serving in any semi-sacerdotal positions. Demonstrating that menstrual taboos have been decisive in keeping women out of positions of power throughout Judeo-Christian history. Only a small percentage of the congregations that uphold that tradition still allow women to be ordained. The taboos are the main justification for prohibiting sexual relations during a woman's menstrual cycle in many Catholic households.[26] Menstruation is typically spoken in whispers and only among women due to the pervasiveness of the taboo. The silence that surrounds the discussion of menstruation prevents most women from educating young girls about their first period due to the stigma attached to it.

In Judaism, menstruating women are perceived as ritually unclean; their 'impure' status often leads to social isolation.[27] Drawn from the *Baraita de-Niddah*,[28] the risks associated with menstruation are explained to those who follow the laws of *niddah*,[29] which are to refrain from baking or cooking for their partners. Also, a menstruating woman is not allowed to serve her husband water or shake the bed. The taboo goes as far as 'even the saliva of menstruating women can pollute her husbands or sons'.[30] Due to her menstruation, she is polluted and can pollute those around her. Menstruating women are not allowed to enter the synagogue until they have completely immersed themselves.[31] Jewish populations were taught the *Baraita de-Niddah* customs to guide their knowledge

[24] R Ruether 'Women's body and blood: The sacred and the impure' in A Joseph (eds) *Through the devil's gateway: Women, religion and taboo* (1990) 7–21.

[25] As above.

[26] Phipps (n 19).

[27] M Jennaway 'Of blood and foetuses: Female fertility and women's reproductive health in a North Balinese village' in PL Rice & L Manderson (eds) *Maternity and reproductive health in Asian societies* (1996) 37–60.

[28] *Baraita de-Niddah* is a rabbinic text about the ritual laws relating to menstruation.

[29] *Niddah* is used in Jewish tradition in relation menstruation; it often refers to a menstruating woman, menstruation, and menstrual impurity.

[30] Koren (n 15).

[31] As above.

of menstruation. Thus, Jewish ideas about the possible risks of menstruation were well-established and were employed to enforce the laws about menstrual impurity.[32]

In Islam, the Quran, chapter 2, verse 222, guides the perception and regulation of menstruation. It states that:

> [A]nd they ask you about menstruation. Say, 'It is harm, so keep away from wives during menstruation'. And do not approach them until they are pure. And when they have purified themselves, then come to them from where Allāh has ordained for you.

The verse indicates that menstruating women are contagiously impure and harmful to their husbands' purity, hence, they should abstain from sexual activity with them. The verse provides for men to stay away from menstruating women because they are impure.[33] Menstruation is considered impure in Islam and for religious purposes.[34] However, Azeem[35] contends that menstruating women are not contagiously unclean, neither untouchable nor cursed, providing a different interpretation of the verse. However, Muslim women who are menstruating are faced with numerous taboos that restrict them from religious practices.

They are not allowed to enter the mosque and engage in religious rituals such as fasting, prayers, or holding the Quran.[36] Menstruating Muslim women are not allowed to fast during Ramadan, participate in the five daily prayers, read from a copy of the Quran, or enter a mosque. Because of their biology, Muslim women are practically prohibited from participating in these acts of prayer on certain days of the month. A woman who is menstruating is considered ritually impure for the duration

[32] Koren (n 15) 35.

[33] EM Whelan 'Attitudes toward menstruation' (1975) 6 *Studies in Family Planning* 106.

[34] AA Engineer '*Status of women in Islam*' (1987).

[35] SA Azeem '*Women in Islam versus women in the Judaeo-Christian tradition: The myth & the reality. Islam*' (1995).

[36] MM Fischer 'Persian women' in L Beck & S Keddie (eds) *Women in the Muslim world* (1978) 204–206.

of her period.[37] As indicated previously, she is prohibited from engaging in sexual activity starting from the moment the bleeding begins. The exemption from these rituals and activities is mandatory because even if a menstruating woman wants to engage in them, she is not permitted to.[38] The basis of these taboos is the attachment of impurity to menstruation, a condition that, unless resolved by a ritual cleansing or purification bath, prohibits a woman from most acts of devotion. After the cleansing, menstruating women are considered clean and are allowed to participate in previously-restricted acts.[39]

Guterman and others[40] assert that all religions, including non-Abrahamic religions, have societal limitations and taboos that target women who are menstruating. For instance, in her 2002 research on Hindu Balinese in Indonesia, Pedersen discovered that a menstruating woman and her blood are explicitly considered to be polluted.[41] The earliest animist beliefs around menstruation may be the source of menstrual taboos. In her research on menstruation, taboos in Western and non-Western cultures, Thomas[42] notes that taboos were historically based on things like the blood pollution that the female body produces. Menstruating women do not only have to practice taboos imposed on them by their cultures, they also have to obey restrictions placed on them by their religions. Many religious faiths still hold onto long-standing ideas and beliefs about menstruation, and there are commonalities in the major religions' views and taboos around menstruation.[43]

[37] B Ahmed 'Bloody hell: Does religion punish women for menstruating?' *Vice* 20 June 2015 https://www.vice.com/en/article/bloody-hell-menstruating-while-religious-235/ (accessed 25 October 2024).

[38] Azeem (n 35).

[39] N Ackbarali 'Why can't a menstruating woman touch the Qur'an? Islam's perspective on menstruation' *IslamQA* 8 October 2010 https://islamqa.org/hanafi/seekersguidance-hanafi/32975/why-cant-a-menstruating-woman-touch-the-quran-islams-perspective-on-menstruation/ (accessed 20 October 2024).

[40] Guterman, Mehta & Gibbs (n 8).

[41] L Pedersen 'Ambiguous bleeding: Purity and sacrifice in Bali' (2002) 41 *Ethnology* 303.

[42] EM Thomas 'Menstruation discrimination: The menstrual taboo as a rhetorical function of discourse in the national and international advances of women's rights' (2007) 28 *Contemporary Argumentation and Debate* 65.

[43] Guterman, Mehta and Gibbs (n 8).

3 An African Feminist Analysis of Menstrual Taboos

Nzegwu[44] establishes that the majority of feminist gender analyses are based on a covert social ideal of equality that governs and directs research and aims to end women's subordination. Drawing from this, this section applies an African feminist lens to religious menstrual taboos to highlight how they perpetuate the oppression and restriction of women and girls in Africa.

Menstrual taboos are not limited to religions, as they also find expression in most African cultures and traditions. Tamale[45] argues that cultural and religious traditions continue to pose significant human rights issues, though not all of them endanger the health and welfare of women and girls. She critiques the idea of culture, arguing that the modern-day conception of culture is the result of colonial construction and re-interpretations with inputs from African male patriarchs.[46] This is because cultural and traditional customs are often detrimental to women's and girls' health and well-being.

Specifically, African feminist analysis of harmful practices recognises how the intersection of patriarchy and gender inequality with other systems of oppression shapes societal structures and power dynamics.[47] It argues that damaging customs like honour killings, child marriage, and female genital mutilation have their roots in patriarchal norms and traditions that uphold the subjugation of women and girls.[48] Menstrual taboos are a means of control and oppression of women and their bodies by patriarchal and capitalist cultures. The insistence of the patriarchy to regulate women's sexuality and reproduction is for two reasons: it controls women's bodies in the domestic space, where they continue to be dependent and subservient in their roles as wives and mothers. Second,

[44] NU Nzegwu '*Family matters: Feminist concepts in African philosophy of culture*' (2005).

[45] S Tamale 'The right to culture and the culture of rights: A critical perspective of women's sexual rights in Africa' (2008) 16 *Feminist Legal Studies* 47.

[46] Tamale (n 45) 153.

[47] J Maluleke 'Culture, tradition, custom, law and gender equality' (2012) 15 *PELJ* 2.

[48] J Geng 'The Maputo Protocol and the Reconciliation of Gender and Culture in Africa' in S Rimmer & K Ogg (eds) *Research handbook on feminist engagement with international law* (2019).

it ensures the continuation of male dominance within the society, which is dependent on the continued oppression, discrimination, and subjugation of women.[49] This is easy to understand when we realise that the patriarchy does not control or regulate men's bodies or sexuality.

Socio-cultural perceptions of menstruation have fed from religious teachings where most communities have the view that menstruating women are unclean, should be excluded from the larger society, and are untouchable.[50] Thomas[51] argues that menstruation was categorised as dirty and dangerous as a means to stigmatise women, their sexuality and reproduction as a threat to men and the socio-cultural order that men represent and control.[52] By separating menstruating women from society, menstrual taboos and restrictions serve as tools to protect men and sustain the patriarchal system.[53]

While menstrual taboos are quite prevalent, modern followers of these religions have raised concerns particularly those who are grappling with their faith and their compatibility with feminist ideals.[54] They find it hard to reconcile the impurity attached to menstruation considering it is a natural and uncontrollable bodily condition. Some religions have changed to be more accepting of women and their menstrual cycles in response to this sentiment, while others—like Islam—have left these matters up to the individual women to resolve.[55]

Misconceptions around menstruation have caused women and girls to be excluded from a variety of roles and environments both historically and globally. Some myths and taboos around menstruation and its

[49] Tamale (n 45).

[50] Y Mohamed and others 'A qualitative exploration of menstruation-related restrictive practices in Fiji, Solomon Islands and Papua New Guinea' (2018) 13 *PLoS ONE* e0208224; P Amatya and others 'Practice and lived experience of menstrual exiles (Chhaupadi) among adolescent girls in far-western Nepal' (2018) 13 *PLoS ONE* e0208260.

[51] Thomas (n 42).

[52] R Franklin & P Bunte 'Animals and humans, sex and death: Toward a symbolic analysis of four southern Numic rituals' (1996) 18 *Journal of California and Great Basin Anthropology* 178.

[53] SZ Syed Abdullah 'Menstrual food restrictions and taboos: A qualitative study on rural resettlement and urban indigenous Temiar of Malaysia' 2022 17 *PLOS One* e0279629.

[54] Ahmed (n 37).

[55] As above.

effects on women and girls include the idea that women should respect their periods and that women cannot manage their periods with dignity if they lack access to safe restrooms and proper hygiene practices.[56] Stigma, marginalisation, and mocking are some of the vices associated with menstruation. Humanitarian crises, extreme poverty, gender discrimination, and destructive customs are some of the activities that make menstruation a nightmare.[57] Menstrual taboos mostly affect women and girls, though they also apply to transgender men and nonbinary people who menstruate. Many countries and societies impose restrictions on women and girls' access to public and cultural life, such as requiring them to separate themselves and forbidding them from handling food or going to places of worship.[58] They diminish the dignity of women and perpetuate negative perceptions about them. They also serve as a reminder of the existing power disparities and structural inequality in civilisations.[59]

The othering of menstruation in most Abrahamic religions finds expression within most African cultures, where menstruating women are seen as impure and unclean. African feminist scholars have sought to theorise the intersection of harmful practices and gender inequality. Using an African feminist lens, I argue that menstrual taboos are rooted in patriarchal dominance over women's bodies and sexual reproductive health. I note further that African feminism enables us to unravel the nuance around menstrual-related taboos and the impugning of women's agency and dignity. By ascribing impurity to menstruation while imposing restrictions on what women can do during their period, I argue that the menstrual taboos limit the full agency of women in society. The restriction and limitations placed on menstruating women and girls is a perpetuation of gender stereotypes and gender inequality. Although founded in religious texts, menstrual-related taboos are very predominant in African cultures and are still prevalent in modern times. I argue that menstrual taboos feed into the multiple levels of oppression that African women are exposed to based on race, gender, coloniality, class, sexuality, and the like. I add another layer to the multiple oppressive systems that African women

[56] S Tellier & M Hyttel 'Menstrual health management in East and Southern Africa: A review paper' (2018).

[57] As above.

[58] MK Uppal, M Rana & A Batta 'Taboos related to menstruation in various cultures' (2022) 13 *Journal of Pharmaceutical Negative Results* 8451.

[59] Maluleke (n 47).

are exposed to, which is religion. I theorise that the impurification of menstruation in Abrahamic religions furthers the systemic oppression that women and girls in Africa are exposed to. I further note that menstrual-related taboos are tools used to inhibit women's SRHR and how they feel about their bodies. The perpetuation of women's systemic oppression, control of their sexual reproductive health and the inhibition of women's agency are fundamental themes that arise when we apply an African feminist lens to understanding menstrual-related taboos within Abrahamic religions.

4 The Impact of Menstrual Taboos on Women and Girls in Africa

This section applies both a human rights and feminist lens to understanding the implication of menstrual-related taboos on African women and girls. It notes that menstrual taboos are predominant in major Abrahamic religions as they all ascribe impurity to menstruation while restricting women from participating in religious ritual activities. It argues that while menstruation has been seen as part of the enjoyment of the right to health, information, dignity and non-discrimination, menstrual taboos infringe on the ability of women and girls to enjoy these rights.

4.1 Right to Non-discrimination

I argue that menstrual taboos perpetuate discrimination against women and girls due to their exclusion from religious rituals, which infringes on their right to non-discrimination. In Islam, it is denoted that women should abstain from Salat (daily prayers), Ramadan fasting and other voluntary fasting, and reading from the holy Quran. These are some of the many restrictions placed on menstruating women and girls, which perpetuates discrimination based on religious ethos. The othering of menstruating women and girls within the religion and exclusion from participating in certain religious rituals is the first testament to the argument of discrimination. Most human rights frameworks and norms provide that no individual should be discriminated against based on any status.[60] I argue that the exclusion of menstruating women and girls from religious rituals and practices within the Abrahamic religion constitutes discrimination based on sex and gender. Menstruation is a natural phenomenon associated with female biology, of which women and girls experience menstruation for almost half of their lifetime. The biology of menstruation is not acknowledged by most Abrahamic religions; rather, it is seen as the consequence of a sin, a wrongdoing, hence the othering. Primarily, menstrual-related taboos in Abrahamic religions affect women and girls, further perpetuating the gendered discrimination that they are exposed to within society. For instance, in Northern Nigeria, which is known to be predominantly Muslim, there is a huge perpetuation of menstrual taboos and stigma such that menstruating women are avoided by their husbands, and some men do not eat their wives' food when she is menstruating.[61] The discrimination against women becomes endemic when religion and religious spaces perpetuate discrimination against women, consolidating the socio-political discrimination they are exposed to. Women are not allowed to hold leadership positions within these religions; this is worse for menstruating women. These menstrual taboos reinforce discriminatory practices that further widen the gender inequality gap. It is safe to argue that the othering of menstruating women is primarily based on gender that is experiencing menstruation rather than the process itself. I argue, therefore, that menstrual-related taboos rooted in Abrahamic religions perpetuate discrimination against women and girls while also excluding them from freely practicing their faith. I note further that this discrimination and exclusion is rooted in gendered identities, thereby explaining why women and girls bear the brunt of menstrual taboos.

[60] Art 2 of the Organisation of African Unity (OAU), African Charter on Human and Peoples' Rights (Banjul Charter), CAB/LEG/67/3 rev 5, 21 ILM 58 (1982), 27 June 1981; art 2 of the UN General Assembly, Universal Declaration of Human Rights, 217 A (III), 10 December 1948.

[61] S Corodova 'Periods through the ages: Nigeria' *Plan International* 22 May 2024 https://www.planusa.org/blog/period-stigma-menstrual-health-stories-nigeria/ (accessed 20 November 2024).

4.2 *Right to Health and Information*

Menstrual health is a fundamental component of the right to health for women and girls, which also intersects with their right to access information about their sexual and reproductive health. I argue that the stigmatisation and othering of menstruation and menstrual-related taboos are in contravention of the SRHR of women and girls, particularly as it affects menstrual health hygiene (MHH). SRHR recognise the importance of menstrual hygiene of women and girls,[62] which is why there are numerous campaigns on MHH seeking to address hindrances to this. I contend that the menstrual-related taboos based on religious ethos are a major hindrance to ensuring MHH due to the impurity and uncleanliness associated with menstruation. Fakomogbon and Egbude[63] explain that apart from financial reasons related to period poverty, taboos, myths, and stigmas associated with menstruation are most responsible for why women in West and Central Africa struggle with their menstrual hygiene. To address this problem, the United Nations Population Fund (UNFPA) organised a campaign on menstrual health in Nigeria to enjoin stakeholders to end taboos and stigma about menstruation.[64] It is important to recognise that the very basis of most Abrahamic religions' othering of menstruation is the belief that menstruation is impure. Though most refer to its spiritual impurity, we can draw a link to the physical purity paradigm of this. How do we rationalise it is only limited to spiritual purity when menstruating women are not allowed into physical spaces of worship, hold the Quran or engage in sexual relations with their partners? We need to unpack the nuance that surrounds the impurity associated with menstruation and the resulting impact on women's SRHR. MHH is embedded within SRHR, which allows women to affirm their agency regarding these rights. I note that menstrual-related taboos infringe on women's ability to make informed decisions and access accurate information about their menstrual hygiene, which can produce negative health

[62] Tellier & Hyttel (n 56).

[63] G Fakomogbon & B Egbude 'We asked girls in Africa about periods and menstrual equity; this is what they said' *Global Citizen* 12 July 2022 https://www.globalcitizen.org/en/content/periods-girls-menstruation-south-africa-nigeria/ (accessed 20 November 2024).

[64] United Nations Population Fund 'End the taboos and stigma about menstruation!' (27 June 2022) https://nigeria.unfpa.org/en/news/end-taboos-and-stigma-about-menstruation (accessed 20 November 2024).

consequences. I explain further that it is difficult for women practicing these faiths to fully enjoy their SRHR due to the inhibitions on their menstruation based on religious ethos. It creates a divide between seeing menstruation as a personal matter which bothers one's SRHR and seeing it as a space that is governed by religious norms. For devout Christian, Muslim, or Jewish women, there is a dichotomy that exists in trying to grapple with their ability to fully affirm their sexual and reproductive rights, ensuring menstrual hygiene while also navigating the restrictions placed on menstruation, which is innate to their gender/sex.

4.3 *Right to Dignity*

The perception of menstruation as impure and unclean affects the dignity of women and girls in Africa. Article 3 of the Maputo Protocol protects women's right to dignity; it notes that 'every woman shall have the right to dignity inherent in a human being'.[65] Other international human rights instruments provide for equality and dignity of all persons, that is, every person shall be treated with dignity.[66] However, women and girls are not afforded this right because of the degrading treatment they are exposed to due to menstrual-related taboos. That religion can prescribe how menstruating bodies should be treated and what they can and cannot do is a relevant point to consider when analysing how menstrual taboos infringe on the right to dignity of women and girls. Importantly, we need to reflect on how these menstrual-related taboos rooted in religious ethos impact the dignity and autonomy of women and girls. That a natural process can be regulated by religion to the extent of determining access and restrictions becomes a necessary avenue for unpacking its effect on women and girls. This argument extends to their autonomy as independent and equal beings rather than impure, unclean, and polluted, showing that women are not regarded as autonomous beings within Abrahamic religions. I argue that menstrual-related taboos do not accord women and girls dignity as prescribed by international and regional human rights norms. I posit further that these taboos hinder women's autonomy and their ability to fully affirm their agency to ensure their self-actualisation.

[65] Art 8 of the Maputo Protocol.

[66] Art 1 of the Universal Declaration of Human Rights; arts 1 and 5 of the African Charter on Human and Peoples' Rights.

The latter allows us to recognise how religion controls women's bodies and imposes restrictions on them while also perpetuating their oppression and discrimination. By understanding the extent of control that menstrual taboos have on women and girls, how they are perceived and the impact it has on their status within society, we can argue that menstrual-related taboos are a tool that subjugates women and girls in Africa. For instance, in Mozambique, menstruating women and girls are treated as less than others; they are not allowed to make food for the family because they are perceived to have blood on their hands, and anything they prepare is not good.[67] This taboo is one of the many restrictions placed on menstruating women that has been normalised as part of tradition. It exemplifies how menstrual taboos perpetuate the othering of women and girls and dictate how they are treated in society.

4.4 *Restriction of Women's Agency*

I argue that menstrual-related taboos are a powerful means of restricting women's agency and expression within society. I further note that shame plays a huge role in how women view menstruation—as unclean and something that prevents them from being fully pure. Feminist works have explored the power of shame and the role that shame plays in controlling women's bodies and expression. Olaitan[68] explores how shame is used to restrict women's dancing bodies in post-colonial Africa. Van Nieuwkerk[69] explains that shame is used to delegitimise women's leisure activities, particularly belly dancing, as a form of economic activity that Egyptian women engage in. I draw on these to extend the argument that shame helps to configure menstrual-related taboos and how they affect menstruating women and girls. Maruapula[70] reports that women in

[67] United Nations Population Fund 'Supporting the dignity of menstruating women and girls displaced by conflict in Mozambique' (25 May 2021) https://mozambique.unfpa.org/en/news/supporting-dignity-menstruating-women-and-girls-displaced-conflict-mozambique-0 (accessed 20 November 2024).

[68] ZM Olaitan 'Dancing the night away: Centering dance as a medium for expressing the liberation of African women' (2024) *Feminist Africa* Special Issue on Reclaiming Women's Play (forthcoming).

[69] K van Nieuwkerk *A trade like any other: Female singers and dancers in Egypt* (1995).

[70] L Maruapula 'Menstruation myth: Why are African women still paying for it?' *World Economic Forum* (9 May 2016) https://www.weforum.org/stories/2016/05/menstruation-myth-why-are-african-women-still-paying-for-it/ (accessed 22 November 2024).

Botswana often speak about their menstruation in hushed tones because the word menstruation comes with a lot of embarrassment. This is rooted in the societal stigma attached to menstruation, which makes it difficult for women to freely speak about it in public. With the spiritual impurity attached to menstruation and the different restrictions placed on menstruating bodies, women and girls are forced to deal with the shame.[71] I argue further that the stigma attached to menstruation, wherein most women and girls find it difficult to talk about it or openly share their experiences, is rooted in menstrual-related taboos based on religious ethos and, in part, cultures. This stigma produces a sort of silencing shame that prevents women from owning menstruation as something natural to their body, not impure, not dirty, just a natural biological process. For instance, a 14-year-old girl in Kenya was shamed for having her menstruation stain her uniform, a trauma she could not live with, leading her to take her life.[72] Also, young girls deliberately refuse to go to school during their menstruation to avoid being humiliated by their peers.[73] Shame and inhibition are important themes to draw out when understanding the impact of menstrual-related taboos based on religious ethos. These themes allow us to interact with a feminist analysis of how shame is often used to silence women and restrict their agency and self-actualisation.

Holistically, these themes come together to paint a full picture of the impact of menstrual taboos based on religious ethos. Interestingly, the three major Abrahamic religions all have menstrual-related taboos rooted in the impurity of menstruation. These taboos propagate the discrimination and exclusion of women within religious spaces and, more broadly, in larger society due to the influence that religious ethos has in informing societal attitudes. Women and girls are left out of most religious rituals, treated as dangerous and perceived as a stain to the purity of these spaces. Furthermore, these taboos are also a way to shame women into silence and inhibit their self-expression within these religious spaces because shame has been used to further the oppression and subjugation of women. Also, these taboos contravene the right to non-discrimination, dignity,

[71] Uppal, Rana & Batta (n 58).

[72] African Health Organisation 'Girls and period shaming' (2017) https://aho.org/health-topics/girls-and-period-shaming/ (accessed 20 November 2024).

[73] United Population Fund 'Menstruation and human rights – Frequently asked questions' (22 May 2022) https://www.unfpa.org/menstruationfaq#Taboos%20and%20Myths%20about%20menstuations (accessed 20 November 2024).

health, information and restrict women's agency. They affect the sexual and reproductive health rights of women and girls as these taboos impede their ability to make informed decisions about their menstrual health and hygiene. Finally, I note that menstrual-related taboos negatively impact the dignity and autonomy of women and girls due to the role that they play in perpetuating discrimination and oppression of menstruating bodies.

5 Previous Efforts at Addressing Menstrual Taboos in Africa

The examination of previous efforts at addressing menstrual taboos will be done under broader attempts to address harmful practices. While negative stereotypes around menstrual taboos have been heavily studied, their impact on women's well-being and dignity is yet to be fully explored. Menstrual taboos rooted in religious ethos and norms are elusive in discussions around harmful practices due to the reverence accorded by most religions. In this section, the chapter focuses on relevant international and African human rights instruments that have been adopted to address negative stereotypes and harmful practices against women and girls in Africa.

The Convention on the Elimination of All Forms of Racial Discrimination (CERD)[74]; the Convention on the Elimination of All Forms of Discrimination Against Women (CEDAW); the Convention against Torture and Other Cruel, Inhuman or Degrading Treatment or Punishment (CAT)[75]; the Convention on the Rights of the Child (CRC)[76]; the Convention on the Rights of Persons with Disabilities (CRPD)[77]; and

[74] UN General Assembly, International Convention on the Elimination of All Forms of Racial Discrimination, United Nations, Treaty Series, vol 660, p 195, 21 December 1965.

[75] UN General Assembly, Convention Against Torture and Other Cruel, Inhuman or Degrading Treatment or Punishment, United Nations, Treaty Series, vol 1465, p 85, 10 December 1984.

[76] UN General Assembly, Convention on the Rights of the Child, United Nations, Treaty Series, vol 1577, p 3, 20 November 1989.

[77] UN General Assembly, Convention on the Rights of Persons with Disabilities: Resolution adopted by the General Assembly, 24 January 2007, UN Doc A/RES/61/106 (2007).

the International Covenant on Civil and Political Rights (ICCPR)[78] were among the first international human rights instruments that addressed issues around discrimination, gender-based violence and ensuring dignity of persons.[79] These instruments ensure that numerous civic, economic and socio-cultural rights are protected, particularly those of women, girls and minorities. Specifically, these instruments forbid discrimination based on any of the following: sex, religion, race, disability, or any other condition that calls for special treatment.[80] Concerning harmful practices and negative stereotypes, CEDAW, the primary international instrument protecting women, took a universal stance rather than a relativist one towards culture and tradition. Article 2(f) of CEDAW ensures that states parties that have ratified the agreement must alter or do away with traditions and practices that discriminate against women and commit to eliminating social and cultural norms that support discrimination against women. Msuya[81] explains that this ensures that states parties cannot use the argument of cultural diversity to justify or legitimise negative social and cultural trends.

In particular, CEDAW requires countries to take all necessary steps to combat gender discriminatory practices and biases.[82] The Joint General Recommendation 31 of the CEDAW Committee and General Recommendation 18 of the Committee on the Rights of the Child on harmful practices notes that harmful practices constitute discrimination against women and girls, they compromise the fundamental rights and freedoms of women and girls and that harmful practices constitute violence against women and girls. This recommendation confirms the thesis that harmful practices are often gendered and based on a skewed notion of superiority and inferiority of sexes with femininity at the lower rung of this supposed hierarchy.[83] Similar views have been voiced by a Joint General

[78] UN General Assembly, International Covenant on Civil and Political Rights, United Nations, Treaty Series, vol 999, p 171, 16 December 1966.

[79] Tamale (n 45).

[80] NH Msuya 'Harmful practices: An obstacle in the realisation of women's rights in Tanzania' (2021) 54 *The Comparative and International Law Journal of Southern Africa* 1.

[81] Mysuya (n 72).

[82] More details please, Article 2 of CEDAW.

[83] Committee on the Elimination of Discrimination against Women & Committee on the Rights of the Child, Joint General Recommendation 31 of the Committee on the

Comment of the African Commission on Human and Peoples' Rights (ACHPR) and the African Committee of Experts on the Rights and Welfare of the Child (ACERWC) on ending child marriage. The Joint General Comment recommends that states parties take necessary legislative, institutional, and other measures to address harmful practices and protect the rights of those at risk or affected by them. Particularly, it acknowledges that harmful practices are often a manifestation of gender inequality, which is the central thesis of this chapter.[84]

The African Charter on Human and Peoples' Rights, the Maputo Protocol, and the African Charter on the Rights and Welfare of the Child are among the pertinent human rights instruments in Africa that address negative gender stereotypes and harmful practices. There are particular provisions about harmful practices in both the African Children's Charter and the Maputo Protocol.[85] In the context of harmful practices, almost every human right is affected and should be protected by these instruments, including the rights to life, dignity, privacy, non-discrimination, health, freedom from torture, and freedom from cruel and degrading treatment.[86]

The Maputo Protocol in article 5 mandates states parties to 'prohibit and condemn all forms of harmful practices which negatively affect women and which are contrary to recognised international standards'. This includes a specific requirement that states parties forbid 'all forms of FGM through legislative measures, backed by sanctions'.[87] This provision is important for regional attempts at preventing and addressing harmful practices. Nabaneh explains further that the provision not only covers

Elimination of Discrimination against Women/General Comment 18 of the Committee on the Rights of the Child (2019) on harmful practices, 8 May 2019, UN Doc CEDAW/C/GC/31/Rev.1CRC/C/GC/18/Rev.1 (2019).

[84] Joint General Comment of the African Commission on Human and Peoples' Rights (ACHPR) and the African Committee of Experts on the Rights and Welfare of the Child (ACERWC) on ending child marriage (2017).

[85] S Nabaneh 'Elimination of harmful practices' in A Rudman, CN Musembi & TM Makunya (eds) *The Protocol to the African Charter on Human and Peoples' Rights in Africa: A commentary* (2023).

[86] Msuya (n 80).

[87] As above.

FGM it also applies to other harmful practices affecting women and girls in Africa.[88]

In addition to article 5, article 17(1) of the Protocol states that 'women shall have the right to live in a positive cultural context and to participate at all levels in the determination of cultural policies'. This article reinforces and strengthens the language of CEDAW while also carrying on the spirit of the African Charter on Human and Peoples' Rights, which emphasises the positive qualities of culture.[89] Rather than a total critique of culture, article 17 highlights its positive aspects and emphasises the need for women to fully and equally participate in deciding what these should be. This article acknowledges the agency of African women to question culture as a notion of power and authority.[90] The Maputo Protocol uses the 'cut and mix' strategy by drawing inspiration from international human rights standards and aligning with African realities; it sets these international norms in the African cultural context.[91] In that regard, it resolves the universalism/relativism conflict in discussing women's rights.[92] While the Maputo Protocol recognises harmful practices and their impact on women and girls' human rights, it takes a cautious stance with culture, even though most harmful practices are rooted in culture and traditions.

5.1 *Challenges That Impede the Effectiveness of Previous Efforts*

Menstrual-related taboos are not a new phenomenon; they are as old as most religions and cultures. At the same time, human rights instruments have been developed to address some of the social stigma and negative impact attached to menstruation and other harmful practices

[88] Nabaneh (n 85).

[89] Tamale (n 45).

[90] T Gashaw 'The interplay between gender and culture: How the African human rights system sought to accommodate universality and cultural relativity of women's rights' *Engenderings* 31 August 2020 https://blogs.lse.ac.uk/gender/2020/08/31/the-interplay-betweengender-and-culture-how-the-african-human-rights-system-sought-to-accommodate-universalityand-cultural-relativity-of-womens-rights/ (accessed 30 October 2024).

[91] Tamale (n 45).

[92] Geng 'The Maputo Protocol and the reconciliation of gender and culture in Africa' (2019).

emanating from the negative perception of menstruation. Although not directly, instruments such as CEDAW and the Maputo Protocol have engaged the need to address practices that are harmful to women and girls. The problem is that, just like FGM, menstrual-related taboos are deeply rooted in religious faith and ethos, thereby posing a huge challenge to the effectiveness of these instruments.

Challenging harmful practices rooted in religious ethos is a herculean task due to the inseparability of religion from everyday life. Like culture, religion is one of the fundamental means through which society guides behaviour.[93] Religion is unique as it hovers around spirituality and the supernatural; hence, it is often seen as off-limits and above critique. Members of a religion have an unshakeable belief in the teachings, norms, and practices attached to that religion as a testament to their faith. They unquestionably follow the directives of the religion often documented in holy books and sub-texts created to guide their spiritual journey. In such situations where it has been prescribed that certain things are taboos for them, it is difficult to reject such directives because of opposing views that are not religiously backed. For instance, FGM has been declared life-threatening by several health organisations such as WHO. It has been criticised based on the negative impact it has on the well-being and health of the girl-child, yet it is still conducted in some parts of the world.[94] So much so that the Parliament of the Gambia almost removed legislation that prohibits this harmful practice.[95] Perpetrators of harmful practices revert to religious teachings as the fundamental justification for their support of such practice.[96] The same can be applied to menstrual-related taboos; they are deeply rooted in religious teachings, so it is difficult to counteract these teachings with human rights instruments or legislation. We can argue that a major challenge to the inefficacy of human rights instruments in addressing harmful practices such as menstrual taboos is the inseparability of this practice from religious faith. The opposition to this practice threatens the foundation of these religions; it is expected that there will be heavy backlash or, worse still, rejection of attempts to address these practices. Additionally, there is a mixing of religion with governance

[93] Koren (n 15).

[94] Msuya (n 80).

[95] Human Rights Watch (n 5).

[96] As above.

wherein most political leaders use religion as a basis for governance, which further exacerbates the problem and legitimises these practices.[97] The state is responsible for ensuring that rights are protected and promoted, however, in the case where the government is co-opting religious teachings as a basis for governance, it becomes challenging for human rights instruments to effectively address these practices.

The deeply ingrained nature of religion informs the culture and tradition of a particular society or people. I highlight the transcending impact that religion has on culture and the extent to which culture is protected by society. I explain that apart from these practices being based on religious teachings, they also find acceptance and expression within cultural norms and traditions. Focusing on the African continent, there are menstrual taboos found within different cultures that reflect the religious-based taboos.[98] The similarity in how religion treats menstruating bodies and how culture treats them impede the effectiveness of previous efforts. Not only are these practices based on religious teachings, but they are also guarded by culture. People are often protective of culture as they see it as a comprehensive way of life that is rooted in their tribal, ethnic, or racial identity. Any attempt at challenging taboos rooted in culture must confront the primacy of culture to everyday life and broader societal operation.

While there needs to be progressive instruments that address harmful practices, the implementation of these instruments determines their effectiveness. Forty-six (46) years after the adoption of CEDAW and 22 years after the adoption of the Maputo Protocol, there have yet to be a widespread reduction in harmful practices.[99] Vices such as FGM, incest, and menstrual taboos are still very much part of everyday reality, although these practices happen mostly in rural areas due to the spread of education in urban areas. However, menstrual taboos are unique because an individual's level of education does not make any difference due to the strong

[97] Olaitan & Isike (n 3).

[98] Tellier & Hyttel (n 56).

[99] AA Ayenew and others 'Prevalence of female genital mutilation and associated factors among daughters aged 0–14 years in sub-Saharan Africa: A multilevel analysis of recent demographic health surveys' (2023) 5 *Frontiers in Reproductive Health; ZM Olaitan 'Using digital technology to address gender-based violence in South Africa' in TA Ojo & B Ndzendze (eds) African Women in the Fourth Industrial Revolution: Change, policies, and approaches (2024).*

bond between religion and personal life. The implementation gap of these instruments creates a leeway for these practices to continue and persist. Without governments taking a committed approach towards ensuring that practices that negatively affect the dignity and autonomy of women and girls are adequately eradicated, these instruments will continue to have a limited success rate.

5.2 *Recommendations*

5.2.1 *Sensitisation on the Nature of Menstruation*

Attempts to address menstrual taboos must start with sensitisation of the biological process of menstruation and its 'naturalness' to female biology. A lot of these taboos are rooted in deep misconceptions filled by religious justification on why women and girls menstruate. These misconceptions can be corrected by educating society about menstruation and what it entails, mainly to dispel the harmful narratives around it. This sensitisation should target every member of society and be based on empirical evidence but communicated in everyday language to avoid excluding certain demographics. Access to the right information about menstruation will challenge the stereotypes and perceptions currently held about it, forcing individuals to do the hard work to reflect on these taboos. Also, this process will help women own their MHH due to the increased information about the process, further instilling confidence in their bodies. Rather than hating their menstruating bodies because of the impurity attached to them, they can begin to accept it as part of a natural process.

5.2.2 *Changing Narratives*

Efforts to address menstrual taboos that do not engage religious leaders are likely to be ineffective. Religious leaders are central to changing the narrative around the impurity of menstruation and the different restrictions placed on menstruating bodies. Based on the sensitisation done, sympathetic religious leaders can be educated on the need to do away with the negative connotations around menstruation and to refrain from discriminating against menstruating bodies. For instance, rather than peddling the notion that the reason menstruating women are not allowed to fast during Ramadan is that they are unclean, a more pragmatic justification is that:

> [I]t is unhealthy for an individual who is menstruating to fast due to the need for energy to survive. To save women and girls from the rigours of having to fast when they are losing blood, they are exempted from fasting.

This justification seems much more plausible and acceptable than blatantly declaring them unclean and, therefore, unfit to fast. Changing the narrative around menstruation will help to address the negative perception associated with it and the social stigma attached to it. Engaging religious leaders in the de-stigmatisation of menstruation goes a long way in addressing menstrual taboos since they symbolise a powerful medium of spirituality and authority. Additionally, it is recognised that not all negative narratives about menstrual taboos can be changed because some are outrightly discriminatory and exclusionary. Hence, more work should be done on finding innovative ways to engage religious leaders to address menstrual taboos.

5.2.3 Continuous Engagement on the Negatives of Menstrual Taboos

More broadly, there needs to be a conscious discussion about the negative impact of menstrual taboos on the well-being and health of women and girls. The discussion should extend to the right to dignity and autonomy of women and girls to draw out the social consequences of these practices. It must be stressed that women and girls continue to suffer from the dangers of these practices, and action must be taken. This strategy will help humanise the advocacy against harmful practices that continue to harm women and girls. Governments have a lot of work to do in addressing menstrual taboos through proper implementation of relevant instruments and ensuring widespread education campaigns. Without implementation, most human rights instruments are good for nothing, hence resources must be mobilised to ensure adequate implementation of these instruments to consolidate their efficacy towards protecting the dignity and autonomy of women and girls.

6 Conclusion

How do we reconcile that all human beings are loved by the Supreme Being and are welcomed to show piety through religious practices, yet women and girls are seen as dangerous because of a natural biological process? This contradiction underpins my analysis of menstrual-related taboos in Abrahamic religions and their impact on women and girls in Africa. Menstrual taboos have been a subject of research focusing mainly on the taboos and how religions have grappled with menstruation. Most Abrahamic religions have a skewed perception of menstruation, which informs how they treat menstruating bodies. Similarities can be found in how Christianity, Islam, and Judaism perceive menstruation as unholy and impure while restricting women from certain religious practices and rituals during their menstruation. Based on studies that have been conducted on religious-based menstrual taboos, my chapter applies an African feminist lens to examine the impact of menstrual taboos on women and girls in Africa. I applied a rights-based approach to unpacking the impact of menstrual taboos as well as an African feminist lens to underpin its analysis. This chapter finds that religious-based menstrual taboos find expression in most African cultures due to the widespread social stigma attached to menstruation. It notes that in addition to the multiple forms of oppression that African women are exposed to, religion is another structure of power that oppresses African women. It finds that menstrual taboos are discriminatory and exclusionary, they weaponise shame as a means to inhibit women's agency. These taboos affect women's menstrual hygiene and broader sexual and reproductive rights, and importantly, they impugn the dignity and autonomy of women and girls. The chapter recognises previous human rights instruments that have been adopted to address harmful practices; it argues that menstrual taboos are too deeply rooted in religious faith to be easily displaced. It recommends that more work needs to be done on changing the narratives around menstruation, an approach that must involve religious leaders. Particularly, the government must adequately commit to ensuring the proper implementation of human rights instruments that address harmful practices to affirm the dignity and agency of women and girls in Africa.

Bibliography

Africa Health Organisation 'Girls and period shaming' (2017) https://aho.org/health-topics/girls-and-period-shaming/ (accessed 20 November 2024)

Amatya, P; Ghimire, S; Callahan, KE; Baral, BK & Poudel, KC 'Practice and lived experience of menstrual exiles (Chhaupadi) among adolescent girls in far-western Nepal' (2018) 13 *PLoS ONE* 12'Anti-rights legislations in Africa: Why South Africa must consolidate its commitment to promoting Human Rights' *University of Pretoria* 20 March 2024 https://www.up.ac.za/news/post_3215877-anti-rights-legislations-in-africa-why-sa-must-consolidate-its-commitment-to-promoting-human-rights- (accessed 29 October 2024)

Ayenew, AA; Mol, BW; Bradford, B & Abeje G 'Prevalence of female genital mutilation and associated factors among daughters aged 0–14 years in sub-Saharan Africa: a multilevel analysis of recent demographic health surveys' (2023) 5 *Frontiers in Reproductive Health*

'Bloody hell: Does religion punish women for menstruating?' *Vice* 20 June 2015 https://www.vice.com/en/article/bloody-hell-menstruating-while-religious-235/ (accessed 25 October 2024)

Engineer, AA '*Status of women in Islam*' (Ajanta Publications: Delhi 1987)

Fischer, MM 'Persian women' in Beck, L & Keddie S (eds) *Women in the Muslim world* (Harvard University Press: Boston 1978)

Franklin, P & Bunte, P 'Animals and humans, sex and death: Toward a symbolic analysis of four southern Numic rituals' (1996) 18 *Journal of California and Great Basin Anthropology* 181

Geng, J 'The Maputo Protocol and the reconciliation of gender and culture in Africa' in Rimmer, S and Ogg, K (eds) *Research handbook on feminist engagement with international Law* (Edward Elgar: Cheltenham 2019)

Guterman, MA; Mehta, P & Gibbs, MS 'Menstrual taboos among major religions' (2007) 5 *The Internet Journal of Wealth and Societal Politics* 3

Human Rights Watch 'Gambia: Bill threatens female genital mutilation ban' (19 April 2024) https://www.hrw.org/news/2024/04/19/gambia-bill-threatens-female-genital-mutilation-ban (accessed 06 November 2024)

International Planned Parenthood Federation 'The rights roll-back is gaining momentum' 18 July 2024 https://eseaor.ippf.org/blogs/rights-roll-back-gaining-momentum (accessed 05 November 2024)

Jennaway, M 'Of blood and foetuses: Female fertility and women's reproductive health in a North Balinese village' in Rice, PL & Manderson, L (eds) *Maternity and reproductive health in Asian societies* (Harwood Academic Publishers: The Netherlands 1996)

Koren, SF 'The menstruant as other in Medieval Judaism and Christianity' (2009) 17 *Nashim: A Journal of Jewish Women's Studies & Gender Issues, Special Issue: Sexuality in Jewish Contexts* 35

Maluleke, J 'Culture, tradition, custom, law and gender equality' (2012) 15 *PELJ* 5

Mohamed, Y; Durrant, K; Huggett, C; Davis, J; Macintyre, A & Menu, S 'A qualitative exploration of menstruation-related restrictive practices in Fiji, Solomon Islands and Papua New Guinea' (2018) 13 *PLoS ONE* 12

Montgomery, R 'A cross-cultural study of menstruation, menstrual taboos and related social variables' (1974) 2 *American Anthropological Association* 140

Msuya, NH 'Harmful practices: An obstacle in the realisation of women's rights in Tanzania' (2021) 54 *The Comparative and International Law Journal of Southern Africa* 20

Nabaneh, S '*Choice and conscience: Lessons from South Africa for a global debate*' (Pretoria University Law Press: Pretoria 2023)

Nabaneh, S 'Elimination of harmful practices' in Rudman, A; Musembi, CN & Makunya, TM (eds) *The Protocol to the African Charter on Human and Peoples' Rights in Africa: A Commentary* (Pretoria University Law Press: Pretoria 2023)

Nzegwu, NU '*Family matters: Feminist concepts in African Philosophy of culture*' (State University of New York Press: New York 2005)

Olaitan, ZM 'Dancing the night away: Centering dance as a medium for expressing the liberation of African women' (2024) *Feminist Africa Special Issue on Reclaiming Women's Play* (forthcoming)

Pedersen, L 'Ambiguous bleeding: Purity and sacrifice in Bali' (2002) 41 *Ethnology* 310

Phipps, W 'The Menstrual Taboo in the Judeo-Christian Tradition' (1980) 19 *Journal of Religion and Health* 300

Plan International 'Periods through the ages: Nigeria' 22 May 2024 https://www.planusa.org/blog/period-stigma-menstrual-health-stories-nigeria/ (accessed 20 November 2024)

'Repealing VAPP Act – A knee-jerk move set to undo Nigeria's decade of progress in protecting the vulnerable' *Africa* 17 September 2024 https://www.africa.com/repealing-vapp-act-a-knee-jerk-move-set-to-undo-nigerias-decade-of-progress-in-protecting-the-vulnerable/ (accessed 05 November 2024)

Ruether, R 'Women's body and blood: The sacred and the impure' in Joseph, A (eds) *Through the devil's gateway: Women, religion and taboo* (SPCK Publishing: London 1990)

Steinem, G 'If men could menstruate' (2019) 6 *Women's Reproductive Health* 151

Steinem, G *Outrageous acts and everyday rebellions* (New American Library: New York 1986)

Syed Abdullah, SZ 'Menstrual food restrictions and taboos: A qualitative study on rural resettlement and urban Indigenous Temiar of Malaysia' 2022 17 *PLOS One* 12

Tamale, S 'The right to culture and the culture of rights: A critical perspective of women's sexual rights in Africa' (2008) 16 *Feminist Legal Studies* 49

'The interplay between gender and culture: How the African human rights system sought to accommodate universality and cultural relativity of women's rights' *Engenderings* 31 August 2020 https://blogs.lse.ac.uk/gender/2020/08/31/the-interplay-betweengender-and-culture-how-the-african-human-rights-system-sought-to-accommodate-universalityand-cultural-relativity-of-womens-rights/ (accessed 30 October 2024)

Thomas, EM 'Menstruation discrimination: the menstrual taboo as a rhetorical function of discourse in the national and international advances of women's rights' (2007) 28 *Contemporary Argumentation and Debate* 70

'Tolerance and tension: Islam and Christianity in sub-Saharan Africa' *Pew Research Center* 15 April 2010 https://www.pewresearch.org/religion/2010/04/15/executive-summary-islam-and-christianity-in-sub-saharan-africa/ (accessed 25 October 2024)

United Nations Population Fund 'End the taboos and stigma about menstruation!' (27 June 2022) https://nigeria.unfpa.org/en/news/end-taboos-and-stigma-about-menstruation (accessed 20 November 2024)

United Nations Population Fund 'Menstrual Health Management in East and Southern Africa; A Review Paper' (2018) https://esaro.unfpa.org/sites/default/files/pub-pdf/UNFPA%20Review%20Menstrual%20Health%20Management%20Final%2004%20June%202018.pdf (accessed 21 October 2024)

United Nations Population Fund 'Menstruation and Human Rights – Frequently Asked Questions' (22 May 2022) https://www.unfpa.org/menstruationfaq#Taboos%20and%20Myths%20about%20menstuations (accessed 20 November 2024)

United Nations Population Fund 'Supporting the dignity of menstruating women and girls displaced by conflict in Mozambique' (25 May 2021) https://mozambique.unfpa.org/en/news/supporting-dignity-menstruating-women-and-girls-displaced-conflict-mozambique-0 (accessed 20 November 2024).Uppal MK; Rana, M & Batta, A 'Taboos related to menstruation in various cultures' (2022) 13 *Journal of Pharmaceutical Negative Results* 8455

Van Nieuwkerk, K *A trade like any other: Female singers and dancers in Egypt* (University of Texas Press: Texas 1995)

'We asked girls in Africa about periods and menstrual equity; this is what they said' *Global Citizen* 12 July 2022 https://www.globalcitizen.org/en/content/periods-girls-menstruation-south-africa-nigeria/ (accessed 20 November 2024)

Whelan, EM 'Attitudes toward menstruation' (1975) 6 *Studies in Family Planning* 106

'Why can't a menstruating woman touch the Qur'an? Islam's perspective on menstruation' *IslamQA* 8 October 2010 https://islamqa.org/hanafi/seekersguidance-Hanafi/32975/why-cant-a-menstruating-woman-touch-the-quran-islams-perspective-on-menstruation/ (accessed 20 October 2024)

World Economic Forum 'Menstruation myth: why are African women still paying for it?' (9 May 2016) http://www.weforum.org/stories/2016/05/menstruation-myth-why-are-african-women-still-paying-for-it/ (accessed 20 November 2024)

World Islamic Network 'Women in Islam versus women in the Judaeo-Christian tradition: The myth & the reality. Islam' (1995) https://www.al-islam.org/women-islam-versus-women-judaeo-christian-tradition-myth-reality-sherif-muhammad-abdel-azeem (accessed 23 October 2024)

African Human Rights Instruments

African Union, Protocol to the African Charter on Human and People's Rights on the Rights of Women in Africa, 11 July 2003

Organisation of African Unity (OAU), African Charter on Human and Peoples' Rights (Banjul Charter), CAB/LEG/67/3 rev 5, 21 ILM 58 (1982)

International Human Rights Instruments

Committee on the Elimination of Discrimination Against Women & Committee on the Rights of the Child, Joint General Recommendation 31 of the Committee on the Elimination of Discrimination against Women/General Comment 18 of the Committee on the Rights of the Child (2019) on harmful practices, (8 May 2019), UN Doc CEDAW/C/GC/31/Rev.1CRC/C/GC/18/Rev.1 (2019)

Joint General Comment of the African Commission on Human and Peoples' Rights (ACHPR) and the African Committee of Experts on the Rights and Welfare of the Child (ACERWC) on Ending Child Marriage (2017)

UN General Assembly, Convention Against Torture and Other Cruel, Inhuman or Degrading Treatment or Punishment, United Nations, Treaty Series, vol 1465, p 85, 10 December 1984

UN General Assembly, Convention on the Elimination of All Forms of Discrimination Against Women, United Nations, Treaty Series, vol 1249, p 13, 18 December 1979

UN General Assembly, Convention on the Rights of Persons with Disabilities: Resolution adopted by the General Assembly, 24 January 2007, UN Doc A/RES/61/106 (2007).

UN General Assembly, Convention on the Rights of the Child, United Nations, Treaty Series, vol 1577, p 3, 20 November 1989
UN General Assembly, International Convention on the Elimination of All Forms of Racial Discrimination, United Nations, Treaty Series, vol 660, p 195, 21 December 1965
UN General Assembly, International Covenant on Civil and Political Rights, United Nations, Treaty Series, vol 999, p 171, 16 December 1966
UN General Assembly, Universal Declaration of Human Rights, 217 A (III), 10 December 1948

CHAPTER 12

Punishing Pregnant Students Through Expulsion from School: A Case Study of Uganda

Rose Wakikona

1 Introduction

Expelling pregnant students from school is a practice that is prevalent at all levels of education in Uganda.[1] Uganda suffers from an epidemic of teenage pregnancies, which is the second leading cause of school dropouts, with over 24% of all adolescent girls below 19 having started childbirth.[2] The country is then left grappling with ensuring continuity of education for pregnant students in the face of deeply seated religious

[1] JA Tushabe and others 'Teenage pregnancy and school dropout in Uganda' (2024) 5 *International Journal of Multidisciplinary Research growth evaluation* 624 at 628.

[2] Uganda Bureau of Statistics 'Uganda Demographic and Health Survey 2022' 75 https://www.unicef.org/uganda/media/16731/file/UDHS-2022-Report.pdf.pdf (accessed 20 October 2024).

R. Wakikona (✉)
Women's Probono Initiative (WPI), Kampala, Uganda
e-mail: counselrose@gmail.com

E. Durojaye et al. (eds.), *Harmful Practices and Human Rights: An International Perspective*, Human Rights Interventions,
https://doi.org/10.1007/978-3-031-90333-5_12

and cultural views that vilify premarital sex and pregnancy.[3] Research has demonstrated that education is the primary way of empowering women and girls to make autonomous decisions and achieve their life goals, it also decreases their vulnerability by opening up opportunities for them to improve their economic and social standing.[4] To deal with the issue of continuity of education for pregnant students who historically have only one recourse, which is expulsion from school, Uganda adopted the 'Revised Guidelines for the Prevention and Management of Teenage Pregnancy in School Settings in Uganda' in 2022 and the 'Health Training Institutions Rules and Regulations' in 2021, which, while claiming to facilitate continuity of education for pregnant students through re-entry, mandate maternity leave for over one year which is a calculated way of authorising the expulsion of pregnant students from school, exacerbating the vulnerability of women and girls by forcing them out of the education space and into early marriages and the grossly underpaid informal work sector, consequently worsening their chances of improving their economic and social standing in society.[5]

These guidelines and regulations standardise a practice already prevalent in primary and secondary schools, religious-based universities, and tertiary institutions like the Uganda Christian University (UCU) and the Islamic University in Uganda (IUIU), all of which mandate the expulsion of pregnant, unmarried students.[6] This practice is embedded within patriarchal religious and cultural norms that seek to control female sexuality and determine the value of a woman based on her sexual purity or virtue;

[3] A Kitooke 'The expulsion of pregnant students in Uganda: Teacher perspectives on a contravention of "education for all"' Master's Thesis, University of Gothenburg, 2021 at 27 https://gupea.ub.gu.se/handle/2077/69369 (accessed 18 November 2024).

[4] Tushabe (n 1) 625.

[5] R Haghes & SH McCarty 'The consequences of forcing pregnant girls out of school: A study focused on Tanzania' (2022) 7 *Journal of Human Rights and Social Work* 23 at 31.

[6] 'University suspension over pregnancy: punishing sin or girls' *Monitor* 5 January 2021 https://www.monitor.co.ug/uganda/lifestyle/reviews-profiles/university-suspension-over-pregnancy-punishing-sin-or-girls--1571628 (accessed 20 October 2024); 'We have values to uphold – IUIU responds to activists objecting to compulsory pregnancy tests' *The Independent* 23 September 2023 https://www.independent.co.ug/we-have-values-to-uphold-iuiu-responds-to-activists-objecting-to-compulsory-pregnancy-tests/ (accessed 20 October 2024).

they reject sex before marriage, emphasise virginity, and promote heterosexual marriages.[7] Uganda is a deeply religious country, with over 72% of the population describing themselves as Christian and 14% describing themselves as Muslim.[8] With widespread religion also comes deeply entrenched religious norms on sexuality, at the forefront of which is encouraging virginity and preserving sex for those who are married.[9] The expulsion of pregnant students from school seeks to control female sexuality by keeping them chaste until marriage and punishes women and girls who fail to live up to this standard by taking away their education regardless of whether the sex leading up to the pregnancy was consensual or not.[10]

Uganda has ratified several human rights instruments that protect the rights of women and girls by recognising freedom from discrimination, the right to sexual and reproductive health, the right to education, and the prohibition of harmful social practices, some of which include the Convention on the Elimination of All Forms of Discrimination Against Women (CEDAW)[11] and the Protocol to the African Charter on Human and Peoples' Rights on the Rights of Women in Africa (Maputo Protocol).[12] Specifically, Uganda has ratified the African Charter on the Rights and Welfare of the Child (African Children's Charter),[13] which in article 21 defines harmful social and cultural practices as those that discriminate on the grounds of sex and any other status and affect the welfare, dignity, normal growth, and development of a child and are prejudicial to their health and life. Equally, the African Committee of Experts

[7] D Latour 'Unbuckling purity culture's chastity belt' (2020) 7 *The Ascendant Historian* 84 at 85.

[8] Uganda Bureau of Statistics (UBOS) 'The National Population and Housing Census 2014 – Main Report' (2016) 19.

[9] Latour (n 7) 85.

[10] *Legal and Human Rights Centre and Centre for Reproductive Rights (on behalf of Tanzanian girls) v United Republic of Tanzania* Communication 0012/Com/001/2019 [2019] ACERWC 2 (17 June 2019) para 42.

[11] UN General Assembly, Convention on the Elimination of All Forms of Discrimination Against Women, United Nations, Treaty Series, vol 1249, p 13, 18 December 1979.

[12] African Union, Protocol to the African Charter on Human and People's Rights on the Rights of Women in Africa, African Union, 11 July 2003.

[13] Organisation of African Unity (OAU), African Charter on the Rights and Welfare of the Child, CAB/LEG/24.9/49 (1990), 11 July 1990.

on the Rights and Welfare of the Child (ACERWC) found in the case of *Legal and Human Rights Centre v United Republic of Tanzania* that the practice of expelling pregnant girls from school is harmful because it interferes with their education and development, thus making it difficult for them to achieve their full potential.[14]

Even with these provisions and standards set against expelling pregnant students from school, Uganda continues to allow this practice, leaving pregnant students vulnerable to violation of their human rights. This chapter will thus discuss the expulsion of pregnant students from school, using the context of Uganda, as a harmful social practice that seeks to control adolescent sexuality and violates the human rights of women and girls, critiquing the current solution of re-entry as insufficient to guarantee continuity of education. The chapter will also consider the prevalence of this practice and its impact on the lives of women and girls in Uganda and make recommendations for the country to begin holistically addressing social protections and guaranteeing the right to education for women and girls as an obligation under human rights standards.

2 Prevalence of Expelling Pregnant Students from Schools in Uganda

Uganda has a population of over 45 million people, 59% of whom are below the age of 19; this means that most of the country's population is underage.[15] The fertility rate remains high at an average of 5.2 children for every woman of reproductive age, which ranges from 15 to 49 years of age.[16] Equally, Uganda grapples with a high teenage pregnancy rate, which has barely seen any change for years. Currently 24% of all adolescent girls below 19 have started childbirth, of these, 18.4% already have a first child or have had multiple births,[17] this is higher than the total sub-Saharan Africa average, which has a teenage pregnancy rate

[14] N 10.

[15] Uganda Bureau of Statistics 'National Population and Housing Census 2024 – Preliminary report' 9 & 17 https://www.ubos.org/wp-content/uploads/publications/National-Population-and-Housing-Census-2024-Preliminary-Report.pdf (accessed 20 October 2024).

[16] Uganda Bureau of Statistics (n 2) 70.

[17] Uganda Bureau of Statistics (n 2) 75.

of 21.36%.[18] This is not surprising since 20% of women in Uganda report having their sexual debut before 15 years of age and 66% before 18 years of age, showing that girls start having sex quite early, putting them at high risk of getting pregnant while still a teenager.[19] The expected age to complete secondary school and join tertiary education in Uganda is 18; this means that most teenage pregnancies occur while girls are still attending primary and secondary school, with many even carrying their second or more pregnancy.[20]

The practice of handling pregnant students in Uganda is that when a girl is found to be pregnant, they are expelled from school regardless of whether the pregnancy arises from sexual violence, this is largely because sexual relations among adolescents are frowned upon, and it is believed that a visibly pregnant girl in school will 'spoil' her friends by making them think that you can have sex, get pregnant, and suffer no repercussions.[21] It is also usually done to protect and maintain the image of the school as having zero tolerance for indiscipline and for the school to escape the perceived responsibilities and risks associated with taking charge of a pregnant student.[22] This has significantly added to the school dropout rates for girls, contributing 22.8% to the school dropouts second only to a lack of resources to continue education due to poverty, and has created a 6% difference in the completion of education rate between boys and girls.[23] The number has also greatly affected the completion rates for girls at school, with only 60% completing the primary level and 40% completing the secondary level, most of them drop out of school because of several reasons, the top being poverty and pregnancy.[24]

[18] MA Zamene and others 'Prevalence and associated factors of teenage pregnancy in sub-Saharan Africa: Multilevel modified Poisson regression analysis' (2024) 14 *SAGE Open* 1 at 4.

[19] Uganda Bureau of Statistics (n 2) 59.

[20] Ministry of Education, Science, Technology and Sports 'A study on linkage between pregnancy and school dropout in Uganda' (August 2016) 10 https://faweuganda.org/wp-content/uploads/2022/07/Study-report-on-Linkages-between-Pregnancy-and-School-dropout.pdf (accessed 20 October 2024).

[21] Ministry of Education, Science, Technology and Sports (n 20) 1.

[22] Kitooke (n 3) 23.

[23] Ministry of Education, Science, Technology and Sports (n 20) 11.

[24] Tushabe and others (n 1) 627.

Initially, the practice was to expel pregnant girls from school with no guarantee of re-entry and with no requirement to expel their male counterparts.[25] To address this and support the continuity of education for pregnant students, in 2015, the Ministry of Education and Sports issued the 'Guidelines for the Prevention and Management of HIV/AIDS and Unintended Pregnancy in School Settings', but these only required schools to allow pregnant students to return and do major exams but did not prohibit the practice of expelling pregnant students from school or guarantee re-entry.[26] Following measures implemented to curb the COVID-19 pandemic, which included the closure of schools for almost two years, the country experienced unprecedented levels of teenage pregnancies, which increased by over 7%, making it impossible for many of these girls to continue with their education,[27] the Ministry of Education and Sports in Uganda decided to revise the 2015 guidelines and issued the 'Revised Guidelines for the Prevention and Management of Teenage Pregnancy in School Settings in Uganda' in 2022 to facilitate the re-entry of teenage mothers in school upon realising that if these girls are not supported to finish their education they will probably drop out of school for good.[28]

The guidelines seek to guarantee continuity of education for pregnant girls by, among others, prohibiting the discrimination and ridicule of pregnant school girls and mothers by fellow students and teachers, providing for the expulsion of boys who make girls pregnant, and ensuring the re-entry of school-going mothers back to school through agreements signed with their parents or guardians to bring them back after six months of breastfeeding; offering counselling to pregnant schoolgirls and their parents with a view of continuing education; and obligating schools to provide age-appropriate sexuality education to students while

[25] Ministry of Education, Science, Technology and Sports (n 20) 1.

[26] Kitooke (n 3) 8.

[27] United Nations Population Fund 'The magnitude of teenage pregnancies in Uganda' (March 2022) 3 https://uganda.unfpa.org/sites/default/files/pub-pdf/issue_brief_19._cost_of_inaction_on_teenage_pregnancy._print_ready_final._8.4._2022.pdf (accessed 21 October 2024).

[28] Ministry of Education and Sports 'Revised Guidelines for the Prevention and Management of Teenage Pregnancy in School Settings in Uganda' (2020) https://www.ungei.org/sites/default/files/2021-02/Revised-Guidelines-Prevention-Management%20-Teenage-Pregnancy-School-Settings-Uganda-2020-eng.pdf (accessed 20 October 2024).

in school as part of the curriculum. The guidelines are thus lauded as a step in the right direction, ensuring continuity of education for pregnant students, but unfortunately, the same guidelines also codify the practice of expelling pregnant girls from school by mandating regular pregnancy check-ups for schoolgirls and, when found pregnant, being placed on mandatory maternity leave only to return after breastfeeding. The guarantee for re-entry has been dismal at best, standing at a measly 8%, many of the schoolgirls who end up pregnant have been forced to get married, take on jobs to look after their new families, and have had to ultimately sacrifice their education at the foot of motherhood, which has greatly limited their life potential.[29]

These revised guidelines follow the 'Health Training Institutions Rules and Regulations', adopted in 2021 by the same Ministry of Education and Sports to guide the conduct of students in health training institutions across the country, which are often at the tertiary level. Regulation 2.9 of these rules, states that pregnancy is a gift from God but discourages it for the school environment; the regulations require self-reporting when a student finds themselves pregnant and for the pregnant student to be expelled from school until the child has been weaned for at least six months, or is six months and has been weaned. They also allow for re-entry but only where the student self-reports the pregnancy and has a good disciplinary record. In the same regulation, the expulsion of male counterparts is dependent on whether they are married to the pregnant student, if they are, they can continue with school, and where they are not, they are expelled.

These guidelines have resulted in health training institutions carrying out mandatory pregnancy tests on their students and expelling them if found pregnant.[30] These regulations are even more perplexing because they are addressed to tertiary institutions that train adults above the age of 18 who are presumed to have reproductive autonomy, and yet they prescribe when a grown woman or man can have sex or have a child,

[29] Ministry of Education, Science, Technology and Sports (n 20) 27.

[30] A Orie 'Ugandan university drops mandatory pregnancy tests for students after outcry' *CNN* 11 November 2022 https://edition.cnn.com/2022/11/11/africa/nursing-students-pregnancy-test-uganda-intl-scli/index.html#:~:text=Ugandan%20university%20drops%20mandatory%20pregnancy%20tests%20for%20students%20after%20outcry,-By%20Amarachi%20Orie&text=A%20university%20in%20Uganda%20has,exams%2C%20after%20facing%20a%20backlash (accessed 21 October 2024).

which is: when they are married; and when they are not in school, indicating a need to control the sexuality of young people also buttressed in regulation 2.10.1 which calls for the dismissal of student(s) found having sex. When the application of these guidelines was brought to the attention of the general public after one of the health training institutions, Kampala International University (KIU), published a memo requiring all their female students to conduct mandatory pregnancy tests and present the results to management before doing exams, there was an uproar that saw women's rights organisations write to KIU and the Ministry of Education and Sports pointing out how this violates the right of women to exercise autonomy over their sexuality and reproductive capacities, KIU was forced to withdraw this memo, but unfortunately, the regulations remain unchanged to date.[31]

Over and above these policy directions, we also have religious-based tertiary institutions that insist on expelling pregnant students from school to uphold the values and morals of the institutions, which often include maintaining sexual purity.[32] Uganda is a deeply religious country where religious institutions are heavily involved in providing education services according to their beliefs and values, they own and control 42.3% of all primary schools, 60.7% of all secondary schools, and 33% of all tertiary institutions, both public and private,[33] these institutions are notorious for expelling unmarried pregnant students from school, a stand often codified in the institutional codes of conduct, because according to them, these students have committed an offence by having premarital sex which goes against the values of their religion, what usually happens is that when a student gets pregnant, the institution demands that they present a marriage certificate to show that the pregnancy arose from the sanctity of marriage, should the student fail to produce a marriage certificate they

[31] 'Lawyers force Ugandan university to cancel mandatory pregnancy tests' *Africa News* 11 November 2022 https://www.africanews.com/2022/11/11/lawyers-force-ugandan-university-to-cancel-mandatory-pregnancy-tests// (accessed 21 October 2024); Business focus 'KIU's internal memo on mandatory pregnancy test irk MPs' 11 November 2022 https://businessfocus.co.ug/kius-internal-memo-on-mandatory-pregnancy-test-irk-mps/ (accessed 21 October 2024).

[32] Kitooke (n 3) 27.

[33] Ministry of Education and Sports 'Education abstract – 2017' 27 https://www.education.go.ug/wp-content/uploads/2019/08/Abstract-2017.pdf (accessed 22 October 2024).

are asked to take a dead year and return after the child is born.[34] This desire to control the sexuality of young people to conform to the patriarchal religious standards where sex is preserved for marriage and any sex outside marriage is punished became obvious when the Parliament of Uganda while discussing mandatory pregnancy tests and expulsion of pregnant students by IUIU, a university based on the Muslim faith, had one of the Muslim MPs, Hon Ibrahim Ssemujju Nganda, state[35]:

> Madam Speaker, we need to be very careful with issues of faith. As Muslims, we do not encourage children to get pregnant before marriage. (..) In our faith, it is Haram; you simply cannot do that.

These policies, regulations, and practices purport to extend to boys and men who make girls and women pregnant by equally calling for their expulsion from school, but most often, their education remains uninterrupted because they are frequently not in the same school as the pregnant woman or girl who also usually chooses to protect the identity of the father of her baby leaving them to continue with their education uninterrupted.[36] The process of expulsion from school, especially for girls in primary and secondary schools, is also usually accompanied by public shaming, where a school assembly is called and informed of the expulsion and the reasons for it.[37] This is supposed to act as a deterrent for other students to keep themselves chaste and not get pregnant, but it has ultimately forced many girls who get pregnant to voluntarily run away from school to escape this humiliating ordeal.[38]

From the above, we can see that the practice of expelling pregnant students from school has become the standard in Uganda across all education levels, disproportionately affecting women and girls whose bodies

[34] Parliament of Uganda 'Parliamentary debates – Hansards' (10 November 2022) https://parliamentwatch.ug/all-hansards/ at 6190 (accessed 22 October 2024).

[35] As above.

[36] J Ahikire & A Madanda 'A survey of pregnant girls in primary and secondary schools in Uganda' *FAWE Uganda* (2011) 24 https://education.go.ug/wp-content/uploads/2019/07/gender_Report-on-Girls-Re-ntry-in-school.pdf (accessed 25 October 2024); Kitooke (n 3) 19.

[37] As above.

[38] As above.

bear the evidence of premarital sex through pregnancy.[39] The standard has been set in policy, regulation, practice, and codes of conduct as mandatory maternity leave with no real guarantee for re-entry, upon expulsion, the majority of students do not come back and instead drop out of school due to stigma, shame, and the lack of a supportive environment to facilitate continuity of their education.[40] Even when the country had an opportunity to adopt a policy that guarantees pregnant students stay in school and continue with their education, they shied away from keeping pregnant girls in school and chose instead to adopt a system of re-entry, which has proved inadequate in bringing girls back to school after giving birth. This has facilitated the violation of the rights of women and girls in Uganda, as shall be discussed below.

3 What Drives the Practice of Expelling Pregnant Students from School?

The foremost driver of this practice is the deeply entrenched religious and cultural values that seek to control young people's sexuality to fit within the patriarchal religious standards of sexual purity.[41] Sylvia Tamale argues that sexuality is set by religion, law, and culture and is often universalised and interpreted through the colonial perspective that finds roots in religion, deciding who can have sex or reproduce and when while using schools, health facilities, and the law to enforce compliance.[42] Religion and culture are set as the supervisors of sexuality, prescribing respectable sex and reproduction as that which is done within heterosexual monogamous marriages rooted in patriarchy where the man has control over his wife and children, this has been used to control women's bodies by demanding abstinence until marriage and by punishing those who do not conform to this standard.[43] For young people, this means being robbed of their sexual agency and an expectation placed on them to remain chaste and display no sexual feelings until they get married.

[39] As above.

[40] Ministry of Education, Science, Technology and Sports (n 20) 11.

[41] Tushabe and others (n 1) 627.

[42] S Tamale 'Exploring the contours of African sexualities: Religion, law and power' (2014) 14 *African Human Rights Law Journal* 150 at 156.

[43] As above.

Desintha Dwi Asriani, while discussing the practice of expelling pregnant girls from school in Indonesia, equally contends that pregnant adolescents are often viewed as a social problem that needs correcting since the transition from girlhood to womanhood is taken to be achieved through marriage marked by sexual intercourse with your husband and childbirth, virginity is therefore expected of girlhood, it is often used as a yardstick to determine the value of a girl where every woman who is not married is viewed as a girl.[44] Pregnant adolescents go against this norm, which is considered a disgrace, leading to social condemnation of such behaviour.[45] Part of the social condemnation is for schools to act as the gatekeepers of morality and expel pregnant students from school to uphold the patriarchal standards of sexuality and reproduction.[46]

Alex Veit and Susan Biecker, while discussing the use of law to police adolescent sexuality in Uganda, noted that Uganda's law on defilement sets a strict age of consent for sexual activity at 18 years, disregarding the sexual agency of many adolescents who dabble in consensual sexual activity on their own volition, they argue that this failure to distinguish between consensual and non-consensual sex among adolescents reflects a desire to control adolescent sexuality using the law and the state machinery tools of enforcement.[47] They note that this is embedded in the patriarchal sentiments about female sexuality, which view females as sexually docile, with women and girls cast as passive and in need of protection from their seducing aggressive male counterparts, this belief paints women and girls as incapable of exercising sexual agency and has been extended to Uganda's laws that criminalise all sexual activity among and with adolescents, serving the dual purpose of controlling adolescent sexuality and punishing sexually active adolescents.[48]

Expelling pregnant girls from school, just like the criminalisation of consensual adolescent sex, is another tool being used by the patriarchy

[44] DD Asriani 'Teenage pregnancy and the quest for a place for pregnant girls: A study on the rule of pregnant student expulsion in Yogyakarta Indonesia' (2018) 22 *Jurnal Ilmu Sosial Dan Ilmu Politik* 74 at 78.

[45] As above.

[46] As above.

[47] A Viet & S Biecker 'Love or crime? Lawmaking and the policing of teenage sexuality in Uganda and the Democratic Republic of Congo' (2022) 16 *Journal of Eastern African Studies* 138.

[48] Viet & Biecker (n 47) 140.

to control young people's sexuality and publicly punish women and girls for failing to remain chaste and virtuous by taking away their education; this tool is so efficient that many students who find themselves pregnant choose to voluntarily drop out of school by running away rather than face this public humiliation.[49] Other pregnant students choose to have unsafe and clandestine abortions, even where it is illegal, to escape society's condemnation and remain in school, by taking away the pregnant body, these girls can then maintain the façade of being a 'good' girl within society.[50]

It does not help that the majority of schools both private and public are religious-based or owned, making them even more vested in upholding these religious patriarchal norms.[51] This shows that the intent of the practice is less about protecting pregnant women or girls and more about controlling their sexuality to fit within the patriarchal religious ideals of female sexuality. It also does not help that the practice has been codified through policy and regulation, which has made it the standard for all primary schools, secondary schools, and health training institutions in that even where a school would have been willing to accommodate pregnant students, they cannot do so because this would be going against policy direction as seen in the incidence of KIU.

Another driver of this practice is the failure to embrace comprehensive sexuality education and access to sexual and reproductive health services for adolescents, which places them at a heightened risk for teenage pregnancies.[52] Uganda has consistently shied away from providing sexual and reproductive health information and services to adolescents ceding the responsibility to parents and religious institutions who emphasise abstinence-only for young people,[53] this has left many young people ignorant about managing their sexual and reproductive health leaving them susceptible to getting pregnant even when they do not intend to, this can be seen in a survey done by the Ministry of Education and Sports

[49] Ahikire & Madanda (n 36) 25.

[50] DM Kakuru, J Nabirye & J Nassimbwa 'Abortion as a muted reality in Uganda: narratives of adolescent girls' agentive experiences with pregnancy termination' (2024) 4 *Youth* 1481 at 1490.

[51] Kitooke (n 3) 27.

[52] FK Muhanguzi & A Ninsiima 'Embracing teen sexuality: Teenager's assessment of sexuality education in Uganda' (2011) 25 *Agenda* 54 at 60.

[53] As above.

in 2016 to establish the link between teenage pregnancy and school dropout where they found that 28% of teenage girls reported being sexually active, of these 80% got pregnant and 97% dropped out of school either through expulsion or self-withdrawal, one of the key reasons given for these teenage pregnancies is the limited knowledge on how to prevent pregnancy.[54]

In 2016, the Parliament of Uganda exacerbated the problem by banning the dissemination of comprehensive sexuality education based on fears that it teaches children deviant practices like masturbation, fornication, abortion, and same-sex sexual conduct,[55] again speaking to the desire to control young people's sexuality by keeping them chaste until marriage, this ban was challenged in the High Court of Uganda in the case of *Center for Health, Human Rights and Development (CEHURD) v Attorney General* and the Court found that the state is obliged to provide age-appropriate sexuality education for adolescents ordering them to put in place a policy for the same.[56] What followed was the adoption of the National Sexuality Education Framework in 2018, which has one of its guiding principles as being God-fearing. It also centres abstinence instead of addressing the needs and lived realities of students and positions sex as only for marriage, and yet many adolescents are already sexually active, just with insufficient knowledge on how to manage their sexuality putting them at heightened risk of getting pregnant.[57] This points to a need to control young people's sexuality rather than addressing their lived realities.

[54] Ministry of Education, Science, Technology and Sports (n 17) 20.

[55] *Center for Health, Human Rights and Development (CEHURD) v Attorney General* High Court Miscellaneous Cause 309 of 2016, paras 5 & 6.

[56] As above.

[57] J Atuhaire, VN Nyakato & CN Murembe 'Teaching sexuality education in secondary schools of Uganda and its implications: A qualitative assessment of the curriculum' (2023) 7 *Journal of Popular Education in Africa* 31 at 42.

4 The Legal Framework Governing the Prohibition of Harmful Practices in Uganda

4.1 International Legal Framework

Uganda has ratified several international human rights instruments that prohibit harmful practices against women and girls, key among which are CEDAW and the CRC.[58] CEDAW prohibits discrimination against women, calling on all states to refrain from and abolish all practices that perpetuate discrimination against women and to ensure that third parties conform to this obligation, it also guarantees equal rights in education, calling on states parties to ensure a reduction of female student dropout rates.[59] The CRC equally recognises the right to education for all children, calling on all states to reduce school dropout rates, it also prohibits discrimination and obliges states to consider the best interests of the child as the primary concern when dealing with children.[60] Even where these treaties do not expressly provide for harmful practices, the provisions mentioned above have been used to successfully challenge harmful practices in Uganda; a key example is when CEDAW was used to successfully challenge the practice of refunding bride price in the Supreme Court of Uganda.[61]

The Committee on the Elimination of Discrimination Against Women, which oversees the implementation of CEDAW, and the Committee on the Rights of the Child, which oversees the implementation of CRC, released a Joint General Recommendation on harmful practices to explain

[58] UN treaty body database 'Ratification status for Uganda' https://tbinternet.ohchr.org/_layouts/15/TreatyBodyExternal/Treaty.aspx?CountryID=182&Lang=EN (accessed 30 October 2024). Uganda ratified the CEDAW on 22 July 1985 and domesticated it under art 33 of the Constitution of the Republic of Uganda, 1995. Uganda also ratified the CRC on 17 August 1990 and domesticated it under art 34 of the Constitution of the Republic of Uganda, 1995 and the Children's Act cap 59.

[59] Arts 2 & 10.

[60] Arts 2, 3 & 28.

[61] *Mifumi (U) Ltd v Attorney General* (2015) UGSC 13 at 13.

how these instruments deal with the issue.[62] The General Recommendation calls on all states to prohibit harmful practices that are deeply rooted in patriarchal norms that seek to subordinate women by exerting control over their sexuality and their bodies.[63] It also establishes parameters for identifying a harmful practice, which include: a practice that results in a denial of dignity for women; a practice that harms individuals by limiting their capacity to reach their full potential; a practice that is traditional, re-emerging, or emerging, and is kept in place by social norms; and a practice that is imposed by family and community regardless of consent.[64] The practice of expelling pregnant girls from school is imposed by society to control female sexuality and punish women and girls for exercising sexual agency by denying them an opportunity to complete their education and limiting their ability to reach their full potential.[65] Moreover, this practice fails to take into consideration the agency of the pregnant student and the circumstances leading up to the pregnancy, if it arose out of sexual violence or if the pregnant student is willing to continue with school even while pregnant, it instead humiliates her and serves to exclude her from society.[66]

Therefore, based on the definition of CEDAW and the CRC, this practice can be qualified as harmful to women and girls, mandating member states like Uganda that have ratified CEDAW and the CRC to eliminate the practice. This was alluded to in the Concluding Observations made by the CEDAW Committee to Uganda on their combined eighth and ninth report in 2022[67] where the Committee acknowledged the disparity in the education completion rates between boys and girls due to teenage pregnancy and called on Uganda to implement measures ensuring retention

[62] Committee on the Elimination of Discrimination Against Women & Committee on the Rights of the Child, Joint General Recommendation 31 of the Committee on the Elimination of Discrimination Against Women/General Comment 18 of the Committee on the Rights of the Child on harmful practices, 14 November 2014, UN Doc CEDAW/C/GC/31-CRC/C/GC/18 (2014) para 5.

[63] Joint General Recommendation 31 (n 62) para 30.

[64] General Recommendation 31 (n 62) para 15.

[65] Tushabe and others (n 1) 627.

[66] Ahikire & Madanda (n 36) 25.

[67] Committee on the Elimination of Discrimination Against Women, Concluding Observations on the combined eighth and ninth periodic reports of Uganda, 1 March 2022, UN Doc CEDAW/C/UGA/CO/8-9 (2022).

and completion of education for pregnant girls while also disseminating comprehensive sexuality education to encourage responsible sexual behaviour.

4.2 *Regional Legal Framework*

Uganda has ratified regional African human rights instruments that protect women and children from harmful practices, Uganda has ratified the Maputo Protocol and the African Children's Charter.[68] The Maputo Protocol calls on member states to combat discrimination against women by, among others, eliminating harmful practices that endanger their health and welfare.[69] It also recognises the right to dignity and equal access to education for women and encourages member states to eliminate harmful practices by prohibiting the same through legislation, creating public awareness, and providing support for victims of such practices.[70] Also, the African Commission on Human and Peoples' Rights (African Commission), in its Concluding Observations to Uganda's combined sixth to eighth report on the African Charter and the Maputo Protocol,[71] noted the struggle to ensure continuity of education for pregnant girls and urged Uganda to strengthen efforts to protect the right to education for pregnant girls by rolling out and funding a national campaign on prevention of teenage pregnancy. The African Children's Charter equally discourages customs and practices that violate the rights of a child, prohibits discrimination, recognises the right to education, requires member states to ensure pregnant girls can continue with their education, and entreats states to protect children from harmful social and cultural practices.[72]

[68] African Union 'Ratifications table' https://www.acerwc.africa/en/member-states/ratifications (accessed 30 October 2024). Uganda ratified the Maputo Protocol on 22 July 2010 and the African Children's Charter on 17 August 1994.

[69] Art 2.

[70] Arts 3, 5 & 12.

[71] ACHPR, Concluding Observations on the Combined 6th-8th Periodic Report of the Republic of Uganda under the African Charter on Human and Peoples' Rights and Initial Report under the Maputo Protocol (2013–2022), 8 March 2024.

[72] Arts 1, 2, 11 & 21.

The above provisions were used by the African Committee of Experts on the Rights and Welfare of the Child (ACERWC) to find the practice of expelling pregnant girls from school as a harmful in the case of *Legal and Human Rights Centre v United Republic of Tanzania*,[73] here the ACERWC discussed the practice of subjecting school-going girls to mandatory pregnancy testing and subsequently expelling them from school if found pregnant in Tanzania. This practice was legitimised through the Education (Expulsion and Exclusion of Pupils from School) Regulations of 2002, which allowed schools to expel school girls who get married and those who engage in immoral behaviour with no re-entry, this was used to subject school girls to mandatory pregnancy tests and expulsion if found pregnant. Tanzania, while defending itself for allowing this practice, argued that it was done to protect African morality, where sexual activity among the young is abhorrent and should be discouraged.[74]

The ACERWC, while discussing this issue, found that this practice amounts to cruel, inhuman, and degrading treatment for girls because no consent is sought, and these pregnancies often arise from sexual violence, expelling a pregnant girl from school, therefore, amounts to punishing them for a perceived moral wrong even where the girl is a victim of sexual violence and compounds their trauma.[75] They also found that the practice amounts to a violation of the right to education because the state should provide every child, with no exception, an opportunity to have an education, this requires them to put in place policies and allocate budgets to ensure continuity of education for pregnant girls.[76] The ACERWC was also of the view that this practice amounts to discrimination on the grounds of gender and health status, here pregnancy, since it is only geared towards girls and perpetuates negative social practices that stigmatise pregnant girls by subjecting them to scrutinisation of their sexuality and punishing them for being sexually active even where the sex is criminal.[77]

[73] *Legal and Human Rights Centre* (n 10) 27.

[74] As above.

[75] *Legal and Human Rights Centre* (n 10) 36.

[76] *Legal and Human Rights Centre* (n 10) 49.

[77] *Legal and Human Rights Centre* (n 10) 56.

The ACERWC also found that the practice violates the right to protection against harmful social practices because it affects the welfare, dignity, development, health, and life of a child.[78] Finally, the ACERWC found that the practice violates the right to health and dignity because the state failed in its obligation to provide comprehensive sexuality education and sexual and reproductive health services for young girls, which increases the risk of teenage pregnancies while also failing to provide access to safe and legal abortion services for survivors of sexual violence.[79] This decision set a standard for countries subscribing to the African human rights system—Uganda being one—that the practice of expelling pregnant girls from school is harmful and must be eliminated.

While the international UN human rights system recognises harmful practices through general recommendations and an expansive interpretation of the covenants, the regional African human rights system expressly addresses harmful practices within its instruments. Within the African human rights system, we also have general comments specifically addressing harmful practices like female genital mutilation and child marriage calling for their elimination, specifically the General Comment on ending child marriage puts an obligation on states to ensure that the education of pregnant students remains uninterrupted.[80] This has given bodies such as the ACERWC a clear opportunity to find the practice of expelling pregnant girls from school as one that violates the African Children's Charter, recognising the harm that such a practice has on the well-being and prospects of girls in Africa.

4.3 National Legal Framework

Uganda has a robust Constitution that recognises the rights of women and children. Specifically, the Constitution recognises the right to equality and freedom from discrimination, the right to dignity, and the right to education for all persons.[81] The Constitution also takes cognisance of the

[78] *Legal and Human Rights Centre* (n 10) 62.

[79] *Legal and Human Rights Centre* (n 10) 87.

[80] Joint General Comment of the African Commission on Human and Peoples' Rights and the African Committee of Experts on the Rights and Welfare of the Child on ending child marriage (2018); ACERWC & ACHPR, Joint General Comment on female genital mutilation (2023).

[81] Constitution of the Republic of Uganda, 1995 arts 21, 24 & 30.

historical marginalisation of women and children seeking to provide extra protections for them as vulnerable groups by placing a specific obligation on the government to provide opportunities necessary to enhance the welfare of women to allow them to reach their full potential, it also requires the government to protect women cognisant of their maternal function and prohibits laws, cultures, customs, and traditions that interfere with the dignity, welfare, and interests of women.[82] The Constitution also forbids depriving children of their education based on religious and other beliefs.[83] These provisions have been used by the Supreme Court and the Constitutional Court to outlaw harmful practices like the refund of bride price[84] and female genital mutilation,[85] which were found to devalue women and take away their dignity.

Uganda also has domestic legislation that protects the rights of children, the law requires that all decisions made concerning children must be based on the best interests principle, recognise freedom from discrimination, and prohibit harmful practices, it defines harmful cultural or customary practices as acts that are mentally, physically, socially, and morally damaging to a child and interfere with their education and social development.[86] These provisions have been used to challenge the practice of expelling pregnant girls from school in the case of *Women With a Mission (WWM) v Busumba Primary School*,[87] where Justice Henry Kawesa Isabirye of the High Court considered a case brought by an organisation on behalf of a pregnant 15-year-old school girl who was expelled from school after being found pregnant by the school management committee following a physical pregnancy check-up, in this case, the school which expelled the pregnant girl conceded to the claim brought by the applicant and entered a consent judgement allowing the girl back in school immediately after childbirth. Although the court did not get an opportunity to delve into the merits of the case and pronounce itself on the matter, the rush of the school to concede to the claim and allow

[82] Art 33 of the Constitution.

[83] Art 34(2) of the Constitution.

[84] *Mifumi* (n 61) 44.

[85] *Law and Advocacy for women in Uganda v Attorney General* Constitutional Petition 8 of 2007, at 12.

[86] Secs 4,7 & 3 of the Children's Act cap 59.

[87] High Court Miscellaneous Cause 001 of 2024, High Court of Uganda.

the student back in school reflects an innate knowledge that their actions were unlawful.

This decision coincides with that of the Constitutional Court of South Africa in the case of *The Head of Department: Department of Education, Free State Province v Welkom High School & Harmony High School*,[88] where the Court considered the constitutionality of school policies that mandate the expulsion of pregnant students from school and held that this constitutes a violation of the Constitution of the Republic of South Africa, 1996 since such policies fail to protect the human rights of students.[89] Specifically, the Court was of the view that expelling pregnant students from school violates their right to education by affecting the ability of pregnant students to complete school and amounts to unfair discrimination because it differentiates between students based on pregnancy and also on sex since it mostly operates against female students.[90] This position stems from express constitutional protections extended to pregnant girls in South Africa and a government policy that forbids the expulsion of pregnant students from school even when teenage pregnancy is frowned upon.

The law in Uganda also criminalises defilement and child-to-child sex here, defilement is defined as performing a sexual act with a child under 18 years of age and carries a maximum sentence of life imprisonment; child-to-child sex has no defined sentence, and punishment depends on the circumstances of the case.[91] Defilement, in this case, disregards the issue of consent, and any sex with a minor is considered illegal, this speaks to the morality of Ugandan society, which insists on viewing adolescents as asexual and incapable of having consensual sex.[92] The Uganda Police Force reports that over 12 818 girls reported cases of defilement in 2023, the majority of who are between the ages of 15 and 17; they also note that of these, 187 were defiled by parents or guardians, and 211 were defiled by teachers, putting all these girls at a heightened risk of getting

[88] 2014 (2) SA 228 (CC).

[89] *Welkom High School* (n 88) para 112.

[90] *Welkom High School* (n 88) paras 113 & 114.

[91] Secs 116 & 117 of the Penal Code Act cap 128.

[92] Viet & Biecker (n 47) 140.

pregnant,[93] and yet the practice of expelling pregnant girls from school ironically presents girls as active participants in sexual relations and disregards the fact that sex with or among minors can never be consensual in the eyes of the law.[94] Instead, the practice demonises pregnant girls by branding them as immoral for losing their sexual purity regardless of whether the sex leading up to the pregnancy was consensual or not, which serves to revictimise survivors of sexual violence and exacerbates their trauma.[95]

5 Recommendations

It is therefore recommended that Uganda consider the findings of the ACERWC that the practice of expelling pregnant students from school is harmful and violates the rights of women and girls and align their laws, policies, and practices to eliminate this practice. The country also needs to put in place social safeguards for women and girls who are victims of this practice to ensure that they can continue with their education and live up to their full potential by ensuring schools have sufficient resources and put in place facilities to accommodate pregnant students and their unique needs.[96]

The country should also reconsider the age of consent to sex for post-pubescent adolescents who are between the ages of 16 and 18 and recognise that post-pubescent adolescents are capable of exercising sexual agency based on the concept of evolving capacities for minors.[97] This will enable Uganda to expand access to sexual and reproductive health information and services for adolescents and adopt a more comprehensive approach to disseminating sexuality education, which will leave adolescents better prepared to prevent pregnancy even as they engage in sexual activity, allowing them to seamlessly continue with their education.[98]

[93] Uganda Police Force 'Annual crime report – 2023' 55 & 56 https://upf.go.ug/wp-content/uploads/2024/09/Official-Annual-Crime-Report-2023-web.pdf (accessed 26 October 2024).

[94] Ahikire & Madanda (n 36) 24.

[95] Ahikire & Madanda (n 36) 25.

[96] Ministry of Education, Science, Technology and Sports (n 20) 35.

[97] Viet & Biecker (n 47) 152.

[98] Atuhaire, Nyakato & Murembe (n 57) 42.

6 Conclusion

In conclusion, the practice of expelling pregnant girls from school in Uganda is a tool used to control female sexuality by punishing women and girls for failing to uphold the patriarchal religious standards of remaining chaste until marriage. The practice has been codified in policy, regulations, and codes of conduct, which has led to many students dropping out of school with very low rates of re-entry. The practice violates the human rights of women and girls, including freedom from discrimination, the right to education, the right to dignity, and their sexual and reproductive health and rights. Uganda, therefore, needs to align its laws, policies, and practices with human rights standards to eliminate this harmful practice and recognise the sexual agency of post-pubescent teenagers.

Bibliography

Ahikire, J & Madanda, A 'A survey of pregnant girls in primary and secondary schools in Uganda' (2011) *FAWE Uganda* 1

Asriani, DD 'Teenage pregnancy and the quest for a place for pregnant girls: A study on the rule of pregnant student expulsion in Yogyakarta Indonesia' (2018) 22 *Jurnal Ilmu Sosial Dan Ilmu Politik* 74

Atuhaire, J; Nyakato, VN & Murembe, CN 'Teaching sexuality education in secondary schools of Uganda and its implications: A qualitative assessment of the curriculum' (2023) 7 *Journal of Popular Education in Africa* 31

Haghes, R & McCarty, SH 'The consequences of forcing pregnant girls out of school: A study focused on Tanzania' (2022) 7 *Journal of Human Rights and Social Work* 23

Latour, D 'Unbuckling purity culture's chastity belt' (2020) 7 *The Ascendant Historian* 84

Kakuru, DM; Nabirye, J & Nassimbwa, J 'Abortion as a muted reality in Uganda: narratives of adolescent girls' agentive experiences with pregnancy termination' (2024) 4 *Youth* 1481

Kitooke, A 'The expulsion of pregnant students in Uganda: Teacher perspectives on a contravention of "education for all"' Masters' Thesis, University of Gothenburg, 2021

Muhanguzi, FK & Ninsiima, A 'Embracing teen sexuality: Teenager's assessment of sexuality education in Uganda' (2011) 25 *Agenda* 54

Orie, A 'Ugandan university drops mandatory pregnancy tests for students after outcry' *CNN* 11 November 2022 https://edition.cnn.com/2022/11/11/africa/nursing-students-pregnancy-test-uganda-intl-scli/index.html#:~:text=Ugandan%20university%20drops%20mandatory%20pregnancy%20tests%20for%20students%20after%20outcry,-By%20Amarachi%20Orie&text=A%20university%20in%20Uganda%20has,exams%2C%20after%20facing%20a%20backlash. (accessed 21 October 2024)

Tamale, S 'Exploring the contours of African sexualities: Religion, law and power' (2014) 14 *African Human Rights Law Journal* 154

Tushabe, JA; Asiimwe, S & Fasco, PS 'Teenage pregnancy and school dropout in Uganda' (2024) 5 *International Journal of Multidisciplinary Research Growth Evaluation* 624

Viet, A & Biecker, S 'Love or crime? Lawmaking and the policing of teenage sexuality in Uganda and the Democratic Republic of Congo' (2022) 16 *Journal of Eastern African Studies* 138

Zamene, MA; Zewde, EA; Ayele, BA; Yimer, TY; Hailemeskei, HS & Tiruneh, S 'Prevalence and associated factors of teenage pregnancy in sub-Saharan Africa: Multilevel modified Poisson regression analysis' (2024) 14 *SAGE Open* 1

Cases

Center for Health, Human Rights and Development (CEHURD) v Attorney General and another High Court Miscellaneous Cause 309 of 2016

Law and Advocacy for Women in Uganda v Attorney General Constitutional Petition 8 of 2007

Legal and Human Rights Centre and Centre for Reproductive Rights (on behalf of Tanzanian girls) v United Republic of Tanzania Communication 0012/Com/001/2019 [2019] ACERWC 2 (17 June 2019)

Mifumi (U) Ltd v Attorney General (2015) UGSC 13

The Head of Department: Department of Education, Free State Province v Welkom High School & Harmony High School 2014 (2) SA 228 (CC)

Women With a Mission (WWM) v Busumba Primary School High Court Miscellaneous Cause 001 of 2024, High Court of Uganda

Laws

Children's Act cap 59

Constitution of the Republic of Uganda, 1995

Penal Code Act cap 128

ACHPR

ACHPR, Concluding Observations on the Combined 6th-8th Periodic Report of the Republic of Uganda under the African Charter on Human and Peoples' Rights and Initial Report under the Maputo Protocol (2013–2022), 8 March 2024

Committee on the Elimination of Discrimination Against Women, Concluding Observations on the combined eighth and ninth periodic reports of Uganda, 1 March 2022, UN Doc CEDAW/C/UGA/CO/8–9 (2022)

African Human Rights Instruments

African Union, Protocol to the African Charter on Human and People's Rights on the Rights of Women in Africa, African Union, 11 July 2003.

Joint General Comment of the African Commission on Human and Peoples' Rights (ACHPR) and the African Committee of Experts on the Rights and Welfare of the Child (ACERWC) on ending child marriage (2017)

Joint General Comment of the African Commission on Human and Peoples' Rights (ACHPR) and the African Committee of Experts on the Rights and Welfare of the Child (ACERWC) on female genital mutilation (2023)

Organisation of African Unity (OAU), African Charter on the Rights and Welfare of the Child, CAB/LEG/24.9/49 (1990), 11 July 1990

UN Human Rights Instruments

Committee on the Elimination of Discrimination Against Women & Committee on the Rights of the Child, Joint General Recommendation 31 of the Committee on the Elimination of Discrimination against Women/General Comment 18 of the Committee on the Rights of the Child (2019) on harmful practices, (8 May 2019), UN Doc CEDAW/C/GC/31/Rev.1CRC/C/GC/18/Rev.1 (2019)

UN General Assembly, Convention on the Elimination of All Forms of Discrimination Against Women, United Nations, Treaty Series, vol 1249, p 13, 18 December 1979

Reports

Ministry of Education, Science, Technology and Sports 'A study on linkage between pregnancy and school dropout in Uganda' (August 2016)

Ministry of Education and Sports 'Education abstract – 2017'

Uganda Bureau of Statistics 'National Population and Housing Census 2014 – Main Report' (2016)

Uganda Bureau of Statistics 'National Population and Housing Census 2024 – Preliminary report'
Uganda Bureau of Statistics 'Uganda Demographic and Health Survey 2022'
United Nations Population Fund 'The magnitude of teenage pregnancies in Uganda' (March 2022)
Uganda Police Force 'Annual crime report – 2023'

CHAPTER 13

Engaging Harmful Traditional Practices from a Supranational Perspective: Reflections from the African Committee of Experts on the Rights and Welfare of the Child

Robert Doya Nanima

1 Introduction

While there is a lot of usable information in Africa, the lack of available disaggregated data affects the deliberate use of current initiatives. There is no available information on statistics on harmful practices in Africa—a situation that affects deliberate appreciation and engagement of harmful

R. D. Nanima (✉)
Faculty of Law, University of the Western Cape, Cape Town, South Africa
e-mail: rnanima@uwc.ac.za

E. Durojaye et al. (eds.), *Harmful Practices and Human Rights: An International Perspective*, Human Rights Interventions,
https://doi.org/10.1007/978-3-031-90333-5_13

practices.[1] As will be shown later, various initiatives point to the engagement of the problem of harmful practices.[2] Africa then looks to other sources such as global partners and civil society. For instance, a report by UNICEF shows that Africa is home to 130 million child brides and nearly 140 million girls and women who have undergone female genital mutilation.[3] The intersection of these two practices is in the fact that over 40 million girls and women in Africa have experienced both harmful practices. This is the cumulative population of either Zambia and Malawi, Somalia and Chad or Morroco and Lesotho.[4] The bigger challenge is that from a global perspective, Africa has the highest levels of both child marriages and female genital mutilation.[5]

This chapter evaluates the argument that the normative guidance from the African Charter on the Rights and Welfare of the Child, the institutional positioning of the African Committee of Experts on the Rights and Welfare of the Child and the developing jurisprudence all form a cycle that to a given degree promotes and protects the child affected by harmful practices. With the aid of three sub-arguments hinged on normative, institutional, and jurisprudential underpinnings, the African Children's Committee's approach is evaluated. The chapter sets the tone as to why this topic is important, followed by a normative evaluation of harmful practices under the African Children's Charter. Consequently, an institutional evaluation of the mechanisms of the African Children's Committee

[1] For the intersession report by the Special Rapporteur on the Rights of Women in Africa (SRRWA) – 79OS (2024) https://achpr.au.int/en/intersession-activity-reports/rights-women-africa (accessed 17 November 2024) hints at the various intersection activities carried out by the mandate holder. The challenge is in the lack of a report with data. There is no similar report on intersession activities by the African Committee of Experts on the Rights and Welfare of the Child.

[2] For instance, the 2030 Sustainable Development Goal Agenda has Goal 5 that seeks to achieve gender equality and empower all women and girls. At its core, Target 5.3 seeks to eliminate all harmful practices, such as child, early and forced marriage and female genital mutilation. In addition, the African Union Agenda 2063 has Aspiration 6 which envisions as Africa whose development is people-driven, relying on the potential of African people, especially its women and youth, and caring for children.

[3] UNICEF 'Towards ending harmful practices in Africa: A statistical overview of child marriage and female genital mutilation' (17 June 2022) https://data.unicef.org/resources/harmful-practices-in-africa/ (accessed 17 November 2024).

[4] Worldometer 'African Countries by population' (2024) https://www.worldometers.info/population/countries-in-africa-by-population/ (accessed 17 November 2024).

[5] UNICEF (n 3).

in relation to dealing with the vice in its working methods follows. A look at the jurisprudence of the African Children's Committee is done to inform the final evaluation of the position of the African Children's Committee. A conclusion and recommendations follow.

The African Children's Committee is established under the African Children's Charter and is mandated to monitor the promotion and protection of the rights of the child in Africa.[6] It is composed of 11 members of high moral standing, integrity, impartiality, and competence and they serve in their personal capacity.[7] This is through the consideration of state party reports, engaging in missions, consideration of communications, conduct of research and development of hard and soft law, and collaboration with stakeholders in the execution of its mandate.[8] As will be shown, in the execution of its mandate, the African Children's Committee uses both country and special (or thematic) rapporteurs.[9] Concerning this contribution, the African Children's Committee has a Special Rapporteur on child marriage and harmful traditional practices, and this will inform the discussion.

2 Setting the Scene: Why (Traditional) Harmful Practices?

The development of the concept of 'traditional harmful practices' has seen a growth and transition in the use of terminology. To this end, in the 1990s, the global community presented an understanding with regard to concepts. The term used to be 'traditional cultural practices'. The Convention on the Elimination of All Forms of Discrimination Against

[6] Art 32 of the Organisation of African Unity (OAU), African Charter on the Rights and Welfare of the Child, CAB/LEG/24.9/49 (1990), 11 July 1990 (African Children's Charter).

[7] Art 33 of the African Children's Charter.

[8] Art 42 of the African Children's Charter.

[9] See Section 4 below. For the 55 African states, there is one rapporteur for every five states. See ACERWC 'Country rapporteurs: Terms of reference for country and thematic rapporteurs of the ACERWC' https://www.acerwc.africa/en/page/country-rapportuers (accessed 28 November 2024). For special rapporteurs, see ACERWC 'Special Rapporteur on child marriage and other harmful practices' https://www.acerwc.africa/en/special-mechanisms/thematic-areas/special-rapporteur-child-marriage-and-other-harmful-practices (accessed 28 November 2024).

Women does not define the concepts of 'harmful', 'traditional'. 'cultural', or 'practice'. It however calls on states to undertake

> to refrain from engaging in any act or practice of discrimination against women and to take all appropriate measures to modify or abolish existing laws, regulations, customs and practices which constitute discrimination against women.[10]

It is important to understand that every social group should identify the traditional cultural practices and beliefs, the point of departure being that while some are beneficial to the members, they may be harmful to others such as women and children.[11] Some of the notable examples include: female genital mutilation; son preference and the implication on the status of the girl child; female infanticide; early marriage and dowry; early pregnancy; nutritional taboos and practices related to child delivery; and violence against women.[12]

Similarly, the African Charter on the Rights and Welfare of the Child does not have the term 'harmful practices' or 'traditional harmful practices'. As such there is no definition to this end.[13] The closest term available in the African Children's Charter is 'harmful social and cultural practices'. It would also then mean that from a quick and close evaluation, the common denominators are 'harmful' and 'practices'. However, there is no definition of the term. The Protocol to the African Charter on Human and Peoples' Rights on the Rights of Women in Africa (Maputo Protocol)[14] is the only continental treaty that defines 'harmful practices'. To this end, it defines 'harmful practices' to mean 'all behaviour, attitudes, and/or practices which negatively affect the fundamental rights of women and girls, such as their right to life, health, dignity, education, and

[10] Art 2(d) and (f) of the UN General Assembly, Convention on the Elimination of All Forms of Discrimination Against Women, United Nations, Treaty Series, vol. 1249, p. 13, 18 December 1979.

[11] OHCHR 'Fact Sheet 23: Harmful traditional practices affecting the health of women and children' (1995) 1.

[12] Fact Sheet 23 at 5, 8, 9 and 11.

[13] Art 21, generally, of the African Children's Charter. A greater silence is evident in the Organisation of African Unity (OAU), African Charter on Human and Peoples' Rights (Banjul Charter), CAB/LEG/67/3 rev. 5, 21 ILM 58 (1982), 27 June 1981.

[14] African Union, Protocol to the African Charter on Human and People's Rights on the Rights of Women in Africa, African Union, 11 July 2003 (Maputo Protocol).

physical integrity'.[15] This may lead one to the irresistible conclusion that is safer to use the term 'harmful practices'. For purposes of this chapter, reference will be to harmful practices.

3 Harmful Practices from a Normative Context

As noted earlier, the African Children's Charter neither has nor defines the concept of 'traditional harmful practices'.[16] The closest is the provision on the wording around the concept. The heading to the article reads 'harmful social and cultural practices'. Before an evaluation is done, it is worth noting that there are three critical terms: 'harmful', 'traditional', and 'practices'. The term 'harmful' is repeated twice in the African Children's Charter and is contextually found in article 21 therein.[17] In addition, the term 'practices' is mentioned five times,[18] and contextually used concerning harmful traditional practices four times.[19] Lastly, the term 'traditional' is mentioned twice and does not contextually refer to harmful practices.[20] Following this normative guidance, a conceptual approach would thus require that an evaluation of 'harmful practices' other than 'harmful traditional practices' is preferred.

Article 21 provides as follows:

Protection Against Harmful Social And Cultural Practices

> 1. States Parties to the present Charter shall take all appropriate measures to eliminate harmful social and cultural practices affecting the welfare, dignity, normal growth and development of the child and in particular:

[15] Art 1(g) of the Maputo Protocol.

[16] This is re-echoed by the African Children's Committee in *Legal and Human Rights Centre and Centre for Reproductive Rights (on behalf of Tanzanian girls) against the United Republic of Tanzania* Communication 0012/Com/001/2019 [2020] ACERWC 1 (1 September 2020) (*Tanzania Communication*) para 62.

[17] Art 21 of the African Children's Charter.

[18] Arts 21 and 27(1)(b) of the African Children's Charter, with regards to sexual exploitative practices.

[19] Art 21 of the African Children's Charter.

[20] Fourth preambular paragraph and art 11(2)(2) with regard to the use of tradition in the enjoyment of the right to education.

> (a) those customs and practices prejudicial to the health or life of the child; and
> (b) those customs and practices discriminatory to the child on the grounds of sex or other status.
>
> 2. Child marriage and the betrothal of girls and boys shall be prohibited and effective action, including legislation, shall be taken to specify the minimum age of marriage to be eighteen years and make registration of all marriages in an official registry compulsory.

A couple of pointers are discernible from this provision from a normative perspective.

3.1 *Mandate on States Parties*

First, the mandate is on states parties. This is an instructive position because the African Children's Charter provides for both states parties and member states. Under the African Children's Charter, the term 'state party' or 'states parties' refers to states that have ratified the African Children's Charter. A closer conceptual look shows that this term is mentioned about 13 times. It is argued that when the term is looked at in context, it refers to obligations of states parties,[21] aspects of parental care and protection,[22] and nomination of experts to serve on the African Children's Committee.[23] Other aspects include the interpretation of the African Children's Charter,[24] submission of state reports,[25] and the recognition of the competence of the African Children's Committee to investigate activities of the state party,[26] and amendments to the African Children's Charter.[27] It is thus not in doubt that the term 'state party' refers to the states in the African Union that have ratified the African Children's Charter.

[21] Art 1(2) of the African Children's Charter.

[22] Art 19(3) & (4) of the African Children's Charter.

[23] Art 35 of the African Children's Charter.

[24] Art 42(iii)(c) of the African Children's Charter.

[25] Art 43(1) & (3) of the African Children's Charter.

[26] Art 45(1) of the African Children's Charter.

[27] Art 48 of the African Children's Charter.

The term 'member state' is used six times in the African Children's Charter and from a contextual background, it refers to member states of the African Union. This is qualified in various parts of the African Children's Charter, such as its first preambular paragraph that refers to African Member States of the Organisation of African Unity,[28] and the nature of their obligations under the African Children's Charter.[29] Other references to the term relate to the submission of reports,[30] signature, and ratification of the Charter.[31]

3.2 Mandatory Obligations

The nature of the obligations is informed by the nature of the wording in the article. The article states that 'states parties shall'. This is an indication that first, the mandate is on states parties. Under the African Children's Charter, the term 'state party' or 'states parties' refers to states that have ratified the African Children's Charter. A closer conceptual look shows that this term indicates that 'states parties shall...'. The wording that follows requires that states parties take appropriate measures to eliminate harmful social and cultural practices that affect the child's well-being in four general aspects of: (1) welfare; (2) dignity; (3) normal growth; and (4) development of the child. It is argued that the engagement of the four areas ensures that the measures taken to eliminate the practice respectively speak to: the holistic well-being of a child that deals with the welfare, normal growth and development of a child; and a human rights approach. The holistic approach would be expected to deal with all aspects like the physical, socio-emotional, and cognitive aspects of the life of the child.[32] A human rights-based approach would then cover the child rights-based approach that is informed by the four principles.[33]

[28] As above.

[29] Art 1(1) of the African Children's Charter.

[30] Art 44(1) of the African Children's Charter.

[31] Art 47(1) & (2) of the African Children's Charter.

[32] JF Zaff and others 'Holistic well-being and the developing child' in MH Bornstein and others (eds) *Well-being: Positive development across the life course* (2003) 23–32.

[33] This includes the principle of non-discrimination (art 3); best interests of the child (art 4); right to life, survival and development (art 5); and consideration of the views of the child (art 7(2)).

In addition, the four aspects that inculcate appropriate measures (as discussed above) have to ensure that these trickle down to dealing with customs and practices that affect the health or life of the child on the one hand, and are discriminatory to the child on grounds of sex or other status.[34] It is thus important that the normative guidance highlights the need to amplify the elimination of harmful practices from the perspective of the enjoyment of the right to health and in a manner that deals with any instances of discrimination.

The mandatory nature of the obligations is also varied and not only placed on the state party. It does not state that the 'state party shall'. Rather, it stated that 'child marriages and betrothal of boys and girls shall be prohibited'. This is important as it retains the mandatory nature of the obligation and by implication places it on every person or entity that is in a position to ensure that child marriages and betrothals do not occur. It may be argued that article 21(2) uses various considerations in handing down normative guidance. First, it takes on a substantive approach by prohibiting child marriage and the betrothal of both girls and boys. Secondly, it takes on a procedural approach by calling for effective action, that latches on one of the added values of the African Children's Charter of the minimum age of marriage as 18 years and the compulsory registration of all marriages in an official registry.

It is argued that if the use of the term 'shall' creates a lot of ambiguity, and it should be discontinued for more appropriate wording such as 'may', 'must' and 'will'. Various instructive examples to show the ambiguity include: the wrongful declaration of a legal result[35]; the misuse of a conditional or relative clause[36]; the creation of a false imperative[37]; and the use of the term 'shall' with no clarity on where the duty falls.[38] To establish the relation of these ambiguities to article 21, a reflection of the foregoing on the wording of the article is important. As such the questions to be posed include whether there is: (1) the existence of a

[34] Art 21(1)(a) and (b) of the African Children's Charter.

[35] For instance, a law that states that: 'It *shall* be [is] unlawful to commit theft'.

[36] For instance, a law that states that: 'If the tenant *shall* [does] not pay the rent on time, the landlord may charge a late fee'.

[37] For instance, a law that states that: 'There *shall* be [is?] created a Department of Legal Studies'.

[38] For instance, a law that states that: 'All lions *shall* be kept in a cage'.

wrongful declaration of legal result; (2) misuse in a conditional clause; (3) the creation of a false imperative; and (4) the use of the term with no clarity on where the duty falls.

Concerning the use of the term 'shall' in the article; the following obligations are created on the part of the state. The article provides that '[s]tate [p]arties to the present Charter shall take appropriate measures to prevent ...'[39] It is argued that the part of the provision neither refers to existing rights nor creates the same. Conversely, there is neither a precatory suggestion nor a conflation of the use of the term 'shall' to refer to another term such as 'should',[40] 'will', or 'may'.[41] This leads to the logical conclusion that the interpretation of article 21 is based on the mandatory obligation on the states parties.[42] It is also clear, that the provision does not have a conditional or relative clause for its application as far as the obligation remains squarely on the state without any condition on any other person or entity.[43] In addition, this provision does not envision the creation of any false imperative or fails to offer clarity concerning the entity that is the duty bearer—in this case, the state.[44] It is clear that the use of the term 'shall' is not a conditional or relative clause for its application—the obligation remains on the state with a resultant qualification that the child is protected. In juxtaposition, it is argued that there is no condition on any other person or entity but rather the protection of the child as a consequence of the state's engagement of its obligations.[45] Clarity also remains on the state as the duty bearer concerning the rights of the child.[46] The mandatory obligation relates to abduction, the sale of, or trafficking of children for any purpose or in any form, and begging.

[39] Art 29 of the African Children's Charter.

[40] Compare with this example, a law that states that: 'It *shall* be [is] unlawful to commit theft'.

[41] RC Wydick *Plain English for lawyers* 5ed (2005) 63–64. See also J Kimble 'The many misuses of shall' (1992) 3 *Scribes journal of legal writing* 61, 70.

[42] As above.

[43] As above.

[44] As above.

[45] As above.

[46] As above.

4 The Institutional Framework of the African Committee of Experts Concerning Traditional Harmful Practices

The African Children's Charter provides for the African Children's Committee, mandated to monitor the promotion and protection of the rights of the child in Africa. In the execution of its mandate, it carries out various activities such as the receipt and consideration of state party reports; the use of missions to states parties, to carry out research in areas that are critical to the African Children's Committee; as well as to interpret the Charter through the consideration of communications; and development of soft law that enhances the understanding of aspects of the African Children's Charter. While this is an instructive institutional development, it is important that it delivers on the actual promotion and protection of the rights of the child. The failure to do this would also mean a failure in its mandate.

From an institutional setting, the African Children's Committee has been quick to set up mechanisms to support the execution of its mandate. The ability to set up mechanisms gets its founding in the Revised Rules of Procedure that allow the appointment of country rapporteurs, special rapporteurs and working groups among others. The appointment of country rapporteurs has seen the appointment of each of the 11 members to monitor the promotion and protection of rights in the 55 countries across Africa. To this end, each member of the Committee is mandated to monitor at least five countries. In hindsight, it is expected that where issues of harmful practices arise in a specific state that is party to the African Children's Charter, the country rapporteur should guide those conversations. The challenge with this approach is that the country rapporteur may end up being a jack of all trades—concerning the promotion and protection of the rights of children in various thematic spaces.

To solve this predicament, the African Children's Committee introduced special rapporteurs as themative leads on specific identifiable thematic areas. To this end, there are 11 thematic areas with thematic rapporteurs to guide the conversations. The thematic areas include: children affected by armed conflict, violence against children, birth registration, name and nationality, child marriage, and other harmful practices and child participation. Others include children in vulnerable situations, health, welfare and development, children on the move, children in conflict with the law, and children without parental care and education. It is worth noting that from an institutional perspective, there is a Special Rapporteur who deals with child marriages and other traditional harmful practices.

It is instructive to mention a few aspects regarding the role of the Special Rapporteur on child marriage and harmful practices. This mechanism was adopted by a resolution at the 39th session of the African Children's Committee and has over time been refined.[47] The mandate was created pursuant to article 38(1) of the African Children's Charter which allows the African Children's Committee to develop its own Rules of Procedures, and Rule 58 of the Revised Rules of Procedure, which allows the ACERWC to establish special mechanisms and assign specific tasks or mandates to either an individual member or group of members.[48] The role of the Special Rapporteur is to analyse the root causes of child marriage and other harmful practices, to seek, receive, examine and act upon information on the situation of child marriage and other harmful practices; and to mobilise action and political support to end child marriage and other harmful practices in Africa.[49] Other roles include the generation of a renewed concern on the harmful effects of child marriage and other harmful practices, to promote behavioural and social change, and to achieve effective progress.[50] The Special Rapporteur is also expected to cooperate and engage in dialogue with member states, National Human Rights Institutions, relevant intergovernmental organisations, international and regional mechanisms, UN Agencies and CSOs to end child marriage and other harmful practices.[51]

[47] African Union, Resolution on the appointment of a Special Rapporteur on child marriage and other harmful practices in Africa (2017) third preambular paragraph. https://www.acerwc.africa/sites/default/files/2022-06/Child-marriage-and-Other-harmful-practices.pdf (accessed 20 November 2024).

[48] Fourth preambular paragraph of the Resolution on the appointment of a Special Rapporteur (n 47).

[49] Roles i–iii, page 2 of the Resolution (n 47).

[50] Role iv, page 2 of the Resolution (n 47).

[51] Role v, page 2 of the Resolution (n 47). You are invited to read the entire resolution to establish the roles of the Special Rapporteur.

The critical question is to what extent the normative and institutional makeup of the African Children's Charter and its Committee have respectively developed jurisprudence on harmful traditional practices. To this question, the chapter now turns.

5 Emerging Jurisprudence on Traditional Harmful Practices

By design, this section will look at specific jurisprudence of the African Children's Committee in light of research that has been done pursuant to concluding observations that have been handed down in state party reports and concluded communications on traditional harmful practices, among others. This will inform the extent to which the African Children's Committee has or has not developed.

Engaging the AU 2063 Agenda and the SDG Agenda. For instance, the 2030 Sustainable Development Goal Agenda has Goal 5 which seeks to achieve gender equality and empower all women and girls. At its core, Target 5.3 seeks to eliminate all harmful practices, such as child, early, and forced marriage and female genital mutilation. In addition, the African Union Agenda 2063 has Aspiration 6 which envisions an Africa whose development is people-driven, relying on the potential of African people, especially its women and youth, and caring for children.[52]

5.1 Concluding Observations on State Party Reports

There are various concluding observations which give guidance to states regarding harmful practices. A look at the same will answer the foregoing question in light of the jurisprudential developments. This is with regard to the narrative that the African Children's Committee puts across in its concluding observations.

First, in all its concluding observations, the African Children's Committee approaches this vice using the terminology in article 21 of the African Children's Charter. To this end, it is referred to as harmful social and cultural practices. This consistency points to the African Children's Committee reading of the normative provisions in the Charter and maintaining this stance. This is an indication that while the for the purpose of

[52] UNICEF (n 3).

this chapter reference is to harmful practices, the terminology with regard to children is maintained as harmful social and cultural practices.

Secondly, the Committee using a carrot and stick method; where it recognised the steps taken by the state party to remedy the vice; and then offers stringent advice. In its Concluding Recommendations to the periodic report of Cameroon, the Committee appreciated the measures taken by the state party in dealing with harmful traditional practices. For instance, in its Concluding Observations of Cameroon, it recognises the collaboration between the religious leaders and the state to eliminate female genital mutilation.[53] Similarly, in its Concluding Observations and Recommendations of the African Children's Committee to the Government of the Republic of South Africa on its Second and Third periodic Report on the Implementation of the African Charter on the Rights and Welfare of the Child,[54] the Committee appreciated various initiatives such as the number of initiatives undertaken by the state party to eliminate harmful social and cultural practices despite their high prevalence in the country, and the development of proposed child protection legislative amendments to ban this practice with regard to all children.[55]

In its Concluding Observation on Botswana's report, the African Children's Committee appreciated the legislative measures made to prohibit and eliminate all forms of harmful traditional practices.[56] It is argued that

[53] Concluding Recommendations by the African Committee of Experts on the Rights and Welfare of the Child (ACERWC) on the Republic of Cameroon's Report on the status of implementation of the African Charter on the Rights and Welfare of the Child (2017) para 25.

[54] Concluding Observations and Recommendations of the African Committee of Experts on the Rights and Welfare of the Child to the Government of the Republic of South Africa on its second periodic report on the implementation of the African Charter on the Rights and Welfare of the Child (2023) para 56.

[55] Concluding Observations on South Africa (n 54) para 56. For instance, in para 57, South Africa adopted the Customary Initiation Act in 2021 to regulate customary initiation practices, prohibit female circumcision and genital mutilation as part of customary initiation practices.

[56] Concluding Observations and Recommendations of the African Committee of Experts on the Rights and Welfare of the Child to the Republic of Botswana on its initial report on the on the implementation of the African Charter on the Rights and Welfare of the Child (2023) para 53. See also Concluding Observations and Recommendations of the African Committee of Experts on the Rights and Welfare of the Child (ACERWC) on the initial report of the Republic of Burundi on the status of the implementation of the African Charter on the Rights and Welfare of the Child para 48.

this recognises the initiative that the state party has done to eliminate the harmful practices.

Regarding the stick method, the African Children's Committee however called on Cameroon to take more action. This included the need to adopt a law on FGM and other forms of serious injury to the privacy of girls, and to take measures against other subtle forms of child marriage like children cohabitation.[57] Regarding South Africa it also called for the adoption of a law on harmful practices and specified FGM and other forms of serious injury to the privacy of girls, it also called on the state party to take measures against other subtle forms of child marriage (children cohabitation).[58] In addition, it went ahead to urge South Africa to intensify the investigation and prosecution of the culprits.[59] With regard to Botswana, the African Children's Committee called on the state party to deal with specific practices such as unsafe male circumcision, son preference over the girl child with regard to inheritance and the prevalent child marriages in the country. Most importantly, the African Children's Committee calls on the state to amend this domestic law on the definition of the child to reflect the position of the African Children's Charter.[60]

Thirdly, there is a move by the African Children's Committee to recognise that there are harmful practices that are not within article 21 but inform the list which the state party should address. In the Concluding Observations on Burundi's report to the African Children's Charter, the African Children's Committee noted a lack of clarity concerning the application of a minimum age of employment. It was observed that while the minimum age was 16 years of age, children between 12 and 16 years of age can engage in hazardous works.[61] This as noted by the Committee led to the violation of other rights such as the right to education.[62] Other violations which were considered harmful yet not part of article 21 included the recruitment of children as domestic workers, and begging

[57] Concluding Recommendations on Cameroon (n 53) para 25.

[58] Concluding Observations on South Africa (n 54) para 58.

[59] Concluding Observations on South Africa (n 54) para 56. For instance, in para 57, South Africa adopted the Customary Initiation Act in 2021 to regulate customary initiation practices, prohibit female circumcision and genital mutilation as part of customary initiation practices.

[60] Para 53 of the Concluding Observations on Botswana.

[61] Para 49 of the Concluding Observations on Burundi.

[62] Para 49 of the Concluding Observations on Burundi.

by children on the streets.[63] The other identifiable harmful practices still formed the usual ones such as child marriages.[64]

5.2 *Communications*

Two decisions have been determined by the African Children's Committee that point to harmful practices.

In *Minority Rights Group International against Mauritania*, it was alleged that two children born to a mother from a Haratine sect were automatically slaves to the El Hassine family.[65] The applicants alleged that the respondent state violated the right to education, prohibition of torture and harmful cultural practices.[66] These children worked seven days a week without pay,[67] were always subjected to corporal punishment and did not go to school.[68] The applicants alleged among others violations, that the use of a culture that upheld slavery of the children amounted to a violation of article 21 on the prohibition on harmful social and cultural practices.[69] The respondent state alluded to a legislative framework that protected children against abuse,[70] a plan of action

[63] Para 50 of the Concluding Observations on Burundi.

[64] Para 51 of the Concluding Observations on Burundi.

[65] *Minority Rights Group International and SOS-Esclaves on Behalf of Said Ould Salem And Yarg Ould Salem v The Republic of Mauritania* Communication 007/Com/003/2015) [2015] ACERWC 3 (15 December 2015).

[66] *Mauritania Communication* (n 65) paras 6–7.

[67] As above.

[68] As above.

[69] Para 12 stated that based on the facts, the complainants alleged that the Republic of Mauritania violated arts 1 (Obligation of State Parties), 3 (Non-Discrimination), 4 (Best Interests of the Child), 5 (Survival and Development), 11 (Education), 12 (Leisure, Recreation, and Cultural Activities), 15 (Protection from Economic Exploitation), 16 (Protection Against Harmful Social and Cultural Practices) and 29 (Prevention of Sale, Trafficking and Abduction of Children) of the African Charter on the Rights and Welfare of the Child.

[70] *Mauritania Communication* (n 65) para 36.

against child labour,[71] the enrolment of children in school,[72] and the prosecution of the perpetrators.[73]

The African Children's Committee used the violation of the principle of non-discrimination as a tool to find a violation of article 21. To this end, it was of the view that there was no legitimate interest by the state that echoed proportional and necessary limitations to counter the violation.[74] In addition, the African Children's Committee created a balancing tool to establish the consequences of a harmful practice. It stated that:

> [A] harmful practice should, among other things, constitute a denial of the dignity and/or integrity of the individual and a violation of human rights and fundamental freedoms enshrined in the [charter].[75]

As such, as long as the identified harmful practice presents a denial of the human dignity of the child and a violation of a right or a freedom, it marked a place of no return with regard to a finding that this constituted a violation of article 21.

This was developed further through a dual approach by the African Children's Committee. First, by extending the context of harmful practices from article 21 (the normative premise) to other articles of the Charter such as article 29 on child labour. Secondly, by relating the violation of article 21 to a failure by the state to uphold the principle of the right to life, survival, and development. The African Children's Committee agreed that child labour negatively affects the welfare, growth, and development of the child.[76] In addition, it states that the practice of slavery as one of the worst forms of child labour impedes the overall well-being of the child.[77] The Committee reiterated its advice to state in concluding observations the extension of the understanding of harmful traditional practices beyond article 21, to the need to consider the holistic development of a child as an important aspect of protection of the right to

[71] *Mauritania Communication* (n 65) para 37.

[72] *Mauritania Communication* (n 65) para 38.

[73] *Mauritania Communication* (n 65) para 39.

[74] *Mauritania Communication* (n 65) para 61.

[75] As above.

[76] *Mauritania Communication* (n 65) para 91.

[77] As above.

life, survival and development. Finally, the Committee used this communication to reiterate the principle of due diligence as one that places an obligation on the state—which is extinguished by an evaluation of the results as a consequence of the implementation of the state obligations.[78]

In the *Centre for Human Rights and La Rencontre Africaine Pour La Defense Des Droits De L'homme (Senegal) v Senegal*, the facts are that many children aged between four and 12 years were sent away by their parents to live in Qur'anic schools known as daaras in the urban centres of Senegal to receive religious education.[79] Furthermore, the children were forced by their instructors (known as marabouts) to work on the streets as beggars.[80] The begging continued as a long-age practice since 1980 despite the existence of provisions in the Penal Code and the Law to Combat Trafficking in Persons and Related Practices and to Protect Victims adopted by the respondent state.[81] The complainants alleged that the state violated: article 4 (best interests of the child); article 5 (the right to survival and development); article 11 (the right to education); article 12 (the right to leisure, recreation and cultural activities); article 14 (the right to health and health services); article 15 (prohibition of child labour); article 16 (protection against child abuse and torture); article 21 (protection against harmful social and cultural practices); and article 29 (prohibition of sale, trafficking and abduction of children) of the Charter.[82]

In dealing with the violation of article 21, the African Children's Committee identified a criterion concerning harmful practices. These included (1) a denial of the dignity and/or integrity of the individual coupled with a human rights violation; (2) constituting discrimination against women or children and are harmful in light of the negative consequences.[83] In addition, the practices are (3) traditional, re-emerging or

[78] As above.

[79] *Centre for Human Rights (University of Pretoria) and La Rencontre Africaine Pour La Defense Des Droits De L'homme (Senegal) v Senegal* Decision 003/Com/001/2012 ACERWC (15 April 2014) (*The Talibes Communication*) paras 1–3.

[80] *The Talibes Communication* (n 79) paras 1–3.

[81] As above.

[82] *The Talibes Communication* (n 79) para 11. For purposes of the conversation, the discussion is limited to the violation of art 21.

[83] *The Talibes Communication* (n 79) para 70.

emerging practices prescribed by social norms that perpetuate male dominance and inequality of women and children, based on sex, gender, age and other intersecting factors.[84] While the use of the criterion is welcomed, it is important that the larger perspective that the African Committee used persuasive jurisprudence from the United Convention on the Rights and Welfare of the Child as well as the Convention on the Elimination of All Forms of Discrimination Against Women.[85] This was an implied application of article 46 as a tool to inform the content (criteria) to identify a harmful practice.[86]

The African Children's Committee called on states parties to take legislative, administrative and other appropriate measures to abolish any practice inconsistent with the Charter. This was extended to the vice of begging prohibited under article 29. In addition, this included the African Children's Charter; and the state was expected to take on all the necessary steps to restrict such practice.[87] By implication, the African Children's Committee reiterates the nature of state party obligations on the state party to take steps to deal with begging.[88] In addition, the African Children Committee also found that the failure of the state to take any measures against these schools led to a compromise of their right to life and development due to injuries from traffic accidents.[89] In a way, the African Children's Committee linked the violation of article 21 to a violation of the right to life, survival, and development as far as the holistic development of the child was stifled by the state party.[90]

84 Art 46 of the African Children's Charter.

85 *The Talibes Communication* (n 79 above) para 70.

86 Art 46 is not directly related to any provisions of the Charter. Rather, it is presents an indirect relationship with all provisions of the Charter because it is an interpretative tool that aids the interpretation of children's rights issue.

87 *The Talibes Communication* (n 79) para 71.

88 This is the context of art 1 of the African Children's Charter. It is further reiterated in the ACERWC & ACHPR, Joint General Comment of the African Charter on the Rights and Welfare of the Child and the African Commission on Human and Peoples' Rights on female genital mutilation (2023). Para 7 reiterates that states parties to the African Children Charter and the Maputo Protocol to take on legislative, institutional, and other measures to protect girls and women from FGM and to eliminate the practice.

89 *The Talibes communication* (n 79 above) para 73.

90 See the discussion on of holistic in Sec 3 above. In addition, read Zaff and others (n 32).

In *Legal and Human Rights Centre and Centre for Reproductive Rights against the Government of Tanzania*,[91] the facts are that primary and secondary school-going girls were subjected to forced pregnancy testing and expulsion from schools.[92] This was compounded by the statistics that showed that over 55 000 female students between 2003 and 2011 dropped out of school due to pregnancy with, 2 433 girls in primary and 4 705 in secondary schools in 2012.[93] In addition, it was alleged that the practice of forced pregnancy testing was done on girls as young as 11 years and it was not done according to the standard procedures.[94] The failure to communicate the results of the testing to the affected girl(s) was alleged to be a violation of the right to privacy.[95] Among the various allegations was the violation of article 21 with regard to harmful practices.[96] The complainants allege that the

> mandatory pregnancy testing, the subsequent expulsion of pregnant and married girls, and the detention of pregnant girls are guided by stereotypes on the role of girls and that their moral status is determined by their virginity,

which violated article 21.[97] According to the African Children's Committee, two issues were critical with regard to the violation of article 21. First, whether the mandatory pregnancy testing, the expulsion of pregnant and married girls, and the detention of girls violated article 21 of the ACRWC; and secondly, whether the measures by the state to eliminate teenage pregnancy and to empower girls are sufficient under article 21 of the African Children's Charter and whether *'on the role of girls and that their moral status is determined by their virginity'* violated article 21.[98]

[91] *Tanzania Communication* (n 16) para 2.

[92] As above.

[93] As above.

[94] *Tanzania Communication* (n 16) para 3.

[95] As above.

[96] *Tanzania Communication* (n 16) para 60.

[97] As above.

[98] *Tanzania Communication* (n 16) para 61.

First, the African Children's Committee underscored four principles that may be used to identify a harmful practice. First, the practice should constitute a denial of the dignity and/or integrity of the individual and a violation of their human rights.[99] Secondly, it should constitute discrimination limiting the capacity of girls to fully participate in society.[100] Thirdly, the practices should be prescribed and/or kept in place by social norms that perpetuate male dominance and inequality of women and children, based on the basis of sex, gender, age, and other intersecting factors.[101] Fourthly, the practice is imposed on women and children by family members, community members, or society regardless of the victim's lack of or inability to consent.[102]

The African Children's Committee stated that the act of the Republic with regard to the expulsion of pregnant girls from school led to negative and discriminatory attitudes which led to harmful practices such as child marriage.[103] As a consequence, an act of a state party that perpetuates negative and discriminatory attitudes and tendencies is a violation of its obligations under the African Children's Charter. It is argued that the African Children's Committee's finding places an agency on the child to have entitlements to rights and freedoms under the African Children's Charter.[104] In addition, the state is expected to actively identify the children who require special measures to remedy their situation.[105] As such, since the state allowed forced pregnancy to continue, it violated the principle of non-discrimination.[106]

[99] *Tanzania Communication* (n 16) para 62.

[100] As above.

[101] As above.

[102] As above.

[103] *Tanzania Communication* (n 16) para 55.

[104] African Committee of Experts on the Rights and Welfare of the Child (ACERWC) General Comment 5 on 'State Party obligations under the African Charter on the Rights and Welfare of the Child (Article 1) and systems strengthening for child protection (2018).

[105] This is beyond the scope of this contribution. See arts 1 and 3 of the African Children's Charter.

[106] The Committee reiterates that this call for dedicated additional resources that should be consciously identified and devoted to implementation of the principle of non-discrimination. See General Comment 5 (n 104) 11.

5.3 5.3General Comments

The African Children's Charter has two specific general comments that deal with specific harmful cultural practices. These are the Joint General Comment by the African Children's Committee and the African Commission on Human and Peoples' Rights on: female genital mutilation,[107] and ending child marriages.[108] The two General Comments have common denominators as they both speak to ending harmful practices,[109] amplification of state party obligations under article 21,[110] the scope of the general comment,[111] both use the child-rights-based approach,[112] the context of the normative framework,[113] and state obligations.[114] The point of departure is in the Joint General Comment on FGM's approach that inculcates other instructive principles that are beyond the child rights-based principles such as gender equality,[115] intersectionality,[116] and respect for bodily integrity.[117]

[107] Joint General Comment by the African Children's Committee and the African Commission on Human and Peoples' RIghs on female genital mutilation (2023) https://www.acerwc.africa/sites/default/files/2023-11/Joint%20General%20Comment_ACHPR-ACERWC_on%20FGM%20%282%29.pdf (accessed 19 November 2024).

[108] Joint General Comment by the African Children's Committee and the African Commission on Human and Peoples' Rights on ending child marriage (2018) https://www.acerwc.africa/sites/default/files/2022-09/Joint_General_Comment_ACERWC-ACHPR_Ending_Child_Marriage_March_2018_English.pdf (accessed 19 November 2024).

[109] Para 1 of the Joint GC on ending child marriages; Para 23 of the Joint JC on FGM.

[110] Para 2 of the Joint GC on ending child marriages; and paras 34–53 of the Joint JC on FGM.

[111] Para 5 of the Joint GC on ending child marriages; and para 7 of the Joint JC on FGM.

[112] Paras 7–14 of the Joint GC on ending child marriages; and paras 9–12 of the Joint JC on FGM.

[113] Paras 16–17 of the Joint GC on ending child marriages; and paras 25–33 of the Joint JC on FGM.

[114] Paras 18–62 of the Joint GC on ending child marriages; and paras 32–42 of the Joint JC on FGM.

[115] Para 13 of the Joint GC on FGM.

[116] Paras 14–16 of the Joint GC on FGM.

[117] Para 17 of the Joint GC on FGM.

In both General Comments, there are essential recommendations of the African Children's Committee and the African Commission on Human and Peoples' Rights. In the Joint General Comment on FGM, it was recommended that states parties use state reporting to indicate progress and share best practices in the implementation of their obligation to eliminate FGM with the aid of the Maputo Protocol and the African Charter on Human and Peoples' Rights.[118] In addition, states parties need to report on measures taken to eliminate FGM under the African Children's Charter and the general principles of children's rights.[119] Furthermore, the state reports ought to provide specific disaggregated information as to the steps that the respective state.[120]

In the Joint General Comment on child marriages, the two human rights monitoring bodies called for legislative reform. The General Comment proposes that states parties ensure that the betrothal and marriage of boys and girls under the age of 18 is prohibited, without exception[121]; ensure personal, full and free consent to marry[122]; and undertake constitutional reforms to specify the minimum age of 18 years for consent and joining of the marriage union.[123] The Joint General Comment also recommends that institutional reforms should extend to ensuring the implementation of verification procedures such as birth registration, age verification and marriage registration[124]; the full enforcement of laws, penalties and sanctions[125]; and institutional reforms around education[126]; health[127]; and access to justice among others.[128]The engagement of these recommendations is instructive in ensuring progress in the elimination of harmful practices.

[118] Para 70 of the Joint GC on FGM.

[119] Para 71 of the Joint GC on FGM.

[120] As above.

[121] Paras 17–20 of the Joint GC on ending child marriages.

[122] Paras 21–23 of the Joint GC on ending child marriages.

[123] Para 24 of the Joint GC on ending child marriages.

[124] Paras 26–28 of the Joint GC on ending child marriages.

[125] Paras 29–30 of the Joint GC on ending child marriages.

[126] Paras 31–33 of the Joint GC on ending child marriages.

[127] Paras 34–38 of the Joint GC on ending child marriages.

[128] Paras 39–42 of the Joint GC on ending child marriages.

5.4 *Agenda 2040*

The African Children's Committee has Agenda 2040 that is birthed out of the African Union's Agenda 2063. At its core, Agenda 2063 has Aspiration 6 which envisages an Africa whose development is people-driven, relying on the potential offered by African people, especially its women and youth, and caring for children.[129] Out of this aspiration is Agenda 2040 which is informed by ten aspirations.[130] With regard to harmful practices, Aspiration 7 envisages that every child is protected against violence, exploitation, neglect, and abuse. Violence against children takes many forms.[131] The narrative of this aspiration indicates that some of the forms of violence include harmful practices such as female genital mutilation, child marriage, virginity testing, breast ironing and child witch killings; gender-based violence; sexual violence; sexual exploitation; pornography; and sexual trafficking.[132]

Some of the notable aspects of the implementation of this Aspiration include the engagement of jurisprudential steps that improved the institutional aspects of the African Children's Committee. First, there was a campaign by the African Union to end child marriage in Africa; and it appointed a Special Rapporteur on child marriage, with a mandate to conduct fact-finding missions on alleged violations, to seek co-operation with states parties, and to develop constructive dialogue with governments, civil society organisations and other actors.[133] This appointment was in line with the competence of the African Children's Committee concerning the establishment of its own Rules of Procedure.[134] Furthermore, it was pursuant to the establishment of special mechanisms to assign specific tasks or mandates to either an individual member or group of

[129] Agenda 2063 https://au.int/en/agenda2063/goals (accessed 20 November 2024).

[130] The Agenda for Children 2040 is a set of ten aspirations for children in Africa to be achieved by 2040. The Agenda was developed after a 2015 conference that assessed the status of children's rights in Africa. The Agenda is based on the African Charter on the Rights and Welfare of the Child, which has been ratified by 51 of the 55 African states. See Agenda 2040|ACERWC—African Committee of Experts on the Rights and Welfare of the Child https://www.acerwc.africa/en/page/agenda-2040 (20 November 2024).

[131] Agenda 2040|ACERWC (n 130).

[132] Agenda 2040|ACERWC (n 130) 37.

[133] As above.

[134] See art 38(1) of the African Children's Charter.

members concerning the preparation of its sessions or the execution of special programmes, studies, and projects.[135]

6 Conclusion

From a normative perspective, the normative guidance with regard to the African Children's Charter presents mandatory obligations that reflect the agency of the child. While there is no definition of harmful practice, most of the guidance on the normative front includes a reading-in of definitions from various instruments such as the Maputo Protocol, the CRC, and the CEDAW. From an institutional process, the presentment of the Special Rapporteur on child marriages and other harmful practices has been instructive in the development of activities and jurisprudence that are tilted towards ending child marriages and female genital mutilation. It may be argued that the jurisprudence showcases a development of two general comments, and communications, concluding observations and the use of Agenda 2040. It would be helpful if the work of the country and special rapporteur were aligned to Agenda 2040 and part of the cyclic link that is informed by the normative, institutional, and jurisprudential founding.

Bibliography

ACERWC 'Country rapporteurs: Terms of reference for country and thematic rapporteurs of the ACERWC' https://www.acerwc.africa/en/page/country-rapportuers (accessed 28 November 2024).

ACERWC 'Special Rapporteur on child marriage and other harmful practices' https://www.acerwc.africa/en/special-mechanisms/thematic-areas/special-rapporteur-child-marriage-and-other-harmful-practices (accessed 28 November 2024).

Agenda 2040 | ACERWC – African Committee of Experts on the Rights and Welfare of the Child https://www.acerwc.africa/en/page/agenda-2040 (20 November 2024).

AU 'Agenda 2063' https://au.int/en/agenda2063/goals (accessed 20 November 2024).

[135] Rule 58 of the Revised Rules of Procedure of the African Committee of Experts on the Rights and Welfare of the Child https://www.acerwc.africa/en/key-documents/working-documents/revised-rules-procedure-african-committee-experts-rights-and (20 November 2024).

Intersession report by the Special Rapporteur on the Rights of Women in Africa (SRRWA) – 79OS (2024) https://achpr.au.int/en/intersession-activity-reports/rights-women-africa (accessed 17 November 2024).

Kimble, J 'The many misuses of shall' (1992) 3 *Scribes journal of legal writing* 61.

UNICEF 'Towards ending harmful practices in Africa A statistical overview of child marriage and female genital mutilation' (17 June 2022) https://data.unicef.org/resources/harmful-practices-in-africa/ (accessed 17 November 2024)

Worldometer 'African Countries by population' (2024) https://www.worldometers.info/population/countries-in-africa-by-population/ (accessed 17 November 2024)

Wydick, RC *Plain English for lawyers* 5ed (Carolina Academy Press 2005)

Zaff, JF; Smith, DC; Rogers, MF; Leavitt, CH; Halle, TG & Bornstein, MH 'Holistic well-being and the developing child' in Bornstein, MH; Davidson, L; Keyes, CLM & Moore, KA (eds) *Well-Being: Positive development across the life course* (Psychology Press, New York 2003).

Cases

Centre for Human Rights (University of Pretoria) and La Rencontre Africaine Pour La Defense Des Droits De L'homme (Senegal) v Senegal Decision 003/Com/001/2012 ACERWC (15 April 2014).

Legal and Human Rights Centre and Centre for Reproductive Rights (on behalf of Tanzanian girls) against the United Republic of Tanzania Communication 0012/Com/001/2019 [2020] ACERWC 1 (1 September 2020).

Minority Rights Group International and SOS-Esclaves on Behalf of Said Ould Salem & Yarg Ould Salem v The Republic of Mauritania Communication 007/Com/003/2015) [2015] ACERWC 3 (15 December 2015).

Laws

Customary Initiation Act in 2021.

ACERWC

Concluding Recommendations by the African Committee of Experts on the Rights and Welfare of the Child (ACERWC) on the Republic of Cameroon's Report on the status of implementation of the African Charter on the Rights and Welfare of the Child (2017).

Concluding Observations and Recommendations of the African Committee of Experts on the Rights and Welfare of the Child to the Republic of Botswana on its initial report on the on the implementation of the African Charter on the Rights and Welfare of the Child (2023).

Concluding Observations and Recommendations of the African Committee of Experts on the Rights and Welfare of the Child to the Government of the Republic of South Africa on its second periodic report on the implementation of the African Charter on the Rights and Welfare of the Child (2023).

General Comment 5 on state party obligations under the African Charter on the Rights and Welfare of the Child (article 1) and systems strengthening for child protection (2018).

Joint General Comment by the African Children's Committee and the African Commission on Human and Peoples' Rights on ending child marriage (2018).

Joint General Comment of the African Charter on the Rights and Welfare of the Child and the African Commission on Human and Peoples' Rights on female genital mutilation (2023).

Revised Rules of Procedure of the African Committee of Experts on the Rights and Welfare of the Child https://www.acerwc.africa/en/key-documents/working-documents/revised-rules-procedure-african-committee-experts-rights-and (20 November 2024).

African Union

African Union, Protocol to the African Charter on Human and Peoples' Rights on the Rights of Women in Africa, African Union, 11 July 2003.

African Union, Resolution on the Appointment of a Special Rapporteur on child marriage and other harmful practices in Africa (2017) https://www.acerwc.africa/sites/default/files/2022-06/Child-marriage-and-Other-harmful-practices.pdf (accessed 20 November 2024).

Organisation of African Unity (OAU), African Charter on Human and Peoples' Rights (Banjul Charter), CAB/LEG/67/3 rev. 5, 21 ILM 58 (1982), 27 June 1981.

Organisation of African Unity (OAU), African Charter on the Rights and Welfare of the Child, CAB/LEG/24.9/49 (1990), 11 July 1990.

UN

OHCHR 'Fact sheet 23: Harmful traditional practices affecting the health of women and children' (1995).

UN General Assembly, Convention on the Elimination of All Forms of Discrimination Against Women, United Nations, Treaty Series, vol 1249, p 13, 18 December 1979.

CHAPTER 14

Cultivating Agency and Claiming Bodily Autonomy: A Response to the Politics of Child Marriage in the African Context

Yumba Bernadette Kakhobwe

1 Introduction

The gravitas of child marriage as a harmful practice within the human rights system has arguably been more recently pronounced. What could be posited is that historically there has been a reluctance to include child marriage amongst what are officially recognised as harmful practices like female genital mutilation and cutting (FGM/C), with its apparent health implications and manifestations of physical injury, and which are more difficult to deny or conceal. The insistence to bluntly refer to FGM/C as 'mutilation' rather than 'cutting' in certain sectors, is meant to convey resounding agreement concerning its recognised brutality, and to be intentionally emotive by provoking a sense of justice, guilt, shame, or concern, depending on where one is situated in relation to the practice.

Y. B. Kakhobwe (✉)
Centre for Human Rights, University of Pretoria, Pretoria, South Africa
e-mail: yumba.kakhobwe@up.ac.za

E. Durojaye et al. (eds.), *Harmful Practices and Human Rights: An International Perspective*, Human Rights Interventions,
https://doi.org/10.1007/978-3-031-90333-5_14

One of the greatest dangers regarding child marriage which contributes to its continuity is that its effects are not as obvious or immediately discernible, especially when compared to FGM/C, hence the lack of consistent or 'resounding agreement' with regards to its recognition as a harmful practice, regionally and internationally. This has possibly contributed to tolerance towards the practice.

Many of the implications of child marriage are health-related, including psychological, and continue to evolve even as girls enter adulthood. The propensity for ill health as a direct result of girls' physical unpreparedness for birth due to their young age, and a lack of autonomy in marriage to make decisions that safeguard their health are some of the very real implications of the custom.[1] Furthermore, these truths are often unacknowledged, and not strongly articulated in the very forums that are meant to effect socio-cultural shifts and yet should be reflected in policies, advocacy campaigns, or interventions that are curated for the eradication of child marriage. Less emphasis is also given to the lack of choice that characterises the induction of girls into the practice, the experiences of isolation that exacerbate the health-related consequences, and exposure to violence.

Approaches towards the eradication of child marriage often take shape based on the focus of international development agendas that are not always translated to speak to the needs of individual contexts.[2] The motivation used to end child marriage has debatably depended on assertions concerning the immorality or appropriateness of the practice due to age, the regurgitation of human rights provisions from instruments that affirm the rights of girls, such as the Convention on the Elimination of All Forms of Discrimination Against Women (CEDAW),[3] and the Protocol to the African Charter on Human and Peoples' Rights on the Rights of

[1] R Gemignani & Q Wodon 'Child marriage and faith affiliation in Sub-Saharan Africa: Stylized facts and heterogeneity' (2015) 13 *The Review of Faith & International Affairs* 41.

[2] NK Mishra & T Tripathi 'Conceptualising women's agency, autonomy and empowerment' (2011) 46 *Economic and Political Weekly* 58.

[3] UN General Assembly, Convention on the Elimination of All Forms of Discrimination Against Women, United Nations, Treaty Series, vol 1249, p 13, 18 December 1979 (CEDAW).

Women in Africa (Maputo Protocol),[4] and a bias towards highlighting the socio-economic implications of child marriage.

As part of generating solutions to end the scourge of child marriage, it is necessary to consider how girls themselves are positioned as stakeholders and how to complement ongoing efforts. It is not only the buy-in of girls that should be deemed essential, but their ability to advocate for themselves despite the inadequacies of legal frameworks, and in spite of their dependency.

If we are to believe in an alleged restraint in advocacy, or an inability to fully illustrate the diverse socio-economic and health-related harms associated with child marriage, and accept that there are various constraints that limit the ability to implement interventions to either eradicate the practice or support girls affected by the practice, and especially outside of the full support of states parties, then it is clear that the crises at hand requires more innovation. The greatest level of impact may hence be achieved not solely from government cooperation but by positioning girls as participants in the realisation of their own rights. This chapter therefore aims to discuss the significance of influencing African girls to have a sense of entitlement as rightsholders. Doing so may assist in facilitating opportunities for them to imagine and aspire for outcomes beyond marriage and its restrictions, the very outcomes that development projections claim they are deprived of. This would require challenging patriarchal norms that govern many African communities, and in which the configurations of gender limit a claim to autonomy by girls, as well as denying a sense of self-ownership, with the privilege of custodial rights traditionally and historically assigned to states, fathers, and eventually husbands.

As a stance that is supported by human rights doctrine, but also has origins within feminism, the importance of cultivating agency and claiming bodily autonomy as a response to child marriage is very much in defiance of the detachment from authority over oneself that affects girls and continues to be restricted, bound and directed by legal frameworks, traditions, customs, and religions across the African continent. Furthermore, the objective is to advance empowering models of advocacy that do not create 'passive victims'.[5] While admittedly intangible and without

[4] African Union, Protocol to the African Charter on Human and People's Rights on the Rights of Women in Africa, African Union, 11 July 2003 (Maputo Protocol).

[5] S Knuckey and others 'Power in human rights advocate and rightsholder relationships: Critiques, reforms, and challenges' (2020) 33 *Harvard Human Rights Journal* 102.

a guarantee that positive practical dividends will be engendered from this, it is about transferring traditional forms of power to girls, beginning with self-definition that is not dependent on marriage and controversially not dependent on parents, culture or community either. This may give girls the tools to reconceptualise how they see themselves, to reimagine their place in their families and communities, even without the evidence of tangible outcomes. The objective would thus be for girls to deem agency and bodily autonomy as innate and inviolable rights for which their very existence justifies a claim, and therefore a potentially powerful form of self-advocacy.

This chapter has seven sections. Following the introduction, child marriage in the African region will be explored, together with its causes and implications. Definitions and the roles of agency and bodily autonomy will be discussed locating their value within contexts where the practice of child marriage persists. The next section will delve into the significance of agency and bodily autonomy as a form of self-advocacy for girls. What is taken into consideration is that despite regional agreements to protect girls' rights, this has not necessarily led to domestic commitments. The chapter will then proceed to discuss interventions that have the potential to be both informative and empowering for girls, such as comprehensive sexuality education (CSE), that create awareness on sexual and reproductive health rights (SRHR) and often promote agency and bodily autonomy. Such initiatives are also supported by various human rights instruments.

Being a regional human rights instrument that focuses solely on bolstering girl's and women's rights, the subsequent section will highlight the Maputo Protocol's alignment with not only protecting girls from child marriage, but promoting their right to an agentive position, which the Protocol implores states to defend. This will be followed by a section that shows appreciation for the sustainable development goals (SDGs) in their affirmation of girls' rights and naming of child marriage as a harmful practice. Like the Maputo Protocol, the SDGs insist that states rework their legislative frameworks to mirror this as part of good governance. In summary, the conclusion argues that until gender equality is prioritised in African jurisdictions, harmful practices such as child marriage will prevail. In the absence of such coverage, girls must therefore lean into self-advocacy.

2 Contextualising Child Marriage and the Role of 'Agency' and 'Bodily Autonomy'

The United Nations Population Fund (UNFPA) estimates that every year 12 million girls are married before they reach the age of 18, with 12% of girls married before the age of 15. It is further reported that '[n]o region is on track to eliminate child, early and forced marriage by 2030, as set out in the 2030 Agenda for Sustainable Development'.[6] Recent data shows that in Ghana, 19% of girls are married before the age of 18, the lowest in the Western and Central African regions;[7] in Ethiopia, 40%;[8] and in Niger, 76%.[9] These figures are shocking, but hardly illustrate the pervasiveness of child marriage, or what can only be described as a crisis.

Varied perceptions prevail concerning the stage at which childhood ends and preparedness for marriage begins, with puberty being a defining factor and rite of passage.[10] Frequently, girls are encouraged to marry in order to avoid pregnancy out of wedlock, for fear of dishonouring their families.[11] Additionally, socio-economic circumstances have made child marriage a poverty alleviating strategy which further contributes to the complexity of ending this tradition. Despite not frequently being highlighted in relation to child marriage, maternal mortality, infant mortality, cases of violence, fistula, HIV/AIDS, STIs, disability from childbirth and depression can all be attributed to child marriage. The young age of

[6] Office of the United Nations High Commissioner for Human Rights (OHCHR) 'Child and forced marriage, including in humanitarian settings' https://www.ohchr.org/en/women/child-and-forced-marriage-including-humanitarian-settings (accessed 2 November 2022).

[7] UNICEF 'Child protection budget' https://www.unicef.org/ghana/media/2301/file/Budget%20Brief%20-%20Child%20Protection.pdf (accessed 4 December 2024).

[8] Girls Not Brides 'Child marriage atlas: Ethiopia' https://www.girlsnotbrides.org/learning-resources/child-marriage-atlas/atlas/ethiopia/ (accessed 4 December 2024).

[9] Girls Not Brides 'Child marriage atlas: Niger' https://www.girlsnotbrides.org/learning-resources/child-marriage-atlas/atlas/niger (accessed 4 December 2024).

[10] EK Naphambo '(Re)constructing the African notion of girls' readiness for marriage: Insights from rural Malawi' PhD thesis, University of Cape Town, 2020 at 4.

[11] G Kangaude 'Adolescent sex and "defilement" in Malawi law and society' (2017) 17 *African Human Rights Law Journal* 527 at 530–534.

girls, their lack of autonomy to safeguard their health, and their immature physiology put them at great risk.[12]

More attention needs to be placed on the evidence of exposure to the diverse forms of harm related to child marriage at the national level, and the diverse pathways to child marriage, rationalised due to the disposability of girls' lives due to gender norms that are embedded within communities and cultures. Therefore, even with the domestication of laws that set 18 years as the legal age of marriage in some African jurisdictions, this is often void of both an understanding of contextual complexities and the benefit of multi-sectoral approaches to support or add substance to this mandate.[13]

It seems believable that girls' narratives are still inadequately featured in the framing and pursuit of gender equality. The sparsity of attention given to child marriage specifically, compared to harmful practices more generally within instruments and agendas is perhaps reflective of the ongoing evolution concerning an understanding of the construction of gender and its lived implications for girls, as well as still deciphering the idea of gender equality, and particularly what it means for girls. Less optimistically, it could simply be a sign of resistance to the notion of girls' rights altogether.

The socio-economic advantages and impact of ending child marriage are certainly cited. The implications of being deprived of education as a result of the practice, for example, are highlighted in development projections that seek to illustrate the socio-economic difference that could be made in African economies, households, girls' well-being and girls' empowerment, if only girls were given an opportunity to bypass marriage and at the very least complete a secondary school education. Mishra and Tripathi, nevertheless, make an interesting observation that not only depicts the murky parameters of the meaning of 'well-being' in early development literature, but the assumption that 'well-being' leads to empowerment. They further reiterate that true empowerment depends on the condition of autonomy, which has not always been foregrounded in development practice.[14]

[12] International Planned Parenthood Federation (IPPF) 'Ending child marriage: A guide for global policy action' (2007) 9-16 https://www.unfpa.org/sites/default/files/pub-pdf/endchildmarriage.pdf (accessed 3 November 2024).

[13] Gemignani & Wodon (n 1) 42.

[14] Mishra & Triparthi (n 2) 58.

Although speaking of women's empowerment, Kabeer takes issue with the common use of 'empowerment' as a gateway to the labour force, without bearing in mind the various conditions of labour, some of which can be disempowering and exploitative, particularly for women. This is certainly vital to consider as we aspire for the emancipation of girls, as well as negotiate and facilitate the conditions for that emancipation. Kabeer notes that 'gender intersects with other kinds of inequalities' and points out that

> once it is acknowledged that women are located at the intersection of inequalities of class, caste, race, ethnicity, legal status and so on, one can begin to locate the quest for women's empowerment within a broader movement for social justice.[15]

There has been much progress in the claiming of agency and bodily autonomy by women. However, in spite of still being contentious and met with resistance, wider support has been garnered over the years, a feat that can be attributed to women's organising and feminist action.[16] The evidence of this can be seen in the diverse roles that women take on in the public space, a space from which they were once excluded and many years on still experience varied forms of hostility, including violence.[17] Knuckey and others speak of the necessity of embarking on 'critically responsive human rights advocacy' which serves to empower persons affected by human rights abuses. This kind of advocacy must be 'rightsholder-centred', it must increase their power and transform their engagement with the very structures at the core of their abuse.[18]

With the encouragement of human rights instruments, mechanisms and advocacy, traction is still to be made with regards to the roles that girls should play in societies, as well as renegotiating the extent to which they

[15] N Kabeer 'Women's empowerment and the question of choice' (2019) 72 *Journal of International Affairs* 209 at 211.

[16] C Lee & A Logan 'Women's agency, activism and organisation' (2019) 28 *Women's History Review* 831 at 831–833.

[17] Mishra & Triparthi (n 2) 61–63.

[18] Knuckey and others (n 5) 102–106.

may govern their own lives.[19] This has required challenging the seemingly natural conferred paternalistic power and authority of states, parents, guardians, and elders, as well as re-adjusting what it means to be a girl in African society, what is means to have rights as a girl, and the degree to which a girl's autonomy can be expressed, even as a dependant.[20]

Previous approaches to the parent/child dynamic assumed that parents largely acted in the best interests of their children. Nevertheless, this may not have factored in the intersection of gender, class, age, and location, a combination which has made girls vulnerable, particularly in the rural contexts where harmful practices are rife.[21] This is not to pathologise rurality or to suggest that it should automatically be linked to the occurrence of harmful norms and practices or harm to girls, but that the frequency of these practices tends to be less prevalent in urban contexts when compared.[22] The intersection certainly tends to shape the parent/child dynamic, and very importantly may influence the kinds of expectations parents have of female children, as well as influence the sense of duty by female children to fulfil these expectations.

The practice of child marriage demonstrates the significance of reviewing the parent/child dynamic in African communities, and the assumption made that guardianship over girls is naturally aligned with protection of girls. It is this supposition that has exposed girls to violence and ill health.[23] Furthermore, this is worsened by the fact that rural areas tend to be the most neglected by the state, compromising the efficient policing of harmful practices even in jurisdictions where they are outlawed. Even so, perhaps what needs to be problematised is how 'guardianship' and 'protection' are framed in different contexts, especially in relation to girls, as there may be conflicting meaning with regards to the nature and parameters of these terms.

[19] B Dube 'The exclusion of black men in South African gender discourses: Rethinking gender, patriarchy and male privilege' (2019) 49 *Africa Insight* 37 at 40–42.

[20] SB Schaffnit '"Child marriage" in context: Exploring local attitudes towards early marriage in rural Tanzania' (2019) 27 *Sexual and Reproductive Health Matters* 93 at 93-94.

[21] A Raj 'When the mother is a child: The impact of child marriage on the health and human rights of girls' (2010) 95 *Archives of Disease in Childhood* 931 at 931.

[22] As above.

[23] As above.

The Convention on the Rights of the Child Committee on General Comment 20 recognised the vulnerability of the child, even those within what should be structures or institutions of care such as families. Moreover, the CRC Committee is supportive of the construction of agentive power, stating that:[24]

> The Committee stresses that engaging adolescents in the identification of potential risks and the development and implementation of programmes to mitigate them will lead to more effective protection. By being guaranteed the right to be heard, to challenge rights violations and to seek redress, adolescents are enabled to exercise agency progressively in their own protection.

Awkwardly, the conservatism of many African societies could explain the hesitancy to commit to the eradication of child marriage by states. The indifference may stem from states' attempts to avoid inserting themselves into what has traditionally been deemed the private domain of the home or family in which the matter of marriage is usually regarded as private too. This may also be an admission to the limits of states' perceived mandate to protect girls, particularly if it may necessitate interfering with parental roles. To this end, developing a sense of agency and bodily autonomy may make the greatest difference, still, it may also be more meaningful, if endorsed at the microcosm of the household, 'the locus of disempowerment',[25] making parents and guardians potent allies. Nevertheless, this would require creating interventions that are curated to include parents and not just girls.

2.1 *'Agency' in Feminist Theory*

Agency, particularly as it relates to gender, has become a politically charged term. This has certainly been the case in the realm of the politics of the female body, women's contentious citizenship, and even the systemic violence women have historically faced, both publicly and privately. Although the term itself and its use may not have originated

[24] Para 19 of the UN Committee on the Rights of the Child (CRC), General Comment 20 (2016) on the implementation of the rights of the child during adolescence, 6 December 2016, UN Doc CRC/C/GC/20 (2016).

[25] Mishra & Triparthi (n 2) 59.

within feminism, its appropriation continues to have weighty meaning in the proclamation of power by women and girls in the face of legal, cultural, and religious opposition to their empowerment. It continues to be both an individual and collective response, and within feminism specifically, it has become a form of active resistance to the systemic and structural patriarchal power that has degraded women and girls across global regions, taking shape based on contextual realities.[26]

Davies describes agency as:

> [T]he discursive constitution of a particular individual as having presence (rather than absence), that is as having access to a subject position in which they have the right to speak and to be heard.[27]

According to Davies,

> [i]ndividuals who are positioned on the female side of the male/female dualism or on the negative side of any other dualism such as black/white, child/adult, mad/sane are rarely heard as legitimate speakers, are rarely positioned as one with agency.[28]

Agency is therefore authority over oneself. It can be a disruptor of the male/female binary wherein girls have been framed, and in which their social and cultural designations have determined them to be less rational and less capable, and thus in need of being steered by a more 'rational' and dominating male presence. It can be active, enacted and embodied, 'crossing boundaries', breaking patterns and shifting consciousness that allows for traversing beyond how one has been discursively constituted. This in turn permits a change in one's discursive positionality. As such, agency constructs a 'protagonist' that defies the strictures of masculinist-centred perspectives of what society, culture, and the law should be,[29] as well as how women and girls should engage with or experience their existence in relation to these.

[26] Kabeer (n 15) 209.

[27] B Davies 'The concept of agency: A feminist poststructuralist analysis' (1991) 30 *Social Analysis: The International Journal of Anthropology* 42 at 51.

[28] Davies (n 27) 52.

[29] As above.

2.2 *'Bodily Autonomy' as a Human Right*

The term bodily autonomy is deceiving, unassuming, and could mistakenly be underestimated or under expressed. Nonetheless, it is a term that simplifies many rights claims, the combination of which indeed amount to bodily autonomy. It is an unnegotiable entitlement to equality, personhood, ownership over oneself, belonging to oneself, and power over oneself.

The most familiar indication of 'bodily autonomy' in human rights doctrine can be observed in the Universal Declaration of Human Rights (Universal Declaration).[30] Although the Universal Declaration does not specifically mention 'bodily autonomy', it is certainly implied in the combination of its provisions, and without distinction based on any status including gender or age.

Bodily autonomy is conferred not just by the Universal Declaration, but other human rights instruments including the International Covenant on Civil and Political Rights (ICCPR),[31] the International Covenant on Economic, Social and Cultural Rights (ICESCR),[32] and even CEDAW.[33] All refer to the 'inherent dignity' of every person in their preambles, and the Universal Declaration emphasises this by stating that '[a]ll human beings are born free and equal in dignity and rights'.[34]

Interestingly, the Universal Declaration also refers to 'security of person',[35] a notion that is loosely defined when contemplated in relation to child marriage in the African context. This is based on the idea that marriage itself is a signifier of security for girls.[36] Although the Universal Declaration also refers to 'consent' within marriage,[37] delving into the complexity of establishing the parameters of 'consent' in the case

[30] UN General Assembly, Universal Declaration of Human Rights, 217 A (III), 10 December 1948 (Universal Declaration).

[31] UN General Assembly, International Covenant on Civil and Political Rights, United Nations, Treaty Series, vol 999, p 171, 16 December 1966 (ICCPR).

[32] UN General Assembly, International Covenant on Economic, Social and Cultural Rights, United Nations, Treaty Series, vol 993, p 3, 16 December 1966 (ICESCR).

[33] CEDAW (n 3) art 12 and others.

[34] Art 1 of the Universal Declaration.

[35] Art 3 of the Universal Declaration.

[36] Schaffnit (n 20) 102.

[37] Art 16(2) of the Universal Declaration.

of underage girls is beyond the scope of this chapter, however, ideally, it should be the product of bodily autonomy, which it very often is not. What can be said is that the grave conditions of child marriages contradict human rights provisions such as those found in the ICCPR, including the right to 'self-determination',[38] protection from servitude,[39] equality before the law,[40] and as stipulated in CESCR, 'enjoyment of physical and mental health',[41] all of which, amongst other rights, make up the essence of bodily autonomy, but are denied by the practice of child marriage.

3 Creating a First Line of Defence for Girls Through Self-advocacy

While a claim of authority over oneself can be made by evoking bodily autonomy; agency is therefore the ability to act on this knowledge, or even defend it, they therefore naturally complement and speak to one another. It could be alleged that there are girls who voluntarily participate in child marriage, for a myriad of reasons, including poverty. Some may claim that this in itself is a demonstration of agency and bodily autonomy. However, what is questionable is whether putting oneself in harm's way for the sake of survival is truly freedom, or making decisions based on a reduced sense of self simply because it is culturally acceptable is true autonomy. This a common conundrum for girls in the African region.

In terms of bodily autonomy especially, who can claim it and to what extent it can be embodied has been contested throughout history, and particularly in relation to women. This has led to restrictions on access to education, ownership of property, employment, with sometimes degrading implications in marriage. And so, it is very much a feminist undertaking. Acknowledging the complexity concerning debates on whether girls who enter child marriages truly 'choose' to do so, Veltman and Piper provide illuminating insight by stating that:[42]

[38] Art 1 of the ICCPR.

[39] Art 8 of the ICCPR.

[40] Art 26 of the ICCPR.

[41] Art 12 of the CESCR.

[42] A Veltman & M Piper 'Introduction' in A Veltman & M Piper (eds) *Autonomy, oppression, and gender* (2014) 1.

> Autonomy provides not only an emancipatory ideal for those who cope with systemic abuse, degradation, domination, or other forms of oppression but also a lens for illuminating philosophical issues surrounding women's desires, choices, and identities. Feminist philosophers working in this area ponder, for instance, whether women can freely or authentically accept conditions that support their own oppression.

Bearing in mind that child marriages are often facilitated by others, gauging the extent of girls' 'consent' or 'choice' may not be as straightforward as we imagine given the power dynamics between elders and children in traditional societies and the tendency to relegate children to a position of submission, subordination and obedience, mainly girls. Therefore, this must be tackled by considering the systemic realities that lead girls to make what can only problematically be termed 'a choice'. The intention is not to be condescending, nor further undermine girls, but to ensure that if a choice is truly being made, it is informed, and further that it is known that it need not be the only choice.

From the perspective of office bearers, activists, and advocates, thought must be spared for the harms associated with child marriage, as well as the few opportunities created to mitigate these harms. A lack of resources plagues most African state coffers, which culminates in the ability to only offer the most basic access to healthcare and social welfare, especially in the mostly rural communities in which child marriage is known to be rampant. The creation of interventions that specifically target girls within child marriage, for the purpose of addressing their unique position as child brides is simply uncommon in most jurisdictions. Moreover, what the responsibility towards girls in child marriages should be regardless of the law remains a puzzle, in spite of their identified vulnerabilities. This is telling of a history of tolerance and nonchalance in relation to child marriage, but also speaks to the abandonment of girls and their widely accepted and even endorsed surrender to others in spite of the potential for harm, whether this may be parents, or in this case, a husband, a typical feature within many African societies.[43] Not only can legal frameworks be implicated in the debasement of girls' lives, gender norms that result in

[43] S Rembe and others 'Child and forced marriage as violation of women's rights, and responses by member states in Southern African Development Community' (2011) 25 *Agenda* 65 at 67–69.

the continued low prestige of girls as constituents in their own jurisdictions, as well as non-commitment towards the realisation of girls' rights in African societies make this possible.

What agency and bodily autonomy provide is that in the absence of provisions to protect girls from child marriage, girls may have some capacity to speak for and defend themselves, admittedly limited and possibly unsupported based on the context, and certainly far from ideal. The lack of enabling environments that could make it easier to avoid child marriage even when it is criminalised, including the inconsistencies related to enforcement of laws banning child marriage means girls must be considered as being an integral participant in challenging gender norms, and therefore also conscious and active agents in their empowerment, liberation and self-protection. In the face of the threat of child marriage, having agency, and claiming bodily autonomy, together with the knowledge of other rights, become an essential first line of defence for girls, particularly in the event of delay or absence of pathways to assistance, or complete lack of redress.

In 2015, the African Union (AU) committed to the African Common Position on the African Union Campaign to End Child Marriage in Africa (the AU Common Position).[44] Yet, the irony of African politicking in relation to an openness to cultural shifts with regard to gender equality has been contradictory and without uniform resolve. This is perhaps inadvertently exhibited in a seeming obsession with policing sexuality, often backed by vociferous rhetoric that particularly targets male culprits who are punished for the abandonment of their so-called masculine roles, and betrayal of a patriarchal brotherhood in which a significant assignment has been to maintain the subordination of girls and women.[45]

A society that shames men by comparing them to women due to their homosexuality also exposes its misogyny and contempt for girls and women. The inconsistency in the application of similar energetic concern

[44] 'African Union Common Position on the Campaign to end child marriage in Africa' https://au.int/sites/default/files/documents/31010-doc-cap_on_ending_child_marriage_-english_0.pdf (accessed 30 October 2024).

[45] A McCool 'Ugandan president calls on Africa to "save the world from homosexuality"' *The Guardian* 3 April 2023 https://www.theguardian.com/global-development/2023/apr/03/ugandan-president-calls-on-africa-to-save-the-world-from-homosexuality (accessed 3 December 2024).

for the plight of girls is on display throughout the continent. Furthermore, the different and hypocritical approaches to 'privacy' is apparent. The precept of 'privacy' and the sanctity of the home are wilfully deserted by law enforcement and permit access to the homes of persons accused or suspected of belonging to the LGBTQ+ community by force, and yet girls are held captive in child marriages in which some form of harm is almost guaranteed with hardly any public condemnation. The same vigour is not used to denounce child marriage in spite of its repercussions, because it is girls who are at the centre of this predicament. What seems to be reaffirmed is a preferred male dominion over girls that contradicts gender equality, and which is dependent on the preservation rather than 'perversion' of a heterosexual order and a determination to conserve a continued gender hierarchy, often narrated as part of the praxis of being African.[46]

More recently, the expression of agency and bodily autonomy is regularly being asserted and debated in response to increased anti-rights movements' mobilisation. The methods used for the advancement of these movements have been insidious and aggressive,[47] threatening to halt the progress that has been made with regards to girls' rights, but also all rights that seem to destabilise conservative right values, including girls' and women's SRHR, LGBTQ+ rights and abortion rights.[48] The threat of increased policing and surveillance of girls' bodies may see a retreat in the progress and stamina to support girls' rights. Therefore, normalising a sense of agency and bodily autonomy for girls is in itself a political act in response to a looming menace.

[46] C Ngwena *What is Africanness? Contesting nativism in race, culture and sexualities* (2018) 197–199.

[47] S Fullagar and others 'Feminist knowledges as interventions in physical cultures' (2019) 41 *Leisure Sciences* 1 at 3.

[48] BR Nyinawagaba 'Reproductive rights as fundamental human rights: A feminist perspective on bodily autonomy and social justice' (2024) 5 *Eurasian Experimental Journal of Humanities and Social Sciences* 9 at 9–10.

4 Invoking Agency and Bodily Autonomy Through Girl-Centred Interventions and Education

In the campaign to eradicate child marriage, girls are certainly not the only stakeholders, but they are arguably the most important, hence, their buy-in is crucial and the reason programme implementation tends to chiefly focus on girls. Campaign slogans to promote the rights of girls such as 'my body, my rights',[49] are curated to facilitate and activate girls' sense of responsibility for the realisation of their own rights, not simply as recipients but active participants.[50] In their own way, these slogans serve as political dialogue that exposes the continued shortcomings in legal frameworks, and community attitudes towards girls' rights. The dissonance between lived experiences and legislative provisions that are meant to safeguard the rights of girls, as well as lack of accountability calls for it.

It would be foolhardy to believe that a single strategy could end child marriage permanently, given the diversity of cultures that rationalise its existence, precarious legislation, and even the politicisation of gender equality, sometimes with negative connotations, or what seem to represent conservative anti-gender equality sentiments. Although agency and bodily autonomy are certainly significant, they are on their own just concepts and are hollow without a wider strategy for delivery that is meaningful to girls' lives, and in the absence of being embedded in culture, religion, and law. It is therefore not the intention of this chapter to suggest that simply advocating for agency and bodily autonomy is in itself the strategy that will lead to a revolutionary shift, rather they are necessary components in any intervention that seeks to elevate girls' lives. Put plainly, for girls to potentially live differently, they must see themselves differently. Interventions must therefore not only resonate with girls' lives, they must challenge how girls have traditionally defined themselves, especially when such definitions lead to harm.

[49] Amnesty International 'My body, my rights' https://www.amnesty.org/en/get-involved/my-body-my-rights/#:~:text=You%20have%20the%20right%20to%20know%20and%20learn%20about%20your,reproductive%20health%20services%20%E2%80%93%20including%20contraception.&text=You%20have%20the%20right%20to%20choose%20your%20partner.,from%20rape%20and%20sexual%20violence. (accessed 3 November 2024).

[50] Spotlight Initiative 'My body is my own' https://www.spotlightinitiative.org/news/my-body-my-own-activists-speak-out (accessed 3 November 2024).

There are numerous campaigns that in their own way have or intend to reroute the trajectory of girls' lives, with part of the purpose or by product being the avoidance of child marriage, by influencing what girls themselves view as their pathways to security. Campaigns that encourage girls to remain in school,[51] afford girls who had previously dropped out of school the opportunity to re-enrol whether they dropped out due to pregnancy, child marriage or other reasons, or programmes that support girls to remain in school until completion with a cash subsidy or other benefits are but some ongoing interventions.[52] These are potentially impactful vehicles for change, but possibly even more so if embedded with messaging or learning that challenges what are acknowledged as norms that diminish girls' lives, including limiting how girls perceive themselves.

In 2018, a Joint United Nations programme called the Spotlight Initiative was launched in Asia, the Caribbean, Latin America the Pacific, and in Africa. The African countries included are Liberia, Malawi, Mali, Mozambique, Niger, Nigeria, Uganda, and Zimbabwe. The programme has sought to advocate for increased capacity building by training relevant government stakeholders, and community outreach workers; working with community-based women's organisations; improving the response to gender-based violence (GBV) and harmful practices by sensitising law enforcement, the judiciary and health sector; as well as tracking occurrences of GBV and harmful practices through the collection of data.[53]

A noteworthy component of the Spotlight Initiative has been a mentorship programme specifically for girls, which includes the formation of 'safe spaces' within their communities. The 'safe spaces' are designed to disseminate evidence-based knowledge concerning SRHR and provide girls with a private domain to have conversations about various social topics. Girls have the opportunity to relate this knowledge and the narratives of their peers to their own lived experiences, and personal struggles. The 'safe spaces' also encourage girls to build self-confidence and instil

[51] Raj (n 21) 934.

[52] S Baird and others 'Cash or condition? Evidence of a cash transfer experiment' (2011) 126 *The Quarterly Journal of Economics* 1709 at 1709–1720.

[53] UN Women 'The spotlight initiative: Ending violence against women and girls' https://www.unwomen.org/en/what-we-do/ending-violence-against-women/spotlight-initiative (accessed 3 November 2024).

self-advocacy, particularly important as knowledge on reporting procedures and pathways for assistance in the face of harm or the threat of child marriage are offered.[54] The camaraderie that is built between girls in 'safe spaces' in the face of shared experiences and vulnerabilities may create a sense of being less isolated. This is based on exposure to a new-found support system that continuously reaffirms that girls' safety, well-being, purpose, respectability, and aspirations do indeed matter and are not hinged on being married.

The African countries that were included in the Spotlight Initiative are of course not the only countries in the region that are devastated by the practice of child marriage, and the Spotlight Initiative is one of the few programmes that has specifically targeted child marriage at this scale. The countries were selected based on data-driven evidence that indicated a rise in GBV, and harmful practices. Individually, despite all being in the African region, they are quite different. Mali and Nigeria, both located in West Africa, for example, are heavily influenced by Islam, and therefore Shari'a law, which has historically led to manifestations of gender inequality, and the difficulty of developing legislation with a determined gender lens. The fact that Nigeria, for example, has a federal dispensation, means that even while having ratified both the Convention on the Rights of the Child (CRC) which mandates states to abolish traditional practices that are harmful to children[55] and the African Charter on the Rights and Welfare of the Child (African Children's Charter) that also supports the eradication of child marriage,[56] this does not mandate individual states to be legally bound to this position.[57] The cultural, legal, and religious distinctions between Nigerian states compound the practice of

[54] Spotlight Initiative 'Create women and girls' safe spaces' https://www.spotlightinitiative.org/create-women-and-girls-safe-spaces#:~:text=The%20Spotlight%20Initiative%20takes%20a,sexual%20and%20reproductive%20health%20information%2C (accessed 3 November 2024).

[55] Art 24(3) of the UN General Assembly, Convention on the Rights of the Child, United Nations, Treaty Series, vol 1577, p 3, 20 November 1989.

[56] Art 21 of the Organisation of African Unity (OAU), African Charter on the Rights and Welfare of the Child, 11 July 1990, UN Doc CAB/LEG/24.9/49 (1990).

[57] TS Braimah 'Child marriage in Northern Nigeria: Section 61 of Part 1 of the 1999 Constitution and the protection of children against child marriage' (2014) 14 *African Human Rights Law Journal* 474 at 475–478.

child marriage, particularly in majority-Muslim states in northern Nigeria, making the eradication of child marriage difficult.[58]

Depending on the context and its particularities, some jurisdictions may require more sensitive navigation than others in order to avoid even further resistance to the incorporation of girls' rights. At the very least, it is hoped that what can be kept intact is the possibility of negotiating gradual or even minimal shifts through advocacy over time, especially if the political or legislative structure cannot be depended on to create traction on its own.

On the surface, Malawi and Zimbabwe, in Southern Africa and Mozambique (a neighbour to both Malawi and Zimbabwe) in the East may not seem too different when compared. They may even appear more amenable to change when measured against Nigeria, based on their legislative frameworks that seem to support gender equality. In all three countries, the legal age for marriage is 18 years and above, and yet in Mozambique, 53% of girls are married before the age of 18,[59] 42% in Malawi,[60] and 34% in Zimbabwe.[61] Their socio-economic conditions, religious and cultural realities make for a complex mixture that should not be underestimated.

The amalgamation of avenues and the lack of a singular or specific element that leads to child marriage in any African jurisdiction contribute to the intricacy of ending the practice. This also means that opportunities to maximise access to stakeholders must still be taken. Additionally, those included in interventions should be influenced to appreciate the necessity of agency and bodily autonomy for girls and become strategic allies, especially when they reside in the very communities where girls who are vulnerable to child marriage belong. Furthermore, being mindful of

[58] KO Mrabure & MK Ovakporae 'Unabated menace of child marriage in Nigeria: The need for an enabling constitutional provision' (2020) 98 *Journal of Law, Policy and Globalization* 179 at 179–185.

[59] Girls Not Brides 'Child marriage atlas: Mozambique' https://www.girlsnotbrides.org/learning-resources/child-marriage-atlas/regions-and-countries/mozambique/ (accessed 3 November 2024).

[60] UNICEF 'Budget scoping on programmes and interventions to end child marriage in Malawi' https://www.unicef.org/esa/media/7446/file/UNICEF-Malawi-End-Child-Marriage-Budget-Scoping-2020.pdf (accessed 6 October 2024).

[61] Girls Not Brides 'Child marriage atlas: Zimbabwe' https://www.girlsnotbrides.org/learning-resources/child-marriage-atlas/regions-and-countries/zimbabwe/ (accessed 3 November 2024).

funding constraints, and lack of state capacity, it has become common in development practice to make use of existing community structures and forums as a way to disseminate information, as well as influence community buy-in and support. This is perhaps feasible and useful for sustainability purposes.

The potential of comprehensive sexuality education (CSE) as a tool to curb child marriage and advocate for the agency and bodily autonomy of girls is met with mixed reactions in parts of the continent, with concerns over the content and composition of programmes. Although not a new innovation, CSE continues to be alluded to as a potentially powerful medium. According to the United Nations Educational, Scientific, and Cultural Organisation (UNESCO) technical guide on CSE:[62]

> Comprehensive sexuality education (CSE) plays a central role in the preparation of young people for a safe, productive, fulfilling life in a world where HIV and AIDS, sexually transmitted infections (STIs), unintended pregnancies, gender-based violence (GBV) and gender inequality still pose serious risks to their well-being.

It is thought that young people could benefit from CSE's dissemination of information regarding sex, sexuality, sexual choices, sexual health, and the responsibilities that come with these, with reference to material that is evidence-based.[63] In addition, UNESCO's guiding notes expressively emphasise that '[i]t is equally critical for all young people to understand consent and how to avoid pressuring others into unwanted situations or actions'.[64]

CSE programmes may be useful for disputing harmful gender norms and practices, as well as incorporating a healthy sense of agency and bodily autonomy for young people, and instilling respect for the agency and bodily autonomy of others. These programmes are not necessarily created

[62] UNESCO 'International technical guidance on sexuality education: An evidence-informed approach' (2018) 12 https://unesdoc.unesco.org/ark:/48223/pf0000260770/PDF/260770eng.pdf.multi (accessed 2 November 2024).

[63] E Miedema, MJ Le Mat & F Hague 'But is it comprehensive? Unpacking the "comprehensive"' in comprehensive sexuality education' (2020) 79 *Health Education Journal* 747 at 751–752.

[64] UNESCO (n 62) 92.

for girls, but young people in general and therefore boys too. In addition, as a strategy to achieve gender equality, the usefulness of including boys as allies continues to be promoted as a way to hasten progress and disrupt gender inequality.[65] This is a transformative endeavour shared with African feminism, 'to disrupt the normalisation of specific notions of masculinities and femininities as part and parcel of a conundrum of citizenship and access to citizenship privilege'.[66] In addition, the intention is to promote 'an ethic of care', a collective sense of co-responsibility, and interconnectedness regardless of gender.[67]

Such a programme would provide an opportunity for boys to reshape how girls are appraised within African society, confronting their own indoctrination and socialisation concerning gender norms, as well as how they relate to girls. An added benefit is that since there is the possibility that boys and girls would receive the same information, whether in single sex or co-education schools, having these conversations openly may become normalised rather than taboo. According to Kangaude:[68]

> As capacity is evolving, children should be protected, and simultaneously, supported to progressively protect themselves. The role of the state, therefore, is to nurture and support the child as the child progressively attains the capacity to avoid and manage risks to sexual health in negotiating sexuality development.

The articles of the African Children's Charter are intentionally woven together to not only appeal to state parties to protect children from harm, but to ensure that children also have the capacity to protect themselves and avoid harm. The African Children's Charter encourages 'to the maximum extent possible, the survival, protection and development of the child';[69] 'fostering respect for human rights and fundamental freedoms

[65] R Makama and others 'The danger of a single feminist narrative: African-centred decolonial feminism for Black men' (2019) 33 *Agenda* 61 at 62–65.

[66] I Dery 'A situated, African understanding of African feminism for men: A Ghanaian narrative' (2020) 27 *Gender, Place & Culture* 1745 at 1747–1748.

[67] GE du Plessis 'Gendered human (in)security in South Africa: What can ubuntu feminism offer?' (2019) 52 *Acta Academica* 41 at 42–44.

[68] Kangaude (n 11) 546–547.

[69] Art 5(2) of the African Children's Charter.

by children;[70] developing 'preventive health care and family life education and provision of service';[71] establishing 'special monitoring units to provide necessary support for the child and for those who have the care of the child, as well as other forms of prevention and for identification, reporting referral investigation, treatment, and follow-up of instances of child abuse and neglect';[72] and protection from 'sexual exploitation and sexual abuse'.[73]

Although yet to gain widespread endorsement, the Southern African Development Community Model Law on eradicating child marriage and protecting children already in marriage (SADC Model Law),[74] was developed to guide SADC states in the domestication of laws for defining, understanding and eradicating child marriage. It may have been designed for the SADC region but is applicable across the continent. Very importantly, 'under the right to education',[75] it mandates states to 'foster respect for human rights and fundamental freedoms';[76] 'promote the child's understanding of the dangers of child marriage';[77] 'promote the child's understanding of the nature, causes, modes of transmission, consequences and means of preventing and managing HIV and AIDS and how to access reproductive rights';[78] and 'promote the child's understanding of the rights and protection of a child who is already in marriage or a victim of a child marriage'.[79] All these provisions when combined should make up some of the aspects of a CSE programme in jurisdictions where child marriage is known to occur. Fortunately, the SADC Model Law

[70] Art 11(b) of the African Children's Charter.

[71] Art 14(f) of the African Children's Charter.

[72] Art 16(1) of the African Children's Charter.

[73] Art 27(a)-(c) of the African Children's Charter.

[74] Southern African Development Community Model Law on eradicating child marriage and protecting children already in marriage (SADC Model Law) https://www.girlsnotbrides.org/documents/484/MODEL-LAW-ON-ERADICATING-CHILD-MARRIAGE-AND-PROTECTING-CHILDREN-ALREADY-IN-MARRIAGE.pdf (accessed 4 December 2024).

[75] Art 9 of the SADC Model Law.

[76] Art 9(2)(b)(ii) of the SADC Model Law.

[77] Art 9(2)(b)(iv) of the SADC Model Law.

[78] Art 9(2)(b)(v) of the SADC Model Law.

[79] Art 9(2)(b)(vi) of the SADC Model Law.

goes further to specifically motivate states to incorporate comprehensive sexuality education.[80]

CSE programmes are offered mainly within the confines of the educational system, making this a low cost and sustainable way to insert healthy norms that may assist in curbing child marriage, GBV amongst other things, if not as a standalone programme, then by possibly merging aspects with other existing subjects that have commonalities.[81]

Interventions that are meant to create cultural shifts, especially those used to tackle the sensitivity of gender norms in African societies must have longevity in mind. They must be easily accessible and embedded within normal, recognisable, and trusted social structures, compared to interventions that have short cycles and are therefore neither memorable, nor as impactful. It is for this reason that CSE continues to be touted as a realistic mode for not only affecting social norms, with the education system as a space for its delivery, and in which the biggest hurdles are acquiring state endorsement, and in some cases, cementing the acceptance of parents and guardians, but must also include the training and sensitisation of educators.

Attempts to popularise CSE have not been without backlash, further exposing existing contradictions and discomfort related especially to girls' knowledge concerning sex and sexuality, a misinformed belief in or desire for their asexuality, and an attachment to the idea that sex for girls is acceptable only after a certain age, or in some cases once having gone through the only supposed legitimate rite of passage for their (often limited) expression of sexuality, marriage.

Miedema and others highlight how negotiating the content of CSE can become a politically contentious process with regards to the type of knowledge that is able to feature in programmes. By unravelling the term 'comprehensive', they seek to 'make more explicit whose political claims are being advanced and whose may be side-lined in these processes'.[82] In certain circumstances, there may be 'variations in conceptualisation'.[83] Programmes may indeed speak to the gender, sex and sexuality needs of young people in a context. Although, in another context, they may

[80] Art 6(b) of the SADC Model Law.

[81] UNESCO (n 62) 94.

[82] Miedema, Le Mat & Hague (n 63) 748.

[83] Miedema, Le Mat & Hague (n 63) 748–749.

also absorb the characteristics and proclivities of a regime, which may lead to a restrained and conservative approach to CSE that may reinforce rather than challenge gender norms,[84] and without a pronounced focus on agency and bodily autonomy, especially for girls. This is best illustrated by a study conducted in Zambia to gauge teacher attitudes towards CSE. The results varied with admissions that teachers do in fact teach aspects they are comfortable with and forego those they find personally problematic.[85] One teacher expressed that '[w]e are a Christian country, so the message for us is no sex before marriage',[86] while another stated that:[87]

> Why should I teach about the steps to using contraception? It's like teaching someone how to fish, they end up always wanting to fish; so, in the case of sex, what will happen when they do have contraception, they will still have sex.

There is a belief that the knowledge extracted from CSE or even safe space programmes might lead girls astray. Assumptions that this exposure would make girls less chaste and likely to be promiscuous may leave girls unprepared and unable to establish boundaries, and even powerless to protect or advocate for themselves from an informed position. Further irony is that while being denied the knowledge to advocate for their agency and bodily autonomy, girls are expected to navigate their way in societies that contradictorily entitle boys and men access to girls' bodies, girls' sexual availability, and their sexual compliance even outside marriage. This makes the status quo predictably dangerous for girls and must prompt greater investment in their ability to self-advocate and the language to do so. In addition, an aversion to girls having a sense of self-ownership is strongly implied and can be assumed not just based on attitudes towards CSE but also to gender equality. This makes girls' claim to agency and bodily autonomy difficult to defend, particularly if it is without support and ally-ship, particularly from the state, key state actors, as well as from the communities that girls belong to.

[84] As above.

[85] JM Zulu and others 'Why teach sexuality education in school? Teacher discretion in implementing comprehensive sexuality education in rural Zambia' (2019) 18 *International Journal for Equity in Health* 1 at 2–7.

[86] Zulu and others (n 85) 6.

[87] Zulu and others (n 85) 5.

5 The Maputo Protocol's Endorsement of Agency and Bodily Autonomy for the Realisation of Girls' Rights and the Elimination of Child Marriage

A three-fold advantage of the Maputo Protocol is its advocacy to end child marriage, its promotion of girls' autonomy, and its unabashed confrontation of the aspects of African culture and society that are detrimental to girls.

As a regionally conceived mechanism, the significance of the Maputo Protocol is based on an alertness to the lived experiences of girls in the African context. While the continent is certainly not homogenous in its traits with regard to the narratives of girls, there are arguably many that are shared, hence the indisputable manifestations of gender inequality that predominantly and negatively affect girls in the region. The composition of the Maputo Protocol is therefore intended to acknowledge these qualities and provide guidance for redress, which includes abolishing harmful cultural practices. It must be stated that the Maputo Protocol in its stance to elevate the status of girls, may be accused of opposing culture. Rather, the Protocol aims to not erase but modify culture in order to contribute to safeguarding the rights and protection of all regional citizens alongside other human rights mechanisms, and particularly for the protection of the most vulnerable such as girls.

The Maputo Protocol elucidates the endangerment of both girls and women separately. It further highlights that women's exposure to harm could also stem from their experiences as girls. In its guiding notes, the Protocol states that 'any practice that hinders or endangers the normal growth and affects the physical and psychological development of women and girls should be condemned and eliminated'.[88] It therefore demonstrates foresight and has the characteristic of being both protective in its advocacy for the prevention of harm, as well as being corrective in the event of harm.

The Maputo Protocol does not name child marriage specifically, although it is deliberate in its recommendation to legalise marriages above 18 years of age.[89] The Protocol therefore clarifies that not only is marriage

[88] Preamble of the Maputo Protocol.

[89] Art 6(b) of the Maputo Protocol.

meant for women and not girls, it underlines that 'choice' is an important condition for marriage.[90] Furthermore, aside from its reference to harmful practices, the Protocol's provisions also stipulate the many points of vulnerability in which girls could become susceptible to harm, thus compelling states to proactively take measures for prevention.

Choice cannot be upheld or becomes questionable without a claim to agency and bodily autonomy, and so the Protocol emphasises states' responsibility to defend it. Interestingly, what is made distinct in the Protocol, is that a claim to agency and bodily autonomy cannot be diminished by age, class, physical, or mental capacity. Very significantly, a call is even made to pay attention to women with disabilities,[91] and women from marginalised populations.[92] This stands as a glaring notification that while states may need to adjust the kind of care they provide based on the circumstances of girls, there is no status that can justify the denigration of their dignity, as well as demonstrating that the most vulnerable also tend to be the most neglected.

The necessity to include a gender lens is also highlighted in order to eliminate discrimination against girls,[93] again allowing for the detection and prevention of harmful practices. All provisions speak to the endorsement of authority over oneself, established simply based on one's human status, regardless of gender, whether referring to the 'right to dignity inherent in a human being',[94] or 'respect for her life, and the integrity and security of her person'.[95] However, the illumination of gender equality in the Maputo Protocol stems from the historical inaccessibility of these rights by girls, and provides measures to counter the violations and exploitation that have resulted from this.

The Maputo Protocol's promotion of the agency and bodily autonomy of girls is indisputable. In fact, the Protocol encourages states to embrace this position as a definitive and defining aspect of leadership and governance in their respective jurisdictions. The Maputo Protocol not only provides guidelines and obligations for states, but delicately accentuates

[90] Art 6(a) of the Maputo Protocol.

[91] Art 23 of the Maputo Protocol.

[92] Art 24 of the Maputo Protocol.

[93] Art 2(c) of the Maputo Protocol.

[94] Art 3 of the Maputo Protocol.

[95] Art 4(1) of the Maputo Protocol.

the known flaws in many African jurisdictions concerning the failure to safeguard the well-being of girls. As a result, the age of marriage has been specified, together with an outline of other meaningful provisions, the lack of which leave girls exposed to a slew of complexities and insecurities, and in which their agency and bodily autonomy may become compromised. Therefore, besides the known 'harmful practices' that are often linked to religion or culture, the Protocol's definition of 'harm' itself is in fact much wider and takes into consideration the diverse ways in which the gendered position of girls makes them predisposed to maltreatment.

Besides complementing other regional and international mechanisms that revere the rights of girls, having articles that complement agency and bodily autonomy is vital for creating regional standards even in the event of non-compliance. They also provide a foundation for activists, advocates, policy makers, and legislators, especially when merged with the evidence of lived experiences which indeed exists in droves, illustrating the diverse ways girls can become vulnerable and violated. These are ideas and knowledge which many African girls are still not privy to, but instead are unwillingly shocked into, hence, the usefulness of programmes like CSE.

In spite of the clarity of the Maputo Protocol in its posture to uphold and promote the rights of girls, and its assumed authority as a regional instrument, the wide ratification of the Protocol (in some cases with reservations) and other human rights mechanisms that complement the Protocol's agenda have not led to inspired subsequent legislative alterations.[96] This is perhaps indicative of an indifference to the instructions of the Protocol by African nation states. Moreover, it seems reasonable to deduce that in some instances, the ratification of the Protocol has been performative, and in truth, the Protocol, as it is currently constituted, is neither palatable nor appealing, but rather contravenes both the ideals and priorities of some jurisdictions.

[96] C d'Orsi 'Are Africans states willing to ratify and commit to human rights treaties? The example of the Maputo Protocol' (2021) 34 *Revue Quebecoise de Droit International* 159 at 180–182.

6 The Significance of the SDGs in Supporting Girl-Centred Advocacy and Ending Child Marriage in the African Region

The SDGs compared to other international development agendas have demonstrated an understanding of the multi-faceted nature of girls' lives, especially by, amongst other things, acknowledging the range of harmful practices that affect them. The SDGs name child marriage specifically in Target 5.3,[97] positioning it as a human rights violation, and one of the barriers to gender equality that thwarts development aspirations.[98] The unambiguous ambitions of the SDGs with regard to gender equality can therefore be referred to and used as additional momentum in the campaigns to eradicate child marriage, as well as an endorsement of the significance of the agency and bodily autonomy of girls.

The pledge to 'leave no one behind' reveals a recognition of the diverse inequities that plague the global community. Singularly, each goal holds importance, but, when combined, they speak to the complex, many-sided and intersectional nature of people's lives. In the same breath, girls who are vulnerable to child marriage may become susceptible to HIV/AIDS, be affected by the implications of climate change, and suffer due to the social and structural barriers to education.[99] As a result, they also become part of a statistical reference point for both the causes and evidence of continued lack of socio-economic growth and development as well as ill health on the African continent. These are all some of the challenges that are represented in the targets of the SDGs, particularly poignant when considered collectively.

It might be tempting to view girls in isolation as a result of having a dedicated goal with specific targets. Nevertheless, while Goal 5 is useful in pointing out challenges that are particular to girls, it is also necessary to further humanise girls by viewing their experiences in relation to the other

[97] The Global Goals '5: Gender equality' https://www.globalgoals.org/goals/5-gender-equality/ (accessed 4 December 2024).

[98] United Nations 'The Sustainable Development Goals Report: Special edition' (2023) 62.

[99] K Haag and others 'Accelerators for achieving the sustainable development goals in sub-Saharan African children and young adolescents—A longitudinal study' (2022) 151 *World Development* 1 at 1–3.

16 Goals. This confirms their right to be viewed as legitimate citizens and constituents of their jurisdictions, but also the world respectively.

Goal 3 of the SDGs refers meaningfully to 'good health and well-being'.[100] This is particularly evocative considering how girls' 'health and well-being' can become unprotected in child marriage due to their gender, age, dependency, location, and lack of agency and bodily autonomy. Target 3.7 refers to 'universal access to sexual and reproductive care, family planning and education',[101] which can become precarious when girls are in child marriages, often at their peril.

Speaking more directly to the purpose of this chapter, Goal 16 illuminates the importance of access to justice and increased youth participation in political decision-making.[102] The claim of agency and bodily autonomy for girls is both a political stance and a demand for social justice, challenging traditionally ingrained gender norms that have been embedded in state governance, law, and culture, and that continue to jeopardise girls' access to the objectives of the SDGs as a whole.

The SDGs' provision of clear indicators that manage to speak to diverse contexts in some form, together with the predetermined goals, adds to the enthusiasm regarding their relevance for guiding the creation of developmental shifts that speak to both the socio-economic and health needs of girls regardless of context. Furthermore, the United Nations notably encourages states to illustrate their solidarity on the SDGs' standpoint on girls, in their legislations, policies, and practices, making the protection of girls a prioritised political agenda that easily supplements other human rights instruments that also revere the rights of girls.

Solving the plight that is child marriage will require the development and deployment of strategies that reflect the multi-layered nature of this practice. The dependence on top-down approaches, which includes state action, must be complemented by bottom-up approaches. They must be empowering, and centre girls' participation in the realisation of their own rights by nurturing an agentive disposition and claim to bodily autonomy despite shortfalls in legislative frameworks, or community resistance. For gender equality to be truly meaningful, together with the innovations and

[100] United Nations (n 95) 60.

[101] The Global Goals '3: Good health and well-being' https://www.globalgoals.org/goals/3-good-health-and-well-being/ (accessed 4 November 2024).

[102] The Global Goals '16: Peace, justice and strong institutions' https://www.globalgoals.org/goals/16-peace-justice-and-strong-institutions/ (accessed 4 December 2024).

interventions that are formulated to achieve it, the strategies used must resonate with girls. Therefore, girls must be thoughtfully engaged in order to situate and imagine themselves within narratives that do not insist that the only pathway to security is marriage.

The development of interventions such as CSE, safe spaces and mentorship programmes have the potential to achieve this, however, they must speak to girls' realities and vulnerabilities. In addition, they must affirm girls' right to protection, self-protection, and self-advocacy, particularly in contexts inconsistently committed to gender equality, and that continue to neglect girls as rights holders.

7 Conclusion

This chapter has sought to expose how the reliance on African states to commit to gender equality and which should be encapsulated in law, policy, culture, and development aspirations has led to insubstantial shifts in girls' lives. This is reflected in the spiralling numbers of child marriages across the region, and the continued neglect of girls as they suffer due to the consequences of this practice, both socio-economically and in terms of their health status.

Throughout the continent, what can be detected is an inconsistent resoluteness towards the eradication of child marriage. While this is disheartening, it should not necessarily be surprising when one considers other variations of harm that affect girls besides child marriage. Child marriage is therefore proof of a systemic issue that is in entrenched in the fabric of most African jurisdictions. What is clear is that without a strong and definitive commitment to gender equality, manifestations of inequality that particularly affect girls have no chance of being abated. In many of the environments in which girls reside, girls are intentionally nurtured to not become agentive persons that embody bodily autonomy, instead they are groomed for servitude, for duty, for obedience and the diminishment of their personhood. As the backlash towards the realisation of girls' rights threatens to terrorise and sabotage the progress that has been made through both human rights and feminist efforts, instilling a sense of agency and bodily autonomy should be pursued with greater urgency.

Bibliography

African Union common position on the campaign to end child marriage in Africa https://au.int/sites/default/files/documents/31010-doc-cap_on_ending_child_marriage_-english_0.pdf (accessed 30 October 2024).

Amnesty International 'My body, my rights' https://www.amnesty.org/en/get-involved/my-body-my-rights/#:~:text=You%20have%20the%20right%20to%20know%20and%20learn%20about%20your,reproductive%20health%20services%20%E2%80%93%20including%20contraception.&text=You%20have%20the%20right%20to%20choose%20your%20partner.,from%20rape%20and%20sexual%20violence (accessed 3 November 2024).

Baird, S; McIntosh, C & Özler, B 'Cash or condition? Evidence of a cash transfer experiment' (2011) 126 *The Quarterly Journal of Economics* 1709.

Braimah, TS 'Child marriage in Northern Nigeria: Section 61 of Part 1 of the 1999 Constitution and the protection of children against child marriage' (2014) 14 *African Human Rights Law Journal* 475.

Davies, B 'The concept of agency: A feminist post-structuralist analysis' (1991) *Social Analysis: The International Journal of Anthropology* 51.

Dery, I 'A situated, African understanding of African feminism for men: A Ghanaian narrative' (2020) 27 *Gender, Place & Culture* 1747–1748.

D'Orsi, C 'Are Africans states willing to ratify and commit to human rights treaties? The example of the Maputo Protocol' (2021) 34 *Revue Quebecoise de Droit International* 159.

Du Plessis, GE 'Gendered human (in)security in South Africa: What can ubuntu feminism offer?' (2019) 52 *Acta Academica* 41.

Dube, B 'The exclusion of black men in South African gender discourses: Rethinking gender, patriarchy and male privilege' (2019) 49 *Africa Insight* 37.

Fullagar, S; Rich, E; Pavlidis, A & Van Ingen, C 'Feminist knowledges as interventions in physical cultures' (2019) 41 *Leisure Sciences* 1.

Gemignani, R & Wodon, Q 'Child marriage and faith affiliation in sub-Saharan Africa: stylized facts and heterogeneity' (2015) 13 *The Review of Faith & International Affairs* 41.

Girls Not Brides 'Child marriage atlas: Ethiopia' https://www.girlsnotbrides.org/learning-resources/child-marriage-atlas/atlas/ethiopia/ (accessed 4 December 2024).

Girls Not Brides 'Child marriage atlas: Mozambique' https://www.girlsnotbrides.org/learning-resources/child-marriage-atlas/regions-and-countries/mozambique/ (accessed 3 November 2024).

Girls Not Brides 'Child marriage atlas: Niger' https://www.girlsnotbrides.org/learning-resources/child-marriage-atlas/atlas/niger (accessed 4 December 2024).

Girls Not Brides 'Child marriage atlas: Zimbabwe' https://www.girlsnotbrides.org/learning-resources/child-marriage-atlas/regions-and-countries/zimbabwe/ (accessed 3 November 2024).

Global Goals '3: Good health and well-being' https://www.globalgoals.org/goals/3-good-health-and-well-being/ (accessed 4 November 2024).

Global Goals '5: Gender equality' https://www.globalgoals.org/goals/5-gender-equality/ (accessed 4 December 2024).

The Global Goals '16: Peace, justice and strong institutions' https://www.globalgoals.org/goals/16-peace-justice-and-strong-institutions/ (accessed 4 December 2024).

Haag, K; Du Toit, S; Rudgard, WE; Skeen, S; Meinck, F; Gordon, SL; Mebrahtu, H; Roberts, KJ; Cluver, L; Tomlinson, M & Sherr, L 'Accelerators for achieving the sustainable development goals in sub-Saharan African children and young adolescents – A longitudinal study' (2022) 151 *World Development* 1.

International Planned Parenthood Federation (IPPF) 'Ending child marriage: A guide for global policy action' (2007) https://www.unfpa.org/sites/default/files/pub-pdf/endchildmarriage.pdf (accessed 3 November 2024).

Kabeer, N 'Women's empowerment and the question of choice' (2019) 72 *Journal of International Affairs* 209.

Kangaude, G 'Adolescent sex and "defilement" in Malawi law and society' (2017) 17 *African Human Rights Law Journal* 527.

Knuckey, S; Hoffman, B; Perelman, J; Reddy, G; Anchieta, A & Jain, M 'Power in human rights advocate and rightsholder relationships: critiques, reforms, and challenges' (2020) 33 *Harvard Human Rights Journal* 1.

Lee, C & Logan, A 'Women's agency, activism and organisation' (2019) 28 *Women's History Review* 831.

Makama, R; Helman, R; Titi, N & Day, S 'The danger of a single feminist narrative: African-centred decolonial feminism for Black men' (2019) 33 *Agenda* 61.

McCool, A 'Ugandan president calls on Africa to "save the world from homosexuality"' *The Guardian* 3 April 2023 https://www.theguardian.com/global-development/2023/apr/03/ugandan-president-calls-on-africa-to-save-the-world-from-homosexuality (accessed 3 December 2024).

Miedema, E; Le Mat, MLJ & Hague, F 'But is it comprehensive? Unpacking the "comprehensive"' in comprehensive sexuality education (2020) 79 *Health Education Journal* 747.

Mishra, NK & Tripathi, T 'Conceptualising women's agency, autonomy and empowerment' (2011) 46 *Economic and Political Weekly* 58.

Mrabure, KO 'Unabated menace of child marriage in Nigeria: The need for an enabling constitutional provision' (2020) 98 *Journal of Law, Policy and Globalization* 179.

Naphambo, EK '(Re)constructing the African notion of girls' readiness for marriage: Insights from rural Malawi' PhD thesis, University of Cape Town, 2020.

Ngwena, C *What is Africanness? Contesting nativism in race, culture and sexualities* (PULP 2018).

Nyinawagaba, BR 'Reproductive rights as fundamental human rights: A feminist perspective on bodily autonomy and social justice' (2024) 5 *Eurasian Experimental Journal of Humanities and Social* Sciences 9.

Office of the United Nations High Commissioner for Human Rights (OHCHR) 'Child and forced marriage, including in humanitarian settings' https://www.ohchr.org/en/women/child-and-forced-marriage-including-humanitarian-settings (accessed 2 November 2022).

Raj, A 'When the mother is a child: The impact of child marriage on the health and human rights of girls' (2010) 95 *Archives of Disease in Childhood* 931.

Rembe, R; Chabaya, O; Wadesango, N & Muhuro, P 'Child and forced marriage as violation of women's rights, and responses by member states in Southern African Development Community' (2011) 25 *Agenda* 65.

Schaffnit, SB; Urassa, M & Lawson, DW '"Child marriage" in context: Exploring local attitudes towards early marriage in rural Tanzania' (2019) 27 *Sexual and Reproductive Health Matters* 93.

Southern African Development Community Model Law on eradicating child marriage and protecting children already in marriage (SADC Model Law) https://www.girlsnotbrides.org/documents/484/MODEL-LAW-ON-ERADICATING-CHILD-MARRIAGE-AND-PROTECTING-CHILDREN-ALREADY-IN-MARRIAGE.pdf (accessed 4 December 2024).

Spotlight Initiative 'Create women and girls' safe spaces' https://www.spotlightinitiative.org/create-women-and-girls-safe-spaces#:~:text=The%20Spotlight%20Initiative%20takes%20a,sexual%20and%20reproductive%20health%20information%2C (accessed 3 November 2024).

Spotlight Initiative 'My body is my own' https://www.spotlightinitiative.org/news/my-body-my-own-activists-speak-out (accessed 3 November 2024).

UNESCO 'International technical guidance on sexuality education: An evidence-informed approach' (2018) https://unesdoc.unesco.org/ark:/48223/pf0000260770/PDF/260770eng.pdf.multi (accessed 2 November 2024).

UNICEF 'Budget scoping on programmes and interventions to end child marriage in Malawi' (2020) https://www.unicef.org/esa/media/7446/file/UNICEF-Malawi-End-Child-Marriage-Budget-Scoping-2020.pdf (accessed 6 October 2024).

UNICEF 'Child protection budget' https://www.unicef.org/ghana/media/2301/file/Budget%20Brief%20-%20Child%20Protection.pdf (accessed 4 December 2024).

United Nations 'The Sustainable Development Goals Report: Special edition' (2023) 62.

UN Women 'The Spotlight Initiative: Ending violence against women and girls' https://www.unwomen.org/en/what-we-do/ending-violence-against-women/spotlight-initiative (accessed 3 November 2024).

Veltman, A & Piper, M 'Introduction' in A Veltman & M Piper (eds) *Autonomy, oppression, and gender* (Oxford University Press 2014).

Zulu, JM; Blystad, A; Haaland, MES; Michelo, C; Haukanes, H & Moland, KM 'Why teach sexuality education in school? Teacher discretion in implementing comprehensive sexuality education in rural Zambia' (2019) 18 *International Journal for Equity in Health* 1.

Human rights instruments

African Charter on the Rights and Welfare of the Child (African Children's Charter) OAU Doc CAB/LEG/24.9/49 (1990).

Committee on the Rights of the Child (CRC), General Comment 20 (2016) on the implementation of the rights of the child during adolescence, 6 December 2016, UN Doc CRC/C/GC/20 (2016).

Convention on the Rights of the Child (CRC) adopted and opened for signature, ratification and accession by GA Res 44/25 of 20 November 1989, entry into force 2 September 1990, in accordance with article 49.

Convention on the Elimination of All Forms of Discrimination Against Women (CEDAW) adopted and opened for signature, ratification and accession by GA Resolution 34/180 of 18 December 1979, entry into force 3 September 1981, in accordance with article 27(1).

International Covenant on Civil and Political Rights (ICCPR) adopted 16 December 1966, GA Res 2200A (XXI), UN Doc A/6316 (1966) 933 UNTS 3, entered into force on 23 March 1976.

International Covenant on Economic, Social and Cultural Rights (ICESCR) adopted and opened for signature, ratification and ascension by GA Res 2200A (XXI) of 16 December, entry into force 3 January 1976, in accordance with article 27.

Protocol to the African Charter on Human and Peoples' Rights on the Rights of Women in Africa (Maputo Protocol) adopted 11 July 2003, entered into force 25 November 2005.

Universal Declaration of Human Rights (Universal Declaration) adopted 10 December 1948, UNGA 217 A (III.

Index

E. Durojaye et al. (eds.), *Harmful Practices and Human Rights: An International Perspective*, Human Rights Interventions,
https://doi.org/10.1007/978-3-031-90333-5

The manufacturer's authorised representative in the EU is Springer Nature Customer Service Centre GmbH, Europaplatz 3, 69115 Heidelberg, Germany. If you have any concerns regarding our products, please contact ProductSafety@springernature.com

Printed and bound by CPI Group (UK) Ltd, Croydon, CR0 4YY
30/09/2026
02225583-0017